California's Channel Islands

The Archaeology of Human-Environment Interactions

Edited by

Christopher S. Jazwa and Jennifer E. Perry

THE UNIVERSITY OF UTAH PRESS

Salt Lake City

The Anthropology of Pacific North America Series

 The Defiance House Man colophon is a registered trademark
of the University of Utah Press. It is based on a four-foot-tall
Ancient Puebloan pictograph (late PIII) near Glen Canyon, Utah.

17 16 15 14 13   1 2 3 4 5

LIBRARY OF CONGRESS CATALOGING-IN-PUBLICATION DATA

California's Channel Islands : the archaeology of human-environment interactions /
edited by Christopher S. Jazwa and Jennifer E. Perry.
    pages cm
  Includes bibliographical references and index.
  ISBN 978-1-60781-271-5 (cloth : alk. paper)
  ISBN 978-1-60781-308-8 (paper : alk. paper)
  ISBN 978-1-60781-272-2 (ebook)
1. Channel Islands (Calif.) — Antiquities.   2. Human ecology — California — Channel
Islands — History.   3. Indians of North America — California — Channel Islands —
Antiquities.   I. Jazwa, Christopher S.   II. Perry, Jennifer E.
  F868.S232C35 2013
  979.4'91 — dc23
                                                                2013014151

Printed and bound by Sheridan Books, Inc., Ann Arbor, Michigan.

Contents

Figures

Tables

Introduction

Christopher S. Jazwa and Jennifer E. Perry

This volume grew out of a symposium that we organized at the 76th Annual Meeting of the Society for American Archaeology in Sacramento, California, in April of 2011. In March of 2010, at the 44th Annual Meeting of the Society for California Archaeology in Riverside, we were lamenting the fact that there were no symposia at that local meeting that were devoted to any or all of Southern California's eight Channel Islands. Rather, papers that were focused geographically on the islands were dispersed among symposia oriented around different theoretical topics and general sessions tied together by other themes.

After some thought, we realized that the reason that there was no Channel Islands session at the 2010 SCA meeting was that island researchers work on such diverse topics that they *could* fit easily into many different theoretical, methodological, ecological, or even geographical realms. Put simply, there is not really a single topic that the majority of the people working on the islands are addressing (e.g., reasons for the collapse of the Classic Maya in Mesoamerica). Rather, the islands represent the opportunity to address a diverse range of questions, and the people who currently work there are doing so in innovative and interesting ways. The 2011 SAA meeting in Sacramento provided us with a perfect opportunity to showcase one of California's greatest natural and cultural treasures. Our goals in organizing the symposium, titled *Small Islands, Big Implications: California's Channel Islands and Their Archaeological Contributions*, were first to present a broad range of interesting and relevant research done by the people working on the islands, and second, to initiate collaborations between participants in the session. By all accounts, this symposium was a great success, and this volume continues along the same course.

This volume includes ten chapters, each of which addresses the archaeology of the California Channel Islands in a unique and timely way. In Chapter 1, we present a summary of the most recent literature on the biogeography and culture history of the islands. Such a compilation for all eight islands did not exist previously. The remaining chapters explore a variety of topics and are written by a combination of "big names" in Channel Islands archaeology and promising up-and-coming scholars in this field. These chapters encompass work that has been done on all of the islands, covering the entire history of their human occupation, and offer a combination of different theoretical and methodological approaches that are relevant throughout archaeology.

Binding the chapters together is an emphasis on reconstructing the dynamic cultural and natural environments that native islanders encountered and interacted with from the end of the Pleistocene through depopulation during the nineteenth century. Hunter-gatherer settlement is a recurring theme throughout the volume, in which factors associated with the natural (e.g., freshwater) and cultural (e.g., ceremonialism, technological developments) environments have been incorporated into models of settlement, travel, and abandonment. In particular, the Channel Islands are ideal bounded contexts in which to evaluate models derived from evolutionary ecology and landscape archaeology, as is evident from previous studies (e.g., Kennett 2005; Braje et al. 2007; Winterhalder et al. 2010; Perry and Delaney-Rivera 2011; Jazwa et al. 2012) and this volume.

The authors of this volume have focused on archaeological, ethnographic, and environmental data at different temporal and spatial scales, from intrasite to inter-island, and from seasons to thousands of years. The scope of this volume also extends beyond subsistence resources to include ritual ones, such as ceremonial items and sacred landscapes (e.g., Bradley 2000; Perry 2007; Perry and Delaney-Rivera 2011; Perry, Chapter 8), thus incorporating different aspects of the cultural environment.

The archaeological literature of the Channel Islands is filled with research on marine resources and transportation, including extensive debates about the role of watercraft (e.g., Arnold 1995; Gamble 2002, 2008). Ames (2002) and others emphasized the importance of watercraft for maritime hunter-gatherer societies throughout the world, with the Chumash and Tongva being no exceptions with respect to boat use for fishing and transportation. The Channel Islands are well suited for evaluating the costs of material conveyance in hunter-gatherer systems because it is possible to identify nonlocal items and to correlate settlement locations with potential travel routes. Evident in this volume is the acknowledgment of transportation, trails, and viewsheds, both maritime and land-based (Perry, Chapter 8; Teeter et al., Chapter 9). Resources and peoples traveled along a combination of routes that had different costs and levels of access (see Perry and Delaney-Rivera 2011; Snead et al. 2009).

In contrast to the emphasis on the maritime aspects of living on the Channel Islands, comparatively little attention has been given to the terrestrial environment. Chapters in this volume address this by explicitly acknowledging the importance to island inhabitants of footpaths, fresh water, plants, tool stone, and other terrestrial resources. Furthermore, it is worth noting that the most complex hunter-gatherer maritime societies in the world, including those encountered historically on the Channel Islands, depended on a combination of both marine and terrestrial resources (Fitzhugh and Habu 2002). Paleoethno-

botanical studies, in particular, have important implications with respect to holistically understanding the development of complex social and political organization in Southern California (Gill, Chapter 7).

Maritime hunter-gatherers tend to stand apart from their exclusively terrestrial counterparts in significant ways (e.g., Fitzhugh and Habu 2002; Kennett 2005; Raab et al. 2009; Yesner 1980). As is evident on the Channel Islands, one thing that distinguishes them from highly mobile foragers is the tendency to occupy permanent residential bases that included houses, ritual features, and other infrastructure. This is particularly true on the coast, where people had access to both marine and terrestrial resources. Several chapters attempt to document, model, and interpret these residential patterns (Gusick, Chapter 3; Glassow, Chapter 4; Jazwa, Kennett, and Winterhalder, Chapter 5). One of these patterns is the tendency for certain places—such as Eel Point on San Clemente Island, and Punta Arena on Santa Cruz Island—to be occupied more intensively and repeatedly for thousands of years (Glassow et al. 2008; Raab et al. 2009). The other is investment in ceremonial spaces, such as sacred enclosures and rock art (Perry, Chapter 8).

Another theme is abandonment of particular sites and islands at different times. The investigation of the ways in which native peoples "mapped" onto the Channel Islands would be incomplete without considering influences of European contact and the eventual abandonment of all of the Channel Islands by the Chumash and Tongva. Islanders suffered severe consequences from European contact, including disease, competition, and annihilation (see Strudwick, Chapter 10). And yet, the islands also served as refuges for traditional lifeways and practices after islanders and mainlanders had been incorporated into Spanish missions, with native people returning to the islands for different reasons (Hudson 1976; Raab et al. 2009:210–211). Facets of these historic transformations and the specific roles the islands played in them are considered in this volume, including the tragic story of island abandonment, but also expressions of ceremonialism and cultural resilience.

Each chapter in this volume takes a different approach to understanding how islanders interacted with their natural and cultural environments. Braje, Erlandson, and Rick (Chapter 2) follow up their recent article in *Science* by discussing the earliest known human occupation of the Channel Islands, which is among the earliest in the Americas, dating between about 13,000 and 11,300 cal BP (Erlandson et al. 2011). They focus in particular on early chipped stone technologies from the Channel Islands and their relationships with mainland Paleoindian traditions. Gusick (Chapter 3) looks at mobility and settlement patterns during the early Holocene, the period immediately following the one discussed by Braje et al. She highlights a series of early sites on Santa Cruz Island, the largest of the Channel Islands, and the conditions unique to different aspects of this environment that influenced early settlement patterns. In Chapter 4, Glassow addresses middle Holocene settlement on the same island, expanding his work on distinctive red abalone middens. Importantly, he lays out a framework for how to test competing settlement models, which has broad implications. Jazwa, Kennett, and Winterhalder (Chapter 5) offer another perspective on settlement in which they use the "ideal free distribution," a promising model borrowed from population ecology that has recently been applied to human populations for the first time. They make a first attempt to apply this model to an archaeological assemblage collected in the field, using excavation data from several sites in a single high-ranked drainage on Santa Rosa Island.

The next three chapters present novel methodological and synthetic approaches to understanding the Channel Islands' prehistory, relating to intrasite activity areas, plants, and evidence of ritual. Guttenberg et al. (Chapter 6) look at the spatial distribution of cultural resources on a smaller scale, using geographic information systems (GIS) software to evaluate artifact distribution at a village site on San Nicolas Island in an interesting and sophisticated way. The use of GIS has become ubiquitous in archaeology, but the use of this technology to look at different activity areas within a single site is less common in hunter-gatherer archaeology. In Chapter 7, Gill assesses the paleoethnobotanical research that has been done on the islands, providing an especially needed and valuable contribution to this volume. Paleoethnobotany is a hot topic in archaeology, and this work adds a new dimension to understanding subsistence, especially on

the Channel Islands, with their long tradition of research on maritime resources. Similarly, in Chapter 8, Perry presents a synthesis of the archaeology of ceremonialism on the islands, a unique and sorely needed contribution to this volume. A pan-island discussion such as this addresses a prominent hole in the existing literature.

In contrast to Santa Cruz, Santa Rosa, and San Miguel Islands, which have been written about extensively, Catalina Island has received less attention in the archaeological literature, despite its significance to the Gabrielino (Tongva), including the availability of steatite (soapstone). In Chapter 9, Teeter, Martinez, and Kennedy Richardson take a landscape approach to precontact settlement on Santa Catalina Island, incorporating site distribution, resource availability, and trail locations. Finally, Strudwick (Chapter 10) looks at the depopulation of Catalina Island using historical records to trace the reasons for depopulation, its timing, and what happened to former Catalina Islanders and their descendants. He incorporates a vast range of data to understand an event that is often relegated to a footnote in the archaeology of the islands.

In the final chapter, Jochim (Chapter 11), who has been at the forefront of hunter-gatherer archaeology for decades (e.g., Jochim 1976), provides a more global perspective. He comments on the research presented in this volume and then addresses current and future directions of Channel Islands archaeology and how the islands fit into hunter-gatherer studies as a whole.

In its far-reaching scope, this volume reveals some of the complex and layered ways in which people have interacted with their environments on the Channel Islands through time, highlighting commonalities that are found not just on the northern and southern island chains, but in coastal societies throughout the world. This volume demonstrates the significance of California's Channel Islands as an archaeological resource and highlights the innovative work that is being done there. Consequently, it has been written not only for Channel Islands or hunter-gatherer archaeologists, but also those who work in other areas but are interested in any of the authors' far-ranging approaches and perspectives.

We would like to thank all of the authors for participating in this project, providing their time and expertise both at the SAA meeting and for this volume. We also appreciate the thoughts and comments of Michael Jochim and Terry Hunt as discussants at the SAA symposium. We would also like to thank Reba Rauch for guid-

ing us through the process of preparing this volume, and Mark Raab and an anonymous reviewer for their helpful comments about the individual chapters and the volume as a whole.

References Cited

Ames, K. M.
2002   Going by Boat: The Forager-Collector Continuum at Sea. In *Beyond Foraging and Collecting: Evolutionary Change in Hunter-Gatherer Settlement Systems*, edited by B. Fitzhugh and J. Habu, pp. 19–52. Kluwer Academic/Plenum Publishers, New York.

Arnold, J. E.
1995   Transportation Innovation and Social Complexity Among Maritime Hunter-Gatherer Societies. *American Anthropologist* 97(4):733–747.

Bradley, R.
2000   *The Archaeology of Natural Places*. Routledge, London and New York.

Braje, T. J., D. J. Kennett, J. M. Erlandson, and B. J. Culleton
2007   Human Impacts on Nearshore Shellfish Taxa: A 7000 Year Record from Santa Rosa Island, California. *American Antiquity* 72(4):735–756.

Erlandson, J. M., T. C. Rick, T. J. Braje, M. Casperson, B. Culleton, B. Fulfrost, T. Garcia, D. Guthrie, N. Jew, D. Kennett, M. L. Moss, L. Reeder, C. Skinner, J. Watts, and L. Willis
2011   Paleoindian Seafaring, Maritime Technologies, and Coastal Foraging on California's Channel Islands. *Science* 441:1181–1185.

Fitzhugh, B., and J. Habu
2002   *Beyond Foraging and Collecting: Evolutionary Change in Hunter-Gatherer Settlement Systems*. Kluwer Academic/Plenum Publishers, New York.

Gamble, L. H.
2002   Archaeological Evidence for the Origin of the Plank Canoe in North America. *American Antiquity* 67(2):301–315.
2008   *The Chumash World at European Contact: Power, Trade, and Feasting among Complex Hunter-Gatherers*. University of California Press, Berkeley.

Glassow, M. A., J. E. Perry, and P. F. Paige
2008   The Punta Arena Site: Early and Middle Holocene Cultural Development on Santa Cruz Island. Santa Barbara Museum of Natural History, Santa Barbara, CA.

Hudson, D. T.
1976   Chumash Canoes of Mission Santa Barbara: The Revolt of 1824. *Journal of California Anthropology* 2(1):5–14.

Jazwa, C. S., D. J. Kennett, and D. Hanson
2012   Late Holocene Subsistence Change and Marine Productivity on Western Santa Rosa Island, California. *California Archaeology* 4(1):69–97.

Jochim, M. A.
1976   *Hunter-Gatherer Subsistence and Settlement*. Academic Press, New York.

Kennett, D. J.
2005   *The Island Chumash: Behavioral Ecology of a Maritime Society*. University of California Press, Berkeley.

Perry, J. E.
2007   Chumash Ritual and Sacred Geography on Santa Cruz Island, California. *Journal of California and Great Basin Anthropology* 27(2):103–124.

Perry, J. E., and C. Delaney-Rivera
2011   Interactions and Interiors of the Coastal Chumash: Perspectives from Santa Cruz Island and the Oxnard Plain. *California Archaeology* 3:103–126.

Raab, L. M., J. Cassidy, A. Yatsko, and W. J. Howard
2009   *California Maritime Archaeology: A San Clemente Island Perspective*. Altamira Press, Lanham, MD.

Snead, J. E., C. L. Erickson, and J. A. Darling
2009   Making Human Space: Archaeology of Travel, Path, and Road. In *Landscapes of Movement: Trails, Paths, and Road in Anthropological Perspective*, edited by J. E. Snead, C. L. Erickson, and J. A. Darling, pp. 1–19. University of Pennsylvania Museum of Archaeology and Archaeology, Philadelphia.

Winterhalder, B., D. J. Kennett, M. N. Grote, and J. Bartruff
2010   Ideal Free Settlement on California's Northern Channel Islands. *Journal of Anthropological Archaeology* 29:469–490.

Yesner, D. R.
1980   Maritime Hunter-Gatherers: Ecology and Prehistory. *Current Anthropology* 21(6):727–735.

1

The Ecological, Environmental, and Cultural Contexts for Island Archaeology

Christopher S. Jazwa and Jennifer E. Perry

California's Channel Islands, a group of eight islands distributed off the coast from Point Conception to the Mexican border, provide a rich abundance and diversity of environmental resources that allowed human populations to live there for at least the past 13,000 years (Figure 1.1; Erlandson et al. 2011). Archaeologists have focused on the role of these resources in human subsistence on the islands in the past. A long-standing debate during much of the twentieth century centered on whether aquatic resources provided lower nutritional returns than terrestrial resources. This raised the question as to whether coastlines would have been settled first by initial colonizers or only after the carrying capacity of the local terrestrial environment had been exceeded (see Erlandson 1994:273 for a discussion). The Channel Islands were one of the case studies used by Erlandson (1988, 1994, 2001; Erlandson et al. 2008) to argue that marine resources were not second-rate food sources, but provided viable dietary staples. Questions about the desirability of coastal environments are no longer in debate. This is especially true when paired with terrestrial plants available on the islands and mainland. Raab et al. (2009) argue that any model in which coastlines are a last resort for human settlement is outdated and a poor fit for the available data. Many researchers working on the Channel Islands are interested in the decisions that people made regarding the resources available on the islands and in surrounding marine ecosystems. These decisions influenced the landscapes and seascapes that we interact with today.

The long history of human settlement on the Channel Islands, which is among the earliest in the Americas, supports the model that the natural resources there were highly regarded. In this chapter we outline the biogeography of the Channel Islands, discussing the environmental conditions and resources that people encountered while living there. We then present a condensed culture history of the islands' human populations. We highlight the similarities between the northern and southern islands to tell a cohesive story of the Channel Islands as a whole, from the terminal Pleistocene through historic contact, while also acknowledging the environmental and historical circumstances unique to the different islands.

Island Biogeography

As one follows the coastline of California from north to south, one of its most prominent features is its eastward trend, starting south of Point Conception near Santa Barbara. This eastward trend defines the northern edge of the California Bight, which extends southward from Point Conception to Baja California (Figure 1.1). On the Channel Islands and in the surrounding ocean waters of the California Bight are a variety of habitats, resources, and opportunities that have attracted people since the terminal Pleistocene. At the northern end of the bight, Point Conception marks the transition between coastal and near-coastal floral and faunal species of Northern and Southern California, their ranges shifting and at times overlapping, depending on sea surface temperature fluctuations and other environmental

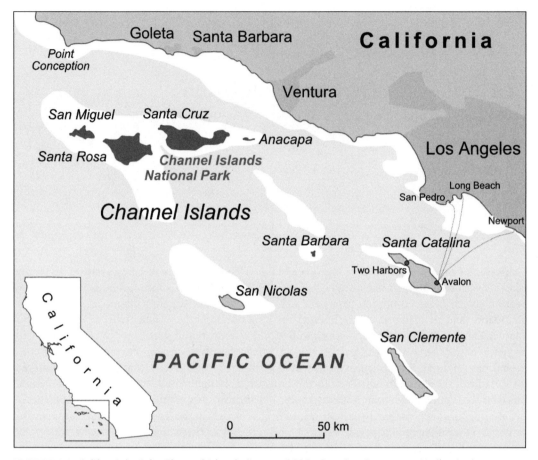

FIGURE 1.1. California's eight Channel Islands (Lencer 2009, Creative Commons Attribution).

and climatic factors. In this area the confluence of the warm California Countercurrent and the cold California Current fluctuates geographically, causing shifts in the distribution of marine species over different time scales (Johnson 2001).

The Santa Barbara Channel region is defined as the area south of Point Conception, including the mainland coastline of Santa Barbara and Ventura, the northern Channel Islands, and the channel waters in between. Prior to European contact and colonization, the Chumash inhabited the Santa Barbara Channel region, whereas the Gabrielino (Tongva) occupied the Los Angeles Basin and southern Channel Islands (McCawley 1996; Figure 1.1). At the time of contact, both populations lived in permanent villages of hunters, gatherers, fishers, and craft specialists who shared aspects of material culture but differed in other important ways. Although not all of the similarities and differences between these societies can be attributed to environmental variation, land-

scapes and resource distribution played important roles in coloring the cultural expressions of coastal peoples in Southern California.

Several attributes of the islands have fostered local variation in ecosystems and, consequently, have influenced the nature of human settlement and subsistence through time. On the Channel Islands these include island location relative to the coast and other islands, island size, topography, and geologic substrate (Keegan and Diamond 1987). Island characteristics that are shaped by these variables include climate, freshwater availability, vegetation communities, terrestrial animals, and marine resources. Smaller islands, such as San Miguel, tend to have less terrestrial diversity and abundance (see Keegan and Diamond 1987), whereas larger islands, such as Santa Cruz and Santa Rosa, have the most abundant and diverse species (Kennett 2005). All of the Channel Islands, however, lack the terrestrial diversity of the adjacent mainland and have been further restricted by the effects of wind, erosion, and significant disturbance by humans and introduced animals (Rick, Erlandson et al. 2005).

The northern and southern Channel Islands differ in their latitude, proximity to the mainland and other islands, freshwater availability, and terrestrial resources. From west to east, the northern island chain includes San Miguel, Santa Rosa, Santa Cruz, and Anacapa; all are located within 21 to 43 km of the mainland and share attributes of the mainland coastal ecosystem (Junak et al. 1995; Figure 1.1). Environmental similarities exist among adjacent northern islands because of their proximity to each other, ranging from 5 to 10 km (Emerson 1982), and the fact that they formed one large island (Santarosae) during a period of lower sea levels in the late Pleistocene (Kennett et al. 2008; Watts et al. 2010; Erlandson et al. 2011; Braje, Erlandson, and Rick, Chapter 2; Gusick, Chapter 3; Jazwa, Kennett, and Winterhalder, Chapter 5). Prior to approximately 10,000 years ago, sea levels were lower than at present (~70–75 m at 13,000 years ago). The subsequent rise in sea level caused a 65 percent decrease in land area. This has important implications for understanding early settlement of the islands because it also potentially submerged, and perhaps destroyed, evidence of early occupation and changed the geographic relationship of different land areas to the ocean. For example, areas that are now on the coast may previously have been further inland (Kennett et al. 2008).

The habitats and species of the southern Channel Islands are more isolated and were never connected to the mainland or each other. Santa Catalina, San Clemente, Santa Barbara, and San Nicolas Islands range from 32 and 97 km from the mainland and 34 to 45 km apart from each other (Junak et al. 1995). San Clemente and Santa Catalina, the largest and closest to the mainland of the southern islands, are 39 km apart and are each oriented on a roughly northwest-southeast axis. Important to understanding cultural variation, transportation costs between the southern islands would have been considerably greater than among the northern island chain throughout prehistory because of greater distances and potentially dangerous ocean conditions (Raab et al. 2009).

Today island size varies dramatically from the less than 2.6 km^2 of Santa Barbara Island to the 250 km^2 of Santa Cruz Island. Among the northern islands, Santa Cruz has the greatest variety of terrestrial resources because of its proximity to the coast, comparatively large size, and topographic variability (Junak et al. 1995; Perry and Delaney-Rivera 2011). The maximum elevation of all of the islands is found on Santa Cruz Island, where the formidable North Ridge reaches nearly 750 m (see Gill, Chapter 7); the only other island with an elevation of more than 600 m is Catalina. In contrast, San Miguel Island is situated farther from the mainland, tops out at about 250 m, and is less than one-sixth the size of Santa Cruz Island. It has limited terrestrial diversity, but a greater abundance of marine resources, including sea mammals (Braje 2010; Kennett 2005); however, on smaller islands, people could reach any location on the island by foot in a day.

Terrestrial Resources

The Mediterranean climate that characterizes Southern California is reflected in mild temperatures on the islands, although there are important geographic differences between them. Drastic changes in the weather can be caused by strong winds, fog, and offshore storm systems. As one travels westward along the northern islands, temperatures are generally cooler and precipitation higher on average. Anacapa Island is the driest; Santa Cruz Island is intermediate; and San Miguel Island is the coldest, wettest, and most windswept of the Channel Islands (Kennett 2005). The southern islands are generally warmer and more arid than the northern chain, with rainfall on San Clemente Island averaging less than 6 inches per year. Because of these climatic differences, cactus and coastal sage scrub are among the dominant vegetation types on San Clemente and Santa Catalina Islands. In contrast, oak woodlands, pine forests, and ironwood stands are present on Santa Cruz and Santa Rosa Islands (Emerson 1982). Common plant communities found on most of the islands include coastal sage scrub, grasslands, dune vegetation, coastal bluff scrub, coyote brush scrub, riparian habitat, and oak woodland (Junak et al. 1995).

Of the factors influencing plant distribution, local variations in temperature, precipitation, and geological substrate are among the most significant. Modern precipitation levels vary considerably on the Channel Islands as a whole, but generally speaking, higher elevations receive higher amounts of precipitation (Junak et al. 1995). In addition to rainfall, the marine fog layer provides substantial moisture for higher-elevation plants, the ceiling of which tends to fluctuate between 200 and 400 m. On Santa Cruz Island, marine fog and moisture-laden air are pushed onto north-facing slopes by the prevailing northwest winds, resulting in overcast conditions along the northern coastline about 50 percent of the time (Junak et al. 1995:4). These conditions support mixed conifer forests at China Pines, on the more arid east end of the island; at Christy Pines, near the head of Cañada Christy on the west end; and along the northern slope of the island's North Ridge.

Although less prolific and diverse than their mainland counterparts, island plant resources were used prehistorically for food, raw materials for making tools and structures (e.g., housing), and sources of firewood (Timbrook 1993). Among the most significant plant communities exploited for these purposes were pine forest, oak woodland, coastal sage scrub, chaparral, and grasslands (Martin and Popper 2001:245). Plants consumed by prehistoric inhabitants include chia (sage seeds) and other seeds; acorns (*Quercus agrifolia*, among others); pine nuts (*Pinus* spp.); islay (island cherry [*Prunus ilicifolia*]); toyon (*Heteromeles arbutifolia*) and manzanita berries (*Arctostaphylos* spp.); as well as a variety of roots, bulbs, and tubers (Timbrook 1993; Glassow 1996:17; Erlandson 1994:28). Aside from food and tool resources, pine, oak, Santa Cruz Island ironwood (*Lyonothamnus floribundus*), and chaparral would also have served as sources of firewood.

California archaeologists have had a tendency to emphasize the role of oak and acorns in subsistence economies (Anderson 2006). It is possible, however, that other habitats, such as coastal sage scrub and grasslands, were more valuable to island occupants because of the variety of seeds, roots, and tubers available (Timbrook 1993, 2007). Of the species dispersed throughout coastal sage scrub and grasslands, blue dicks bulbs (*Dichelostemma capitatum*) and seeds from red maids (*Calandrinia ciliata*) were harvested in large quantities according to ethnographic accounts (Timbrook 1993:51). Blue dicks, onion (*Allium praecox*), and other bulbs are significant

sources of carbohydrates and are easy to identify, collect, and prepare in large quantities, making them attractive plant resources (see Gill, Chapter 7).

Of the resources available on the islands, terrestrial animals are limited not only in diversity and abundance, but also in size. The largest indigenous land mammal is the island fox (*Urocyon littoralis*), which is similar in size to the domestic cat. Other native species are the spotted skunk (*Spilogale putorious*), deer mice (*Peromyscus* spp.), birds, and a variety of reptiles and amphibians, such as frogs, salamanders, lizards, and snakes (Emerson 1982; Colten 2001). Although terrestrial animals did not comprise a substantial amount of the prehistoric diet, people were able to rely upon a combination of marine animals and terrestrial plants. Marine species provide sufficient amounts of protein and fat but are generally lacking in carbohydrates. Therefore, reliance on plant foods, which were consistently available and obtainable with low costs, would have been important to maintain a balanced diet (Erlandson 1988).

Lithic Sources

In addition to its influence on plant communities, geologic substrate is important with respect to the kinds of lithic materials available on the islands. Obsidian is not present in the Santa Barbara Channel region or the Los Angeles Basin, but it was imported from the Coso Mountains in eastern California, hundreds of kilometers to the northeast (Rick, Skinner et al. 2001). Islanders relied primarily on locally available materials such as Monterey and Franciscan cherts, basalts and other igneous stone, fused shale, sandstone, and quartz (Arnold 1987, 2011; Conlee 2000; Perry and Jazwa 2010; Pletka 2001). On San Clemente, San Miguel, and San Nicolas Islands, people used sandstone and volcanic materials to manufacture bowl mortars at a large enough scale that some were exported to other islands. Other resources are more geographically circumscribed, such as soapstone, or steatite, which is found only on Catalina Island. Soapstone was exported to other islands and the mainland in the form of bowls, comals (heating stones), and effigies (see Perry, Chapter 8; Strudwick, Chapter 10; Teeter, Martinez, and Richardson, Chapter 9; McCawley 1996).

The lithic material that receives the most attention in the archaeological literature is chert, which was used to manufacture drills (for shell beads) and other tools (Arnold 1987; Perry and Jazwa 2010). Like soapstone, it was used to make a variety of exchange items but is limited in its geographic distribution. Although chert occurs on Santa Rosa and San Miguel Islands, it is most abundant on eastern Santa Cruz Island. Known as Santa Cruz Island blonde chert because of its usual color range from tan to brown, it is well suited for flint-knapping because of its high silica content (Arnold et al. 2001:115). In all, there are at least 30 known chert outcrops on Santa Cruz Island that have evidence of prehistoric quarrying activities, although smaller chert outcrops are present elsewhere, such as Cico and Tuqan chert on San Miguel Island and Wima chert on Santa Rosa Island (Erlandson et al. 1997; Erlandson et al. 2012; Perry and Jazwa 2010). Given the abundance of chert in multiple accessible locations, it seems plausible that these outcrops were quarried throughout the occupation of the islands. Supporting this hypothesis are the recent attempts to generate a chronology for human use of chert quarries. Some of the oldest and most recent radiocarbon dates on Santa Cruz Island are associated with these outcrops (see Gusick, Chapter 3; Arnold 1987; Kennett 2005; Perry and Jazwa 2010). This suggests the strong influence of terrestrial resources such as tool stone on human decisions about site location on the islands through time.

Freshwater Availability

Among all of these vital resources, the most important factor influencing and constraining island occupation was freshwater availability (see Jazwa, Kennett, and Winterhalder, Chapter 5; Kennett 2005; Kennett et al. 2009; Raab and Yatsko 1990; Winterhalder et al. 2010). On an inter-island scale, accessibility to freshwater influenced the population size and length of habitation of a particular island. An island may have been occupied permanently, or visitors from other islands may have exploited its resources temporarily, whether seasonally or during stopovers. Freshwater sources on Santa Cruz Island consist of abundant perennial streams and springs. This contrasts with the lack of surface freshwater on Anacapa and Santa Barbara Islands (Emerson 1982; Junak et al. 1995). Between these extremes are natural freshwater catchments and seasonal springs on San Clemente Island (Raab et al. 2009), as well as springs and seeps on San Miguel Island. With their large size, resource abundance, and reliable freshwater sources, Santa Cruz, Santa Rosa, and Catalina were able to support large and/or long-term human occupations. Yatsko (2000) has argued that San Clemente Island, where freshwater is more limited, was partially abandoned during periods of droughts during the Medieval Climatic Anomaly. Furthermore, Anacapa and Santa Barbara could not support permanent settlements because of their small size and limited freshwater; however, it appears that temporary camps were established on these islands to exploit marine resources such as sea mammals and sea birds, and as stopovers along travel routes, among other possibilities (Arnold 1992a; Erlandson et al. 1992; Rick 2001, 2006; Rick and Erlandson 2001; Rick et al. 2009; Rozaire 1978).

Although freshwater was a significant limiting factor with respect to site location, people were able to range farther afield by carrying water in baskets. Archaeological evidence for this on the islands is primarily in the form of asphaltum tarring pebbles, which were used to seal basketry to make it watertight (Hudson and Blackburn 1983). Given such observations, it is important to consider the location of all potential freshwater sources—large and small alike, and at different times in the past—as one of the most significant variables in shaping how people used the landscape, whether directly or indirectly.

Marine Resources

Because of the limited availability of terrestrial resources and relative abundance of marine ones, the ocean environment was the primary focus of prehistoric subsistence activities on the Channel Islands. Although plant resources, whether local or imported, were important sources of carbohydrates, most protein requirements were satisfied through exploitation of shellfish, fish, and sea mammals. Resources were obtained from several marine habitats, including rocky intertidal, nearshore sandy bottom, rocky bottom, kelp bed, and pelagic waters (see Jazwa, Kennett, and Winterhalder, Chapter 5; Kennett 2005; Kennett et al.

2009; Winterhalder et al. 2010; Strudwick 1986). Differences in island location, sea temperature, and marine habitat affect the variability and availability of specific habitats and species, thereby influencing local food choices. Selection of particular marine animals depends on search costs, pursuit costs, and yield. Predictability, accessibility, abundance, and technological investment are among the factors considered when evaluating the contribution of different marine resources to island inhabitants' diet (Jochim 1976). These environmental and technological factors changed over time, influencing human decisions about settlement and subsistence. Similarly, overexploitation of marine resources influenced their relative availability and quality (Kennett 2005; Braje et al. 2007; Raab 1992; Raab et al. 2009; Winterhalder et al. 2010; Jazwa, Kennett, and Winterhalder, Chapter 5).

The marine environment of the Santa Barbara Channel region includes a complex interaction of warm- and cold-water currents that form a counter-clockwise gyre of mixed temperatures between the islands and mainland. The resulting nutrient-laden waters support abundant and diverse marine species that have sustained large human populations (Kennett 2005). The warm California Countercurrent traveling northward along the Southern California Bight intersects with the cold California Current moving southward in the channel area. This had several important consequences for the islands' prehistoric inhabitants. The trajectories of these currents generally result in colder waters to the northwest, around San Miguel Island, whereas warmer waters occur to the southeast, near the southeastern shores of Santa Cruz and Anacapa Islands, as well as around the islands farther south (Johnson 2001). In addition to creating tremendous variations in temperature and habitat, the mixing of these currents promotes the upwelling of nutrient-laden waters from the bottom of the channel, which supports the diversity and proliferation of the region's marine species (Caviedes 2001).

The distribution of specific marine resource patches and resident species in the California Bight depends on variations in microhabitat characteristics, including geologic composition, slope and orientation of substrate, temperature, salinity, and intensity of wave action (Engle 1994).

Important shellfish species harvested from rocky intertidal habitats include California mussel (*Mytilus californianus*), barnacle (*Balanus* spp.), black abalone (*Haliotis cracherodii*), black turban (*Tegula funebralis*), and a variety of limpets. Lower intertidal and subtidal species include red abalone (*Haliotis rufescens*), wavy top (or turban) (*Lithopoma undosum*), Norris top (*Norissia norissii*), and brown turban (*Tegula brunnea*). Shellfish harvested from sandy-bottomed areas include clams (*Protothaca staminea, Tivela stultorum*) and purple olive snails (*Olivella biplicata*). With limited terrestrial game, shellfish provided an alternative protein source that was predictable, abundant, and could be harvested with minimal search costs and risks. In addition, shell can be used for containers, fishhooks, and ornamental items. Most shellfish can be accessed by virtually any member of a population with minimal technological investment and experience (Glassow 1993a). Children, adults, and elderly people could procure large amounts of intertidal shellfish with the aid of a digging stick or other tools to pry shell off of rocks (Perry and Hoppa 2012).

Fish exploitation requires the greatest investment in pursuit costs by requiring the construction and maintenance of specialized technologies (Glassow 1993a); however, the development of these technologies makes fishing a highly intensifiable source of protein (Raab 1992). Occupying the range of marine habitats—including open ocean, kelp beds, and sandy and rocky shores—the strategies for catching fish vary widely depending on the context (Kennett 2005). Low-investment methods of obtaining fish in nearshore areas include spear fishing or grabbing fish by hand, with limited search and handling time, and minimal technological investment (Raab and Yatsko 1990). The waters above rocky substrates are common residences for multiple species of rockfish (*Sebastes* sp.) and California sheephead (*Semiocossyphus pulcher*), whereas sandy habitats support surfperch (Family Embiotocidae), flatfishes (Order Pleuronectiformes), bat rays (*Myliobatis californica*), and sharks (*Triakis semifasciata, Galeorhinus galeus*). More costly options include the use of nets, basketry traps, poison, bow and arrow, and hook and line (Strudwick 1986). The introduction of the single-piece fishhook, J-shaped and later circular, to the Channel Islands by no later than 2,500 years ago allowed inhabitants to more efficiently rely upon abundant and predictable resources (Rick et al. 2002). In addition to the manufacture and maintenance costs of specialized tools, fishing from watercraft on the open ocean has the greatest pursuit costs because of the technology and distances involved; however, especially with the use of boats, kelp forests are rich habitats with resources such as fish and sea mammals that could be exploited with minimal risk and low search costs. As is evident in the archaeological record, kelp forest fish were important resources throughout human occupation of the islands (Kinlan et al. 2005). The most extensive kelp beds are found along the southern coasts of Santa Cruz and Santa Rosa Islands (Kennett 2005).

Aside from shellfish and fish, sea mammals were also important resources because they are predictable and produce large meat packages providing protein, vitamins, and fat. In addition, the bones and skins were used to make structures, clothing, tools, and other items. Sea mammals inhabiting the open ocean and kelp beds surrounding the Channel Islands include California sea lion (*Zalophus californianus*), Guadalupe and northern fur seals (*Arctocephalus townsendi, Callorhinus ursinus*), harbor seals (*Phoca vitualina*), and sea otters (*Enhydra lutris*), as well as dolphins and cetaceans (Kennett 2005). Resident dolphins that were hunted by islanders include Pacific white-sided (*Lagenorhynchus obliquidens*), common (*Delphinus delphis*), bottlenose (*Tursiops truncata*), and Risso's (*Grampus griseus*) (Glassow 2005; Glassow et al. 2008; Porcasi and Fujita 2000). Migratory sea mammals such as the northern elephant seal (*Mirounga angustirostris*), dolphins, and porpoises also provided seasonal resources for island populations (Colten 2001; Yesner 1980).

Primary determinants of sea mammal exploitation are accessibility and abundance, which vary depending on location and season (Glassow 1993a). Search and pursuit costs limit reliance on mobile sea mammals, and their large size requires collective efforts to capture and process the meat (Yesner 1980). The more reliable method for sea mammal exploitation involving the lowest risk and largest potential returns would be to club or spear individuals on shore. Rookeries and haulouts on the islands provided predictable locations of aggregated individuals during certain times of the year, especially summer (Kennett 2005). Currently, the largest rookery is at Point Bennett on western San Miguel Island, where harbor seals, northern fur seals, California sea lions, elephant seals, and other species come to breed. The most prolific rookeries have always been adjacent to the colder waters near San Miguel and Santa Rosa Islands, although they also exist farther south on Santa Barbara and San Clemente Islands.

Influencing the distribution of marine animals are spatial and temporal variations in sea temperature. Temporal variation occurs on three general scales of duration and intensity. First, sea temperature varies seasonally, resulting in annual fluctuations in the distribution and abundance of marine species (Raab et al. 1995). Second, El Niño-Southern Oscillation (ENSO) events elevate sea surface temperature over a period of one to three years because of the intrusion of warmer waters and suppression of the thermocline. This results in significant declines in upwelling and concomitant decreases in primary productivity and therefore resident marine populations (Caviedes 2001; Kennett 2005). Increases in sea temperature can harm kelp beds, which in turn can lead to starvation and reproductive disruption among species dependent on them. During ENSO events, when upwelling of cool, nutrient-rich water decreases, fish and sea mammal species from southern waters migrate into the Channel Islands. This would have offered different food choices for island inhabitants but would not have compensated for the mass mortality or migration of certain species (Arnold 1992a). Third, cycles in sea temperature occurring over decades and centuries would have influenced decision making over multiple human generations. The temporal and spatial variability that characterizes the Channel Islands required its inhabitants to interact with a dynamic and ever-changing environment over the course of their occupation of the islands.

Island Chronology

Given the similar environmental conditions encountered by occupants of the northern and southern Channel Islands, there were some fundamental commonalities between the island Chumash and island Gabrielino (Tongva). Meighan (2000:7–8), for example, has argued that the archaeology of the southern islands is more similar to that of the northern islands than it is to the adjacent mainland. This is perhaps most apparent in the strong maritime focus of both populations (e.g., Kennett 2005; Erlandson et al. 2008; Erlandson et al. 2011; Raab et al. 2009). This is, in turn, likely related to the rich marine resources and comparatively limited terrestrial resources available on the islands. There are, however, important differences between the two island groups, both at the time of contact and earlier, many of which have been highlighted in recent literature (Salls 1992; Raab et al. 1994; Raab et al. 2009; McCawley 1996; Vellanoweth and Erlandson 1999; Meighan 2000; Altschul and Grenda 2002; Cassidy et al. 2004; Rick, Erlandson et al. 2005). For example, Vellanoweth and Erlandson (1999) found that fishing intensified on San Nicolas Island as early as 5,000 years ago, similar to what was found on the other southern islands (e.g., Raab 1997), but perhaps earlier than was the case on the northern islands, where it is usually associated with the late Holocene (Braje et al. 2007:741; Colten 2001; Glassow 1993a; Kennett and Kennett 2000; Kennett 2005; Raab et al. 1995; Rick 2007; Rick et al. 2008:81). Raab et al. (2009:181–189) have also argued that the existing archaeological record does not support a model in which the island Gabrielino were organized as redistributive chiefdoms to the same degree as the island Chumash.

On a finer scale, there were cultural differences between people living on different islands, in part related to many of the factors already described. Nevertheless, a brief discussion of the culture history of the islands as a whole is a valuable contribution given the similarities that existed throughout the islands. The body of literature on the northern Channel Islands is expansive compared to that of the southern islands (see Raab et al. 1994:243; see bibliography in Glassow 2010), although there have been recent compilations focused on the island Gabrielino (Altschul and Grenda 2002; Raab et al. 2009). Nonetheless, the northern and southern Channel Islands have certainly been intertwined throughout their occupation and therefore share much of their prehistoric past. The Channel Islands have become a fixture in high-profile journals and have been explicitly tied to some of the most pressing questions in American archaeology, such as the debate over the routes that people took when first entering the Americas (e.g., Erlandson 1994, 2002; Erlandson et al. 2007; Erlandson et al. 2011; Braje, Erlandson, and Rick, Chapter 2) and complexity among hunter-gatherer societies (e.g., Arnold 1991, 1992a, 1993, 1995, 2001a).

The Terminal Pleistocene and Earliest Inhabitants

The evidence for occupation of the Channel Islands during the terminal Pleistocene (before 10,000 cal BP) is confined to the northern islands, whereas the earliest evidence for settlement of the southern islands dates to the early Holocene (Raab 1992; Goldberg et al. 2000; Salls 2000; Altschul and Grenda 2002; Cassidy et al. 2004; Raab et al. 2009). There is strong evidence that people have visited and seasonally exploited the resources of the northern islands since at least 13,000 cal BP (Erlandson et al. 2007; Erlandson et al. 2008; Erlandson et al. 2011; Johnson et al. 2002; Kennett 2005; Kennett et al. 2008). None of the Channel Islands were ever connected to the mainland, even during the periods of lowest sea level during the Quaternary. This has been interpreted as evidence for the early use of boats in the Americas (Cassidy et al. 2004; Erlandson 2002; Erlandson et al. 2007; Erlandson et al. 2011; Raab et al. 2009).

When the Pleistocene island Santarosae existed, its occupants had a significantly shorter distance (9 km at the closest point) to travel across water to reach the mainland, which was not the case for the southern islands (Vedder and Howell 1980; Porcasi et al. 1999; Kennett et al. 2008; Raab et al. 2009). As a result of eustatic sea level rise, the islands of Santarosae were separated by the time of the earliest evidence for permanent settlement at approximately 8,000 years ago (Winterhalder et al. 2010). This rise in sea level caused a 65 percent decrease in land area, which may have submerged evidence of early permanent settlement (Kennett et al. 2008). Because of this significant change, it is unclear whether the early, ephemeral sites that have been found were part of a broader settlement system that included more-permanent sites on the mainland or other islands (Kennett 2005).

The earliest human presence on the northern Channel Islands is associated with the terminal Pleistocene. Arlington Man, a partial skeleton found beneath 11 m of sediment near the mouth of a canyon on the northern coast of Santa Rosa

Island, has been dated to between 13,000 and 12,900 cal BP (Johnson et al. 2002; Agenbroad et al. 2005). Because this is an isolated find, it is difficult to interpret settlement or subsistence, with the exception of the inference of maritime abilities (Erlandson et al. 2008).

The cultural record on the Channel Islands starts on San Miguel Island, with the sites at Daisy Cave and Cardwell Bluffs (Rick, Erlandson, and Vellanoweth 2001; Erlandson et al. 2008; Erlandson et al. 2011), and on Santa Rosa Island, at CA-SRI-512W, located near Arlington Springs (Erlandson et al. 2011). Both San Miguel sites have clear evidence for the use of maritime resources in shell lenses that date to the late Pleistocene (Erlandson et al. 2008; Erlandson et al. 2011). The assemblage from CA-SRI-512W, however, appears to be dominated by bird bone (Erlandson et al. 2011). Substantial recent work has also been done to identify late Pleistocene lithic technologies on the Channel Islands (e.g., Erlandson et al. 2011; Braje, Erlandson, and Rick, Chapter 2). These include chipped stone crescents, Channel Island Barbed (CIB; a.k.a. Arena) points, and Amol points, which reliably date to the terminal Pleistocene and early Holocene on the northern Channel Islands (Erlandson et al. 2011; Erlandson and Braje 2008a, 2008b; Glassow et al. 2008).

Early Holocene

The number of sites on the northern Channel Islands dating to the early Holocene (10,000–7500 cal BP) dwarfs what has been found on the southern islands. More than 50 shell midden sites on the northern islands date to the terminal Pleistocene and early Holocene (Erlandson et al. 2011). On the southern islands, evidence of early Holocene occupation is primarily limited to Eel Point (CA-SCLI-43), on the western side of San Clemente Island (Raab and Yatsko 1990; Cassidy et al. 2004; Byrd and Raab 2007; Raab et al. 2009), which was first occupied at least 9,000 years ago. Additionally, there is some evidence that San Nicolas Island may have been first settled around 8,000 years ago. Crescents, which date to the terminal Pleistocene and early Holocene, have been recovered from both Santa Catalina and San Nicolas Islands (Jertberg 1986; Erlandson et al. 2008).

On the northern Channel Islands, there is evidence for a diverse faunal assemblage, including fish, shellfish, and sea mammals. On San Miguel Island, Daisy Cave, which was first occupied during the terminal Pleistocene, was also inhabited throughout the early Holocene. It is located within 2 km of an important "Cico" chert source and one of the island's few reliable freshwater sources, both of which are likely among the reasons for its continued occupation throughout much of human habitation of the islands (Erlandson et al. 1997:127). Because of its surrounding steep topography, Daisy Cave remained within a few hundred meters of the coast throughout the late Pleistocene and early Holocene (Kennett 2005:117). Shell middens on the Channel Islands have also yielded evidence of fishing-related technologies that date to this period. At least 30 whole or fragmentary bone gorges have been recovered from early Holocene levels in Daisy Cave, making this some of the earliest evidence for hook-and-line fishing on the Pacific Coast of the Americas (Rick, Erlandson, and Vellanoweth 2001:605; Erlandson et al. 2005:679; Erlandson et al. 2008; Kennett 2005:122). These gorges were manufactured from bird, sea mammal, and land mammal bones and retain evidence of scoring or asphaltum from where they were tied to a fishing line. Almost 2,000 pieces of woven sea grass cordage were recovered from these strata and have been interpreted as fishing line or even nets (Connolly et al. 1995:313; Rick, Erlandson, and Vellanoweth 2001:605). Additional sea grass appears to have been woven into twined basketry.

Dietary reconstructions conducted on the material excavated from Daisy Cave suggest that fish composed between 50 and 65 percent of the edible meat at this site during the beginning of the early Holocene (Rick, Erlandson, and Vellanoweth 2001:609). There were also *Olivella* shell beads and a large shellfish assemblage dominated by California mussels, black abalones, and turban snails (Erlandson et al. 2008). Despite this, it appears that Daisy Cave is an outlier among sites dating to the early Holocene; in nearly every other island site of this period, shellfish represent by far the most abundant dietary constituent. During the early Holocene, fish were usually a distant second, and other meat sources such as sea mammals and birds rank an even more distant third (Glassow 1993a; Rick, Erlandson et al. 2005:185; Erlandson 1994:259–260). Many other early sites on the northern Channel Islands are located near freshwater springs and may have been seasonal campsites. *Olivella* beads and bone gorges similar to the ones found at Daisy Cave have been found at some of these early middens (Erlandson et al. 2008).

Although Eel Point is one of the few sites on the southern Channel Islands with an early Holocene occupation, it has extensive cultural components with evidence for residential permanence (i.e., well-defined house features) (Cassidy et al. 2004; Raab et al. 2009). During this period, the occupants of the site depended heavily on relatively large sea mammals (including seals, sea lions, and dolphins) and California mussels, with small contributions from fish (Goldberg et al. 2000; Cassidy et al. 2004). What is perhaps most notable about the cultural assemblage from Eel Point is the suite of lithic tools found there. Cassidy et al. (2004) and Raab et al. (2009) have argued that the early Holocene tool kit from this site is strikingly similar to assemblages dating to the late Holocene that have been associated with the construction of plank canoes. This may provide the best proxy that still exists for the form of early boats, since the wooden boats themselves would only survive in extremely favorable conditions that have yet to be discovered archaeologically. Cassidy et al. (2004; also Raab et al. 2009) argue that there is no reason to think that the boats that people took to arrive at the Channel Islands prior to the plank canoes of the late Holocene were not technologically sophisticated. Rather, the challenge of traveling to and between the southern islands, in particular, would have required sturdy ocean-going boats. They argue that the assemblage at Eel Point suggests the use of plank technology with sophisticated features that maximized the utility of the craft.

Middle Holocene

The first known evidence for persistent residential bases on both the northern and southern islands dates to the middle Holocene (7500–2600 cal BP); if earlier coastal settlements existed, they may now be underwater (Winterhalder et al. 2010). The first evidence for a residential base on the islands is on the north coast of Santa Rosa Island near the mouth of Tecolote Canyon, where the cemetery at CA-SRI-3, a large site that also contains a later midden component, has been

radiocarbon dated to between 8,000 and 7,000 years ago (Orr 1968; Erlandson 1994; Winterhalder et al. 2010). There is a significant increase in the number of archaeological sites dating to the middle Holocene, suggesting demographic expansion. On the northern Channel Islands, settlement expansion is evident on the north and east coasts of Santa Rosa Island (e.g., CA-SRI-41, -116, and -187), and the south and west coasts of Santa Cruz Island (CA-SCRI-333, -109) (Glassow et al. 2008; King 1990; Wilcoxon 1993; Winterhalder et al. 2010; Glassow, Chapter 4). This period is also associated with large interior middens, potentially associated with the seasonal collection of plant resources (Perry 2003; Kennett and Clifford 2004; Kennett 2005; Perry and Delaney-Rivera 2011). On the southern Channel Islands, there is clear evidence for occupation of Catalina (e.g., Little Harbor site; Meighan 1959; Salls et al. 1993; Raab et al. 1994; Raab et al. 1995) and San Nicolas (e.g., Bird Blind site; Vellanoweth and Erlandson 1999; Altschul and Grenda 2002; Cassidy et al. 2004), and expansion of settlement on San Clemente (e.g., Nursery site) (Raab et al. 1994; Raab et al. 2009; Goldberg et al. 2000).

Coinciding with settlement expansion is the earliest evidence of residential sedentism on the islands, as represented by whale bone house structures. On the southern islands, Salls et al. (1993; also Raab et al. 1994; Raab et al. 2009) describe middle Holocene house features at Eel Point and the Nursery site (CA-SCLI-1215) on San Clemente Island. They argue that the adoption of substantial residential structures was a trend that influenced a large area at the same time. Features that have been identified as house pits are evident at roughly the same time at CA-SCRI-333 on the western end of Santa Cruz Island (Salls et al. 1993; Wilcoxon 1993; Jazwa et al. 2013). Additionally, the middle Holocene was characterized by a large interaction sphere in which *Olivella* grooved rectangle beads were traded long distances. The distribution of these beads suggests that this interaction sphere linked the southern Channel Islands with the mainland, extending as far as the Great Basin and Oregon (Howard and Raab 1993; Jenkins and Erlandson 1996; Raab et al. 2009).

Along with these changes in settlement during the middle Holocene are several interesting dietary trends associated with diversification. A unique case occurred on the eastern end of Santa Rosa Island, where a substantial estuary was present during the early and middle Holocene. This is the location of SRI-187, a residential base with evidence for the consumption of estuarine shellfish (Cole and Liu 1994; Rick, Kennett, and Erlandson 2005; Rick et al. 2006; Wolff et al. 2007; Rick 2009; Winterhalder et al. 2010:484; Jazwa, Kennett, and Winterhalder, Chapter 5). There were numerous such environments on the mainland California coast, many of which were the focus of human settlement because of their high productivity, but no others of this scale existed on the northern Channel Islands (Bickel 1978; Inman 1983; Erlandson 1994).

More generally, an emphasis on hunting dolphins has been noted on both the northern (Glassow 2005; Glassow et al. 2007; Glassow et al. 2008) and southern (Meighan 1959; Raab et al. 1995; Raab et al. 2009; Cassidy et al. 2004; Porcasi and Fujita 2000; Porcasi et al. 2004) islands during this period. Glassow et al. (2007; 2008) attribute the hunting of dolphins at the Punta Arena (SCRI-109) site on the south coast of Santa Cruz Island to the proximity of a deep, steep-sided submarine canyon that does not exist elsewhere on the northern islands, but does occur on the southern islands near Eel Point on San Clemente Island and the Little Harbor site on Catalina Island (Porcasi and Fujita 2000). Raab et al. (2009: 100) suggest that dolphin hunting seems to have peaked during the middle Holocene for reasons yet to be explained, although it did occur both before and after to lesser extents. Potential techniques for capturing dolphins without harpoons include striking stones together underwater to disrupt their echolocators and drowning them in nets (Raab et al. 1995; Raab et al. 2009; Porcasi and Fujita 2000).

The prevalence of red abalone (*Haliotis rufescens*) in many midden sites throughout the islands indicates another dietary trend during parts of the middle Holocene. Historically, red abalones prefer to live in subtidal environments in Southern California but will live in intertidal regions during periods of cooler water (Raab 1992). Glassow (1993b, Chapter 4; Glassow et al. 1988; Glassow et al. 1994; Glassow et al. 2008; also Raab 1992; Salls 1992) has argued that red abalone

middens dating to between 6300 and 5300 BP were in part related to cooler water temperatures during this period when compared to both immediately earlier and later time intervals (Kennett 2005:66; Kennett et al. 2007:354). He also suggests that the comparatively lower human population densities during this period would have limited the depletion of stocks of abalone and other large gastropods from overpredation, while the later expansion of human populations may have had deleterious effects on these high-ranked resources (Glassow, Chapter 4).

There appears to be a similar pattern on the southern Channel Islands with respect to the emphasis on large gastropods during the middle Holocene. For example, of comparable importance to red abalone in warmer waters are wavy top (*Lithopoma undosum*), a large snail that lives in lower intertidal and subtidal waters (Perry and Hoppa 2012). Salls (1992) notes that it is common for shell middens on the southern Channel Islands to exhibit shifts from energy-efficient dietary staples to less efficient ones over time, which may be related to population growth and/ or changes in mobility. For example, Meighan (1959) observed a change on Santa Catalina Island from abalone to mussel, and Raab (1992; Raab et al. 2009) documented a shift on San Clemente from large abalone to small turban snails (*Tegula* spp.).

The transition from the middle to late Holocene is characterized by a further diversification of subsistence activities and technologies throughout the Channel Islands. Changes in hunting and fishing strategies are manifested in faunal and artifact records of middle and late Holocene sites, including the introduction of stone net weights, contracting stem points, and circular shell fishhooks (Erlandson 1997; Glassow 1997; Glassow et al. 2007; Rick et al. 2002). Also evident, in the form of tarring pebbles and asphaltum impressions, is the use of asphaltum for a variety of purposes, including making watertight baskets. When this evidence is considered along with mortars and pestles and other technologies, it is evident that by the end of the middle Holocene, islanders had diversified their subsistence and economic activities, particularly with respect to fishing, and were participating in spheres of interaction that extended to the mainland interior.

Late Holocene

During the late Holocene (after 2600 cal BP), important interrelated environmental, technological, economic, and sociopolitical changes occurred on the Channel Islands (Rick, Erlandson et al. 2005; Glassow 2010). One of the most significant trends in the Santa Barbara Channel region was the intensification of marine fishing. This was pronounced in island contexts, where fish and sea mammals became particularly important (Braje et al. 2007:741; Colten 2001; Glassow 1993a; Kennett 2005; Kennett and Kennett 2000; Kennett and Conlee 2002; Raab et al. 1995; Rick 2007; Rick et al. 2008:81; Jazwa et al. 2012). On the southern islands, there is similar evidence of fishing intensification (Raab 1997; Vellanoweth and Erlandson 1999; Cassidy et al. 2004; Raab et al. 2009), although it may have occurred somewhat earlier, around 5000 cal BP. This trend may have been related in part to the development of plank canoe technology, the earliest clear evidence for which dates to the early part of this period. This allowed more extensive targeting of pelagic fish.

Most of the current evidence suggests that the Chumash *tomol* provided residents of the Santa Barbara Channel region with more reliable oceanic transportation than what was available earlier, although Cassidy et al. (2004; also Raab et al. 2009) argue that sturdy boats must have been used previously. Nonetheless, this development may have allowed islanders to travel more quickly, farther from shore into pelagic waters, and with larger amounts of cargo, while also providing a more stable platform for fishing and sea mammal hunting (Arnold 1992a, 1995, 2001a; Gamble 2002; Fagan 2004). The Gabrielino *ti'at*, a similarly constructed plank canoe, was developed for travel among the southern Channel Islands and adjacent mainland (Raab et al. 2009). Given the labor and material costs of making such watercraft, their ownership was limited to chiefs and other wealthy individuals, a circumstance that has inspired lively discussion regarding the role of these boats in promoting complexity (Arnold 1992a, 1995; Arnold and Bernard 2005; Arnold et al. 1997; Gamble 2002).

Beginning around AD 650, there was accelerated population increase and growth in the number of permanent settlements on the northern Channel Islands (Arnold 2001a; Kennett 2005;

Kennett and Conlee 2002; Winterhalder et al. 2010). Institutionalized differences in social status appeared at this time as well (Kennett et al. 2009). One period in particular, the Middle to Late period transition (MLT; 800–650 BP), has been associated with important changes that facilitated sociopolitical complexity (Arnold 1991, 1992a, 1997, 2001b; Arnold and Tissot 1993; Arnold et al. 1997; Jazwa et al. 2012, Kennett 2005; Kennett and Conlee 2002; Raab and Larson 1997). Arnold and her collaborators originally associated these changes with a period of elevated sea surface temperature (SST) inferred from changing radiolaria assemblages in sediments from the adjacent Santa Barbara Basin (Pisias 1978). They further argued that increased SSTs reduced marine productivity and the overall extent of kelp forests. Kelp is particularly sensitive to elevated SSTs, and the reduction in the distribution of offshore kelp forests and associated biota would have had serious consequences for islanders. Increased SSTs would also have changed the distribution of various dietary species, including fish, shellfish, and sea mammals (Arnold 1992a, 2001a; Colten 2001; Pletka 2001). This, in turn, led to the resource stress that stimulated sociopolitical change on the islands during the MLT.

Raab and Larson (1997), on the other hand, argued that the archaeological record in the Santa Barbara Channel region during the MLT is not consistent with marine resource depression because of warm SST and reduced marine productivity; instead, they associated this period with drought conditions that occurred during the Medieval Climatic Anomaly (Kennett 2005; Jones et al. 1999; Jones and Schwitalla 2008; Raab and Larson 1997; Stine 1994; Yatsko 2000). These widespread droughts gave rise to the nutritional and social stress indicators evident in the bioarchaeological record at this time (Lambert and Walker 1991; Lambert 1993). These include disease, malnutrition, and violence, which they argue was related to shrinking supplies of freshwater and terrestrial foods on the islands and mainland. They also extend the time over which these trends developed beyond the MLT (Raab and Larson 1997:331–334). A well-dated oxygen isotope SST record from the Santa Barbara Basin indicates that the MLT also occurred at the tail end of a longer climatic interval (AD 450–1300) characterized by cooler and more variable SSTs (Kennett and Kennett 2000; Kennett 2005). In any case, there are relatively few well-documented and precisely dated sites on the islands that have been associated with the MLT (Arnold 1991:956, 1992a:76, 1992b:142; Raab and Larson 1997; Yatsko 2000; Munns and Arnold 2002:133; Perry 2003; Kennett 2005; Rick, Erlandson et al. 2005; Rick 2007; Glassow 2010:2.27; Jazwa et al. 2012).

The *Olivella biplicata* shell bead industry, the product of which served as a medium of exchange throughout Southern California, also grew significantly on the northern Channel Islands during the MLT (Arnold 1987, 1990, 1992a, 1992b, 2001a; Arnold and Munns 1994; Munns and Arnold 2002:132–133; Kennett 2005; King 1990; Rick 2007). Early on, the dominant bead production technique was to make multiple beads from the walls of each individual *Olivella* shell. By the end of this period, another form was introduced and became the predominant type. This was a more labor intensive and resource-wasteful technique that produced one bead from the thicker callus portion of each shell (Arnold and Graesch 2001; Arnold and Munns 1994). Associated changes in chert microblades and microdrills used in the manufacture of these beads occur at this time as well (Arnold 1987, 1990, 1992a; Arnold et al. 2001; Kennett 2005; Perry and Jazwa 2010; Preziosi 2001). The dramatic increase in microblade, microdrill, and *Olivella* bead manufacture—particularly with respect to the increased standardization associated with triangular prepared microliths and callus beads—is often cited as evidence of craft specialization and increased complexity in the Santa Barbara Channel region (Arnold 1987, 1992a, 1993, 2001a, 2001b; Arnold and Graesch 2001; Dietler 2003; Preziosi 2001).

The southern Channel Islands show analogous settlement and economic patterns; there is an increase in permanent coastal villages during the late Holocene, with an apparent lack of sites during the period associated with the MLT (Raab et al. 1994; Yatsko 2000). There is, however, some debate as to whether the island Gabrielino were organized as chiefdoms in a manner similar to the Chumash (Raab et al. 2009). Raab and colleagues (Raab et al. 2002; Raab et al. 2009) have argued that many of the factors that characterize the complex chiefdoms of the northern Channel Islands, including warfare, territoriality, and health problems, appear to be missing from the archaeological record on the southern islands, leaving the case for social complexity more ambiguous. Williams and Rosenthal (1993) showed that steatite artifact manufacture on Santa Catalina Island was not specialized to the degree of *Olivella* shell bead production on the northern islands. Raab et al. (2009:194) argue that this lack of specialized production or centralized control suggests that the southern Channel Islands reflect a pattern of "weak complexity" in comparison with that of the northern islands, which was referred to historically as the "Island Province" (Hudson et al. 1977; Hudson and Underhay 1978); however, this difference may be related to the fact that less archaeological work has been done on the southern islands, and indicators of complexity have yet to be found. Additionally, on San Clemente and San Nicolas Islands, military operations, specifically the use of safe harbors for boat travel and training, have damaged or destroyed cultural resources, including coastal village sites and traditional boats.

Other elements of late Holocene complexity relate to island ceremonialism, which is documented in the historic and ethnographic literature, including accounts written by Spanish priests at missions where islanders were continuing to practice their own rituals (such as mourning ceremonies). Among the specialists who resided in island communities were healers, singers, dancers, undertakers, and members of the Chumash 'antap and the Tongva Chingichngish (Johnson 2001; Perry, Chapter 8). Both the 'antap and Chingichngish were pan-regional ritual organizations that incorporated members from different villages and societies (McCawley 1996). They have been interpreted as "crisis religions" that spread in response to dramatically changing circumstances after European contact (Perry, Chapter 8; Strudwick, Chapter 10; Hudson and Underhay 1978; Raab et al. 2009).

Overall, what the ethnohistoric and archaeological data depict are the dynamic ways in which people on the islands were connected to each other and mainlanders through subsistence, trade, marriage, and ceremonial life. Their collective study helps to enrich our understanding of island lifeways, mainland connections, and cultural transformations through time, from the end of the Pleistocene through European contact and after.

Conclusion

California's Channel Islands and the surrounding ocean waters have a wide variety of subsistence and other resources that have supported human populations in some capacity over the course of at least 13,000 years. At the time of European contact in 1542, the islands were densely populated compared to other areas in California, to hunter-gatherers in general, and to earlier periods on the islands (Moratto 1984; Kelly 1995; Winterhalder et al. 2010). To varying degrees, the islands' residents lived in large coastal villages under the control of chiefs. They were also part of an extensive trade network that included nonfood items such as shell beads and steatite artifacts (King 1976, 1990; Johnson 1982, 1993; Arnold 1992a, 2001a; Williams and Rosenthal 1993; Raab et al. 2002; Raab et al. 2009; Kennett 2005).

As discussed above, however, the cultural systems that existed on the Channel Islands at European contact were the end product of at least 13,000 years of changing patterns of human subsistence and settlement. The changes that occurred were related to environmental adaptations, historical contingencies, and other factors beyond the grasp of archaeological research. Soon after the permanent settlement of California by the Spanish, and through several different mechanisms, the islands were quickly depopulated (Raab et al. 2009; Strudwick, Chapter 10). Because of the long history of occupation and unique adaptive systems of the human inhabitants of California's Channel Islands, they provide an excellent opportunity to address many of the most pressing and interesting questions in present-day American archaeology, including those about initial colonization and cultural complexity. Furthermore, these long-term perspectives offer insights that are relevant to the current issues of cultural preservation and ecological restoration (e.g., Braje 2010; Rick and Erlandson 2008a, 2008b).

Acknowledgments

We thank Michael Glassow for reading through a draft of this chapter and pointing out inconsistencies with the archaeological literature. This chapter also benefitted from comments from Mark Raab and an anonymous reviewer.

References Cited

Agenbroad, L. D., J. R. Johnson, D. Morris, and T. W. Stafford, Jr.

2005   Mammoths and Humans as Late Pleistocene Contemporaries on Santa Rosa Island. In *Proceedings of the Sixth California Islands Symposium*, edited by D. K. Barcelon and C. A. Schwemm, pp. 3–7. Institute for Wildlife Studies, Arcata, CA.

Altschul, J. H., and D. R. Grenda

2002   *Islanders and Mainlanders: Prehistoric Context for the Southern California Bight*. SRI Press, Tucson.

Anderson, M. K.

2006   *Tending the Wild: Native American Knowledge and the Management of California's Natural Resources*. University of California Press, Berkeley.

Arnold, J. E.

1987   *Craft Specialization in the Prehistoric Channel Islands, California*. University of California Press, Berkeley.

1990   Lithic Resource Control and Economic Change in the Santa Barbara Channel Region. *Journal of California and Great Basin Anthropology* 12(2):158–172.

1991   Transformation of a Regional Economy: Sociopolitical Evolution and the Production of Valuables in Southern California. *Antiquity* 65:953–962.

1992a   Complex Hunter-Gatherer-Fishers of Prehistoric California: Chiefs, Specialists, and Maritime Adaptations of the Channel Islands. *American Antiquity* 57(1):60–84.

1992b   Early-Stage Biface Production Industries in Coastal Southern California. In *Stone Tool Procurement, Production, and Distribution in California Prehistory*, edited by Jeanne E. Arnold, pp. 67–130. Perspectives in California Archaeology Vol. 2. Cotsen Institute of Archaeology, University of California, Los Angeles.

1993   Labor and the Rise of Complex Hunter-Gatherers. *Journal of Anthropological Archaeology* 12:75–119.

1995   Transportation Innovation and Social Complexity Among Maritime Hunter-Gatherer Societies. *American Anthropologist* 97(4): 733–747.

1997   Bigger Boats, Crowded Creekbanks: Environmental Stresses in Perspective. *American Antiquity* 62:337–339.

2001a   The Chumash in World and Regional Perspectives. In *The Origins of a Pacific Coast Chiefdom: The Chumash of the Channel Islands*, edited by J. E. Arnold, pp. 1–20. University of Utah Press, Salt Lake City.

2001b   Social Evolution and the Political Economy in the Northern Channel Islands. In *The Origins of a Pacific Coast Chiefdom: The Chumash of the Channel Islands*, edited by J. E. Arnold, pp. 287–296. University of Utah Press, Salt Lake City.

2011   Technological Decision Making: Fused Shale Tool Production in California. *North American Archaeologist* 32(1):15–48.

Arnold, J. E., and J. Bernard
2005   Negotiating the Coasts: Status and Evolution of Boat Technology in California. *World Archaeology* 37:109–131.

Arnold, J. E., R. H. Colten, and S. Pletka
1997   Contexts of Cultural Change in Insular California. *American Antiquity* 62(2): 300–318.

Arnold, J. E., and A. P. Graesch
2001   The Evolution of Specialized Shellworking among the Island Chumash. In *The Origins of a Pacific Coast Chiefdom: The Chumash of the Channel Islands*, edited by J. E. Arnold, pp. 71–112. University of Utah Press, Salt Lake City.

Arnold, J. E., and A. Munns
1994   Independent or Attached Specialization: The Organization of Shell Bead Production in California. *Journal of Field Archaeology* 21(4):473–489.

Arnold, J. E., A. M. Preziosi, and P. Shattuck
2001   Flaked Stone Craft Production and Exchange in Island Chumash Territory. In *The Origins of a Pacific Coast Chiefdom: The Chumash of the Channel Islands*, edited by J. E. Arnold, pp. 113–132. University of Utah Press, Salt Lake City.

Arnold, J. E., and B. N. Tissot
1993   Measurement of Significant Paleotemperature Variation Using Black Abalone Shells from Prehistoric Middens. *Quaternary Research* 39:390–394.

Bickel, P. M.
1978   Changing Sea Levels along the California Coast: Anthropological Implications. *The Journal of California Anthropology* 5:6–20.

Braje, T. J.
2010   *Modern Oceans, Ancient Sites: Archaeology and Marine Conservation on San Miguel Island, California.* University of Utah Press, Salt Lake City.

Braje, T. J., D. J. Kennett, J. M. Erlandson, and B. J. Culleton
2007   Human Impacts on Nearshore Shellfish Taxa: A 7,000 Year Record from Santa Rosa Island, California. *American Antiquity* 72(4):735–756.

Byrd, B. F., and L. M. Raab
2007   Prehistory of the Southern Bight: Models for a New Millennium. In *California Prehistory, Colonization, Culture and Complexity*, edited by T. L. Jones and K. A. Klar, pp. 215–226. Altamira, Lanham, MD.

Cassidy, J., L. M. Raab, and N. A. Kononenko
2004   Boats, Bones, and Biface Bias: The Early Holocene Mariners of Eel Point, San Clemente Island, California. *American Antiquity* 69(1): 109–130.

Caviedes, C. N.
2001   *El Nino through History: Storming through the Ages.* University Press of Florida, Gainesville.

Cole, K. L., and G. Liu
1994   Holocene Paleoecology of an Estuary on Santa Rosa Island, California. *Quaternary Research* 41:326–335.

Colten, R. H.
2001   Ecological and Economic Analysis of Faunal Remains from Santa Cruz Island. In *The Origins of a Pacific Coast Chiefdom: The Chumash of the Channel Islands*, edited by J. E. Arnold, pp. 199–219. University of Utah Press, Salt Lake City.

Conlee, C. A.
2000   Intensified Middle Period Ground Stone Production on San Miguel Island. *Journal of California and Great Basin Anthropology* 22(2):374–391.

Connolly, T., J. M. Erlandson, S. E. Norris
1995   Early Holocene Basketry from Daisy Cave, San Miguel Island, California. *American Antiquity* 60:309–318.

Dietler, J. E.
2003   The Specialist Next Door: Microblade Production and Status in Island Chumash Households. Master's thesis. Department of Anthropology, University of California, Los Angeles.

Emerson, M. J.

1982   The Unique Plants and Animals of the
        Northern Channel Islands, California. Mas-
        ter's thesis. University of California, Santa
        Barbara.

Engle, J. M.

1994   Perspectives on the Structure and Dynamics
        of Nearshore Marine Assemblages of Califor-
        nia Channel Islands. In *The Fourth California
        Islands Symposium: Update on the Status of
        Resources*, edited by W. L. Halvorson and G. J.
        Maender, pp. 13–26. Santa Barbara Museum
        of Natural History, Santa Barbara, CA.

Erlandson, J. M.

1988   The Role of Shellfish in Prehistoric Econo-
        mies: A Protein Perspective. *American Antiq-
        uity* 53(1):102–109.

1994   *Early Hunter-Gatherers of the California
        Coast*. Plenum Press, New York.

1997   The Middle Holocene on the Western Santa
        Barbara Coast. In *Archaeology of the Califor-
        nia Coast During the Middle Holocene*, edited
        by J. M. Erlandson and M. A. Glassow, pp. 91–
        109. Cotsen Institute of Archaeology, Univer-
        sity of California, Los Angeles.

2001   The Archaeology of Aquatic Adaptations:
        Paradigms for a New Millennium. *Journal of
        Archaeological Research* 9(4):287–350.

2002   Anatomically Modern Humans, Maritime
        Adaptations, and the Peopling of the New
        World. In *The First Americans: The Pleisto-
        cene Colonization of the New World*, edited
        by N. Jablonski, pp. 59–92. Memoirs of
        the California Academy of Sciences, San
        Francisco.

Erlandson, J. M., and T. J. Braje

2008a   Five Crescents from Cardwell: Context and
        Chronology of Chipped Crescents at CA-
        SMI-679. *Pacific Coast Archaeological Society
        Quarterly* 40(1):35–45.

2008b   A Chipped Stone Crescent from CA-SMI-
        681, San Miguel Island, California. *Journal
        of California and Great Basin Anthropology*
        28(2):58–62.

Erlandson, J. M., T. J. Braje, T. C. Rick, and J. Peterson

2005   Beads, Bifaces, and Boats: An Early Maritime
        Adaptation on the South Coast of San Miguel
        Island, California. *American Anthropologist*
        107(4):677–683.

Erlandson, J. M., M. A. Glassow, C. Rozaire, and
D. Morris

1992   4,000 Years of Human Occupation on Santa
        Barbara Island, California. *Journal of Califor-
        nia and Great Basin Anthropology* 14(1):85–
        93.

Erlandson, J. M., D. J. Kennett, R. J. Behl, and I. Hough

1997   The Cico Chert Source on San Miguel Island,
        California. *Journal of California and Great
        Basin Anthropology* 19(1):124–130.

Erlandson, J. M., T. C. Rick, T. J. Braje, M. Casperson,
B. Culleton, B. Fulfrost, T. Garcia, D. Guthrie, N. Jew,
D. Kennett, M. L. Moss, L. Reeder, C. Skinner, J. Watts,
and L. Willis

2011   Paleoindian Seafaring, Maritime Technol-
        ogies, and Coastal Foraging on California's
        Channel Islands. *Science* 441:1181–1185.

Erlandson, J. M., T. C. Rick, T. J. Braje, A. Steinberg,
and R. L. Vellanoweth

2008   Human Impacts on Ancient Shellfish: A
        10,000 Year Record from San Miguel, Cali-
        fornia. *Journal of Archaeological Science* 35:
        2144–2152.

Erlandson, J. M., T. C. Rick, and N. P. Jew

2012   Wima Chert: ~12,000 Years of Lithic Re-
        source Use on California's Northern Channel
        Islands. *Journal of California and Great Basin
        Anthropology* 32(1):76–85.

Erlandson, J. M., T. C. Rick, T. L. Jones, and J. F. Porcasi

2007   One If by Land, Two If by Sea: Who Were the
        First Californians? In *California Prehistory:
        Colonization, Culture and Complexity*, edited
        by T. L. Jones and K. A. Klar, pp. 53–62. Alta-
        mira, Lanham, MD.

Fagan, B.

2004   The House on the Sea: An Essay on the An-
        tiquity of Planked Canoes in Southern Cali-
        fornia. *American Antiquity* 69(1):7–16.

Gamble, L. H.

2002   Archaeological Evidence for the Origin of the
        Plank Canoe in North America. *American
        Antiquity* 67(2):301–315.

Glassow, M. A.

1993a   Changes in Subsistence on Marine Resources
        through 7,000 Years of Prehistory on Santa
        Cruz Island. *Archaeology on the Northern
        Channel Islands of California*, edited by M. A.
        Glassow, pp. 75–94. Coyote Press Archives of
        California Prehistory, Vol. 34. Coyote Press,
        Salinas, CA.

1993b   The Occurrence of Red Abalone Shells in
        Northern Channel Island Archaeological
        Middens. In *Third California Island Sym-
        posium: Recent Advances in Research on the
        California Islands*, edited by F. G. Hochberg,
        pp. 567–576. Santa Barbara Museum of Natu-
        ral History, Santa Barbara, CA.

1996   The Significance to California Prehistory of
        the Earliest Mortars and Pestles. *Pacific Coast
        Archaeological Society* 32(4):14–26.

1997   Middle Holocene Development in the Central Santa Barbara Coastal Region. In *The Archaeology of the California Coast During the Middle Holocene*, edited by J. M. Erlandson and M. A. Glassow, pp. 73–90. Cotsen Institute of Archaeology, University of California, Los Angeles.

2005   Prehistoric Dolphin Hunting on Santa Cruz Island, California. In *The Exploitation and Cultural Importance of Sea Mammals*, edited by G. Monks, pp. 107–120. Oxbow Books, Oxford.

2010   *Channel Islands National Park Archaeological Overview and Assessment*. Prepared for and on file at the Cultural Resources Division, Channel Islands National Park, Ventura, CA.

Glassow, M. A., L. H. Gamble, J. E. Perry, and G. S. Russell

2007   Prehistory of the Northern California Bight and the Adjacent Transverse Ranges. In *California Prehistory, Colonization, Culture, and Complexity*, edited by T. L. Jones and K. A. Klar, pp. 191–213. Altamira, Lanham, MD.

Glassow, M. A., D. J. Kennett, J. P. Kennett, and L. R. Wilcoxon

1994   Confirmation of Middle Holocene Ocean Cooling Inferred from Stable Isotopic Analysis of Prehistoric Shells from Santa Cruz Island, California. In *The Fourth California Islands Symposium: Update on the Status of Resources*, edited by W. L. Halvorson and G. J. Maender, pp. 223–232. Santa Barbara Museum of Natural History, Santa Barbara, CA.

Glassow, M. A., J. E. Perry, and P. F. Paige

2008   The Punta Arena Site: Early and Middle Holocene Cultural Development on Santa Cruz Island. Santa Barbara Museum of Natural History, Santa Barbara, CA.

Glassow, M. A., L. R. Wilcoxon, and J. M. Erlandson

1988   Cultural and Environmental Change During the Early Period of Santa Barbara Channel Prehistory. In *The Archaeology of Pacific Coastlines*, edited by G. N. Bailey and J. Parkington, pp. 64–77. Cambridge University Press, Cambridge.

Goldberg, C., M. Titus, R. Salls, and R. Berger

2000   Site Chronology on San Clemente Island, California. *Pacific Coast Archaeological Society Quarterly* 36(1):31–40.

Howard, W. J., and L. M. Raab

1993   Olivella Grooved Rectangle Beads as Evidence of a Mid-Holocene Southern Channel Islands Interaction Sphere. *Pacific Coast Archaeological Society Quarterly* 29:1–11.

Hudson, D. T., and T. C. Blackburn

1983   *The Material Culture of the Chumash Interaction Sphere*, Vol. 2: *Food Preparation and Shelter*. Ballena Press, Santa Barbara, CA.

Hudson, D. T., T. Blackburn, R. Curletti, and J. Timbrook

1977   *The Eye of the Flute: Chumash Traditional History and Ritual as Told by Fernando Librado Kitsepawit to John P. Harrington*. Malki Museum Press, Banning, CA.

Hudson, D. T., and E. Underhay

1978   *Crystals in the Sky: An Intellectual Odyssey Involving Chumash Astronomy, Cosmology, and Rock Art*. Anthropological Papers No. 10, edited by L. J. Bean and T. C. Blackburn. Ballena Press, Socorro, NM.

Inman, D. L.

1983   Application of Coastal Dynamics to the Reconstruction of Paleocoastlines in the Vicinity of La Jolla, California. In *Quaternary Coastlines and Marine Archaeology: Towards the Prehistory of Land Bridges and Continental Shelves*, edited by P. M. Masters and N. C. Flemming, pp. 1–49. Academic Press, London.

Jazwa, C. S., L. H. Gamble, and D. J. Kennett

2013   A High-Precision Chronology for Two House Features at an Early Village Site on Western Santa Cruz Island, California, USA. *Radiocarbon* 55(1):185–199.

Jazwa, C. S., D. J. Kennett, and D. Hanson

2012   Late Holocene Subsistence Change and Marine Productivity on Western Santa Rosa Island, California. *California Archaeology* 4(1):69–97.

Jenkins, D. L., and J. M. Erlandson

1996   Olivella Grooved Rectangle Beads from a Middle Holocene Site in the Fort Rock Valley, Northern Great Basin. *Journal of California and Great Basin Anthropology* 18(2):296–302.

Jertberg, P. M.

1986   The Eccentric Crescent: Summary Analysis. *Pacific Coast Archaeological Society Quarterly* 22:35–64.

Jochim, M. A.

1976   *Hunter-Gatherer Subsistence and Settlement: A Predictive Model*. Academic Press, New York.

Johnson, J. R.

1982   An Ethnographic Study of the Island Chumash. Master's thesis. Department of Anthropology, University of California, Santa Barbara.

1993   Cruzeño Chumash Social Geography. In

Archaeology on the Northern Channel Islands of California, edited by Michael A. Glassow, pp. 19–46. Coyote Press, Salinas, CA.

2001   Ethnohistoric Reflections of Cruzeño Chumash Society. In *The Origins of a Pacific Coast Chiefdom: The Chumash of the Channel Islands*, edited by J. E. Arnold, pp. 21–52. University of Utah Press, Salt Lake City.

Johnson, J. R., T. W. Stafford, Jr., H. O. Ajie, and D. P. Morris

2002   Arlington Springs Revisited. In *The Fifth California Islands Symposium*, edited by D. R. Brown, K. C. Mitchell, and H. W. Chaney, pp. 541–545. Santa Barbara Museum of Natural History, Santa Barbara, CA.

Jones, T. L., G. M. Brown, L. M. Raab, J. L. McVicar, W. G. Spaulding, D. J. Kennett, A. York, and P. L. Walker

1999   Environmental Imperatives Reconsidered: Demographic Crises in Western North America During the Medieval Climatic Anomaly. *Current Anthropology* 40(2):137–170.

Jones, T. L., and A. Schwitalla

2008   Archaeological Perspectives on the Effects of Medieval Drought in Prehistoric California. *Quaternary International* 188:41–58.

Junak, S., T. Ayers, R. Scott, D. Wilken, and D. Young

1995   *A Flora of Santa Cruz Island*. Santa Barbara Botanic Garden, Santa Barbara, CA.

Keegan, W., and J. Diamond

1987   Colonization of Islands by Humans: A Biogeographical Perspective. *Advances in Archaeological Method and Theory* 10:49–91.

Kelly, R. L.

1995   *The Foraging Spectrum: Diversity in Hunter-Gatherer Lifeways*. Smithsonian Institution Press, Washington, DC.

Kennett, D. J.

2005   *The Island Chumash: Behavioral Ecology of a Maritime Society*. University of California Press, Berkeley.

Kennett, D. J., and R. A. Clifford

2004   Flexible Strategies for Resource Defense on the Northern Channel Islands of California: An Agent-Based Model. In *Voyages of Discovery: The Archaeology of Islands*, edited by S. M. Fitzpatrick, pp. 21–50. Praeger, Westport, CT.

Kennett, D. J., and C. A. Conlee

2002   Emergence of Late Holocene Sociopolitical Complexity on Santa Rosa and San Miguel Islands. In *Catalysts to Complexity: Late Holocene Societies of the California Coast*, edited by J. M. Erlandson and T. L. Jones, pp. 147–

165. Cotsen Institute of Archaeology, University of California, Los Angeles.

Kennett, D. J., and J. P. Kennett

2000   Competitive and Cooperative Responses to Climatic Instability in Coastal Southern California. *American Antiquity* 65(2):379–395.

Kennett, D. J., J. P. Kennett, J. M. Erlandson, and K. G. Cannariato

2007   Human Responses to Middle Holocene Climate Change on California's Channel Islands. *Quaternary Science Reviews* 26:351–367.

Kennett, D. J., J. P. Kennett, G. J. West, J. M. Erlandson, J. R. Johnson, I. L. Hendy, A. West, B. J. Culleton, T. L. Jones, and T. W. Stafford, Jr.

2008   Wildfire and Abrupt Ecosystem Disruption on California's Northern Channel Islands at the Ållerød-Younger Dryas Boundary (13.0–12.9 ka). *Quaternary Science Reviews* 27:2528–2543.

Kennett, D. J., B. Winterhalder, J. Bartruff, and J. M. Erlandson

2009   An Ecological Model for the Emergence of Institutionalized Social Hierarchies on California's Northern Channel Islands. In *Pattern and Process in Cultural Evolution*, edited by S. Shennan, pp. 297–314. University of California Press, Berkeley.

King, C. D.

1976   Chumash Inter-village Economic Exchange. In *Native Californians: A Theoretical Perspective*, edited by L. J. Bean and T. C. Blackburn, pp. 289–318. Ballena Press, Ramona, CA.

1990   *Evolution of Chumash Society: A Comparative Study of Artifacts Used for Social System Maintenance in the Santa Barbara Channel Region before AD 1804*. Garland, New York.

Kinlan, B. P., M. H. Graham, and J. M. Erlandson

2005   Late Quaternary Changes in the Size and Shape of the California Channel Islands: Implications for Marine Subsidies to Terrestrial Communities. In *Proceedings of the Sixth California Islands Symposium*, edited by D. K. Garcelon and C. A. Schwemm, pp. 119–130. Institute for Wildlife Studies, Arcata, CA.

Lambert, P. M.

1993   Health in Prehistoric Populations of the Santa Barbara Channel Islands. *American Antiquity* 58:509–522.

Lambert, P. M., and P. L. Walker

1991   Physical Anthropological Evidence for the Evolution of Social Complexity in Coastal Southern California. *Antiquity* 65:963–973.

Martin, S. L., and V. S. Popper

2001   The Chumash in World and Regional Perspectives. In *The Origins of a Pacific Coast*

Chiefdom: The Chumash of the Channel Islands, edited by J. E. Arnold, pp. 1–19. University of Utah Press, Salt Lake City.

McCawley, W.
1996   *The First Angelinos: The Gabrielino Indians of Los Angeles*. Malki Museum Press, Banning, CA.

Meighan, C. W.
1959   The Little Harbor Site, Catalina Island: An Example of Ecological Interpretation in Archaeology. *American Antiquity* 24(4):383–405.
2000   Overview of the Archaeology of San Clemente Island, California. *Pacific Coast Archaeological Society Quarterly* 36(1):1–17.

Moratto, M. J.
1984   *California Archaeology*. Academic Press, New York.

Munns, A. M., and J. E. Arnold
2002   Late Holocene Santa Cruz Island: Patterns of Continuity and Change. In *Catalysts to Complexity: Late Holocene Societies of the California Coast*, edited by J. M. Erlandson and T. L. Jones, pp. 127–146. Cotsen Institute of Archaeology, University of California, Los Angeles.

Orr, P. C.
1968   *Prehistory of Santa Rosa Island*. Santa Barbara Museum of Natural History, Santa Barbara, CA.

Perry, J. E.
2003   Changes in Prehistoric Land and Resource Use among Complex Hunter-Gatherer-Fishers on Eastern Santa Cruz Island, California. PhD dissertation. University of California, Santa Barbara.

Perry, J. E., and C. Delaney-Rivera
2011   Interactions and Interiors of the Coastal Chumash: Perspectives from Santa Cruz Island and the Oxnard Plain. *California Archaeology* 3:103–126.

Perry, J. E., and K. M. Hoppa
2012   Subtidal Shellfish Exploitation on the California Channel Islands: Wavy Top (*Lithopoma undosum*) in the Middle Holocene. In *Exploring Methods of Faunal Analysis: Perspectives from California Archaeology*, edited by M. A. Glassow and T. L. Joslin, pp. 65–86. Cotsen Institute of Archaeology, University of California, Los Angeles.

Perry, J. E., and C. S. Jazwa
2010   Spatial and Temporal Patterning in Chert Exploitation on Eastern Santa Cruz Island, California. *American Antiquity* 75(1):177–198.

Pisias, N. G.
1978   Paleo-oceanography of the Santa Barbara Basin during the Last 8,000 Years. *Quaternary Research* 10:366–384.

Pletka, S.
2001   Bifaces and the Institutionalization of Exchange Relationships in the Chumash Sphere. In *The Origins of a Pacific Coast Chiefdom: The Chumash of the Channel Islands*, edited by J. E. Arnold, pp. 133–150. University of Utah Press, Salt Lake City.

Porcasi, J. F., and H. Fujita
2000   The Dolphin Hunters: A Specialized Prehistoric Maritime Adaptation in the Southern California Channel Islands and Baja California. *American Antiquity* 65(3):543–566.

Porcasi, J. F., T. L. Jones, and L. M. Raab
2004   Trans-Holocene Marine Mammal Exploitation on San Clemente Island: A Tragedy of the Commons Revisited. In *Prehistoric California: Archaeology and the Myth of Paradise*, edited by L. M. Raab and T. L. Jones, pp. 73–85. University of Utah Press, Salt Lake City.

Porcasi, P., J. F. Porcasi, and C. O'Neill
1999   Early Holocene Coastlines of the California Bight: The Channel Islands as First Visited by Humans. *Pacific Coast Archaeological Society Quarterly* 35(2–3):1–24.

Preziosi, A. M.
2001   Standardization and Specialization: The Island Chumash Microdrill Industry. In *The Origins of a Pacific Coast Chiefdom: The Chumash of the Channel Islands*, edited by J. E. Arnold, pp. 151–164. University of Utah Press, Salt Lake City.

Raab, L. M.
1992   An Optimal Foraging Analysis of Prehistoric Shellfish Collecting on San Clemente Island, California. *Journal of Ethnobiology* 12(1):63–80.
1997   The Southern Channel Islands During the Middle Holocene: Trends in Maritime Cultural Evolution. In *The Archaeology of the California Coast During the Middle Holocene*, edited by Jon M. Erlandson and Michael A. Glassow, pp. 23–34. Cotsen Institute of Archaeology, University of California, Los Angeles.

Raab, L. M., K. Bradford, J. F. Porcasi, and W. J. Howard
1995   Return to Little Harbor, Santa Catalina Island, California: A Critique of the Marine Paleoenvironmental Model. *American Antiquity* 60(2):287–308.

Raab, L. M., K. Bradford, and A. Yatsko
1994   Advances in Southern Channel Islands Archaeology: 1983 to 1993. *Journal of California and Great Basin Anthropology* 16(2):243–270.

Raab, L. M., J. Cassidy, A. Yatsko, and W. J. Howard
2009   *California Maritime Archaeology: A San Clemente Island Perspective*. Altamira, Lanham, MD.

Raab, L. M., and D. O. Larson
1997   Medieval Climatic Anomaly and Punctuated Cultural Evolution in Coastal Southern California. *American Antiquity* 62(2):319–336.

Raab, L. M., and A. Yatsko
1990   Prehistoric Human Ecology of Quinquina: A Research Design for Archaeological Studies on San Clemente Island, Southern California. *Pacific Coast Archaeological Society Quarterly* 26(2–3):10–37.

Raab, L. M., A. Yatsko, T. S. Garlinghouse, J. F. Porcasi, and K. Bradford
2002   Late Holocene San Clemente Island: Notes on Comparative Social Complexity in Coastal Southern California. In *Catalysts to Complexity: Late Holocene Societies of the California Coast*, edited by J. M. Erlandson and T. L. Jones, pp. 13–26. Cotsen Institute of Archaeology, University of California, Los Angeles.

Rick, T. C.
2001   The Archaeology of Santa Barbara Island: Past Projects and Future Directions. *Pacific Coast Archaeological Society Quarterly* 37(3): 57–72.
2006   A 5,000 Year Record of Coastal Settlement on Anacapa Island, California. *Journal of California and Great Basin Anthropology* 26:65–72.
2007   The Archaeology and Historical Ecology of Late Holocene San Miguel Island, California. Cotsen Institute of Archaeology, University of California, Los Angeles.

Rick, T. C., and J. M. Erlandson
2001   Late Holocene Subsistence Strategies on the South Coast of Santa Barbara Island. *Journal of California and Great Basin Anthropology* 23(2):297–307.
2008a   Archaeology, Historical Ecology, and the Future of Ocean Ecosystems. In *Human Impacts on Ancient Marine Ecosystems: A Global Perspective*, edited by T. C. Rick and J. M. Erlandson, pp. 297–307. University of California Press, Berkeley.
2008b   Historical Ecology and Human Impacts on Coastal Ecosystems of the Santa Barbara Channel Region, California. In *Human Impacts on Ancient Marine Ecosystems: A Global Perspective*, edited by T. C. Rick and J. M. Erlandson, pp. 77–102. University of California Press, Berkeley.

Rick, T. C., J. M. Erlandson, T. J. Braje, J. A. Estes, M. H. Graham, and R. L. Vellanoweth
2008   Historical Ecology and Human Impacts on Coastal Ecosystems of the Santa Barbara Channel Region, California. In *Human Impacts on Ancient Marine Ecosystems*, edited by T. C. Rick and J. M. Erlandson, pp. 77–101. University of California Press, Berkeley.

Rick, T. C., J. M. Erlandson, and K. E. Horton
2009   Marine Shellfish Harvest on Middle and Late Holocene Santa Barbara Island. *California Archaeology* 1(1):109–123.

Rick, T. C., J. M. Erlandson, and R. L. Vellanoweth
2001a   Paleocoastal Marine Fishing on the Pacific Coast of the Americas: Perspectives from Daisy Cave, California. *American Antiquity* 66(4):595–613.

Rick, T. C., J. M. Erlandson, R. L. Vellanoweth, and T. J. Braje
2005a   From Pleistocene Mariners to Complex Hunter-Gatherers: The Archaeology of the California Channel Islands. *Journal of World Prehistory* 19:169–228.

Rick, T. C., D. J. Kennett, and J. M. Erlandson
2005b   Preliminary Report on the Archaeology and Paleoecology of the Abalone Rocks Estuary, Santa Rosa Island, California. In *Proceedings of the Sixth California Islands Symposium*, edited by D. Garcelon and C. Schwemm, pp. 55–63. National Park Service Technical Publication CHIS-05-01. Institute for Wildlife Studies, Arcata, CA.

Rick, T. C., J. A. Robbins, and K. M. Ferguson
2006   Stable Isotopes from Marine Shells, Ancient Human Subsistence, and Environmental Change on Middle Holocene Santa Rosa Island, California, USA. *Journal of Island and Coastal Archaeology* 1:233–254.

Rick, T. C., C. E. Skinner, J. M. Erlandson, and R. L. Vellanoweth
2001b   Obsidian Source Characterization and Human Exchange Systems on California's Channel Islands. *Pacific Coast Archaeological Society Quarterly* 37(3):27–44.

Rick, T. C., R. L. Vellanoweth, J. M. Erlandson, and D. J. Kennett
2002   On the Antiquity of a Single-Piece Shell Fishhook: AMS Radiocarbon Evidence from the Southern California Coast. *Journal of Archaeological Science* 29:933–942.

Rozaire, C. E.
1978   *Archaeological Investigations of Anacapa Island*. Los Angeles County Museum of Natural History, Los Angeles.

Salls, R. A.

1992   Prehistoric Subsistence Change on California's Channel Islands: Environmental or Cultural? In *Essays on the Prehistory of Maritime California*, edited by Terry Jones, pp. 150–172. Center for Archaeological Research at Davis, Davis, CA.

2000   The Prehistoric Fishery of San Clemente Island. *Pacific Coast Archaeological Society Quarterly* 36(1):53–72.

Salls, R. A., L. M. Raab, and K. G. Bradford

1993   A San Clemente Island Perspective on Coastal Residential Structures and the Emergence of Sedentism. *Journal of California and Great Basin Anthropology* 15(2):176–194.

Stine, S.

1994   Extreme and Persistent Drought in California and Patagonia During Mediaeval Time. *Nature* 369:546–549.

Strudwick, I. H.

1986   Temporal and Areal Considerations Regarding the Prehistoric Circular Fishhook of Coastal California. Master's thesis. California State University, Long Beach.

Timbrook, J.

1993   Island Chumash Ethnobotany. *Archaeology on the Northern Channel Islands*, edited by M. A. Glassow, pp. 47–62. Coyote Press Archives of California Prehistory, Vol. 34. Coyote Press, Salinas, CA.

2007   *Chumash Ethnobotany: Plant Knowledge among the Chumash People of Southern California*. Santa Barbara Museum of Natural History, Santa Barbara, CA.

Vedder, J. G., and D. G. Howell

1980   Topographic Evolution of the Southern California Borderland During Late Cenozoic Time. In *The California Islands: Proceedings of a Multi-Disciplinary Symposium*, edited by D. M. Power, pp. 7–31. Santa Barbara Museum of Natural History, Santa Barbara, CA.

Vellanoweth, R., and J. M. Erlandson

1999   Middle Holocene Fishing and Maritime Adaptations at CA-SNI-161, San Nicholas Island, California. *Journal of California and Great Basin Anthropology* 21(2):257–274.

Watts, J., B. Fulfrost, and J. M. Erlandson

2010   Searching for Santarosae: Surveying Submerged Landscapes for Evidence of Paleocoastal Habitation Off California's Northern Channel Islands. In *The Archaeology of Maritime Landscapes*, edited by B. Ford, pp. 11–26. Springer, New York.

Wilcoxon, L. R.

1993   Subsistence and Site Structure: An Approach for Deriving Cultural Information from Coastal Shell Middens. In *Archaeology on the Northern Channel Islands of California*, edited by Michael A. Glassow, pp. 137–150. Coyote Press, Salinas, CA.

Williams, S. L., and E. J. Rosenthal

1993   Soapstone Craft Specialization at the Upper Buffalo Springs Quarry, Santa Catalina Island. *Pacific Coast Archaeological Society Quarterly* 29:22–50.

Winterhalder, B., D. J. Kennett, M. N. Grote, and J. Bartruff

2010   Ideal Free Settlement on California's Northern Channel Islands. *Journal of Anthropological Archaeology* 29:469–490.

Wolff, C. B., T. C. Rick, and A. Aland

2007   Middle Holocene Subsistence and Land Use on Southeast Anchorage, Santa Rosa Island, California. *Journal of California and Great Basin Anthropology* 27:44–56.

Yatsko, A.

2000   From Sheepherders to Cruise Missiles: A Short History of Archaeological Research at San Clemente Island. *Pacific Coast Archaeological Society Quarterly* 36(1):18–24.

Yesner, D. R.

1980   Maritime Hunter-Gatherers: Ecology and Prehistory. *Current Anthropology* 21(6): 727–735.

2

Points in Space and Time
The Distribution of Paleocoastal Points and Crescents on the Northern Channel Islands

Todd J. Braje, Jon M. Erlandson, and Torben C. Rick

By at least 13,000 years ago, Paleoindians were inhabiting continental North America from the Pacific to Atlantic coasts (Waters and Stafford 2007). Part of the subsistence economies of these first Americans included the hunting of terrestrial megafauna (mammoths, mastodons, bison, etc.) with sophisticated chipped stone technologies (Waguespack and Surovell 2003). Fluted Clovis and later Paleoindian projectile points found across North America and stemmed points from the Western Pluvial Lakes Tradition (WPLT) in the Far West have helped archaeologists track the spread and lifeways of these New World pioneers (e.g., Anderson and Gillam 2000; Beck and Jones 2010).

Since the discovery and dating of Monte Verde II in Chile to ~14,000 years ago (Dillehay et al. 2008; Erlandson, Braje, and Graham 2008), and because of the growing likelihood that some of the first migrants to the New World arrived in boats, archaeologists have intensified their search for the first Americans along the Pacific Coast. Due to the effects of rising postglacial sea levels, earthquakes, tsunamis, isostatic adjustments, coastal erosion, and other landscape changes, terminal Pleistocene (>11,500 cal BP) and early Holocene (11,500–7500 cal BP) coastal sites have been difficult to identify in many areas.

California's northern Channel Islands are one location where archaeologists have successfully documented a relatively high density of sites more than 7,500 years old (Rick et al. 2005), including Paleocoastal occupations dated between about 13,000 and 11,300 cal BP (see Erlandson,

Moss, and Des Lauriers 2008; Erlandson, Rick et al. 2011; Johnson et al. 2002). Until recently, however, Channel Island archaeologists had found little evidence for formal chipped stone technologies that might help identify the relationship of these early maritime peoples with mainland Paleoindian traditions such as Clovis, WPLT, or San Dieguito. New discoveries on Santa Cruz, Santa Rosa, and San Miguel islands have demonstrated that Channel Islanders possessed sophisticated maritime hunting technologies as early as 12,200 to 7,800 years ago (Erlandson, Rick et al. 2011; Glassow et al. 2008). Along with chipped stone crescents, two types of stemmed projectile points, Channel Island Barbed (CIB; aka Arena) and Amol points, now appear to be reliable terminal Pleistocene and early Holocene time markers on the northern Channel Islands (Erlandson 2013; Erlandson, Rick et al. 2011; Erlandson and Braje 2008a, 2008b; Glassow et al. 2008, n.d.).

As the antiquity, context, and significance of these distinctive early maritime technologies have become clearer, the number of known Paleocoastal sites has grown significantly. Given the fact that all paleoshorelines and more than 80 percent of the coastal lowlands that once surrounded the northern Channel Islands have been lost to rising postglacial seas and coastal erosion, the number (n=11 greater than 11,000 cal BP) of early sites that have been recorded is remarkable (Erlandson, Moss, and Des Lauriers 2008). This has led us to suspect that there may have been considerably more Paleocoastal people on the islands than anyone might have guessed a decade or two ago. The number of Paleocoastal sites that have been excavated and described is still small, however, and is limited primarily to small samples from shell middens where radiocarbon (^{14}C) dates can be easily obtained. Numerous lithic sites where Paleocoastal artifacts have been found but no reliable ^{14}C dates are available have not yet been described, a problem we address in this chapter. Specifically, we compile published and unpublished data on northern Channel Island sites, dated or undated, that have produced diagnostic Paleocoastal points and crescents. In discussing these early technologies we also explore some recent ideas about their functions and their relationships to other early cultural traditions in western North America and around the Pacific Rim.

Environmental and Cultural Overview of the Northern Channel Islands

Located between 20 and 42 km off the coast of Santa Barbara, California's northern Channel Islands—Anacapa, Santa Cruz, Santa Rosa, and San Miguel—range in size from 2.9 to 249 km^2. The islands are an extension of the mainland Santa Monica Mountains, an east-west trending line that forms the southern boundary of the Santa Barbara Channel. All of the islands are characterized by a Mediterranean climate with mild, dry summers and cooler, wetter winters. The terrestrial environments and topography vary across the islands, but modern vegetation communities are composed primarily of coastal sage scrub, island chaparral, and valley and foothill grassland (Junak et al. 2007). Santa Cruz and Santa Rosa Islands exhibit the highest diversity of terrestrial resources and topography, including small stands of oak woodland and pine forests, and significant interior mountain peaks. Sparse freshwater sources, a dearth of trees, and a limited terrestrial flora and fauna contribute to a relatively impoverished terrestrial environment, especially on Anacapa and San Miguel Islands. Historical overgrazing appears to have exacerbated these conditions, but island vegetation communities and aquifers are beginning to show signs of recovery.

Island shorelines consist of a mix of rocky intertidal and sandy beach habitats, with extensive and highly productive nearshore kelp forests and other deep-water marine habitats. Santa Barbara Channel waters are characterized by intensive marine upwelling and are located at the intersection of warm southerly and cool northerly ocean currents, which support diverse populations of shellfish, fishes, seabirds, and sea mammals (Schoenherr et al. 1999). This productive marine environment has provided sustenance for maritime hunter-gatherers for at least the last 13,000 years (Erlandson, Rick et al. 2011; Johnson et al. 2002), culminating in the sophisticated Chumash culture encountered by Europeans after AD 1542 (see Arnold 2001; Gamble 2008; Kennett 2005; Rick 2007).

The northern Channel Islands contain some of the earliest evidence of maritime adaptations in North America. Several sites are now relatively well known: Arlington Springs (CA-SRI-173) on Santa Rosa Island, with human bones dated to ~13,000 years old (Johnson et al. 2002); CA-SRI-512W, located near Arlington Springs, with abundant bird bone and a variety of artifacts dated between ~11,800 and 11,300 years ago (Erlandson, Rick et al. 2011); Daisy Cave (CA-SMI-261) on San Miguel Island, with multiple Paleocoastal occupations dated between about 11,600 and 8,600 years ago (Erlandson et al. 1996; Rick et al. 2001); and the Cardwell Bluffs sites (CA-SMI-678 and CA-SMI-679) on eastern San Miguel, with large assemblages of stone tools and shellfish remains dated between ~12,200 and 11,300 years ago (Erlandson and Braje 2008a; Erlandson, Rick et al. 2011).

During the terminal Pleistocene, when sea levels were as much as 75 m lower than today, the northern Channel Islands were connected by a series of land bridges into one large island known as Santarosae (Orr 1968; Porcasi et al. 1999; see Figure 2.1), the eastern end of which was roughly 10 km from the mainland coast. Rapid postglacial sea level rise reduced the size of Santarosae (and the northern Channel Islands) roughly 75 percent, with Anacapa (ca. 10,900 cal BP), Santa Cruz (9300 cal BP), and Santa Rosa-San Miguel (9000 cal BP) separating in step-wise fashion near the end of the Pleistocene (Kennett et al. 2008:2532). By about 6,000 years ago, the outline of the northern Channel Islands was similar to the modern geography, although significant landscape changes have continued to the present day.

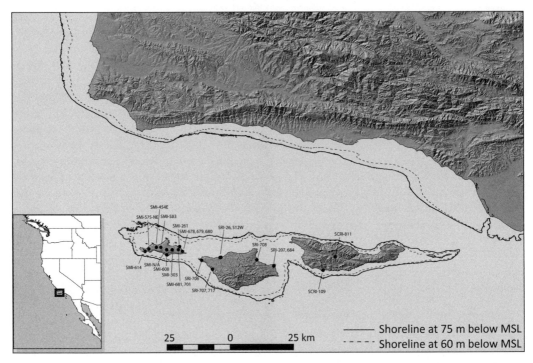

FIGURE 2.1. Map showing localities discussed in the text relative to the reconstructed terminal Pleistocene paleogeography, including the –60 m (dark shading) and –50 m (lighter shading) submarine contours, which approximate the shorelines of 12,500 and 11,000 years ago (base map by L. Reeder).

In the last two decades, intensive surveys of late Pleistocene and early Holocene soils, a refined understanding of landscape changes and settlement histories, and an extensive program of radiocarbon dating have helped identify more than 50 sites on the northern Channel Islands ^{14}C dated between about 13,000 and 8000 cal BP (see Erlandson, Moss, and Des Lauriers 2008; Reeder et al. 2008; Rick et al. 2005; Gusick 2012, Chapter 3). While much less abundant, a handful of sites on the southern Channel Islands have been dated between 10,000 and 8000 cal BP (Raab et al. 2009). Until recently, most of these early sites could be characterized as relatively small, low-density shell middens featuring scatters of California mussel (*Mytilus californianus*), black abalone (*Haliotis cracherodii*), and other rocky intertidal shellfish remains. Most of these sites produced relatively few artifacts, and chipped stone points and bifaces were particularly rare (e.g., Braje and Erlandson 2006; Erlandson et al. 1999; Erlandson et al. 2004). Thus, little was known about the nature of chipped stone technologies

made and used by early maritime peoples on the northern Channel Islands.

The Antiquity of Paleocoastal Points and Crescents

Chipped stone crescents and CIB points from the Channel Islands (Figure 2.2) were first illustrated and described by Wardle (1913) and George Heye (1921), founder and director of the Museum of the American Indian. Heye funded a four-and-a-half-month-long collecting expedition to San Miguel Island in 1919, led by Ralph Glidden, an antiquarian who worked extensively on the Channel Islands during the early twentieth century. Heye's 1921 book is an ahistorical description of the artifacts that Glidden's team recovered, most of which were associated with 343 human burials exhumed from at least 21 localities. In it, he illustrated a crescent and two CIB points, one intermingled with 13 other chipped stone points (Heye 1921: Plate 39, top row, third from the left) and one by itself. Of this second point, Heye (1921:68) wrote:

FIGURE 2.2. Channel Island Barbed (Arena) points and crescents from two lithic sites on San Miguel Island, CA-SMI-303 (*top*) and CA-SMI-454 (*bottom*) (digital scan by J. Erlandson; scale in cm).

Of all the chipped implements from San Miguel, the finest example is shown in pl. XLII. It is of a light-brown, semi-transparent chalcedony, and at its thickest part measures only an eighth of an inch. The object is of entirely too delicate a character to have been utilitarian; it may have hung from a neck as a pendant, although its shape would seem to preclude its use as such, or it was possibly set in a bone shaft and used as a hair-ornament.

Heye (1921) described this point as one of the finest examples of flint-knapping in North America, but never speculated on the age of CIB points (or any of the other technologies he identified on San Miguel), leaving that task for future researchers more interested in cultural histories than collecting museum-quality relics.

Over the next eighty years, archaeologists employing increasingly rigorous field and laboratory methods conducted research on the northern

Channel Islands and adjacent mainland. Scores of sites were excavated, and cultural historical sequences were established and refined. By the mid-twentieth century, the Oak Grove, or Milling Stone, horizon represented the earliest well-defined cultural stage in the Santa Barbara Channel area. This horizon is characterized by an emphasis on the gathering of small seeds and shellfish, the heavy use of grinding stones (manos and metates), and the occasional use of relatively crude projectile points (Rogers 1929; Wallace 1955). Now known to date to as many as 9,000 years ago along the Santa Barbara mainland coast, the lack of Milling Stone sites on the islands led some researchers to assume that the northern Channel Islands were settled relatively late (see Olson 1930; Rogers 1929). Even after Orr (1968) established that the islands were occupied as early as 10,000 RYBP, it seemed logical to assume that the earliest islanders focused heavily on shellfish and had crude projectile point technologies similar to their neighbors across the channel.

Therefore, when Justice (2002:264) first formally defined CIB points, he considered them to be a late Holocene technology. These ultra-thin, relatively long stemmed, intricately barbed, and often needle-tipped points were much more similar to small, thin, and delicately knapped arrow points dated to the last 1,500 years than they were to the large, thick, and cruder bifaces found in many island and mainland sites dating to the early and middle Holocene. Recognizing the lack of good chronological control, however, Justice (2002:264) cautiously concluded that:

> This type is thought to date roughly from ca. 1000 BC to ca. AD 1000 or later, although there is little evidence to bring to bear on the question of age of the Channel Islands Barbed type since no dated contexts with this type in association are presently known. Thus, the type probably appears in the latter part of the late Archaic period and perhaps persists throughout the Intermediate period and into the late Prehistoric period.... Based on overall design and extremely thin and delicate features, this type places chronologically late in the stemmed point tradition of the southern California coast.

The first indication that CIB points had a greater antiquity on the islands came from excavations conducted by Michael Glassow on western Santa Cruz Island (Glassow et al. 2008). His work at the deeply stratified Punta Arena site (CA-SCRI-109) produced three CIB points from deposits dating between ~8500 and 7800 cal BP. Years before, in an unpublished report, Rozaire (1978: Plate 14B) depicted a similar point found deeply buried in a stratified shell midden at Daisy Cave on eastern San Miguel Island, a point Erlandson assumed to be intrusive until Glassow first documented the antiquity of CIB points (Erlandson and Jew 2009). A recent review of Rozaire's field notes led Erlandson to conclude that the CIB point may be associated with the terminal Pleistocene occupation of Daisy Cave, dated to ~11,500 cal BP. More recent work at Daisy Cave also produced the first chipped stone crescent from the Channel Islands found in a stratified and dated context, a specimen recovered from a shell midden stratum dated between ~10,000 and 8600 cal BP (Erlandson 2005).

Soon after the early Holocene age of CIB points and crescents was recognized at Punta Arena and Daisy Cave, CIB points were discovered at two other well-dated sites on San Miguel Island, including a single point from a 9,600–8,600–year-old shell midden at CA-SMI-608 (Braje 2010: Figure 4.5; Erlandson et al. 2005:679) and five point fragments from an 8,600–8,400–year-old midden at CA-SMI-575-NE (Erlandson and Braje 2007). We recently found numerous leaf-shaped biface preforms, crescents, and CIB and Amol points at several lithic workshop and camp sites on eastern San Miguel Island (the Cardwell Bluffs sites: CA-SMI-678, -679, -680, and -701), many of them associated with low- or moderate-density shell midden loci dated between ~12,200 and 11,300 cal BP (Erlandson, Rick et al. 2011; Erlandson, Braje, Snitker 2008). Shell and bone middens of similar age have also been identified on Santa Rosa Island (CA-SRI-26, CA-SRI-512W, CA-SRI-706; see Erlandson, Rick et al. 2011; Erlandson, Rick, and Jew 2011; Rick and Erlandson 2011). At many of these sites, CIB points are found with crescents, but some sites have produced only one or the other. Based on currently available evidence, CIB points may have been used for as many as 4,000 years, from ~11,700 to 12,200 cal BP. Crescents appear to have a similar antiquity, but there is currently no evidence that they persisted beyond about 9000 cal BP on the northern Channel Islands.

Also found at Cardwell Bluffs is a new Paleocoastal stemmed point type that Erlandson (2012) has dubbed "Amol" (Figure 2.3). These relatively small and thin points are similar to CIB points but lack prominent barbs and generally have serrated blade margins. Although relatively few Amol points have been found so far, their associations with CA-SMI-678 and CA-SMI-679 middens dated to ~12,000 cal BP and a midden at CA-SRI-26 on Santa Rosa Island dated to 11,300 cal BP (Erlandson, Rick, and Jew 2011) led Erlandson (2013) to propose that they might be a shorter-lived point type that was a precursor to the more elaborate and abundant CIB points. Additional research is necessary to better document the age of Amol points and their relationship to CIB points.

FIGURE 2.3. Composite image of an Amol point from CA-SRI-26 (digital scan by J. Erlandson and K. Hamm).

The Distribution of Paleocoastal Stemmed Points and Crescents

For the northern Channel Islands, chipped stone crescents and Channel Island Barbed points have long been known from museum collections (see Heye 1921; Jones 1956; Mohr and Fenenga 2010; Wardle 1913) gathered by early antiquarians and archaeologists. Much smaller numbers of chipped stone crescents have been found on the southern Channel Islands of San Nicolas and Santa Catalina (Davis et al. 2010), but CIB and Amol points are currently only known from the northern islands.

Just a decade ago, none of these distinctive artifacts could be linked to known sites on the islands, and although crescents were widely regarded to be early Holocene markers in California and the Great Basin, the antiquity of CIB points was generally assumed to be limited to the late Holocene (Justice 2002:264). Since Glas-

sow first found CIB points in the early Holocene contexts at CA-SCRI-109 (Glassow et al. 2008), the number of stemmed Paleocoastal points and crescents found at specific sites has grown rapidly, and many of those sites have now been ^{14}C dated between ~12,000 and 7800 cal BP.

In Table 2.1, we present data on 125 CIB points, 25 Amol points, and 78 crescents (including whole specimens, diagnostic fragments, and preforms) found within the boundaries of at least 23 recorded sites on San Miguel, Santa Rosa, and Santa Cruz Islands (Figure 2.1). Several isolated points or crescents, along with scores of museum specimens with only general provenience, are not included. Currently, the largest number of Paleocoastal points and crescents comes from San Miguel Island (n = 113, 49.6 percent), with all but 14 of those recovered from the Cardwell Bluffs sites. Santa Rosa has produced a roughly equal number (n = 110, 48.2 percent), with 86 of these

TABLE 2.1. Terminal Pleistocene and early Holocene sites on the northern Channel Islands with Channel Island Barbed and Amol points

Site #	# CIB Pts	# Amol Pts	# of Crescents	Associated 14C Age (cal BP)	Site Description	Reference
San Miguel Island						
SMI-N/A	1	—	—	None	Small shell and lithic scatter in interdune swale on south slope of San Miguel Hill	This chapter
SMI-261	1	—	1	11,600–8500	Multicomponent cave site with diverse faunal, artifact, and paleontological remains	Erlandson 2005; Erlandson and Jew 2009; Rozaire 1978
SMI-303	2	—	1	None	Low-density lithic scatter with 2 CIB point fragments, 1 crescent preform	This chapter
SMI-454E	3	—	1	8500?	Lithic scatter and low-density midden eroding from Simonton Soil	This chapter
SMI-575-NE	5	—	—	8600–8300	Small shell midden located on ancient dune ridge above Point Bennett	Erlandson and Braje 2007
SMI-583/H	2	—	2	None	Lithic scatter with >30 points and biface preform fragments	This chapter
SMI-608	1	—	—	9600–8600	Early Holocene residential base with a diverse faunal and artifact assemblage	Braje 2010; Erlandson et al. 2005
SMI-614	1	—	1	None	Multicomponent site deflated on beach at Adams Cove; early Holocene to Historic	Braje and Erlandson 2008
SMI-678	13	—	14	12,250–11,300	Large lithic scatter on bluffs above Cardwell Point; with 4 intact shell midden loci	Erlandson et al. 2011
SMI-679	18	—	16	12,000–11,400	Large lithic quarry/workshop at Cardwell Bluffs; 1 shell midden, scores of biface preforms	Erlandson and Braje 2008a; Erlandson et al. 2011
SMI-680	—	—	2	None	Multicomponent lithic scatter at Cardwell Bluffs, numerous biface preforms	Erlandson, Braje, and Snitker 2008
SMI-681	1	—	1	None	Low-density lithic scatter with 1 crescent fragment and 1 CIB preform	Erlandson and Braje 2008b
SMI-701	—	—	2	11,700	Lithic scatter with rare shell fragments, leaf-shaped bifaces	Erlandson 2010
Subtotal	48	3	24	41		

Santa Rosa Island

Site					Description	Reference
SRI-717	1	—	2	None	Large lithic scatter with some in situ red abalone shells	This chapter
SRI-26	2	1	3	11,800–11,200	Deeply buried lithic and bone scatter with small amounts of marine shell	Erlandson, Rick, and Jew 2011
SRI-207	1	—	1	None	Small lithic scatter located on the bluffs overlooking Bechers Bay	Rick 2008
SRI-512W	67	—	19	11,800–11,500	Deeply buried midden with abundant bird bone and chipped stone tools	Erlandson et al. 2011
SRI-684	—	—	1	None	One crescent fragment made from Monterey or Tuqan chert	This chapter
SRI-706	—	—	4	11,560–11,210	Large lithic scatter with one in situ red abalone shell, several biface preforms	This chapter
SRI-707	2	—	4	None	Large, low-density, multicomponent lithic scatter overlooking southwest coast	This chapter
SRI-708	1	—	1	11,190–11,120	Large shell and lithic scatter on coastal terrace overlooking Bechers Bay	This chapter
Subtotal	74	1	35			
Santa Cruz Island						
SCRI-109	3	—	—	8500–7800	Large, multicomponent shell midden with diverse molluscan remains	Glassow et al. 2008
SCRI-811	—	—	2	None	Low-density lithic scatter, Central Valley area	Glassow 2009
Subtotal	3	0	2			
Total	125	25	78			

found at CA-SRI-512W. There are currently just three CIB points and two crescents reported from Santa Cruz Island sites (2.2 percent), the former from the Punta Arena site (CA-SCRI-109), and the latter believed to be from CA-SCRI-811, a lithic scatter located in the central valley (Glassow 2009). No Paleocoastal sites are known for Anacapa Island, and no CIB points or crescents from that small island have been identified in museum collections.

The density of these Paleocoastal artifacts (number divided by the modern land area of each island) tells a somewhat different story, with San Miguel having a much higher value (3.2/km²) than Santa Rosa (0.51/km²) or Santa Cruz (0.02/km²) islands. These values appear to be generally consistent with the abundance of crescents and CIBs from San Miguel and Santa Rosa found in museum collections. The higher densities on San Miguel and Santa Rosa may result from greater exposure and visibility, more intensive research on the Paleocoastal period, and the larger number of terminal Pleistocene and early Holocene sites identified on these western islands. Historically, livestock grazing on San Miguel, and to a lesser extent Santa Rosa, destabilized extensive dune fields, exposing large areas where Paleocoastal artifacts have been collected by antiquarians and archaeologists. Current research by Amy Gusick (Chapter 3) and Michael Glassow (Chapter 4) on early Santa Cruz Island sites should help balance Paleocoastal research efforts on the northern Channel Islands and develop a better understanding of variability in early technologies, settlement, and adaptations across the archipelago.

On San Miguel, a systematic search of caves, freshwater springs, and chert sources has identified numerous early shell middens and lithic scatters. Reconnaissance of the rim of the island's steep escarpment, which offers commanding views of much of the island's coastline, has added additional early sites that may have been used as strategic overlooks to monitor the movement of game (sea mammals) or people. Targeting these features has been exceptionally fruitful in identifying terminal Pleistocene and early Holocene sites. Recent reconnaissance work has also identified several lithic sites (e.g., CA-SMI-303,

CA-SMI-454, CA-SMI-681) containing Paleocoastal stemmed points or crescents located outside these geographic features in unexpected locations.

We should also note that several lithic scatters on San Miguel and Santa Rosa have produced assemblages that we suspect may be of Paleocoastal age, which would increase the number of Paleocoastal sites on the northern Channel Islands, but no clearly diagnostic points or crescents have yet been found. Numerous shell middens dated between about 10,200 and 7800 cal BP have also been identified but have produced no diagnostic Paleocoastal artifacts. With further monitoring, surface collections, and excavations, some of these lithic scatters and shell middens may produce crescents or CIB/Amol points that will expand our understanding of the number, distribution, and function of Paleocoastal settlements and adaptations on the islands.

The Function of Paleocoastal Points and Crescents

Among archaeologists, no consensus has been reached on the function of crescents and Paleocoastal stemmed points. In the Far West, crescents come in a variety of shapes that have been interpreted as everything from surgical tools to scrapers and transverse projectile points to zoomorphic effigies or amulets (e.g., Erlandson and Braje 2008a, 2008b; Koerper and Farmer 1987; Mohr and Fenenga 2010; Tadlock 1966; Wardle 1913). Strongly associated with lake, marsh, and coastal habitats in the Far West, the bilaterally symmetrical lunate crescents seem most likely to be related to the hunting of waterfowl and/or seabirds, although they may also have been used for other purposes by early or later peoples. On the northern Channel Islands, where land animals and plant resources are relatively limited, an association with bird hunting seems most likely, especially given their association with thousands of waterfowl and seabird bones at CA-SRI-512W (Erlandson, Rick et al. 2011).

In contrast, there is little doubt that most CIB points were used as projectile tips in hunting. They come in a variety of sizes, persist for ~4,000 years, and are found in sites containing a variety of faunal assemblages. It seems most likely that these ultra-thin bifaces with delicate barbs, serrations, and needle-like tips were used primarily in marine hunting, where they would have been less likely to fracture. Glassow et al. (2008) suggested that CIB points may have been used in fishing, but some larger specimens seem more likely to have been used in hunting sea mammals, and numerous very small specimens have been found at CA-SRI-512W, where they may have been used to hunt birds.

So far, most crescents and Paleocoastal points recovered on the Channel Islands have come from surface contexts where sandblasting has rendered microwear and residue analyses impossible or inconclusive. Substantial numbers of Paleocoastal points and crescents have been recovered from stratified contexts in recent years, but there has not yet been any systematic study of breakage patterns, microwear traces, or residues that might help illuminate their specific function.

Even where they are found in sites with good faunal preservation, one problem with reconstructing the function of Paleocoastal points and crescents is that the sites were all located between 1 and 10 (or more) km from contemporary Paleocoastal shorelines, and that their contents (and interpreted function) may have been differentially affected by the distance to marine habitats and the Schlepp Effect. If CIB or Amol points were used to hunt marine mammals or catch fish, for instance, it is possible (perhaps likely) that carcasses were processed on distant beaches and that parts of the animals were not brought back to the site. This may be the case at CA-SMI-575-NE, CA-SMI-608, CA-SMI-678, CA-SMI-679, and the terminal Pleistocene component at Daisy Cave, where shellfish dominate the faunal assemblages but were clearly not the prey targeted by maritime hunters armed with stemmed points and crescents. This issue is particularly problematic at the Cardwell Bluff sites, where hundreds of bifaces have been recovered (including dozens of Paleocoastal crescents and stemmed points), but the recovered faunal assemblages consist entirely of shellfish remains (Erlandson, Rick et al. 2011).

The faunal assemblage at CA-SRI-512W tells a very different story. Here, the 67 CIB points and 19 crescents reported from the site were found with more than 5,000 bone fragments domi-nated by waterfowl such as Canada goose (*Branta canadensis*) and snow goose (*Chen caerulescens*), as well as seabirds such as cormorant (*Phalacrocorax* spp.), albatross (*Phoebastria albatrus*), and the extinct flightless sea duck, *Chendytes lawi* (Erlandson, Rick et al. 2011:1182–1183). Smaller numbers of pinniped and undifferentiated marine mammal bones were also recovered, along with some nearshore fish remains, but no shellfish. This faunal assemblage suggests that CIB points and crescents were used in the hunting or processing of vertebrates, especially birds (Erlandson, Rick et al. 2011), but questions remain about their specific functions.

Far West and Circum-Pacific Technological Connections?

Just as projectile points have been used to track movements of Clovis and later Paleoindian peoples in North America, recent discoveries related to crescents and stemmed Paleocoastal points on the northern Channel Islands provide evidence for potential links between WPLT assemblages throughout the Far West, as well as more speculative links to stemmed point traditions from much of the Pacific Rim region. Beck and Jones (2010) reinvigorated a long-standing debate about whether stemmed points and crescents found in many WPLT sites in the Great Basin and Far West may be as old or older than Clovis points found in the Central Plains and American Southwest. Beck and Jones (2010) also suggested that stemmed points might be related to a coastal migration into the Americas, an argument that is much less contentious since the discovery, dating, and widespread acceptance of Monte Verde II as a pre-Clovis site (Dillehay et al. 2008).

Erlandson and Braje (2011) expanded on this idea, noting a circum-Pacific distribution of broadly similar stemmed points extending from Japan to Kamchatka, to Oregon and California, and into coastal South America. The hypothesis that crescents and stemmed points from the northern Channel Islands and Far West may be related to a coastal migration from Asia to the Americas remains speculative at this point, primarily because major gaps in the trans-Pacific distribution of stemmed points exist, the dating of many of these technological traditions needs refinement, and detailed morphological comparisons are generally lacking. Still, there are intriguing similarities in chronology, with stemmed (aka "tanged," "pedunculate") points dated to 16,000 years ago in Japan, 13,000 years ago in Kamchatka, and between ~13,000 and 8,000 years ago along the Pacific Slope in North and South America. Especially striking is the morphological similarity between tanged points from Japan, dated between ~16,000 and 13,800 years ago (Nagai 2007), and CIB points.

For now, the technological and cultural linkages between Paleocoastal peoples of the northern Channel Islands and their WPLT neighbors in California and the Great Basin seem reasonably well established. Further research is needed to determine if these similarities mark a common origin linked to a coastal migration from Asia into the Americas, and if similarities in late Pleistocene stemmed point traditions around the Pacific Rim result from such a common origin or adaptive and technological convergence among early maritime peoples.

Conclusions

In this chapter, we presented data on the distribution and age of Paleocoastal stemmed points and crescents on the northern Channel Islands, including numerous lithic sites that have not been ^{14}C dated but contain diagnostic artifacts dated elsewhere between ~12,200 and 7800 cal BP. These lithic sites add to the inventory of Paleocoastal sites on the islands and support an emerging view that Santarosae and the northern Channel Islands were home to larger populations of early maritime peoples than earlier accounts have suggested. The fact that the number of such Paleocoastal sites on the islands continues to grow rapidly further supports this idea, especially when we consider that all paleoshorelines and as much as 75 percent of the land area of Santarosae have been lost to postglacial sea level rise and coastal erosion.

Until recently, we knew relatively little about the lifeways of Santarosae's earlier Paleocoastal peoples. Most early island sites are small shell scatters containing only limited technology, sug-

gesting that populations were mobile and relied on intertidal shellfish as their primary source of protein (Rick et al. 2005). In the last few years, a broader picture has emerged as Paleocoastal technologies have been identified and terminal Pleistocene sites on Santa Rosa Island have produced faunal assemblages dominated by waterfowl, seabirds, marine mammals, and fish remains. Recent discoveries suggest that Paleocoastal technologies, subsistence, and settlement patterns were more diverse than once thought, calling into question much of what we thought we knew about the earliest Channel Islanders.

The recognition of sophisticated Paleocoastal technologies in terminal Pleistocene and early Holocene island sites also raises interesting questions about the relationship of these early islanders and Milling Stone peoples along the adjacent mainland coast, two technological traditions that appear to overlap in time, at least between ~9,000 to 7,800 years ago. On the other hand, the stemmed points and crescents found in terminal Pleistocene and early Holocene Paleocoastal sites also establish technological links with WPLT assemblages throughout much of the Far West, which contain similar crescents and stemmed points. At Cardwell Bluffs and CA-SRI-512W, these links can be dated to at least 12,200 to 11,300 cal BP. An obsidian artifact from the latter site established the existence of exchange between island Paleocoastal and WPLT peoples in eastern California by ~11,700 years ago.

Finally, the dating of crescents and stemmed CIB and Amol points to the terminal Pleistocene and early Holocene may provide even broader links between Paleocoastal and WPLT peoples of the Far West and the migration of maritime peoples around the Pacific Rim, from Asia to the Americas. The colonization of the New World was a dynamic and complex process, with archaeological signatures left by a variety of populations moving by land and by sea. Reconstructing these migrations requires a creative, interdisciplinary group of scientists from both sides of the Pacific intent on piecing together a more complete mosaic of archaeological, genetic, and paleoecological data.

Acknowledgments

We thank Chris Jazwa and Jenn Perry for organizing the 2011 Society for American Archaeology session and the resulting edited volume that inspired us to start and finish this manuscript. We also thank Mark Raab and an anonymous reviewer for their insightful comments, and the editors for their logistical help in the production of this volume. We also have benefitted tremendously by communicating regularly with Michael Glassow about issues related to Paleocoastal technologies and adaptations on the islands.

References

Anderson, D. G., and J. C. Gillam
2000   Paleoindian Colonization of the Americas: Implications from an Examination of Physiography, Demography, and Artifact Distribution. *American Antiquity* 65(1):43–66.

Arnold, J. E. (editor)
2001   *The Origins of a Pacific Coast Chiefdom: The Chumash of the Channel Islands.* University of Utah Press, Salt Lake City.

Beck, C., and G. T. Jones
2010   Clovis and Western Stemmed: Population Migration and the Meeting of Two Technologies in the Intermountain West. *American Antiquity* 75(1):81–116.

Braje, T. J.
2010   *Modern Oceans, Ancient Sites: Archaeology and Marine Conservation on San Miguel Island, California.* University of Utah Press, Salt Lake City.

Braje, T. J., and J. M. Erlandson
2006   CA-SMI-623: An Early Holocene Site from the South Coast of San Miguel Island, California. *Current Research in the Pleistocene* 23:80–81.

Davis, T. W., J. M. Erlandson, G. L. Fenenga, and K. Hamm
2010   Chipped Stone Crescents and the Antiquity of Maritime Settlement on San Nicolas Island, Alta California. *California Archaeology* 2(2):185–201

Dillehay, T. D., C. Ramírez, M. Pino, M. B. Collins, J. Rossen, and J. D. Pino-Navarro
2008   Monte Verde: Seaweed, Food, Medicine, and the Peopling of South America. *Science* 320 (5877):784–786.

Erlandson, J. M.
2005   An Early Holocene Eccentric Crescent from Daisy Cave, San Miguel Island, California. *Current Research in the Pleistocene* 21:45–47.
2013   Amol Points: Stemmed and Serrated Paleocoastal Points from Terminal Pleistocene Sites on California's Santarosae Island. *California Archaeology*, in press.

Erlandson, J. M., and T. J. Braje
2007   Early Maritime Technology on California's San Miguel Island: Arena Points from CA-SMI-575-NE. *Current Research in the Pleistocene* 24:85–86.
2008a   Five Crescents from Cardwell: Context and Chronology of Chipped Crescents at CA-SMI-679. *Pacific Coast Archaeological Society Quarterly* 40(1):35–45.
2008b   A Chipped Stone Crescent from CA-SMI-681, San Miguel Island, California. *Journal of California and Great Basin Anthropology* 28(2):58–62.
2011   From Asia to the Americas by Boat? Paleogeography, Paleoecology, and Stemmed Points of the Northwest Pacific. *Quaternary International* 239:28–37.

Erlandson, J. M., T. J. Braje, and M. H. Graham
2008   How Old is MVII? Seaweeds, Shorelines, and Chronology at Monte Verde, Chile. *Journal of Island and Coastal Archaeology* 3:277–281.

Erlandson, J. M., T. J. Braje, T. C. Rick, and J. Peterson
2005   Beads, Bifaces, and Boats: An Early Maritime Adaptation on the South Coast of San Miguel Island, California. *American Anthropologist* 107(4):677–683.

Erlandson, J. M., T. J. Braje, and G. Snitker
2008   Two Chipped Stone Crescents from CA-SMI-680, Cardwell Bluffs, San Miguel Island, California. *Current Research in the Pleistocene* 25:46–47.

Erlandson, J. M., and N. Jew
2009   An Early Maritime Biface Technology at Daisy Cave, San Miguel Island, California: Reflections on Sample Size, Site Function, and Other Issues. *North American Archaeologist* 30(2):145–165.

Erlandson, J. M., D. J. Kennett, B. L. Ingram, D. A. Guthrie, D. P. Morris, M. A. Tveskov, G. J. West, and P. L. Walker
1996   An Archaeological and Paleontological Chronology for Daisy Cave (CA-SMI-261), San Miguel Island, California. *Radiocarbon* 38(2):355–373.

Erlandson, J. M., M. L. Moss, and M. Des Lauriers
2008   Life on the Edge: Early Maritime Cultures of the Pacific Coast of North America. *Quaternary Science Reviews* 27:2232–2245.

Erlandson, J. M., T. C. Rick, and M. R. Batterson
2004   Busted Balls Shell Midden: An Early Coastal Site on San Miguel Island, California. *North American Archaeologist* 25(3):251–272.

Erlandson, J. M., T. C. Rick, T. J. Braje, M. Casperson, B. Culleton, B. Fulfrost, T. Garcia, D. A. Guthrie, N. Jew, D. J. Kennett, M. L. Moss, L. Reeder, C. Skinner, J. Watts, and L. Willis

2011   Paleoindian Seafaring, Maritime Technologies, and Coastal Foraging on California's Channel Islands. *Science* 331:1181–1185.

Erlandson, J. M., T. C. Rick, and N. Jew

2011   CA-SRI-26: A Terminal Pleistocene Site on Santa Rosa Island, California. *Current Research in the Pleistocene* 28:35–36.

Erlandson, J. M., T. C. Rick, R. L. Vellanoweth, and D. J. Kennett

1999   Maritime Subsistence at a 9300 Year Old Shell Midden on Santa Rosa Island, California. *Journal of Field Archaeology* 26:255–65.

Gamble, L. H.

2008   *The Chumash World at European Contact: Power, Trade, and Feasting Among Complex Hunter-Gatherers.* University of California Press, Berkeley.

Glassow, M. A.

2009   Archaeological Site Record for CA-SCRI-811. On file, Department of Anthropology, University of California, Santa Barbara.

Glassow, M. A., J. M. Erlandson, and T. J. Braje

n.d.   A Typology of Channel Islands Barbed Points. *Journal of California and Great Basin Anthropology* (in review).

Glassow, M. A., J. E. Perry, and P. F. Paige

2008   *The Punta Arena Site: Early and Middle Holocene Cultural Development on Santa Cruz Island.* Contributions in Anthropology No. 3. Santa Barbara Museum of Natural History, Santa Barbara, CA.

Gusick, A. E.

2012   Behavioral Adaptations and Mobility of Early Holocene Hunter-Gatherers, Santa Cruz Island, California. Ph.D. dissertation. University of California, Santa Barbara.

Heye, G. G.

1921   *Certain Artifacts from San Miguel Island, California.* New York: Museum of the American Indian, Heye Foundation, New York.

Johnson, J. R., T. W. Stafford, Jr., H. O. Ajie, and D. P. Morris

2002   Arlington Springs Revisited. In *Proceedings of the Fifth California Islands Symposium*, edited by D. Brown, K. Mitchell, and H. Chaney, pp. 541–545. Santa Barbara Museum of Natural History, Santa Barbara, CA.

Jones, P. M.

1956   Archaeological Investigations on Santa Rosa Island in 1901. *University of California Anthropological Records* 17(2):203–280.

Junak, S., D. A. Knapp, J. R. Haller, R. Philbrick, A. Schoenherr, and T. Keeler-Wolf

2007   The California Channel Islands. In *Terrestrial Vegetation of California*, 3rd ed., edited by M. Barbour and T. Keeler-Wolf, and A. A. Schoenherr, pp. 229–252. University of California Press, Berkeley.

Justice, N. D.

2002   *Stone Age Spear and Arrow Points of California and the Great Basin.* Indiana University Press, Bloomington.

Kennett, D. J.

2005   *The Island Chumash: Behavioral Ecology of a Maritime Society.* University of California Press, Berkeley.

Kennett, D. J., J. P. Kennett, G. J. West, J. M. Erlandson, J. R. Johnson, I. L. Hendy, A. West, B. J. Culleton, T. L. Jones, and T. W. Stafford, Jr.

2008   Wildfire and Abrupt Ecosystem Disruption on California's Northern Channel Islands at the Allerød-Younger Dryas Boundary (13.0–12.9 ka). *Quaternary Science Reviews* 27:2528–2543.

Koerper, H. C., and M. F. Farmer

1987   A Bear-Shaped Crescentic from Northern San Diego County, California. *Journal of California and Great Basin Anthropology* 9:282–288.

Mohr, A. D., and G. L. Fenenga (with contributions by F. A. Riddell)

2010   Chipped Crescentic Stones from California. In *A Riddle Wrapped in a Mystery Inside an Enigma: Three Studies of Chipped Stone Crescents from California*, edited by G. L. Fenenga and J. N. Hopkins, pp. 5:93–280. Contributions to Tulare Lake Archaeology. Coyote Press, Salinas, CA.

Nagai, K.

2007   Flake Scar Patterns of Japanese Tanged Pints: Toward an Understanding of Technological Variability During the Incipient Jomon. *Anthropological Science* 115:223–226.

Olson, R. L.

1930   Chumash Prehistory. *University of California Publications in American Archaeology and Ethnology* 28:1–21.

Orr, P. C.

1968   *Prehistory of Santa Rosa Island.* Santa Barbara Museum of Natural History, Santa Barbara.

Porcasi, P., J. F. Porcasi, and C. O'Neill

1999   Early Holocene Coastlines of the California Bight: The Channel Islands as First Visited by Humans. *Pacific Coast Archaeology Society Quarterly* 35:1–24.

Raab, L. M., J. Cassidy, A. Yatsko, and W. J. Howard

2009   *California Maritime Archaeology: A San Cle-mente Island Perspective*. Altamira Press, Lanham, MD.

Reeder, L., T. C. Rick, and J. M. Erlandson

2008   Forty Years Later: What Have We Learned about the Earliest Human Occupations of Santa Rosa Island, California? *North American Archaeologist* 29(1):37–64.

Rick, T. C.

2007   *The Archaeology and Historical Ecology of Late Holocene San Miguel Island*. Cotsen Institute of Archaeology, University of California, Los Angeles.

2008   An Arena Point and Crescent from Santa Rosa Island, California. *Current Research in the Pleistocene* 25:140–142.

Rick, T. C., and J. M. Erlandson

2011   Kelp Forests, Coastal Migrations, and the Younger Dryas: Late Pleistocene and Earliest Holocene Human Settlement, Subsistence, and Ecology on California's Channel Islands. In *Hunter-Gatherer Behavior: Human Response During the Younger Dryas*, edited by M. Eren, pp. 79–110. Elsevier, New York.

Rick, T. C., J. M. Erlandson, and R. L. Vellanoweth

2001   Paleocoastal Marine Fishing on the Pacific Coast of the Americas: Perspectives from Daisy Cave, California. *American Antiquity* 66(4):595–613.

Rick, T. C., J. M. Erlandson, R. L. Vellanoweth, and T. J. Braje

2005   From Pleistocene Mariners to Complex Hunter-Gatherers: The Archaeology of the California Channel Islands. *Journal of World Prehistory* 19:169–228.

Rogers, D. B.

1929   *Prehistoric Man of the Santa Barbara Coast*. Santa Barbara Museum of Natural History, Santa Barbara, CA.

Rozaire, C. E.

1978   Archaeological Investigations on San Miguel Island. Unpublished manuscript. Los Angeles County Museum of Natural History.

Schoenherr, A. A., C. R. Feldmeth, and M. J. Emerson

1999   *Natural History of the Islands of California*. University of California Press, Berkeley.

Tadlock, W. L.

1966   Certain Crescentic Stone Objects as a Time Marker in the Western United States. *American Antiquity* 31(5):662–675.

Waguespack, N. M., and T. A. Surovell

2003   Clovis Hunting Strategies, or How to Make Out on Plentiful Resources. *American Antiquity* 68(2):333–352.

Wallace, W. J.

1955   A Suggested Chronology for Southern California Coastal Archaeology. *Southwestern Journal of Anthropology* 11:214–230.

Wardle, H. N.

1913   Stone Implements of Surgery from San Miguel Island, California. *American Anthropologist* 15:656–660.

Waters, M. R., and T. W. Stafford

2007   Redefining the Age of Clovis: Implications for the Peopling of the Americas.

3

The Early Holocene Occupation
of Santa Cruz Island

Amy E. Gusick

The study of early maritime migration and adaptation has become an increasingly important research area within New World archaeology. The discovery of numerous sites dating in excess of 10,000 BP along the eastern Pacific coastline has pushed this region to the forefront of study on early human coastal migration in the Americas (Braje et al., Chapter 2; Dillehay 1997; Erlandson et al. 1996, 2011; Fujita 2008; Johnson et al. 2002; Keefer et al. 1998; Núñez et al. 1994; Sandweiss et al. 1998; Stothert 1985). While the exact nature and timing of a late Pleistocene human migration into the New World is still in contention, new research on the development of settlement and foraging organization during the early Holocene (7500–10,000 cal BP) has helped to define how California's early inhabitants utilized the abundant resources and spacious landscape they encountered after their initial migration into the Americas. One region that has been a focus of this research is the northern Channel Islands. Though settlement and foraging organization on these islands have been widely studied with respect to later time periods (Arnold 1987, 1992; Erlandson and Jones 2002; Kennett and Conlee 2002; Glassow 2002), researchers are just beginning to consider what these were like during earlier periods of occupation on the northern Channel Islands (Glassow, Chapter 4; Glassow et al. 2008; Jazwa et al., Chapter 5; Kennett 2005; Rick et al. 2005).

The northern Channel Islands include four landmasses: Anacapa, Santa Cruz, Santa Rosa, and San Miguel. They are currently located 21 to 43 km off the mainland of California, in the northern waters of the Southern California Bight (Power 1980) (Figure 3.1). Previous researchers have suggested that reduced residential mobility and logistical organization existed during the early Holocene on these islands (Kennett 2005: 224). Cited evidence for this proposition derives largely from Santa Rosa Island. CA-SRI-3 is located among a complex of sites with early Holocene components (CA-SRI-3, -4, -5, -6, -26, -173), all centered on the north coast of Santa Rosa Island (Kennett 2005: Map 8). Because this site complex represents the most concentrated set of early Holocene activities that have been discovered on the northern Channel Islands, is associated with a variety of artifacts, and includes a cemetery, Kennett (2005:123) concludes that this site complex is evidence of "a certain degree of sedentism" among early Holocene hunter-gatherers on the islands, and that the location is a "central place that people returned to with relative frequency." Expanding this model, Kennett (2005:224) also suggests that logistical organization existed on Santa Cruz, the largest and most ecologically diverse of the northern Channel Islands, as early as 8,500–7,500 years ago, with central-place locales predicted to be on the western and northeastern sectors of the island; however, data from Santa Cruz Island supporting this proposition is lacking.

This lack of data is problematic because though the mainland of California and each of the Channel Islands share the general characteristics of a coastal ecosystem, sea surface temperature, climate, wind, land area, topography, and ocean

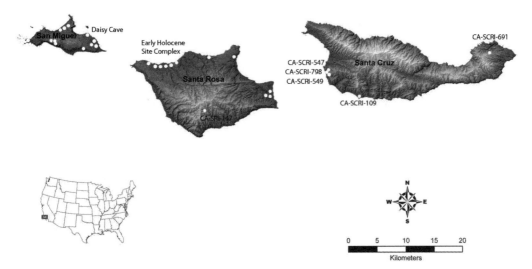

FIGURE 3.1. Location map of the northern Channel Islands. White circles show the general locations of early Holocene sites and sites discussed in text.

currents differ between the islands. These differences create a distribution and abundance of terrestrial and marine resources that are unique to each island (see Junak et al. 1995; Kennett et al. 2008; Rick 2002; Rick et al. 2005). Prehistorically, these unique distributions likely affected how hunter-gatherers moved across the landscape, as degree of mobility is directly related to resource distribution and abundance. It is therefore necessary to evaluate the archaeological record in relation to local environmental variants, as these can play crucial roles in shaping mobility and subsistence strategies (Jochim 1983; Koyama and Uchiyama 2006; Jazwa et al., Chapter 5).

Recent excavations at the five known early Holocene sites on Santa Cruz Island (CA-SCRI-109, -547, -549, -691, and -798) have yielded data that provide details on the lifeways of early maritime peoples on the island. The resulting data show that local resources were paramount in settlement and subsistence decisions during the early Holocene, with no evidence for a more complex, logistically organized settlement system during this early time period (Glassow 2006 and Chapter 4; Glassow et al. 2008; Gusick 2008, 2010, 2011, 2012).

Background

The Santa Barbara Channel region, like the rest of the Pacific Rim, underwent major environmental shifts during the early Holocene as a result of sea

level rise and marine and terrestrial climatic fluctuation (Aikens and Akazawa 1996; Borrero 1996; Erlandson and Moss 1996; Kennett 2005; Peltier 2002; Scavia et al. 2002). This variation affected both biodiversity and the distribution of resources on each of the northern Channel Islands, which would have influenced human group mobility, foraging, and settlement patterns.

Late Quaternary glaciation diminished the volume of global oceans; because water was locked up in ice sheets, sea level between 17,000 and 13,000 cal BP was approximately 120 m lower than it is today (Fairbanks 1989; Peltier 2002). There was a subsequent rise in sea level until approximately 7000 cal BP (Inman 1983), which resulted in the loss of 20,000 km^2 of land along the mainland California coast (Bickel 1978:16). The northern Channel Islands also experienced massive inundation of coastal landscapes. With seas at lowered levels, the northern Channel Islands formed one large landmass known as Santarosae (Johnson 1983; Kennett et al. 2008; Porcasi et. al 1999). Though a land bridge from this landmass to mainland California did not exist during the Quaternary, the channel separating the eastern end of Santarosae from the mainland was only ~7 km wide, compared to the ~20 km separation today (Kennett et al. 2008). Around 10,900 cal BP, eustatic sea level rise began inundating Santarosae, separating Anacapa from the larger landmass. By 9300 cal BP, Santa Cruz was separated from the other islands, and by ~9000 cal BP, Santa Rosa and San Miguel had separated, becoming the independent islands known today (Kennett et al. 2008).

Much like the other northern Channel Islands, the marine environments around Santa Cruz are very productive, but this productivity is variable geographically and over time. Major climatic shifts in the Santa Barbara Channel region during the early Holocene caused variation in biological productivity. Fluctuation in sea surface temperature (SST) directly affects available resources because marine productivity is influenced principally by rates of cold, upwelling, nutrient-rich water (Kinlan et al. 2005:125). Although upwelling makes the waters off the mainland coast and surrounding the islands of California extremely productive, millennial-scale oscillations in SST (Kennett and Kennett 2000; Kennett 2005:66, Figure 11A) greatly affected marine productivity during the early Holocene. During a distinct cold-water cycle (9600 to 8200 cal BP), marine productivity was high; however, during the subsequent warm-water cycle (8200 and 6300 cal BP) there was a significant drop in productivity (Kennett 2005:66, Figure 11B; Glassow et al. 2008:37). Yet, even with changes in marine productivity, the Santa Barbara Channel region has high marine biodiversity due to converging currents in the Southern California Bight: the cold, southward flowing California Current and the warmer, northward flowing California Countercurrent (Browne 1994; see Jazwa and Perry, Chapter 1).

Santa Cruz Island is the "most ecologically diverse of the four northern Channel Islands because of its large size, rugged topography, complex geology, availability of ground water, and presence of a central valley" (Jones et al. 1993:97). The presence of an interior central valley is unique to Santa Cruz Island, resulting in the greatest diversity in climate and relief of any of the northern Channel Islands (Junak et al. 1995). The climatic diversity and topographic complexity have produced the largest number of plant taxa found on any of the northern Channel Islands (Junak et al. 1995:46), in part due to the island's microclimatic and precipitation variation (Brumbaugh 1983:19; Glassow et al. 2008:15; Junak et al. 1995:9; Kennett 1998: Table 3.3).

The Early Holocene on Santa Cruz Island

Excavations and subsequent material analysis at the five known early Holocene sites on Santa Cruz Island have provided a more complete view of the settlement, mobility, and subsistence patterns of maritime hunter-gatherer-fishers during this early phase of island occupation. Material used for this analysis was collected from test units, column samples, and bulk samples. Test units were sifted over ⅛-inch mesh in the field and water screened in the processing area at the University of California, Santa Barbara (UCSB). Column and bulk samples were flotation-processed at the Collections Processing Lab at UCSB. Deposit and sample size varied significantly between some sites; therefore, in order to present a meaningful intersite comparison of site function, density data and percentages were calculated in mass or count per liter of soil excavated. Intrasite ratios of different faunal classes and lithic size grades were also calculated and used for comparison on an intersite basis.

The Christy Beach Sites (CA-SCRI-547, -549, and -798)

These three early Holocene deposits are currently located at or near the edge of a sea cliff on the western side of Santa Cruz Island, and all share similar depositional contexts (Figure 3.2). Each deposit consists of a single shell lens located approximately 6–8 m from the surface as exposed on the sea cliff face or gully wall. There are numerous shell lenses located stratigraphically above these early Holocene deposits, and all lenses are separated by sterile alluvial flow. Samples from CA-SCRI-547 and -549 include both test units and column samples, while those from CA-SCRI-798 include only bulk samples due to the limited amount of material available for collection at that site (Table 3.1). A total of five ^{14}C dates derived from well-preserved California mussel (*Mytilus californianus*) provide a 2σ date range of 8660–8013 cal BP for the three sites (Table 3.2).

Faunal Remains
Faunal samples from all of the Christy Beach sites are very similar and include mostly marine shell with small amounts of fish, sea mammal,

FIGURE 3.2. Image of CA-SCRI-549 showing typical depositional context of all known early Holocene sites located on the sea cliffs on the west end of Santa Cruz Island. Early Holocene dated shell lens is at the depth of excavator and tools.

TABLE 3.1. Total volume of samples collected from each site

Site	Sample Type	Sample Size (cm)	Volume (liters)
109	Test Unit 1	120 × 50	60
	Test Unit 2	100 × 50	77.5
	Test Unit 3	100 × 50	77.75
	Bulk Sample 1	35 × 35	21
	Bulk Sample 2	35 × 35	21
Total			257.25
547	Test Unit 1	N/A	74.2
	Bulk Sample 1	25 × 25	13.75
Total			87.95
549	Test Unit 1	100 × 50	25
	Test Unit 2	50 × 22	12.5
	Bulk Sample 1	25 × 25	12.5
	Bulk Sample 2	35 × 35	23.28
Total			73.28
691	Test Unit 1	100 × 50	98.43
	Test Unit 2	100 × 50	50
	Bulk Sample 1	25 × 25	15
	Bulk Sample 2	25 × 25	6.25
Total			169.68
798	Bulk Sample 1	52 × 30	36.27
	Bulk Sample 2	50 × 50	56.25
Total			92.52

and other bone. The excavations at the three sites yielded 30.8 kg of marine shell: CA-SCRI-547, 7.1 kg; CA-SCRI-549, 17.4 kg; and CA-SCRI-798, 6.2 kg. The CA-SCRI-549 sample contained the greatest weight of shell and the highest density of marine shell in the site assemblage. At least 18 taxa were identified at all sites, and California mussel dominates all assemblages, making up 90–96 percent of the total shell weight (Table 3.3). Acorn barnacle (*Balanus* spp.) is the next most abundant taxon; however, most specimens were from small species and were most likely incidentally introduced into the midden (see Moss and Erlandson 2010). Black abalone (*Haliotis*

cracherodii) and Pismo clam (*Tivela stultorum*) are the next most abundant species in the deposits, but their contributions are minimal. All other taxa comprise less than 0.5 percent of the total shell weight at each site.

Vertebrate remains are scarce at these sites, with 540 bone fragments weighing just 63.8 g. The most abundant animal remains at all sites are of fish, totaling 403 fragments. CA-SCRI-549 yielded well over half of these remains (259 NISP), with CA-SCRI-547 and CA-SCRI-798 yielding relatively similar amounts (81 NISP and 63 NISP, respectively). Other vertebrate remains include mammal, sea mammal, and bird. All are

TABLE 3.2. Radiocarbon dating results

Site	Sample	Radiocarbon Age (BP)	Calendar Year BP (1 sigma)	Calendar Year BP (2 sigma)	Material	Lab No.	Note
SCRI-109	U2 LV 3	7850 ± 40	8143–8026	8183–7967	*Mytilus ca.*	OS-79395	Gusick 2012
SCRI-109	U3 LV 3	7280 ± 40	7580–7491	7628–7442	*Mytilus ca.*	OS-76957	Gusick 2012
SCRI-109	U1 LV1	7780 ± 35	8058–7950	8129–7927	*Mytilus ca.*	OS-79618	Gusick 2012
SCRI-109	CS1 42 cm	7940 ± 40	8267–8134	8306–8046	*Mytilus ca.*	OS-82416	Gusick 2012
SCRI-109	CS1 49 cm	8300 ± 40	8588–8466	8656–8403	*Mytilus ca.*	OS-82417	Gusick 2012
SCRI-109	CS2	7980 ± 40	8286–8173	8343–8116	*Mytilus ca.*	OS-82418	Gusick 2012
SCRI-109	17A	8270 ± 70	8577–8414	8704–8352	*Haliotis crac.*	Beta-122000	Glassow 2008
SCRI-109	18A	8520 ± 70	8973–8743	9024–8596	*Lithopoma und.*	Beta-119187	Glassow 2008
SCRI-109	19	7570 ± 210	8001–7598	8234–7425	*Mytilus ca.*	UCR 0390	Glassow 2008
SCRI-109	19B	7780 ± 80	8111–7934	8191–7837	*Mytilus ca.*	Beta-119192	Glassow 2008
SCRI-109	EU 8	8220 ± 60	8520–8387	8591–8332	*Haliotis crac.*	Beta-148733	Glassow 2008
SCRI-547	U1	8240 ± 35	8518–8415	8569–8380	*Mytilus ca.*	OS-84076	Gusick 2012
SCRI-549	Stra. 6	7930 ± 60	8100–8272	8317–8013	*Mytilus ca.*	Beta-122011	Glassow 2006
SCRI-549	U1	8230 ± 35	8509–8408	8560–8373	*Mytilus ca.*	OS-79675	Gusick 2012
SCRI-549	U2	8250 ± 35	8529–8424	8578–8386	*Mytilus ca.*	OS-79676	Gusick 2012
SCRI-691	CS 1	8140 ± 50	8990–8860	8521–8265	*Mytilus ca.*	Beta-261911	Gusick 2010
SCRI-691	U1 50 cm	8610 ± 40	9064–8924	9120–8790	*Mytilus ca.*	OS-86773	Gusick 2012
SCRI-691	U1 60 cm	9400 ± 40	10091–9902	10146–9790	*Mytilus ca.*	OS-86774	Gusick 2012
SCRI-691	U2 69 cm	9120 ± 40	9596–9489	9679–9458	*Mytilus ca.*	OS-86777	Gusick 2012
SCRI-798	CS1	8270 ± 60	8650–8370	8660–8365	*Mytilus ca.*	Beta-242819	Gusick 2008

Note: The calibrated dates were obtained using the CALIB program and a local correction for marine upwelling of −225 ± 25 years (Stuiver et al. 1986; Stuiver and Reimer 1993).

TABLE 3.3. Total shell weight and percentage shell weight from the sites discussed in text

	SCRI-109	SCRI-547	SCRI-549	SCRI-691	SCRI-798
Sum of weight (g)					
Abalone	356.03	—	0.76	0.87	12.03
Acorn Barnacle	8183.47	462.80	363.17	1688.74	148.44
Black Abalone	794.67	31.64	133.31	30.36	43.20
Black Turban	133.64	—	4.94	22.80	20.93
California Mussel	67547.99	6456.28	16454.92	18667.53	5624.68
Leaf Barnacle	119.11	1.10	97.31	178.59	4.84
Owl Limpet	73.77	11.70	45.77	—	—
Pismo Clam	175.69	—	7.58	1.64	121.18
Red Abalone	575.78	—	3.94	—	3.10
Sea Urchin	75.63	—	0.14	17.35	1.07
Wavy Top Turban	216.58	—	5.37	114.70	50.48
Percentage contribution to overall weight					
Abalone	<0.00	—	<0.00	<0.00	0.19
Acorn Barnacle	10.32	0.06	2.09	8.03	2.38
Black Abalone	1.00	0.44	0.77	0.14	0.69
Black Turban	0.17	—	0.03	0.11	0.34
California Mussel	85.20	90.50	94.60	88.79	90.05
Leaf Barnacle	0.15	0.02	0.56	0.85	0.08
Owl Limpet	0.09	0.16	0.26	—	—
Pismo Clam	0.22	—	0.04	0.01	1.94
Red Abalone	0.73	—	0.02	—	0.05
Sea Urchin	0.10	—	0.00	0.08	0.02
Wavy Top Turban	0.27	—	0.03	0.55	0.81

minor contributors found in similar abundances at all three sites (Table 3.4).

Looking at the sites as a whole, the subsistence economy was focused on collection of California mussel, with varying degrees of other fauna contributing to the overall dietary pattern. Early hunter-gatherer-fishers utilizing this section of the landscape focused on local resources and habitats, including marine animals from the rocky intertidal and kelp bed habitats that were present in the nearshore environment during the time of site occupation.

Technology
All three sites have limited chipped stone debris, with low weight and count densities per liter of excavated soil: 0.78 g/0.55 count per liter at

CA-SCRI-547, 1.29 g/1.53 count per liter at CA-SCRI-798, and 1.54 g/1.31 count per liter at CA-SCRI-549. Most of the lithic debitage is volcanic[1] angular and flake shatter in the ⅛-inch sample, and only 16 lithic flakes (classified by the presence of a striking platform) were identified between the three sites, 8 of Monterey chert and 8 of volcanic rock. One lightly used hammer stone made of local volcanic stone was recovered from CA-SCRI-547, and one small core fragment of Monterey chert was identified at CA-SCRI-798 (Table 3.5).

All chipped stone artifacts are made of rock available on Santa Cruz Island. Evidence for a formal technological strategy is minimal, and raw material was mainly collected from the local volcanic stone that is abundant throughout much of

TABLE 3.4. Vertebrate total NISP and percentage NISP from sites discussed in text

	Aves	Mammal	Sea Mammal	Teleostei	Unident. Bone
Vertebrate NISP					
SCRI-109	20	11	259	1,464	10
SCRI-547	3	3	4	81	0
SCRI-549	33	1	25	259	16
SCRI-691	6	3	73	95	40
SCRI-798	5	3	18	63	26
Percentage NISP					
SCRI-109	1.13	0.62	14.68	82.99	0.57
SCRI-547	3.3	3.3	4.4	89.01	—
SCRI-549	9.88	0.30	7.49	77.54	4.79
SCRI-691	1.40	1.41	34.11	44.39	18.69
SCRI-798	4.35	2.61	15.65	54.78	22.6

Note: Percentages include only vertebrate assemblage.

TABLE 3.5. Chert and volcanic lithic components from sites discussed in text

	SCRI-109	SCRI-691	SCRI-547	SCRI-549	SCRI-798
Chert					
Biface	2	9	—	—	—
Core	—	4	—	—	1
Shatter	124	2,635	9	25	47
Flake	32	537	—	4	4
Flake tool	6	1	—	—	—
Count Totals	164	3186	9	29	52
Chert density	0.61	18.70	0.10	0.33	0.55
Volcanic					
Core	6	—	—	—	—
Shatter	187	7	38	83	87
Flake	38	4	1	3	4
Hammer stone	—	—	1	—	—
Ground stone	—	—	—	1	—
Count Totals	231	11	40	87	91
Volcanic density	0.87	0.06	0.44	0.98	0.98

Note: Densities are count per liter of soil excavated at each site.

the island and is plentiful in fluvial and marine deposits in the form of clasts eroded from breccias exposed along sea cliffs above Christy Beach. Conversely, known outcrops of Monterey chert on Santa Cruz Island are found only in the Monterey Formation that occurs on the isthmus and east end of the island (Arnold 1987; Arnold et al. 2001; Perry and Jazwa 2010). The chert found in the samples from the Christy Beach sites is the only nonlocal material present and indicates that

FIGURE 3.3. CA-SCRI-109, pictured covering the entire promontory. The location of excavation of the early Holocene deposit is indicated by excavators.

the groups occupying these sites transported this important tool stone from the source on the east end of the island. The dominance of volcanic debris at the sites suggests that most tools were expediently manufactured from local stones.

Three unique artifacts recovered from CA-SCRI-549—a small metate rim fragment, a bone point, and an *Olivella biplicata* spire-lopped bead—suggest that a variety of activities occurred at this site. These observations, combined with the site's overall density and diversity, which are greater than at the other two Christy Beach sites, indicate that CA-SCRI-549 was more frequently used and appears to have been a focus of habitation and processing activities in the Christy Beach vicinity on Santa Cruz Island during the early Holocene.

CA-SCRI-109

CA-SCRI-109 is a large site consisting of a shell midden deposit covering the upper terrace of a prominent promontory along the south coast of Santa Cruz Island (Figure 3.3). A ravine bisecting the midden has exposed an erosional profile a few hundred meters in length. This profile shows that most of the midden accumulated in broad lenses, typically no more than 20 cm thick and not always clearly defined (Glassow et al. 2008:13). The site is near one of the highest-ranked watersheds

on Santa Cruz Island (Kennett et al. 2009) and has extensive middle Holocene deposits, suggesting that this was an important residential base during this later time period (Glassow, Chapter 4; Glassow et al. 2008).

The most substantial excavations focused solely on the early Holocene stratum previously identified at the site (Glassow et al. 2008). The sloping surface of the erosional profile allowed placement of units in such a way that the upper strata, which have been dated to the middle Holocene, were left undisturbed. Samples collected from CA-SCRI-109 included material from three test units and two column samples (Table 3.1). Shells for ^{14}C AMS dating were collected from the basal level of all test units and column samples. The occupation identified through the analysis for the current research has a 2σ range of 8656–7442 cal BP, encompassing the latter half of the early Holocene. Previous studies placed the date of initial occupation early as 9024–8596 cal BP (Table 2; Glassow et al. 2008:20).

Faunal Remains

The faunal sample from CA-SCRI-109 includes marine shell, fish, sea mammal, land mammal, and bird bone (Glassow et al. 2008). Excavations at the site yielded 79.3 kg of marine shell, with a density of about 308 g per liter. Though the

TABLE 3.6. Vertebrate densities for sites discussed in text, presented as NISP per liter of excavated soil

	Vertebrate Densities				
	SCRI-109	SCRI-547	SCRI-549	SCRI-798	SCRI-691
Teleostei	5.69	0.92	2.95	0.68	0.56
Sea mammal	1.01	0.05	0.29	0.19	0.43
Mammal	0.04	0.03	0.01	0.03	—
Aves	0.08	0.03	0.38	0.05	0.02
Unident. bone	0.04	—	0.18	0.28	0.24

Note: Densites are NISP per liter of soil excavated at each site.

TABLE 3.7. Meat weight percentages of vertebrates from sites discussed in text

	Aves	Mammal	Sea Mammal	Teleostei	Elasmobranchii	Unident. Bone
SCRI-798	8.49	1.97	33.01	48.48	—	8.04
SCRI-549	4.76	0.06	35.29	53.72	4.4	1.77
SCRI-547	9.94	1.44	6.47	82.14	—	—
SCRI-109	1.81	1.6	31.37	58.71	4.37	2.14
SCRI-691	1.49	—	54.83	39.17	—	4.52

density of shell at this site is greater than at the Christy Beach sites, the diversity of the shell assemblage is very similar. California mussel dominates the assemblage, comprising 87 percent of the total shell weight. Yet by removing the species such as smaller barnacles and limpets that were likely accidentally introduced into the midden as "riders" on the mussel shells, and focusing on just the 12 species that are most abundant and known for their economic importance, California mussel comprises 96.3 percent of the assemblage, with black abalone (1.1 percent), red abalone (*Haliotis rufescens*) (0.8 percent), wavy top turban (*Lithopoma undosum*) (0.3 percent), and Pismo clam (0.3 percent) the next most abundant species. This variety of species is similar to what was identified at CA-SCRI-798, with a combination of nearshore rocky intertidal, midtidal, and sandy beach species (Table 3.3).

Vertebrate remains at CA-SCRI-109 are varied and include the same types found at the Christy Beach sites; however, the density of vertebrate remains is more than double that at CA-SCRI-109, with the exception of Aves. Bird bone densities at all sites are low and relatively similar. The most abundant vertebrate at CA-SCRI-109 is fish (1,464

NISP). There is almost double the density of fish bone at this site than at any of the Christy Beach sites (Table 3.6); however, meat weight calculated for the vertebrates at all sites indicates that fish provided the highest percentage contribution of the vertebrate meat at another site, CA-SCRI-549 (Table 3.7).

Sea mammal remains, though not dense, do appear with relative consistency and are found in higher densities here than at other sites. While most of the identified sea mammal is likely pinniped, including California sea lion (*Zalophus californianus*), bones from sea otter (*Enhydra lutris*) and two dolphin (Delphinidae) otoliths were also identified. Data from previous excavations at CA-SCRI-109 show that dolphin remains are dense in deposits dating to 6300–5300 cal BP, suggesting a focus on hunting these animals during that period of the middle Holocene (Glassow et al. 2008:32). This pursuit was likely facilitated by the presence of a submarine canyon just offshore from CA-SCRI-109. The upwelling along the canyon edge fosters high productivity, providing a food source at the edge of the canyon (Bradford 1996; Porcasi and Fujita 2000).

Whether the early Holocene inhabitants of

the site had organized hunting parties focused on exploiting this submarine canyon is questionable and cannot be determined from current data; however, other sites of the same antiquity on San Clemente Island display a focus on dolphin hunting and suggest that this may be have been a widespread trend among island communities off the California mainland. Similar to CA-SCRI-109, analyses at the trans-Holocene site of Eel Point (CA-SCLI-43) on San Clemente Island show dolphin hunting beginning during the early Holocene and increasing in importance throughout the middle Holocene (Raab et al. 2009:100).

Though the contribution from species other than California mussel is small, the emerging subsistence patterns indicate that inhabitants of CA-SCRI-109 practiced an adaptive subsistence strategy focused on the varied marine habitats found locally. These habitats include a variety of intertidal and midtidal habitats, such as rocky substrate and kelp beds, and sandy beaches. Heavy use of rocky intertidal habitats with more infrequent, or perhaps opportunistic, exploitation of midtidal and sandy beach habitats is consistent with the finding from both previous and current research on all identified early Holocene sites on Santa Cruz Island (Glassow 2002; Glassow et al. 2008; Gusick 2008).

Technology
CA-SCRI-109 has a greater diversity of chipped stone artifacts than the Christy Beach sites. Lithic count density is similar, 1.48 count per liter, but lithic weight density is more than double those of any of the Christy Beach sites (2.67 g per liter), indicating that larger pieces of lithic debris are present at CA-SCRI-109. Of the 381 pieces of debitage, 20 percent are classified as formal flakes, including 6 large utilized flakes. The remaining artifacts include 6 cores, one biface preform, and one almost complete Channel Island Barbed (CIB) projectile point (Figure 3.4). The cores and 225 pieces of debitage are of local volcanic stone, while all flake tools, the biface preform, the projectile point, and 156 pieces of debitage are of Monterey chert. One small obsidian flake also is in the sample (Table 3.5).

The six cores identified at CA-SCRI-109 are all of volcanic stone, and all can be classified as expedient. Two are multidirectional cores, two are

FIGURE 3.4. Channel Island Barbed point found in the early Holocene stratum at CA-SCRI-109.

possible bipolar cores, and two are cobble cores, or tested cores, that had been broken in half with one or two flakes removed. All of these cores are informal and represent an expedient reduction strategy.

Bipolar cores are typically small, informal cores that are placed on another rock (anvil) and reduced. This creates two opposed striking platforms and produces a lot of shatter. Though bipolar cores have been linked to sedentism (Hiscock 1996) and sparse raw material availability (MacDonald 1999), Parry and Kelly (1987:301) describe the bipolar reduction strategy as "wasteful," an example of an expedient technology. Studies of bipolar cores have shown that they are typically smaller than other cores found at a site, suggesting that they are prepared cores, used to maximize the number of useable flakes that can be removed (Andrefsky 1994a). The possible bipolar cores at CA-SCRI-109 differ from this pattern and are larger in size than all other cores, with the exception of one of the tested cobbles. They are not small, exhausted cores typical of a reduction strategy focused on prepared cores and formal tool creation.

FIGURE 3.5. Location of CA-SCRI-691 on inland hilltop, covered in grasses. Center of site is indicated by pin flag and GPS unit.

One small obsidian flake also is in the sample. Obsidian is not available on any of the northern Channel Islands, so this small flake is likely derived from an obsidian object brought from the mainland. Recent sourcing on obsidian samples from CA-SRI-147 on Santa Rosa Island indicates that the material originated from the Coso Volcanic Field in Inyo County, California (Rick et al. 2001). CA-SRI-147 is roughly contemporaneous with the stratum in which the obsidian was found at CA-SCRI-109, and the obsidian may be from the same source. Although the presence of the obsidian does indicate some sort of contact with the mainland, it is premature to suggest that a trade network existed at this early time period. The presence of obsidian at early Holocene sites is, however, an indication of the "ancient…interaction spheres of Native American peoples" (Rick et al. 2001:41).

CA-SCRI-691

CA-SCRI-691 is the only identified early Holocene site on Santa Cruz Island currently located on an inland hilltop rather than a coastal terrace (Figure 3.5). Recent excavations were positioned at a section of the site known to contain early Holocene material (Clifford 2001; Gusick 2010). Samples came from two test units and two column samples (Table 3.1). The chronology for the site is based on 10 ^{14}C AMS dates of California mussel shell. The early Holocene component of the midden deposit is beneath strata that date to the middle Holocene (~3600 RYBP); therefore, defining the site's stratigraphic chronology was integral in identifying the early Holocene strata. Four of the 10 ^{14}C AMS samples dated to the early Holocene, and one sample returned a 2σ date range of 10,146–9790 cal BP (OS-86774), making CA-SCRI-691 the oldest known midden deposit on Santa Cruz Island and among the oldest archaeological sites on the northern Channel Islands (Table 3.2).

Faunal Remains

The density of both marine shell and fish bone is greater here than at CA-SCRI-547 and CA-SCRI-798, two of the deposits from the Christy Beach sites. The diversity of the marine shell, however, is similar to all other early Holocene sites on the island, with California mussel and acorn barnacle comprising most of the shell weight, and black abalone and wavy top turban next most abundant (Table 3.3).

Vertebrate remains at CA-SCRI-691 are not as diverse as at the other early Holocene sites on Santa Cruz Island. Fish bone is not as dense as at some of the other sites, but it does appear consistently. Sea mammal bone density is similar or greater than the densities at the Christy Beach sites. Interestingly, the meat weight contribution for sea mammal exceeds that of fish at CA-SCRI-691, comprising 55 percent of the meat weight for the vertebrate assemblage at that site. This trend is not apparent at any other known early Holocene site on Santa Cruz Island. While not main foci, fishing and sea mammal hunting provide supplements to the main shellfish diet at CA-SCRI-691 (Table 3.4).

Technology

The collection of raw material and manufacture of tools was a primary activity at CA-SCRI-691. The density of lithic debris at the site is unprecedented among early Holocene sites on Santa Cruz Island (18.7 count/liter). A total of 3,183 pieces of lithic debitage, weighing 1104.76 g, were identified in the sample. The overwhelming proportion of lithic material is Monterey chert (99.65 percent). The amount of chert in the sample is not surprising given that CA-SCRI-691 is less than 2 km from an identified chert quarry, CA-SCRI-610, the largest and most intensively used chert quarry known on the northern Channel Islands (Kennett 1998; Perry and Jazwa 2010). While there are a few pieces of volcanic debris in the sample from CA-SCRI-691, all formal and informal tools are of chert and include one leaf-shaped biface, seven biface production failures, one scraper, four utilized flakes, and four chert cores (Table 3.5).

The assemblage of chert debitage at CA-SCRI-691 reflects a range of lithic reduction activities, from the first stage of cobble reduction to nearly finished bifaces. The density of chert at this site indicates a more intensive use of this locale for tool manufacturing and cobble processing activities; however, the intrasite size-grade percentages for debitage is very similar to what has been calculated for CA-SCRI-549 and CA-SCRI-109 (Figure 3.6).

Despite being close to a chert source, CA-SCRI-691 is like the other early Holocene sites on the island in that its occupants performed routine subsistence activities there (Beck and Jones 1990; Jones et al. 2003; Kelly and Todd 1988). CA-SCRI-691 shows similar site function to all other early Holocene sites on Santa Cruz Island. There was focus on collection of locally available subsistence and material resources, with an emphasis on California mussel and, to a lesser degree, fish and sea mammal. These subsistence pursuits targeted the rocky intertidal habitat present at the base of the coastal headlands that surround the site (Kennett 1998: Figure 13.3).

Discussion

The subsistence and technological data presented above provide a framework for examining settlement, mobility, and subsistence decisions of early Holocene hunter-gatherer-fishers on Santa Cruz Island. The general resource procurement patterns identified from the data analyses are consistent with those of other early Holocene sites on the northern Channel Islands (see Erlandson 1994; Erlandson et al. 2007; Glassow 1993; Glassow et al. 2008; Kennett 2005). California mussel was the main meat resource consumed by the early islanders, and fish from nearshore habitats also contributed to the diet. Evidence for sea mammal exploitation, though present, is not abundant, even though this resource is plentiful around all of the northern Channel Islands (Colten and Arnold 1998, 2002; Kennett 2005) and increases in importance later in time (Glassow 1993; Perry and Hoppa 2012; Walker et al. 2000). Terrestrial resources, including tool stone, were also collected from local sources, with the exception of the location-restricted chert.[2] The relationship between the five known early Holocene sites on Santa Cruz Island and how they contribute to a broader settlement pattern can be inferred by both a more focused analysis of the lesser dietary patterns and consideration of the artifact diversity identified at each site.

Though all sites are functionally similar, the density, size, and diversity of material at CA-SCRI-109 suggest that this site was the most frequently used among the known early Holocene sites on Santa Cruz Island, owing most likely to its central location with respect to a variety of marine habitats. Though waters adjacent to CA-SCRI-109 are relatively warm (Browne 1994), the marine environment is one of the island's most productive, rivaled only by Forney's Cove at the west end (Glassow et al. 2008:8). The promontory on which the site is located is surrounded on

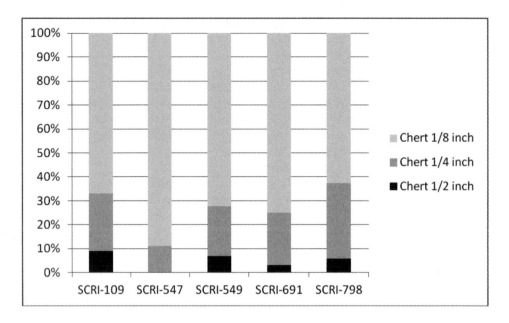

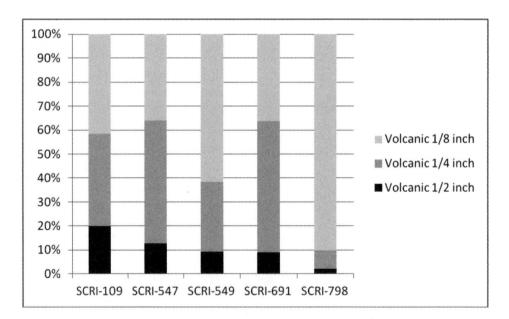

FIGURE 3.6. Graphs show percentage of lithic debitage (shatter and flakes) in each size grade. Top chart is chert debris and bottom chart is volcanic debris.

three sides by bedrock shelves that are productive for California mussel and most other marine shell species found in the midden sample. Numerous fish species also inhabit nearshore waters with rocky substrates, as well as the kelp forests located offshore from CA-SCRI-109 (Love 1996). West of the site is Playa Larga, a 2.5 km sandy beach (Glassow et al. 2008), a habitat known for both Pismo clam and pinniped colonies. A small perennial stream 1 km northeast of the site may also have influenced site location (Glassow et al. 2008).

The central location of CA-SCRI-109, combined with the extensive midden deposits and the diversity of material identified in the samples, suggests that this site was an important locale for island peoples, but no data currently available indicate that this was a central base site in a logistically organized settlement system. A central base site should, for example, be functionally differentiated from other contemporaneous sites and should show signs of year-round habitation, such as the presence of seasonally available but distant resources (Binford 1980; Torrence 1983).

The smaller and less dense Christy Beach sites are all likely seasonal residential bases (Binford 1980) given their size and density of material. This type of low-density shell midden with expedient flakes, cores, and occasional beads and bone awls is consistent with other early Holocene sites that have been sampled on Santa Rosa and San Miguel Islands (Braje et al. 2004, 2007; Erlandson 1994; Erlandson et al. 1999; Erlandson et al. 2004; Erlandson et al. 2005). The location of the sites, 2 km from the shoreline at the time of occupation, suggests that a limited and location-specific resource influenced settlement decision. Few archaeobotanical remains were identified in the assemblages (Gusick 2012), though they are plentiful in the grasslands that surround the site, which would have provided edible plants such as seeds, roots, and bulbs. In particular, blue dicks (*Dichelostemma capitatum*) often are very common in grasslands, and their corms are edible (Gill, Chapter 7). Blue dicks produce a purple flower that makes them visible during the spring, with dried stalks and flowers still visible into the summer (Kennett 1998:101; Glassow et al. 2008). The metate fragment identified at CA-SCRI-549 indicates that plant resources were processed at that site and may have been an influential factor in settlement location. Additionally, there is a freshwater source in a ravine just south of CA-SCRI-549. Today this ravine has water from late winter to early spring and may have been a perennial stream at the time of site occupation.

Though the three Christy Beach sites were likely all seasonal residential bases given size and density of material, the relatively high density and diversity of material at CA-SCRI-549 suggest that this site was a focus of habitation activity in this region of the island. Though the general patterning is functionally similar to CA-SCRI-549, both CA-SCRI-547 and CA-SCRI-798 may be

"locations" (Binford 1980:9) associated with CA-SCRI-549, making the three sites functionally linked rather than three distinct habitation locales. Alternatively, CA-SCRI-547 and CA-SCRI-798 may be seasonal residential bases that were simply not used as frequently as CA-SCRI-549. Indeed, the lithic assemblages at all of the sites vary in density but are similar in proportional frequencies. These lithic data do not support distinguishing CA-SCRI-547 and CA-SCRI-798 as functionally different from CA-SCRI-549 (Hayden 1978:109–191).

Much like the Christy Beach sites, the samples from CA-SCRI-691 indicate that settlement location was largely dependent on a location-specific resource: chert from the Monterey Formation. This type of high-quality tool stone has been shown to affect hunter-gatherer mobility and settlement decisions (Andrefsky 1994b; Bamforth 1990, 1991; Kelly and Todd 1988; Perry and Jazwa 2010). Additionally, there is a small ravine with a freshwater seep approximately 150 m north of the site. Although this seep is part of the site's current environmental context, paleoenvironmental conditions were cooler and wetter than at present (Moratto 1984:34–36; Kennett et al. 2008: Figure 12). This seep was likely present and perennial during the early Holocene, providing another important resource that may have influenced settlement of CA-SCRI-691.

The site's hilltop location facilitates access to inland chert sources; however, though the density and diversity of chert chipped stone at CA-SCRI-691 are greater than at other sites, the percentage of pieces in each size grade is similar to all other sites, particularly CA-SCRI-549, and is not much different from CA-SCRI-109 (Figure 3.6). These data suggest that similar raw material procurement and lithic reduction strategies were practiced at each of the sites, with CA-SCRI-691 a focus for chert reduction due to the local availability of that raw material (Andrefsky 1994b). The several biface production failures in the assemblage, coupled with the exhausted cores and first-stage production flakes, suggest that all stages of tool production occurred at CA-SCRI-691. The lack of heavily used and discarded chert tools indicates that the tools created at the site were likely part of mobile tool kits that were transported around Santa Cruz Island. Yet, as mentioned, CA-SCRI-691 is like other identified early Holocene sites on Santa Cruz Island and elsewhere in that site occupants carried out routine subsistence activities, the difference being that local stone material was procured as well (Beck and Jones 1990; Jones et al. 2003; Kelly and Todd 1988).

The high elevation of CA-SCRI-691 does increase the cost for transportation of shellfish and sea mammal from the coast to the site (Perlman 1980; Winterhalder 1981). Interestingly, the vertebrate meat weight percentage for sea mammal at CA-SCRI-691 is greater than at all other known early Holocene sites on Santa Cruz Island, suggesting that sea mammal was an important caloric supplement to the main shellfish diet (Table 3.7). A similar subsistence economy relying on both shellfish and sea mammal has been identified at CA-SCRI-724, a site close to CA-SCRI-691, in a similar high-elevation position (Perry and Hoppa 2012). This increased focus on sea mammal despite the increased transportation costs is possibly due to their greater abundance and easier access to the coast near the locality than is currently recognized.

Both CA-SCRI-691 and the Christy Beach sites were less frequently used than CA-SCRI-109; however, all sites were possibly inhabited seasonally, with CA-SCRI-109 being used for longer periods of time per occupation, or more consistently over the years. This same general trend has been assumed for the early Holocene occupation at Daisy Cave (CA-SMI-261) on San Miguel Island. Daisy Cave contains an ephemeral late Pleistocene stratum under denser and more diverse early Holocene material. The density of early Holocene material at Daisy Cave is likely due to "repeated short-term occupations of the site...by maritime peoples who relied heavily on marine resource like shellfish, fish and sea mammals" (Erlandson et al. 1996:364, 370). The environmental context of Daisy Cave is similar to that of CA-SCRI-109 in that it is centrally located to a variety of productive nearshore habitats. The value of this location on Santa Cruz Island is also evident in the increasingly dense middle Holocene deposits that accumulated after long-term and repeated use of the site (Glassow et al. 2008).

Even considering the less dense Christy Beach and CA-SCRI-691 site deposits, the value of

their locations on the landscape is also apparent through evidence of repeated use throughout the Holocene. CA-SCRI-691 has dense middle Holocene–aged deposits stratigraphically above the early Holocene strata, and the Christy Beach sites have numerous shell lenses above the early Holocene deposits that date to both the middle and late Holocene. Early island inhabitants and their descendants repeatedly selected these locales from the vast landscape of Santa Cruz Island. This repeated use of locales that are either centrally located to a variety of habitats or located adjacent to key location-restricted resources such as high-quality tool stone or freshwater, is consistent with sites containing early Holocene components on all of the Channel Islands.

Aside from Daisy Cave on San Miguel Island, the large trans-Holocene site of CA-SRI-147 on Santa Rosa Island is located at the confluence of two drainages and a series of caves and rock-shelters (Braje et al. 2007). This deeply stratified midden was occupied for at least 5,600 years, starting at the end of the early Holocene (Braje et al. 2007:742). Similarly, the Eel Point site (CA-SCLI-43) on San Clemente Island has a "remarkably well-preserved sequence of maritime cultural development, ranging in time from the early Holocene to European contact" (Raab et al. 2009:76). Raab et al. (2009:83) posit that the cultural features in the early Holocene component at Eel Point indicate a "substantial degree of residential permanence," with a settlement strategy more akin to Binford's (1980) "collectors" than "foragers." It is difficult to draw firm conclusions on early settlement pattern on the island because information from additional contemporaneous sites is lacking, but the importance of Eel Point on the San Clemente landscape is apparent and is consistent with many other multicomponent California island sites.

Conclusions

The archaeological record for the early Holocene on the northern Channel Islands previously included a disproportionate number of deposits on Santa Rosa Island and San Miguel Island, with few Santa Cruz Island sites contributing to the overall picture of the early Holocene on the islands. I have used the midden samples analyzed as part of the current research to attempt to close this information gap and provide the first data set from Santa Cruz Island that can contribute to a framework with which to identify mobility and adaptations of early Holocene inhabitants on all of the Channel Islands. These data have demonstrated that subsistence and settlement decisions were based on locally available resources, and the more complex, logistically organized settlement systems of later time periods probably had not yet developed by the end of the early Holocene on Santa Cruz Island. As always, further research and more extensive sampling are needed to refine the conclusions developed in this chapter.

Notes

1. The term *volcanic* is used to refer to basalt, andesite, and/or rhyo-dacite. Further distinction between these volcanic stones was not made for this analysis.
2. The term *location-restricted* indicates that the resource is found only in certain areas of the island; for instance, high-quality chert has been found only on its eastern end.

Acknowledgments

First and foremost, I would like to thank Michael Glassow for his guidance and support during all phases of this project, from inception to publication. Thank you also to the many people who assisted me in the field, working long hours and carrying heavy bags: Kristina Gill, Kristin Hoppa, Jennifer Perry, Matthew Edwards, Terry Joslin, Heather Thakar, Don Morris, Gretchen Hess, Paula Pugh, Natalie Ortega, and Macduff Everton. I am grateful to Chris Jazwa and Jennifer Perry for their helpful comments on this manuscript and their editorial work on this volume. The excavations at CA-SCRI-691 would not have occurred without support from Ann Huston and Kelly Minas at Channel Islands National Park, as well as the members of the Tribal Elders Council of the Santa Ynez Band of Chumash Indians. This work was generously supported by the National Science Foundation (Grant No. 0946603); the Peter Paige Memorial Fund at the University of California, Santa Barbara; the Mildred E. Mathias Foundation; and the Lewis and Clark Fund for Exploration and Field Research from the American Philosophical Society.

References Cited

Aikens, C. M., and T. Akazawa
1996   The Pleistocene-Holocene Transition in Japan and Adjacent Northeast Asia: Climate and Biotic Change, Broad-Spectrum Diet, Pottery, and Sedentism. In *Humans at the End of the Ice Age*, edited by L. Straus, B. V. Eriksen, J. Erlandson, and D. R. Yesner, pp. 215–227. Plenum Press, New York.

Andrefsky, W., Jr.
1994a   The Geological Occurrence of Lithic Material and Stone Tool Production Strategies. *Geoarchaeology* 9(5):375–391.
1994b   Raw-material Availability and the Organization of Technology. *American Antiquity* 59(1):21–34.

Arnold, J. E.
1987   *Craft Specialization in the Prehistoric Channel Islands, California*. University of California Press, Berkeley.
1992   Complex Hunter-Gatherer-Fishers of Prehistoric California: Chiefs, Specialists, and Maritime Adaptations of the Channel Islands. *American Antiquity* 57:60–84.

Arnold, J. E., A. M. Preziosi, and P. Shattuck
2001   Flaked Stone Craft Production and Exchange in Island Chumash Territory. In *The Origins of a Pacific Coast Chiefdom: The Chumash of the Channel Islands*, edited by J. E. Arnold, pp. 113–131. University of Utah Press, Salt Lake City.

Bamforth, D. B.
1990   Settlement, Raw Material, and Lithic Procurement in the Central Mojave Desert. *Journal of Anthropological Archaeology* 9(1):70–104.
1991   Technological Organization and Hunter-Gatherer Land Use: A California Example. *American Antiquity* 56(2):216–234.

Beck, C., and G. T. Jones
1990   Toolstone Selection and Lithic Technology in Early Great Basin Prehistory. *Journal of Field Archaeology* 17(3):283–299.

Bickel, P.
1978   Changing Sea Levels Along the California Coast. *Journal of California Anthropology* 5:6–20.

Binford, L. R.
1980   Willow Smoke and Dogs' Tails: Hunter-Gatherer Settlement Systems and Archaeological Site Formation. *American Antiquity* 45:4–20.

Borrero, L. A.
1996   The Pleistocene-Holocene Transition in

Southern South America. In *Humans at the End of the Ice Age*, edited by L. Straus, B. V. Eriksen, J. Erlandson, and D. R. Yesner, pp. 339–354. Plenum Press, New York.

Bradford, K. G.
1996   Influence of Submarine Canyons on Fish Species Found in Coastal Archaeological Sites. *Pacific Coast Archaeological Society Quarterly* 32(1):37–49.

Braje, T. J., J. M. Erlandson, and T. C. Rick
2004   Reassessing Human Settlement on the South Coast of San Miguel Island, California: The Use of ¹⁴C Dating as a Reconnaissance Tool. *Radiocarbon* 47(1):11–19.

Braje, T. J., D. J. Kennett, J. M. Erlandson, and B. J. Culleton
2007   Human Impacts on Nearshore Shellfish Taxa: A 7,000 Year Record from Santa Rosa Island, California. *American Antiquity* 72(4):735–756.

Browne, D. R.
1994   Understanding the Oceanic Circulation In and Around the Santa Barbara Channel. In *The Fourth California Islands Symposium: Update on the Status of Resources*, edited by W. L. Halvorson and G. J. Maender, pp. 27–34. Santa Barbara Museum of Natural History, Santa Barbara, CA.

Brumbaugh, R. W.
1983   Hillslope Gullying and Related Changes, Santa Cruz Island, California. PhD dissertation. Department of Geography, University of California, Los Angeles.

Clifford, R. A.
2001   Middle Holocene Hilltop and Ridgeline Settlement on the Northern Channel Islands of California: A Study of Evolutionary Stability. Master's thesis. Department of Anthropology, California State University, Long Beach.

Colten, R. H., and J. E. Arnold
1998   Prehistoric Marine Mammal Hunting on California's Northern Channel Islands. *American Antiquity* 63:679–701.

2002   Native Uses of Marine Mammals on Santa Cruz and San Miguel Islands. In *Proceedings of the Fifth California Islands Symposium*, edited by D. R. Browne, K. L. Mitchell and H. W. Chaney, pp. 623–627. U.S. Department of the Interior Minerals Management Service, Pacific OCS Region.

Dillehay, T. D.
1997   *Monte Verde: A Late Pleistocene Settlement in Chile, vol. 2: The Archaeological Context and Interpretation*. Smithsonian Institution Press, Washington, DC.

Erlandson, J. M.
1994   *Early Hunter-Gatherers of the California Coast*. Plenum Press, New York.

Erlandson, J. M., and T. L. Jones (editors)
2002   *Catalysts to Complexity: Late Holocene Societies of the California Coast*. Cotsen Institute of Archaeology, University of California, Los Angeles.

Erlandson, J. M., and M. L. Moss
1996   The Pleistocene–Holocene Transition Along the Pacific Coast of North America. In *Humans at the End of the Ice Age*, edited by L. Straus, B. V. Eriksen, J. M. Erlandson, and D. R. Yesner, pp. 277–301. Plenum Press, New York.

Erlandson, J. M., T. C. Rick, T. J. Braje, M. Casperson, B. Culleton, B. Fulfrost, T. Garcia, D. A. Guthrie, N. Jew and D. J. Kennett
2011   Paleoindian Seafaring, Maritime Technologies, and Coastal Foraging on California's Channel Islands. *Science* 331(6021):1181–1185.

Erlandson, J. M., T. C. Rick, J. A. Estes, M. H. Graham, T. J. Braje, and R. L. Vellanoweth
2005   Sea Otters, Shellfish, and Humans: A 10,000 Year Record from San Miguel Island, California. In *Proceedings of the Sixth California Islands Symposium*, edited by D. Garcelon and C. Schwemm, pp. 9–21. National Parks Service Technical Publication CHIS-05-01. Institute for Wildlife Studies, Arcata, CA.

Erlandson, J. M., T. C. Rick, T. L. Jones, and J. F. Porcasi
2007   One If by Land, Two If by Sea: Who Were the First Californians? In *California Prehistory: Colonization, Culture, and Complexity*, edited by T. L. Jones and K. A. Klar, pp. 53–62. Altamira, Lanham, MD.

Erlandson, J. M., T. C. Rick, and R. Vellanoweth
2004   Human Impacts on Ancient Environments: A Case Study from California's Northern Channel Islands. In *Voyages of Discovery: The Archaeology of Islands*, edited by S. M. Fitzpatrick, pp. 51–83. Praeger, Westport, CT.

Erlandson, J. M., T. C. Rick, R. L. Vellanoweth, and D. J. Kennett
1999   Maritime Subsistence at a 9300 Year Old Shell Midden on Santa Rosa Island, California. *Journal of Field Archaeology* 26(3):255–265.

Erlandson, J. M., M. Tveskov, D. J. Kennett, and B. L. Ingram
1996   Further Evidence for a terminal Pleistocene Occupation of Daisy Cave, San Miguel Island, California. *Current Research in the Pleistocene* 13:13–15.

Fairbanks, R. G.

1989　A 17, 000-year Glacio-Eustatic Sea Level Record: Influence of Glacial Melting Rates on the Younger Dryas Event and Deep-Ocean Circulation. *Nature* 342(6250):637–642.

Fujita, H.

2008　Late Pleistocene and Early Holocene Occupations at El Pulguero and on Espíritu Santo, Baja California Sur. Paper presented at the annual meeting of the Southern California Archaeological Society, Modesto.

Glassow, M. A.

1993　Changes in Subsistence on Marine Resources Through 7,000 Years of Prehistory on Santa Cruz Island. In *Archaeology on the Northern Channel Islands of California: Studies of Subsistence, Economics, and Social Organization,* edited by M. A. Glassow, pp. 75–94. Coyote Press, Salinas, CA.

2002　Prehistoric Chronology and Environmental Change at the Punta Arena Site, Santa Cruz Island, California. In *Proceedings of the Fifth California Islands Symposium,* edited by D. R. Browne, K. L. Mitchel, and H. W. Chaney, pp. 555–562. Santa Barbara Museum of Natural History, Santa Barbara.

2006　Early to Middle Holocene Occupation on Santa Cruz Island. Paper presented at the 40th annual conference of the Society for California Archaeology, Ventura.

Glassow, M. A., J. E. Perry, and P. Paige

2008　*The Punta Arena Site: Early and Middle Holocene Development on Santa Cruz Island.* Contributions in Archaeology. Santa Barbara Museum of Natural History, Santa Barbara, CA.

Gusick, A. E.

2008　Early Maritime Hunter-Gatherer Occupation and the Initial Human Migration into the New World, Santa Cruz Island, California. Report submitted to the Mildred E. Mathias Foundation.

2010　Punta Arena: The Early Years. Paper presented at the 75th annual meeting of the Society for American Archaeology, St. Louis.

2011　The Early Holocene on Santa Cruz Island, Paper presented at the 76th annual meeting of the Society for American Archaeology, Sacramento.

2012　Behavioral Adaptations and Mobility of Early Holocene Hunter-Gatherers, Santa Cruz Island, California. PhD dissertation. Department of Anthropology, University of California, Santa Barbara.

Hayden, B.

1978　Snarks in Archaeology: Or Inter-assemblage Variability in Lithics (a View from the Antipodes). In *Lithics and Subsistence: The Analysis of Stone Use in Prehistoric Economies,* edited by D. L. Davis, pp. 179–198. Publications in Anthropology 20. Vanderbilt University, TN.

Hiscock, P.

1996　Mobility and Technology in the Kakadu Coastal Wetlands. *Bulletin of the Indo-Pacific Prehistory Association* 15:151–157.

Inman, D. C.

1983　Application of Coastal Dynamics to the Reconstruction of Paleocoastlines in the Vicinity of La Jolla, California. In *Quaternary Coastlines and Marine Archaeology: Towards the Prehistory of Land Bridges and Continental Shelves,* edited by P. M. Masters and N. C. Flemming, pp. 1–50. Academic Press, London.

Jochim, M. A.

1983　Optimization Models in Context. In *Archaeological Hammers and Theories,* edited by J. A. Moore and A. S. Keene, pp. 157–172. Academic Press, New York.

Johnson, D. L.

1983　The California Continental Borderland: Landbridges, Watergaps and Biotic Dispersal. In *Quaternary Coastlines and Marine Archaeology: Towards the Prehistory of Land Bridges and Continental Shelves,* edited by P. M. Masters and N. C. Flemming, pp. 481–528. Academic Press, London.

Johnson, J. R., T. W. Stafford Jr., H. O. Ajie, and D. P. Morris

2002　Arlington Springs Revisited. In *The Fifth California Islands Symposium,* edited by D. R. Brown, K. C. Mitchell, and H. W. Chaney, pp. 541–545. U.S. Department of the Interior Minerals Management Service, Pacific OCS Region.

Jones, G. T., C. Beck, E. E. Jones, and R. E. Hughes

2003　Lithic Source Use and Paleoarchaic Foraging Territories in the Great Basin. *American Antiquity* 68(1):5–38.

Jones, J. A., S. A. Junak, and R. J. Paul

1993　Progress in Mapping Vegetation on Santa Cruz Island and a Preliminary Analysis of Relationships with Environmental Factors. In *Third California Islands Symposium: Recent Advances in Research on the California Islands,* edited by F. G. Hochberg, pp. 97–104. Santa Barbara Museum of Natural History, Santa Barbara.

Junak, S., T. Ayers, R. Scott, D. Wilken, and D. Young
1995   *A Flora of Santa Cruz Island*. Santa Barbara Botanic Garden in collaboration with the California Native Plant Society, Santa Barbara.

Keefer, D. K., S. D. deFrance, M. E. Moseley, J. B. I. Richardson, D. R. Satterlee, and A. Day-Lewis
1998   Early Maritime Economy and El Niño Events at Quebrada Tacahuay, Peru. *Science* 281 (5384):1833–1835.

Kelly, R. L., and L. C. Todd
1988   Coming into the Country: Early Paleoindian Hunting and Mobility. *American Antiquity* 53(2):231–244.

Kennett, D. J.
1998   Behavioral Ecology and the Evolution of Hunter-Gatherer Societies on the Northern Channel Islands, California. PhD dissertation. Department of Anthropology, University of California, Santa Barbara.
2005   *The Island Chumash: Behavioral Ecology of a Maritime Society*. University of California Press, Berkeley.

Kennett, D. J., and C. A. Conlee
2002   Emergence of Late Holocene Sociopolitical Complexity on Santa Rosa and San Miguel Islands. In *Catalysts to Complexity: Late Holocene Societies of the California Coast*, edited by J. M. Erlandson and T. L. Jones, pp. 147–165. Cotsen Institute of Archaeology, University of California, Los Angeles.

Kennett, D. J., and J. P. Kennett
2000   Competitive and Cooperative Responses to Climatic Instability in Coastal Southern California. *American Antiquity* 65(2):379–395.

Kennett, D. J., J. P. Kennett, G. J. West, J. M. Erlandson, J. R. Johnson, I. L. Hendy, A. West, B. J. Culleton, T. L. Jones, and T. W. Stafford Jr.
2008   Wildfire and Abrupt Ecosystem Disruption on California's Northern Channel Islands at the Ållerød-Younger Dryas Boundary (13.0–12.9 ka). *Quaternary Science Reviews* 27(27–28):2530–2545.

Kennett, D., B. Winterhalder, J. Bartruff, and J. M. Erlandson
2009   An Ecological Model for the Emergence of Institutionalized Social Hierarchies on California's Northern Channel Islands. In *Pattern and Process in Cultural Evolution*, edited by S. Shennan, pp. 297–314. University of California Press, Los Angeles.

Kinlan, B. P., M. H. Graham, and J. M. Erlandson
2005   Late Quaternary Changes in the Size and Shape of the California Channel Islands: Implications for Marine Subsidies to Terrestrial Communities. In *Proceeding of the Sixth California Islands Symposium, Ventura, California, December 1–3, 2003*, edited by D. K. Garcelon and C. A. Schwemm, pp. 119–130. Institute for Wildlife Studies, Arcata, CA.

Koyama, S., and J. Uchiyama
2006   Why "Beyond Affluent Foragers"?: Looking Back at the Original Affluent Foragers Concept. In *Beyond Affluent Foragers: Rethinking Hunter-Gatherer Complexity*, edited by C. Grier, J. Kim, and J. Uchiyama, pp. 1–3. Oxbow Books, Oxford.

Love, M.
1996   *Probably More Than You Want to Know about the Fishes of the Pacific Coast*. Really Big Press, Santa Barbara, CA.

MacDonald, D. H.
1999   Modeling Folsom Mobility, Mating Strategies, and Technological Organization in the Northern Plains. *Plains Anthropologist* 44 (168):141–161.

Moratto, M.
1984   *California Archaeology*. Academic Press, San Diego.

Moss, M. L., and J. M. Erlandson
2010   Diversity in North Pacific Shellfish Assemblages: The Barnacles of Kit'n'Kaboodle Cave, Alaska. *Journal of Archaeological Science* 37(12):3359–3369.

Núñez, L., J. Varla, R. Casamiquela, and C. Villagrán
1994   Reconstrucción multidisciplinaria de la ocupación prehistórica de Quero, Centro de Chile. *Latin American Antiquity* 5:99–118.

Parry, W. J., and R. L. Kelly
1987   Expedient Core Technology and Sedentism. In *The Organization of Core Technology*, edited by J. K. Johnson, pp. 285–304. Westview Press, Boulder.

Peltier, W. R.
2002   On Eustatic Sea Level History: Late Glacial Maximum to Holocene. *Quaternary Science Reviews* 21:377–396.

Perlman, S. M.
1980   An Optimum Diet Model, Coastal Variability, and Hunter-Gatherer Behavior. *Advances in Archaeological Method and Theory* 3:257–310.

Perry, J. E., and K. Hoppa
2012   Subtidal Shellfish Exploitation on the California Channel Islands: Wavy Top (*Lithopoma undosum*) in the Middle Holocene. In *Exploring Methods of Faunal Analysis: Insights from California Archaeology*, edited by M. A. Glassow and T. L. Joslin, pp. 65–86. Cotsen Institute of Archaeology, University of California, Los Angeles.

Perry, J. E., and C. S. Jazwa

2010   Spatial and Temporal Variability in Chert Exploitation on Santa Cruz Island, California. *American Antiquity* 75(1):177–198.

Porcasi, J. F., and H. Fujita

2000   The Dolphin Hunters: A Specialized Prehistoric Maritime Adaptation in the Southern California Channel Islands and Baja California. *American Antiquity* 65(3):543–566.

Porcasi, P., J. F. Porcasi, and C. O'Neill

1999   Early Holocene Coastlines of the California Bight: The Channel Islands as First Visited by Humans. *Pacific Coast Archaeology Society Quarterly* 35(2–3):1–14.

Power, D. M.

1980   Introduction. In *The California Islands: Proceeding of a Multidisciplinary Symposium*, edited by D. M. Power, pp. 1–4. Santa Barbara Museum of Natural History, Santa Barbara, CA.

Raab, L. M., J. Cassidy, A. Yatsko, and W. J. Howard

2009   *California Maritime Archaeology: A San Clemente Island Perspective.* Altamira, Lanham, MD.

Rick, T.

2002   Eolian Processes, Ground Cover, and the Archaeology of Coastal Dunes: A Taphonomic Case Study from San Miguel Island, California, USA. *Geoarchaeology* 17(8):811–833.

Rick, T. C., D. J. Kennett, and J. M. Erlandson

2005   Early-Holocene Land Use and Subsistence on Eastern Santa Rosa Island, California. *Current Research in the Pleistocene* 22:60–62.

Rick, T. C., C. E. Skinner, J. M. Erlandson, and R. L. Vellanoweth

2001   Obsidian Source Characterization and Human Exchange Systems on California's Channel Islands. *Pacific Coast Archaeology Society Quarterly* 37(3):27–44.

Sandweiss, D. H., H. McInnis, R. L. Burger, A. Cano, B. Ojeda, R. Paredes, M. C. Sandweiss, and M. D. Glascock

1998   Quebrada Jaguay: Early South American Maritime Adaptations. *Science* 281(5384): 1830–1832.

Scavia, D., J. C. Field, D. F. Boesch, R. W. Buddemeier, V. Burkett, D. R. Cayan, M. Fogarty, M. A. Harwell, R. W. Howarth, and C. Mason

2002   Climate Change Impacts on US Coastal and Marine Ecosystems. *Estuaries* 25(2):149–164.

Stothert, K. E.

1985   The Preceramic Las Vegas Culture of Coastal Ecuador. *American Antiquity* 50(3):613–637.

Torrence, R.

1983   Time Budgeting and Hunter-Gatherer Technology. In *Hunter-Gatherer Economy in Prehistory: A European Perspective*, edited by G. N. Bailey, pp. 11–22. Cambridge University Press, Cambridge.

Walker, P. L., D. J. Kennett, T. L. Jones, and R. DeLong

2002   Archaeological Investigations at the Point Bennett Pinniped Rookery on San Miguel Island. In *Proceedings of the Fifth California Islands Symposium*, edited by D. R. Browne, K. L. Mitchell, and H. W. Chaney, pp. 628–632. Santa Barbara Museum of Natural History, Santa Barbara, CA.

Winterhalder, B.

1981   Optimal Foraging Strategies and Hunter-Gatherer Research in Anthropology: Theory and Models. In *Hunter-Gatherer Foraging Strategies: Ethnographic and Archeological Analyses*, edited by B. Winterhalder and E. A. Smith, pp. 13–35. University of Chicago Press, Chicago.

4

Settlement Systems on Santa Cruz Island Between 6300 and 5300 BP

Michael A. Glassow

Archaeological deposits at prehistoric sites on western Santa Cruz Island dating between 6300 and 5300 BP are characterized by the presence of abundant quantities of red abalone (*Haliotis rufescens*) shells, which are very rare in deposits dating earlier and later in time. (All dates in this chapter are calibrated years BP.) I have referred to these deposits as red abalone middens (Glassow 1993b), and at present, 13 on Santa Cruz Island have been radiocarbon dated. Red abalone middens also occur on the northern Channel Islands to the west: Santa Rosa and San Miguel (Braje et al. 2009: Table 1; Rick et al. 2005: Tables 2–3); however, they span broader intervals of times on these islands (Glassow 1993b; Braje et al. 2009:912).

Most red abalone middens are small in area—generally less than 75 m in maximum dimension—and their deposits are typically less than 40 cm thick. Two red abalone middens, SCRI-109 and SCRI-333, are much larger, with areal dimensions of more than 150 m and thicknesses of more than a meter. This contrast suggests complexity among settlement systems during the 6300–5300 BP period in that the larger sites may have articulated with settlement systems in different ways than did the smaller sites. The issue considered here, therefore, is determining which methods are appropriate for gaining insight into the character and degree of complexity within settlement systems of this period.

Background

With a land area of 249 km², Santa Cruz Island (Figure 4.1) is the largest of the four northern Channel Islands comprising the southern mar-gin of the Santa Barbara Channel. It is 30 km from the mainland, and its Mediterranean climate supports diverse flora, including oak woodlands, chaparral, and scrublands (Junak et al. 1995 13–26). Shellfish, fish, and marine mammals are available and locally abundant around the perimeter of the island, but there are no terrestrial game animals (Schoenherr et al. 1999:299–300). At the time of Spanish colonization of California in the late eighteenth century, Santa Cruz Island and the other northern Channel Islands were occupied by the Island Chumash, who spoke a language distinct from, but related to, that of their Chumash neighbors on the other side of the Santa Barbara Channel (Johnson 1982). The Chumash's central base–focused, relatively sedentary settlement system (Landberg 1965; Gamble 2008) appears to have come into existence sometime between 3000 and 2000 BP, when midden deposits began to accumulate relatively rapidly at some coastal locations (Kennett 2005:169; Glassow et al. 2007:202; Kennett et al. 2009).

On Santa Cruz Island, known red abalone middens are distributed between Forney's Cove, near its western extreme, and Punta Arena, on its south coast (Figure 4.1). The two largest red abalone middens, SCRI-109 and SCRI-333, are located at the eastern and western extremes of the distribution, respectively. Most of these middens, including the two largest, are at or very near the coast, although a few are as far as 1.9 km inland. Although red abalone shells are conspicuous in these middens due to their large size and frequent occurrence as whole or nearly whole shells, other shellfish taxa are more abundant. As is true at most sites on the island, California mus-

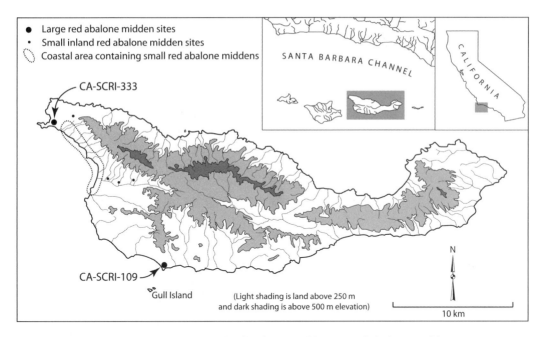

FIGURE 4.1. Santa Cruz Island, showing the distribution of known red abalone middens.

sel (*Mytilus californianus*) predominates, and shells of other abalone species (black abalone [*H. cracherodii*] and pink abalone [*H. corrugata*]), wavy top (*Lithopoma undosum*), and purple sea urchin (*Strongylocentrotus purpuratus*) also may be abundant, sometimes more so than red abalone shells. Bones of fish and sea mammals also are present, but their abundance at the smaller red abalone middens generally is minimal. The two larger middens, however, contain substantially more bone, although proportional abundance among the faunal remains still is lower than is typical of coastal middens dating after about 3000 BP (Glassow 1993a).

The occurrence of abundant red abalone shells in middens of the 6300–5300 BP period is due in part to cooler water temperatures during this period as compared to both immediately preceding and later time intervals (Glassow et al. 1994; Kennett 2005:66; Kennett et al. 2007:354; Glassow et al. 2012). Red abalone prefer waters cooler than do other California coastal abalone species such as black abalone. In modern times, red abalone has been mainly a subtidal species around the northern Channel Islands, with limited occurrence in the lower intertidal zone. The cooler waters of the 6300–5300 BP period presumably fostered more red abalone in the intertidal and shallow subtidal zones around the island. Another likely factor accounting for red abalone middens is the apparently low numbers of humans living on the Channel Islands during the 6300–5300 BP period (Kennett 2005:153). Red abalone would have been a high-ranked shellfish (Braje and Erlandson 2007), but it could not have been an important dietary component during cool-water intervals of late prehistoric times, when much larger populations would have had to supplement red abalone with lower-ranked shellfish species.

The occurrence of red abalone middens on western Santa Cruz Island, but not in the central and eastern sectors of the island, probably is due to two factors. First, the coast of western Santa Cruz Island contains extensive stretches of bedrock shelves within the intertidal zone and in shallow subtidal waters. These are ideal habitats for abalone. In contrast, the central and eastern sectors of the island largely lack such habitats. Second, nearshore waters are increasingly warmer west to east along the length of the island. Most likely these warmer waters would have prevented red abalone from occupying waters shallow enough for easy access by human populations. Instead, on eastern Santa Cruz Island, some sites dating to the 6300–5300 BP period (and later in time) contain relatively abundant shells of wavy top, a large gastropod that prefers warmer waters (Glassow et al. 2008:81, 84; Perry and Hoppa 2012). Even though red abalone middens are restricted to the western sector of the island, coeval sites are distributed throughout the island (although quantities so far documented are very low). This fact has important implications for understanding island settlement systems during the 6300–5300 BP period.

Two Alternative Models of Settlement Systems During the 6300–5300 BP Period

Archaeologists working on the northern Channel Islands have proposed two contrasting settlement system models to account for the nature and distribution of red abalone middens. Each has strengths and weaknesses in accounting for currently available data. The models contrast with respect to degree of mobility and functional differentiation between sites.

Kennett (2005:129, 151; Kennett et al. 2007:356) proposed that populations during the 6300–5300 BP period (and generally during the Middle Holocene) were relatively sedentary and obtained resources logistically. He argued that this fit the pattern of maritime hunter-gatherers worldwide, during all time periods (Kennett 2005:30). This is a position taken by other archaeologists with regard to populations dependent on aquatic resources (Yesner 1980:730; Binford 1990:139; Kelly 1995:132; Ames 2002:19–20). In Kennett's model, large sites such as SCRI-333 were "primary villages"; that is, central locations for residence and a variety of social and economic activities. "Secondary villages" are similar to primary villages but lack a cemetery. He classified SCRI-109 at Punta Arena as a secondary village. "Interior residences" were occupied to obtain and process plant foods, and he felt the large size of some interior residential sites indicates that they may have been occupied for extended lengths of time. "Logistical encampments" are sites where resources were acquired and processed for return to a primary village. He placed the small red abalone middens on Santa Cruz Island and the other Channel Islands in this category. Although he proposed that island populations of the 6300–5300 BP period were logistically mobile, he seems to include some degree of residential mobility as well, specifically with respect to the occupation of both coastal and larger interior sites.

My colleagues and I have advocated a contrasting model (Glassow et al. 2008:74). We proposed that island populations during the 6300–5300 BP period were residentially rather than logistically mobile. We argued that the two larger red abalone midden sites, SCRI-109 and SCRI-333, were occupied for longer lengths of time per visit than was the case at the small red abalone midden sites, and that the smaller and larger sites were essentially comparable with regard to their places within a settlement system. The unusually large size of SCRI-109 and SCRI-333, as well as the greater proportional abundance of fish and sea mammal remains within their deposits, suggests unusually high marine productivity of the intertidal zones and nearshore waters adjacent to these sites. In fact, no other locations around the island are comparable. It is possible that SCRI-333 was a winter habitation site.

As previously noted, these two large sites are not centrally located, at least not with regard to the known distribution of red abalone middens on the island. Our interpretation also was based on the distribution of smaller red abalone middens and, to some extent, their contents. Four of the smaller red abalone midden sites are located inland (CA-SCRI-426, -568, -796, and Temp CWS-11). If these were logistical camps for acquiring and processing red abalone and other marine resources for return to a central base, we reasoned that all would be located adjacent to the coast. Finally, we noted that a smaller red abalone midden site at which a small-scale investigation has taken place (Glassow 2005b) has yielded digging-stick weights, a mortar fragment, and a complete pestle. These artifacts imply plant food acquisition and processing for on-site consumption rather than for transport to a central base.

These facts alone, however, are not sufficient for rejecting Kennett's proposal that populations during the 6300–5300 BP period practiced logistical mobility. Central bases may have been located for reasons other than centrality within a territory from which resources were acquired. Furthermore, the inland location of some smaller red abalone middens may be related to acquiring plant food resources, or possibly freshwater, rather than acquiring marine resources. Finally, if a logistical camp was occupied for extended periods of time—on the order of several days or weeks, for instance—it would be expected to contain evidence of food processing for immediate consumption. Consequently, on the basis of currently available evidence, neither settlement system model can be rejected. In fact, other, more complicated models also may be proposed.

Theoretical Considerations

Before delving further into alternative models of settlement systems during the 6300–5300 BP period, the theoretical underpinnings of settlement system models must be explicated in order to give direction to their development. Binford's (1980) distinction between residential and logistical mobility was the first serious attempt to explicate not only structural differences between hunter-gatherer settlement systems but also how these differences related to environmental variation. Since publication of Binford's article, archaeologists have looked to behavioral ecological theory for developing models of hunter-gatherer subsistence and explanations of hunter-gatherer mobility patterns. Kelly's (1983, 1995:111–160) careful consideration of the determinants of variation in mobility patterns still stands as a definitive treatment of the subject.

For a variety of reasons, however, archaeologists have considerable difficulty explicating the nature of hunter-gatherer settlement systems and changes in their characteristics over time (Chatters 1987). One reason for this, as Kelly (1992: 43) points out, is the challenge of relating material culture to mobility patterns. In addition, hunter-gatherer settlement systems readily adjust to seasonal and annual fluctuation in availability of food resources, and loci where activity occurs have varying visibility. Indeed, some sites may have been occupied only a few times over the course of a decade, whereas other sites may have been occupied almost every year. In short, although broad patterns of settlement may have persisted over a period several hundred years long, most likely there was an underlying complexity that, from an archaeologist's perspective, resulted in a good deal of "noise" that distracts from identifying the broad patterns.

Nonetheless, archaeologists have expended considerable effort to understand the determinants of the degree of hunter-gatherer mobility (or sedentism), often through comparative analysis of ethnographic data. The most obvious determinants are size of territory available to a foraging group in relation to its population size (Binford 1980:17; Bettinger 1991:72; Kelly 1995:152; Kennett et al. 2009:305–308), spatial variation in the distribution and abundance of food resources (Binford 1980, 1990; Kelly 1983, 1992, 1995:111–160), seasonal variation in their availability (Kelly 1983: 292–293), degree of dependence on storage and storage facilities (Binford 1980, 1990; Kelly 1995: 146–147), and the need to socialize for mate selection and resource acquisition (Kelly 1995:147). The operation of determinants often has been couched from the perspective of foraging theory, particularly central-place foraging theory (Orians and Pearson 1979; Bettinger et al. 1997; Bird 1997; Kennett 2005:29–32). Especially important factors are the time-energy costs of continuing to forage from a residential base relative to the costs at a new residential base some distance away (Kelly 1995:136–138, 141–142), the costs of transporting food resources back to a residence (and cost of field processing before transport) (Metcalfe and Barlow 1992; Barlow and Metcalfe 1996), and the costs of moving residence to a new location (Kelly 1995:139).

Another determinant potentially affecting mobility, as well as placement of residential bases, is the temporal consistency in the acquisition of different kinds of food resources. Some foods, such as shellfish, can provide consistent amounts of food on a daily basis—that is, they are relatively low risk foods—whereas others, such as sea mammals, may be successfully acquired only occasionally—that is, they are higher-risk foods even though they typically are high-ranked with respect to caloric return once encountered. Moreover, women tend to focus their food acquisition efforts on low-risk food resources, whereas men tend to focus on higher-risk resources, in large part because food acquisition goals differ between women and men (Jackson 1991; McGuire and Hildebrandt 1994; Elston and Zeanah 2002; Zeanah 2004; Codding et al. 2011). Differences between women's and men's food acquisition efforts can influence location of residential bases if the foods on which each sex focuses are in different locations.

Just as archaeologists have difficulty explicating the nature of hunter-gatherer settlement systems, they also have difficulty knowing enough about the operation of these determinants for developing case-specific explanations, even if they were able to develop explicit models of mobility patterns within a particular region. Nonetheless, the archaeological literature abounds with models of settlement systems (i.e., settlement patterns) or particular aspects of them, as well as explanations for settlement system variability (see Billman and Feinman 1999; Kowalewski 2008). The more successful of these are based on large databases accumulated over a number of years (e.g., Bettinger 1999).

Elaboration of Alternative Models

Despite the opinion previously cited that hunter-gatherers dependent on aquatic resources tend to be logistically mobile, many archaeologists have noted that mobility varied among such societies. Ethnographic and archaeological data from various parts of the world support this recognition. Kelly (1995:125–126), for instance, notes that ethnographically documented groups dependent on aquatic resources living in relatively lower primary-biomass settings were more mobile than those in relatively higher primary-biomass settings, and that all groups that practice low residential mobility live in high primary-biomass settings (see also Binford 1990). Similarly, Yesner (1980:130) notes that at lower latitudes some populations dependent on aquatic resources "could not have been completely sedentary" and that some sites in such settings were seasonally occupied. Fitzhugh (2002) proposes a similar situation among high-latitude populations during early prehistoric periods.

Ethnography provides instances of highly mobile hunter-gatherers living on marine resources. The Alacaluf and Yahgan of the Tierra del Fuego region appear to have practiced a classic form of residential mobility (Bird 1946:58; Cooper 1946:84). Although this pattern appears to have developed during the historic period as a result of disruption accompanying contacts with European populations and their overhunting of pinnipeds (Yesner 2004:77), the aquatic adaptation recorded ethnographically may be one of relatively low density hunter-gatherers similar to those of early prehistoric periods, assuming historic population decline. It is reasonable to suspect that

settlement systems of coast-living people were much different earlier during prehistory, particularly because population density expectably was much lower. The diversity of resources important to the diet would have been lower, predation pressure on resources generally would have been lower, and technology for their acquisition likely would have been simpler.

The five alternative models (Figure 4.2) presented below incorporate aspects of both Kennett's model and the one that my colleagues and I have proposed. They are more elaborate than either, and they all account for currently available data derived from Santa Cruz Island red abalone middens. They do not exhaust the possibilities, however. All of the models assume that differences in the foods acquired by women and men, and their significance within the diet, do not substantially affect either degree of mobility or the placement of residential bases. This is because all marine resources reflected in faunal remains in red abalone middens are largely coincident along the western Santa Cruz Island coast; consequently, women's and men's food acquisition activities would not have been in conflict. However, as more is learned about variation in food resource remains among red abalone middens, particularly those in the interior of the island, this assumption will need to be revisited.

Refinement of the Logistical Mobility Model

A site such as SCRI-333, near the western end of the island, indeed may have been a central base occupied by logistical foragers, even though it is not centrally located. The location of a central base on Santa Cruz Island may have been determined more by the abundance of reliable food resources than by centrality within the territory regularly exploited by its population. As mentioned, intertidal and nearshore waters adjacent to SCRI-333 exhibit unusually high marine productivity. Foraging here for marine resources would have entailed lower energy and transport costs than from other locations around the island, even if some foraging required round trips of 10 km or more. In other words, the average foraging distance traveled would have been less than if the central base was located near the center of the territory in which foraging took place. It is possible that the foraging territory of the

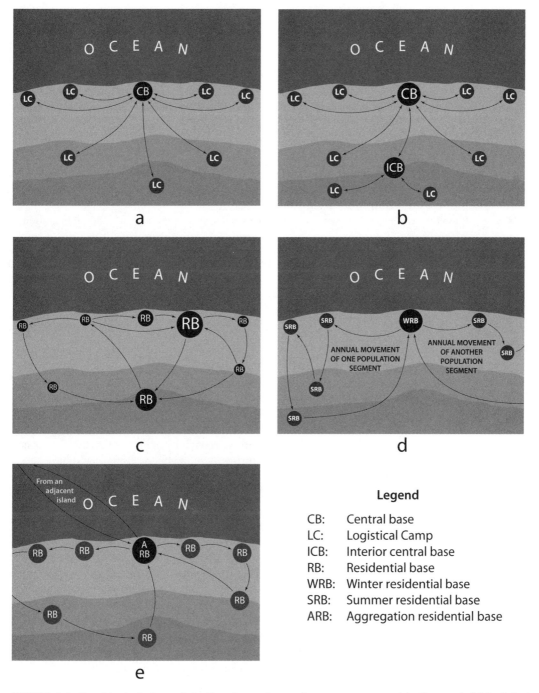

FIGURE 4.2. Graphic depictions of the five alternative settlement system models discussed: (a) logistical mobility; (b) seasonal shifts of a central base; (c) residential mobility; (d) seasonal variation in degree of mobility; (e) aggregation for social interaction and exchange.

site's occupants also included eastern Santa Rosa Island, which would mean that SCRI-333 was, in fact, in a central location. This possibility is unlikely, however, assuming that the nature of watercraft during the 6300–5300 BP period did not allow frequent travel across the 10.2 km passage between the islands, the waters of which frequently are rough.

The smaller red abalone middens—Kennett's "logistical camps"—may not have served for acquiring and processing shellfish for transport to the central base. Instead, the shellfish may have been consumed on-site, and fish, sea mammals, and/or plant foods may have been the resources acquired for transport. The low quantities of these remains at the small sites may be the product of minimal processing prior to transport such that their remains would be at the central base, not at the logistical camps. Those logistical camps located inland would have been occupied for acquiring plant foods, and the shellfish remains at these sites represent the foods eaten at these sites while plant resources were being acquired and possibly processed. This revision of Kennett's model would have difficulty accommodating the fact that some small red abalone middens are located within 2 km of SCRI-333. These sites are within a distance radius that would have precluded the need for logistical camps. It is conceivable, however, that such sites were satellites of the central base, occupied for brief periods of time by families that were socially separated from the rest of the central base population.

A Model Based on Seasonal Shifts of a Central Base

Kennett indicated that larger interior sites appear to have been occupied for relatively long periods of time. It is possible that such sites served as central bases occupied when various productive plant food resources were at peak abundance. A variety of plant food resources would have been available for varying lengths of time from late spring through early fall, and a strategically placed central base would allow access to multiple productive localities. However, to satisfy protein needs, an interior-living population always would have visited the coast to acquire marine foods, particularly shellfish, which would have been the quickest and most predictable resource to acquire. In contrast, coastal sites such as SCRI-333 may have been central bases occupied during those portions of the year when plant food resources were minimally available; the focus instead would have been on marine resources. Occupation of two or more central bases over the course of the year, each used for acquiring resources logistically, may have been an optimal solution assuming that costs of movement from one base to another and construction or maintenance of shelter were low.

Elaboration of the Residential Mobility Model

A settlement system based on residential mobility, in which each red abalone midden site was a residential base from which resources in the immediate vicinity were acquired, undoubtedly would have involved occupation episodes of varying lengths of time. Consequently, rates of midden accumulation would vary, leading to variation in area sizes of sites and midden volumes. The uniqueness of the marine habitats adjacent to SCRI-333 and SCRI-109 would have resulted in the contrast between larger and smaller red abalone middens. The particular combination of food resources acquired and their relative importance would reflect the variety available in the immediate vicinity of the site and the costs of acquiring them. Some locations would have had a greater variety of resources than others, and some would have had distinctive resources, such as dolphins near SCRI-109 (Glassow 2005a) and particular species of plant foods at interior locations.

Variation in area and volume of red abalone midden deposits also may be related to the number of people occupying the site. Many of the small red abalone middens give the impression that just one or two small family groups occupied them. The large middens, in contrast, may have been produced by aggregates of several family groups, and this pattern of fission and fusion may have been tied to the seasons.

A Model Based on Seasonal Variation in Degree of Mobility

Ethnographic data indicate that a common pattern in aboriginal California and in the Pacific Northwest was relatively sedentary occupation at a central residential base during winter months, November through March, and varying degrees of dispersal to, and mobility between, logistical camps or small residential bases during summer months. This was the case, for instance, among mainland coastal Chumash populations (Landberg 1965). This ethnographic pattern may have derived from a settlement system in which a population was logistically mobile during winter months and residentially mobile during summer months. Although winters are relatively mild in coastal Southern California, they are cool enough, and rains are prevalent enough, that relatively substantial dwellings would be desirable, especially on western Santa Cruz Island, where winds occasionally range 8 to 10 on the Beaufort scale. Furthermore, because plant productivity would be lowest during winter months, greater dependence on marine resources would be expected, which would favor occupation at locations where marine productivity is highest, such as that of SCRI-333. Winter foraging would have been within an area large enough that logistical camps sometimes would have been occupied for acquiring resources for transport back to the central base. In this model, many of the smaller red abalone midden sites would have been residential bases occupied during warmer months of the year, perhaps when the population had divided into smaller groups. However, some of the smaller red abalone middens may have been winter logistical camps.

A Model Incorporating Aggregation for Social Interaction and Exchange

Ethnography of low-density hunter-gatherers of the Great Basin indicates that local groups periodically aggregated for social interaction and consequent large-scale food consumption (Steward 1938:237), as did many groups in California (Blackburn 1974), including the Chumash (Gamble 2008:180–181, 224–225). Noah (2005: 242–283) and Perry and Delaney-Rivera (2011: 118) have built strong cases from archaeological data for large-scale feasting events at a coastal and an interior site on Santa Cruz Island. For groups living at a relatively low population density, periodic aggregation undoubtedly would have been the most effective mechanism for mate selection. Kennett (2005:153) estimates that only 400 to 600 people lived on the northern Channel Islands during the middle Holocene, an estimate that is

probably within an order of magnitude of being correct. Not only would the abundant marine resources available near SCRI-333 have provided food for groups of 100 or more people, at least for periods of a few weeks, but blue dicks (*Dichelostemma capitatum*) corms probably were very abundant nearby during spring to early summer and could have been collected in large quantities.

This model is not truly an alternative type of settlement system; it is an elaboration of any of the alternatives just presented. Regardless of whether a territorial population was logistically or residentially mobile, people may have aggregated with neighboring populations for purposes of information exchange, mate selection, economic exchange, and maintenance of intersocietal relations through ritual and ceremonial activities (e.g., feasting).

Information Needed to Evaluate the Models

As mentioned, explication of hunter-gatherer settlement systems is fraught with difficulty, and available data on red abalone middens, whether on Santa Cruz Island or on the other northern Channel Islands, do not allow favoring one of the models proposed over the others. In attempts to evaluate the models, three distinctions are important:

1. A central base of a logistically mobile group versus a residential base of a residentially mobile group visited more frequently or for longer periods than other residential bases.
2. A small residential base occupied for short periods per episode versus a logistical camp occupied for periods of comparable duration.
3. A residential base of either a logistically or residentially mobile population where no regional aggregation of politically autonomous groups occurred versus a residential base where such aggregation did occur.

In addition, the season or seasons during which a site was occupied is critical information for determining which model may be correct, specifically those that entail a seasonal pattern of movement.

First to be considered is distinguishing between a central base of a relatively sedentary population and a popular residential base of a mobile one. Kennett (2005:129) emphasized large area and thick deposits as well as the presence of a cemetery at sites he classified as primary villages (central bases), and SCRI-333 did have a cemetery, which was excavated in 1927, dating to the 6300–5300 BP period (Olson 1930; Glasgow 1977: 111, 114–115). However, the simple presence of a cemetery may not be a firm indication of a central base. Approximately 45 individuals dating to the 6300–5300 BP period were exhumed from the cemetery (King 1990:269–275). Based on radiocarbon dates, the habitation deposits pertaining to this period date between 5700 and 5300 BP (Wilcoxon 1993; unpublished dating results). If the burials were distributed over this 400-year period, roughly one individual was interred every nine years, on average. Isolated burials have been discovered eroding from deposits at two other red abalone middens, and the concentration of burials within what appears to be a formal cemetery at SCRI-333 may be related to the site's topography. The burials are at the top of the knoll on which the site is located. It is plausible, therefore, that the cemetery at SCRI-333 was created by a residentially mobile population that frequently visited the site and resided there for several weeks per episode. In fact, if the site was a central base of a logistically mobile population, presumably the cemetery would be larger, assuming use over the entire 400-year period.

A central base and a popular residential base would be superficially similar. Both would contain substantial midden deposits with relatively well preserved constituents. Distinguishing between the two must be based on specific information derived from food remains, artifact categories, features related to food processing, kinds of dwellings present, and indicators of season of occupation. These are considered in turn.

1. In addition to remains of local food resources, a central base may contain remains of food resources that come from localities more than a day's convenient foraging radius of the site, although if the resources in these localities are the same as those existing close to the central base, they are unlikely to be distinguishable.

2. Both kinds of sites would be expected to contain artifacts reflecting subsistence activities focused on abundant and productive resources near the site. However, a central base may contain few or no artifacts related to processing demonstrably nonlocal food resources even though their remains are present at the central base. Instead, those resources would have been processed at a logistical camp. However, if there is no distinction between local and nonlocal food resources, this measure would not apply.

3. Both may contain features resulting from processing food resources, although if nonlocal food resources were processed elsewhere and evidence of their processing is absent, this would indicate that the site was a central base. This assumes that a distinctive kind of feature is a product of processing a specific resource.

4. A central base most likely would contain remains of relatively substantial dwellings, ones meant to last over the long term, whereas dwellings at a residential base, if they are discoverable, are less likely to be substantial.

5. Indicators of season of occupation, if they are diverse, would be distributed throughout the year at a central base, but they may also be so at a residential base if there was no strong seasonality to when the site was occupied. However, if seasonal indicators cluster during a particular season, the site most likely was a residential base of a group that was residentially mobile for at least part of the year.

The second key distinction—between a small residential base occupied by a residentially mobile population and a logistical camp—also involves some ambiguity. Both would be expected to be small in area and to have relatively thin deposits. Both should contain artifacts related to obtaining food resources in the immediate vicinity of the site, and the remains of food resources would reflect the same. Moreover, indicators of season of occupation at both may indicate occupation during a specific season or multiple seasons.

Whether an identifiable distinction exists most likely depends on the length of occupation episodes. For instance, if a logistical camp is occupied only for a few hours or days, whereas a residential base is occupied for weeks, the likelihood of a distinction undoubtedly would be strong. If, however, both are occupied for at least several days per episode, a distinction may not be apparent. Possible distinctions between the two are the following:

1. If food resource remains are dominated by unusable portions of relatively few taxa of plants or animals, with few other food remains present, a logistical camp would be indicated. However, if these few taxa are especially abundant in the site vicinity whereas others are not, both kinds of sites would exhibit similar remains. With regard to large animals such as sea mammals, however, if the bone assemblage is dominated by elements associated with minimal amounts of meat, this would be a clear indicator that high-value portions of animal carcasses were transported to the central base (Perkins and Daly 1968; Reitz and Wing 1999:204–205).

2. Artifacts at a logistical camp may be narrowly focused on processing one or very few food resources acquired for transport back to a central base, whereas a residential base would be expected to contain artifacts related to acquiring and processing the variety of food resources readily available in the site vicinity. Furthermore, artifacts at a residential base related to activities other than food acquisition and processing may be prominent in the assemblage, including artifacts related to construction of shelters and manufacture and maintenance of tools.

3. Features resulting from processing food resources may exist at both kinds of sites, but they could be anomalously abundant at a logistical camp that otherwise has no evidence of longer-term occupation episodes.

4. A residential base occupied by a residentially mobile group may have some evidence of shelters if an occupation episode lasted a period of weeks, whereas a logistical camp is unlikely to contain obvious evidence of shelter, assuming that occupation episodes would have been much shorter.

The final distinction is between a site at which only routine residential activities—such as food processing and consumption, construction and use of dwellings—took place and a site of this sort at which periodic aggregation of groups also occurred for social and economic reasons. Both categories would have substantial deposits containing a variety of artifacts, food remains, features related to food production, and perhaps evidence of dwellings. If a site also served for regional aggregation, it may also have the following:

1. Unusually large and discrete concentrations within habitation deposits of the remains of particular kinds of food, probably those that could be acquired in relatively large quantities. These would be expected not only if an unusually large number of people occupied the site for a short period, but also if feasting events occurred.

2. Features related to unusually large scale food-processing events, such as baking pits, large hearths, and concentrations of heat-altered stones.

3. Unusually large numbers of artifacts related to ritual activity, including items that may have been components of special regalia, such as distinctive ornaments.

4. Seasonal indicators restricted to a particular season of the year associated with large concentrations of food remains and features related to large-scale food production. The season indicated most likely would be one during which at least some food resources were especially abundant.

However, regional aggregation sites may not exhibit any of these characteristics if social activities of aggregated groups were on the casual end of the spectrum, which would be expected if regional population density was relatively low, with perhaps only 100 or so individuals congregating at a site. As well, social status distinctions in such situations would have been minimal, which likely translated into minimally elaborate ritual paraphernalia.

Discussion and Conclusions

Efforts to understand the degree of mobility of populations living on Santa Cruz Island between 6300 and 5300 BP depends ideally on data from a number of sites distributed across a large proportion of the island. At present, however, the data are too scanty to gain greater confidence in any of the alternative models, nor is there an obvious theoretically based argument for favoring a particular one. On the basis of the available data, it is apparent that settlement systems on western Santa Cruz Island exhibited some degree of complexity, as is evident in the distinction between the two large sites, SCRI-333 and SCRI-109, and the more numerous small ones. In addition, variation exists among the smaller sites with regard to volume of deposits and variety of artifacts present. At this stage of research, however, the nature of these differences still must be explicated. As efforts move forward to expand understanding of settlement systems during the 6300–5300 BP period, data will need to be acquired in the following ways.

First, samples must be obtained from a larger number of sites dating within this period, not just from known red abalone middens, all of which are in the western sector of the island, but also from sites in the central and eastern sectors, as well as the island's interior. At present, excavated samples exist for only eight red abalone middens (Glassow 2005b; Glassow et al. 2008; Ballantyne 2006; Heather B. Thakar, personal communication, 2012), and data from some of these are too limited in quantity and variety for evaluating the alternative models.

Second, larger sample sizes per site must be obtained, large enough for characterizing variation in artifact assemblages, food remains, and features related to food processing. Aside from two units at SCRI-333 (Wilcoxon n.d., 1993) that extended into the red abalone midden deposits at this site, two units excavated at SCRI-109 (Glassow et al. 2008), and a single unit at an interior site (Ballantyne 2006:27, 31–33), only column or auger samples have been acquired from red abalone middens. Samples on the order of 2–3 m³ will be necessary for generating needed data, particularly those derived from artifacts and domestic features.

Third, greater emphasis must be placed on acquiring information about season of occupation. Species and age at death represented among faunal remains commonly have been used to infer season (e.g., Glassow et al. 2008:72–73), but other indicators of season of occupation are becoming popular as well. Kennett (2005:151–152; see also Braje 2010:107–109) used oxygen isotope values of mussel shells to distinguish between year-round and seasonal occupation, but his data do not allow the specific season of occupation to be ascertained. Because profiles of values along the length of the shell reflect annual cycles of sea surface temperature variation, identifying season of occupation (specifically, the season during which mussels were collected) is possible (Killingley 1981). In addition, season of occupation may be indicated by the kinds of floral remains present, given that many seeds and nuts are available only during particular seasons. The possibility of storage of seeds and nuts for periods beyond their availability complicates the utility of this measure; nonetheless, occupation may be argued to have occurred at least during the season when the seed or nut was available.

Fourth, insight into the determinants of settlement systems on western Santa Cruz Island during the 6300–5300 BP period would be facilitated through comparable studies on the other Channel Islands. Each of the island populations had to adapt to a set of environmental circumstances distinctive, in many respects, of their home island. The most obvious realms in which distinctiveness occurs are land area, nature and abundance of plants that could serve as foods, productivity of different taxa of marine fauna in waters surrounding the island, and exposure to adverse weather conditions. Perhaps it is not surprising, for instance, that evidence of middle Holocene sedentism, in the form of house floors, is most evident on San Clemente Island (one of the southern Channel Islands), which offered few plant food resources because of its aridity and minimal natural protection from strong winds (Raab 2009:115, 119–120).

Despite the elusiveness of information pertinent to inferring the nature of settlement systems to which red abalone midden sites were articulated, the prospects for gaining an understanding of their structure are high, even though substantially more data, and a greater diversity of data, must be acquired. Surely, settlement systems of the 6300–5300 BP period differed substantially from those that existed at the beginning of Spanish colonization. The manner in which settlement systems changed in response to growing population numbers and changes in subsistence will deepen our understanding of cultural development on California's Channel Islands.

Acknowledgments

The ideas expressed in this chapter grew out of many conversations with UCSB archeology graduate students who at the time this was written were carrying out dissertation research on Santa Cruz Island, including Carola Flores Fernandez, Kristina Gill, Amy Gusick, Elizabeth Sutton, and Heather Thakar. To varying degrees, they also are attempting to understand the nature of settlement systems on the island during various periods of prehistory. I thank them for stimulating my thinking about settlement systems and the various ways in which they can be elucidated. Comments on an earlier draft by Mark Raab and an anonymous reviewer helped me to clarify parts of the chapter and to consider other factors affecting the nature of settlement systems. I also thank Christopher Jazwa and Jennifer Perry, not only for their comments that helped me improve the chapter, but also for encouraging me to participate in the SAA symposium they organized and to bring this work to fruition.

References Cited

Ames, K. M.
2002   Going by Boat: The Forager-Collector Continuum at Sea. In *Beyond Foraging and Collecting: Evolutionary Change in Hunter-Gatherer Settlement Systems*, edited by B. Fitzhugh and J. Habu, pp. 19–52. Kluwer Academic/Plenum, New York.

Ballantyne, K. E.
2006   An Analysis of Buried Archaeological Sites on Western Santa Cruz Island. Master's thesis. Department of Anthropology, University of California, Santa Barbara.

Barlow, K. R., and D. Metcalfe
1996   Plant Utility Indices: Two Great Basin Examples. *Journal of Archaeological Science* 23: 351–371.

Bettinger, R. L.
1991   *Hunter-Gatherers: Archaeological and Evolutionary Theory*. Plenum, New York.
1999   From Traveler to Processor, Regional Trajectories of Hunter-Gatherer Sedentism in the Inyo-Mono Region, California. In *Settlement Pattern Studies in the Americas: Fifty Years Since Virú*, edited by B. R. Billman and G. M. Feinman, pp. 39–55. Smithsonian Institution Press, Washington, DC.

Bettinger, R. L., R. Malhi, and H. McCarthy
1997   Central Place Models of Acorn and Mussel Processing. *Journal of Archaeological Science* 24:887–899.

Billman, B. R., and G. M. Feinman (editors)
1999   *Settlement Pattern Studies in the Americas: Fifty Years Since Virú*. Smithsonian Institution Press, Washington, DC.

Binford, L. R.
1980   Willow Smoke and Dogs' Tails: Hunter-Gatherer Settlement Systems and Archaeological Site Formation. *American Antiquity* 45:4–20.
1990   Mobility, Housing, and Environment: A Comparative Study. *Journal of Anthropological Research* 46(2):119–152.

Bird, D. W.
1997   Behavioral Ecology and the Archaeological Consequences of Central Place Foraging among the Meriam. In *Rediscovering Darwin: Evolutionary Theory in Archaeological Explanation*, edited by C. M. Barton and G. A. Clark, pp. 291–306. American Anthropological Association, Washington, DC.

Bird, J.
1946   The Alacaluf. In *Handbook of South American Indians*, Vol. 1: *The Marginal Tribes*, edited by J. H. Steward, pp. 55–80. Smithsonian Institution, Bureau of American Ethnology Bulletin 143. Government Printing Office, Washington, DC.

Blackburn, T.
1974   Ceremonial Integration and Social Interaction in Aboriginal California. In *'Antap: California Indian Political and Economic Organization*, edited by L. J. Bean and T. F. King, pp. 95–110. Ballena Press, Ramona, CA.

Braje, T. J.
2010   *Modern Oceans, Ancient Sites: Archaeology and Marine Conservation on San Miguel Island, California*. University of Utah Press, Salt Lake City.

Braje, T. J., and J. M. Erlandson
2007   Measuring Subsistence Specialization: Comparing Historic and Prehistoric Abalone Middens on San Miguel Island, California. *Journal of Anthropological Archaeology* 26: 474–485.

Braje, T. J., J. M. Erlandson, T. C. Rick, P. K. Dayton, and M. B. A. Hatch
2009   Fishing from Past to Present: Continuity and Resilience of Red Abalone Fisheries on the Channel Islands. *Ecological Adaptations* 19(4):906–919.

Chatters, J. C.
1987   Hunter-Gatherer Adaptations and Assemblage Structure. *Journal of Anthropological Archaeology* 6:336–375.

Codding, B. F., R. Bliege Bird, and D. W. Bird
2011   Provisioning Offspring and Others: Risk-Energy Trade-offs and Gender Differences in Hunter-Gatherer Foraging Strategies. *Proceedings of the Royal Society B* 278:2502–2509.

Cooper, J. M.

1946   The Yahgan. In *Handbook of South American Indians*, Vol. 1: *The Marginal Tribes*, edited by J. H. Steward, pp. 81–106. Smithsonian Institution, Bureau of American Ethnology Bulletin 143. Government Printing Office, Washington, DC.

Elston, R. G., and D. W. Zeanah

2002   Thinking Outside the Box: A New Perspective on Diet Breadth and Sexual Division of Labor in the Prearchaic Great Basin. *World Archaeology* 34(1):103–130.

Fitzhugh, B.

2002   Residential and Logistical Strategies in the Evolution of Complex Hunter-Gatherers on the Kodiak Archipelago. In *Beyond Foraging and Collecting: Evolutionary Change in Hunter-Gatherer Settlement Systems*, edited by B. Fitzhugh and J. Habu, pp. 257–304. Kluwer Academic/Plenum, New York.

Gamble, L. H.

2008   *The Chumash World at European Contact: Power, Trade, and Feasting among Complex Hunter-Gatherers*. University of California Press, Berkeley.

Glassow, M. A.

1977   An Archaeological Overview of the Northern Channel Islands, California, Including Santa Barbara Island. Unpublished report. Department of Anthropology, University of California, Santa Barbara.

1993a   Changes in Subsistence on Marine Resources through 7,000 Years of Prehistory on Santa Cruz Island, California. In *Archaeology on the Northern Channel Islands of California*, edited by M. A. Glassow, pp. 75–94. Archives of California Prehistory 34. Coyote Press, Salinas, CA.

1993b   The Occurrence of Red Abalone Shells in Northern Channel Island Archaeological Middens. In *Third California Island Symposium: Recent Advances in Research on the California Islands*, edited by F. G. Hochberg, pp. 567–576. Santa Barbara Museum of Natural History, Santa Barbara, CA.

2005a   Prehistoric Dolphin Hunting on Santa Cruz Island, California. In *The Exploitation and Cultural Importance of Sea Mammals*, edited by G. Monks, pp. 107–120. Oxbow Books, Oxford.

2005b   Variation in Marine Fauna Utilization by Middle Holocene Occupants of Santa Cruz Island. In *Proceedings of the Sixth California Islands Symposium*, edited by D. K. Garcelon

and C. A. Schwemm, pp. 23–34. National Park Service Technical Publication CHIS-05-01. Institute for Wildlife Studies, Arcata, CA.

Glassow, M. A., L. H. Gamble, J. E. Perry, and G. S. Russell

2007   Prehistory of the Northern California Bight and the Adjacent Transverse Ranges. In *California Prehistory: Colonization, Culture, and Complexity*, edited by T. L. Jones and K. A. Klar, pp. 191–213. Altamira, Lanham, MD.

Glassow, M. A., D. J. Kennett, J. P. Kennett, and L. R. Wilcoxon

1994   Confirmation of Middle Holocene Ocean Cooling Inferred from Stable Isotopic Analysis of Prehistoric Shells from Santa Cruz Island, California. In *The Fourth California Islands Symposium: Update on the Status of Resources*, edited by W. L. Halvorson and G. J. Maender, pp. 223–232. Santa Barbara Museum of Natural History, Santa Barbara, CA.

Glassow, M. A., J. E. Perry, and P. F. Paige

2008   *The Punta Arena Site: Early and Middle Holocene Cultural Development on Santa Cruz Island*. Contributions in Anthropology 3. Santa Barbara Museum of Natural History, Santa Barbara, CA.

Glassow, M. A., H. B. Thakar, and D. J. Kennett

2012   Red Abalone Collecting and Marine Water Temperature During the Middle Holocene Occupation of Santa Cruz Island, California. *Journal of Archaeological Science* 39:2574–2582.

Jackson, T. L.

1991   Pounding Acorn: Women's Production as Social and Economic Focus. In *Engendering Archaeology: Women and Prehistory*, edited by J. M. Gero and M. W. Conkey, pp. 301–325. Blackwell, Oxford.

Johnson, J. R.

1982   An Ethnohistoric Study of the Island Chumash. Master's thesis. Department of Anthropology, University of California, Santa Barbara.

Junak, S., T. Ayres, R. Scott, D. Wilken, and D. Young

1995   *A Flora of Santa Cruz Island*. Santa Barbara Botanic Garden, Santa Barbara, CA.

Kelly, R. L.

1983   Hunter-Gatherer Mobility Strategies. *Journal of Anthropological Research* 39(3):277–306.

1992   Mobility/Sedentism: Concepts, Archaeological Measures, and Effects. *Annual Review of Anthropology* 21(43–66):43–66.

1995   *The Foraging Spectrum: Diversity in Hunter-*

Gatherer Lifeways. Smithsonian Institution Press, Washington, DC.

Kennett, D. J.
2005   *The Island Chumash: Behavioral Ecology of a Maritime Society*. University of California Press, Berkeley.

Kennett, D. J., J. P. Kennett, J. M. Erlandson, and K. G. Cannariato
2007   Human Responses to Middle Holocene Climate Change on California's Channel Islands. *Quaternary Science Reviews* 26:351–367.

Kennett, D. J., B. Winterhalder, J. Bartruff, and J. M. Erlandson
2009   An Ecological Model for the Emergence of Institutionalized Social Hierarchies on California's Northern Channel Islands. In *Pattern and Process in Cultural Evolution*, edited by S. Shennan, pp. 297–314. University of California Press, Berkeley.

Killingley, J. S.
1981   Seasonality of Mollusk Collecting Determined from O-18 Profiles of Midden Shells. *American Antiquity* 46:152–158.

King, C. D.
1990   *Evolution of Chumash Society: A Comparative Study of Artifacts Used for Social System Maintenance in the Santa Barbara Channel Region Before A.D. 1804*. Garland, New York.

Kowalewski, S. A.
2008   Regional Settlement Pattern Studies. *Journal of Archaeological Research* 16:225–285.

Landberg, L. C. W.
1965   *The Chumash of Southern California*. Papers 19. Southwest Museum, Los Angeles.

McGuire, Kelly R., and William R. Hildebrandt
1994   The Possibilities of Women and Men: Gender and the California Millingstone Horizon. *Journal of California and Great Basin Anthropology* 16(1):41–59.

Metcalfe, D., and K. R. Barlow
1992   A Model for Exploring the Optimal Trade-off Between Field Processing and Transport. *American Anthropologist* 94:340–356.

Noah, A. C.
2005   Household Economies: The Role of Animals in a Historic Period Chiefdom on the California Coast. PhD dissertation. Department of Anthropology, University of California, Los Angeles.

Olson, R. L.
1930   Chumash Prehistory. *University of California Publications in American Archaeology and Ethnology* 28(1):1–21.

Orians, G. H., and N. E. Pearson
1979   On the Theory of Central Place Foraging. In *Analysis of Ecological Systems*, edited by D. J. Horn, G. R. Stairs, and R. D. Mitchell, pp. 155–177. Ohio State University Press, Columbus.

Perkins, D., Jr., and P. Daly
1968   A Hunters' Village in Neolithic Turkey. *Scientific American* 219(5):96–105.

Perry, J. E., and C. Delaney-Rivera
2011   Interactions and Interiors of the Coastal Chumash. *California Archaeology* 3(1):103–125.

Perry, J. E., and K. M. Hoppa
2012   Subtidal Shellfish Exploitation on the California Channel Islands: Wavy Top (*Lithopoma undosum*) in the Middle Holocene. In *Exploring Methods of Faunal Analysis: Insights from California Archaeology*, edited by M. A. Glassow and T. L. Joslin, pp. 65–86. Cotsen Institute of Archaeology, University of California, Los Angeles.

Raab, L. M.
2009   This Old House. In *California Maritime Archaeology: A San Clemente Island Perspective*, edited by L. M. Raab, J. Cassidy, A. Yatsko, and W. J. Howard, pp. 109–121. Altamira, Lanham, MD.

Reitz, E. J., and E. S. Wing
1999   *Zooarchaeology*. Cambridge University Press, Cambridge.

Rick, T. C., D. J. Kennett, and J. M. Erlandson
2005   Preliminary Report on the Archaeology and Paleoecology of the Abalone Rocks Estuary, Santa Rosa Island, California. In *Proceedings of the Sixth California Islands Symposium, December 1–3, 2003*, edited by D. K. Garcelon and C. A. Schwemm, pp. 55–63. Institute for Wildlife Studies, Arcata.

Schoenherr, A. A., C. R. Feldmeth, and M. J. Emerson
1999   *Natural History of the Islands of California*. University of California Press, Berkeley.

Steward, J. H.
1938   *Basin-Plateau Aboriginal Sociopolitical Groups*. Smithsonian Institution, Bureau of American Ethnology Bulletin 120. Government Printing Office, Washington, D.C.

Wilcoxon, L. R.
n.d.   Field notes pertaining to archaeological excavation at site CA-SCRI-333. On file at the Repository for Archaeological and Ethnographic Collections, Department of Anthropology, University of California, Santa Barbara.

1993   Subsistence and Site Structure: An Approach for Deriving Cultural Information from Coastal Shell Middens. In *Archaeology on the Northern Channel Islands of California*, edited by M. A. Glassow, pp. 137–151. Archives of California Prehistory 34. Coyote Press, Salinas, CA.

Yesner, D. R.
1980   Maritime Hunter-Gatherers: Ecology and Prehistory. *Current Anthropology* 21(6): 727–750.

2004   Prehistoric Maritime Adaptations of the Subarctic and Subantarctic Zones: The Aleutian/ Fuegian Connection Reconsidered. *Arctic Anthropology* 41(2):76–97.

Zeanah, D. W.
2004   Sexual Division of Labor and Central Place Foraging: A Model for the Carson Desert of Western Nevada. *Journal of Anthropological Archaeology* 23:1–32.

5

The Ideal Free Distribution and Settlement History at Old Ranch Canyon, Santa Rosa Island

Christopher S. Jazwa, Douglas J. Kennett, and Bruce Winterhalder

The decisions that people make about where to settle on a landscape are influenced by climate, resource distribution, religion, cultural and economic factors, technological developments, defensive requirements, and the distribution of other human populations. These decisions are often strategic, with the goal of attaining specific economic, social, and political ends (Jochim 1976, 1981). A behavioral ecology model, the ideal free distribution (IFD), has been used to address questions about the relationships between environment, economy, and population distribution (Åström 1994; Fretwell and Lucas 1969; Fretwell 1972; Sutherland 1983, 1996; Tregenza 1995).

Potential settlement locations are ranked by their suitability based on attaining specific economic, social, or political ends. The model assumes that people are knowledgeable about their environment and predicts that they will first settle in the most suitable location. As the population grows, overcrowding, resource depression, and other effects of local competition will cause the suitability of the first-ranked location to decline. When the suitability of the settlement location falls, a portion of subsequent growth will expand into the second-ranked location. Progressively lower ranked locations are filled in order by the same mechanism. Occupancy of low-ranked areas signals lessened marginal economic returns across the full suite of occupied locations and thus, by the diet breadth model, predicts low-ranked resources in the diet. In the IFD, individuals always move if it offers any advantage, equalizing marginal suitability across all occupied settlement locations.

The IFD is scalable and can be used to predict changes in landscape use on scales both large (e.g., continental [Fitzhugh and Kennett 2010; Allen and O'Connell 2008]) and small (e.g., islands and regions [Kennett et al. 2006; Culleton 2012]). On California's northern Channel Islands, it has been used to model the establishment and persistence of 46 permanent settlements (Kennett et al. 2009; Winterhalder et al. 2010); however, these pioneering studies did not take into account details of environmental change and individual site history that allow for a more localized and environmentally sensitive refinement and appraisal of IFD predictions.

We analyzed the faunal record of two sites at Old Ranch Canyon (ORC), Santa Rosa Island, to show how environmental, economic, and cultural change influenced settlement decisions in the past. The suitability of ORC was enhanced with respect to other locations during the early Holocene and beginning of the middle Holocene because a resource-rich estuary existed at the mouth of the canyon. Sediment infilling of this small estuary started as sea level stabilized between 6,000 and 5,000 years ago, decreasing the suitability of OCR for primary human settlement. The stratigraphy and chronology of multiple sites at the mouth of Old Ranch Canyon suggests that the resident population decreased for several millennia after the estuary was largely infilled. We hypothesize that the canyon's inhabitants moved

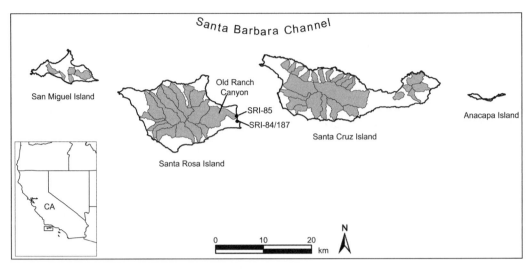

FIGURE 5.1. California's northern Channel Islands and the sites SRI-84/187 and SRI-85. Watersheds ranked by Winterhalder et al. (2010) are highlighted in gray.

to other, more suitable locations as the resource potential of the estuarine environment decreased. When ORC settlement expanded 3,000 years later, subsistence was more focused on rocky intertidal resources.

The record from ORC shows that during the late Holocene, *Olivella biplicata* shell bead production increased, paralleling the rising importance of regional trade. The long sandy beach at the mouth of the canyon would have been a good source of *Olivella* shells and provided a convenient landing place for plank canoes (*tomols*), an important technological innovation that facilitated trade with the mainland and other island communities after AD 500 (Arnold 1992a, 1995, 2001a; Gamble 2002; Fagan 2004). We argue that this increased the suitability of this location and provides an example of how localized changes in the environment or economy can impact settlement decisions and the distribution of population regionally.

California's Northern Channel Islands

The four northern Channel Islands are separated from the California mainland by the Santa Barbara Channel. From west to east they are San Miguel, Santa Rosa, Santa Cruz, and Anacapa (Figure 5.1; Jazwa and Perry, Chapter 1). These islands are an excellent test case for the IFD for several reasons. They have remained separated from the mainland, throughout the Quaternary, when

sea levels were periodically lower, and therefore represent a bounded sampling universe. The earliest visible evidence of permanent settlement on the islands is approximately 8000–7000 cal BP (Kennett et al. 2009); however, people had been visiting and seasonally exploiting the resources available on the islands since at least 13,000 cal BP (Erlandson et al. 2007; Erlandson et al. 2008; Erlandson et al. 2011; Johnson et al. 2002; Kennett 2005; Kennett et al. 2008). Thus, the initial permanent occupants likely understood habitat suitability and were prepared to make informed decisions about the best settlement locations on the islands. Because islands are inherently sensitive to natural and human-induced changes (Fitzhugh and Hunt 1997:381–382), fluctuations in resource availability may be more readily documented in the archaeological record.

The terrestrial resources on islands also tend to be more limited; this is certainly the case on the northern Channel Islands (Rick et al. 2005). Because of this, the inhabitants had a strong intertidal and maritime focus from the earliest occupation (Erlandson et al. 2011). Although there is no direct evidence for boat use dating to the period of early occupation, ocean-going watercraft would have been required to reach any of the islands (Erlandson et al. 2008; Raab et al. 2009). At historic contact, island populations were primarily concentrated in large coastal villages governed by chiefs (Johnson 1982, 1993). Earlier settlements also are largely either coastally located or coastally oriented (Winterhalder et al. 2010:478), and coastal resources factor highly in the ranking of settlement locations on these islands (Kennett et al. 2009; Winterhalder et al. 2010).

Although Winterhalder et al. (2010) did not include environmental change in their regional application of the IFD, the model is well suited to address temporal dynamics in habitat suitability. At the time of earliest occupation, 13,000 years ago, sea level was ~70–75 m below its present level. The four islands were all connected to form one land mass, Santarosae. The rise in sea level through the early settlement period caused a 65 percent decrease in land area, potentially submerging evidence of early settlement (Kennett 2005; Kennett et al. 2008). There have been more than 50 nonresidential shell middens and other sites found on the islands that date to the Late Pleistocene or early Holocene, before the earliest available evidence for permanent settlement about 8,000 years ago (Erlandson et al. 2008; Erlandson et al. 2011:1181–1182; Rick et al. 2005).

Early permanent habitation sites are associated with a diverse faunal assemblage, including fish, shellfish, and sea mammals, all present to varying degrees throughout the archaeological record on the islands. There is a general increase in the amount of fishing and a decrease in the relative contribution of shellfish through time. Fish and sea mammals became particularly important during the late Holocene (Braje et al. 2007:741; Colten 2001; Glassow 1993; Kennett 2005; Kennett and Kennett 2000; Kennett and Conlee 2002; Raab et al. 1995; Rick 2007; Rick et al. 2008:81).

There were important demographic changes on the islands over time. The earliest evidence for permanent settlement is from the mouth of Tecolote Canyon (SRI-3), a high-ranked drainage on the northern coast of Santa Rosa Island. We define *permanent settlement* by the presence of substantial residential middens, cemeteries, or houses (see Winterhalder et al. 2010). There is evidence for population expansion during the middle Holocene, particularly along the north and east coasts of Santa Rosa Island and the west and south coasts of Santa Cruz Island (Glassow et al. 1988, 2008; King 1990; Wilcoxon 1993; Winterhalder et al. 2010). It is this expansion that is addressed by Winterhalder et al. (2010). Large inland middens appeared at this time, potentially

associated with seasonal exploitation of inland plant resources (Kennett 2005; Kennett and Clifford 2004; Perry 2003).

Important technological and social changes occurred during the late Holocene, many of them beginning during the Middle period (2250–800 cal BP) as occupants of the islands began to exploit fish and sea mammals more intensively (Arnold 1992a:65; Glassow 1977). This may have been related to the development of the *tomol*, which appeared after 1500 cal BP (Arnold 1992a, 1995, 2001a; Gamble 2002; Fagan 2004). Population increase and growth in the number of permanent settlements on the islands accelerated during the late Middle period (1300–800 cal BP) (Arnold 2001a; Kennett 2005; Kennett and Conlee 2002; Winterhalder et al. 2010). Also beginning at this time and continuing through the Middle to Late period transition (MLT; 800–650 cal BP) and Late period (650–168 cal BP) were institutionalized differences in social status (Arnold 2001a; Kennett et al. 2009). The MLT, in particular, has been associated with important sociocultural, economic, and technological change (Arnold 1991, 1992a, 1997, 2001b; Arnold and Tissot 1993; Arnold et al. 1997; Jazwa et al. 2012, Kennett 2005; Kennett and Conlee 2002; Raab and Larson 1997). The *Olivella biplicata* shell bead industry, which served as a medium of exchange at historic contact, also grew significantly during the MLT (Arnold 1987, 1990, 1992a, 1992b, 2001a; Arnold and Munns 1994; Munns and Arnold 2002:132–133; Kennett 2005; King 1990; Rick 2007).

Anthropogenic and climate-driven environmental changes have been well studied on the northern Channel Islands and are thought to have influenced sociopolitical developments there during the Holocene (e.g., Arnold 1992a, 2001a; Arnold and Graesch 2004; Arnold and Tissot 1993; Braje et al. 2007; Erlandson and Jones 2002; Jazwa et al. 2012; Kennett 2005; Kennett and Kennett 2000; Kennett et al. 2007; Kennett et al. 2008; Raab and Larson 1997). We demonstrate here that the IFD can contribute to such interpretations.

The Channel Islands Ideal Free Distribution Model

The IFD has its roots in population ecology (Fretwell and Lucas 1969; Fretwell 1972; Sutherland 1983, 1996; Åström 1994; Tregenza 1995). Like other human behavioral ecology models, it

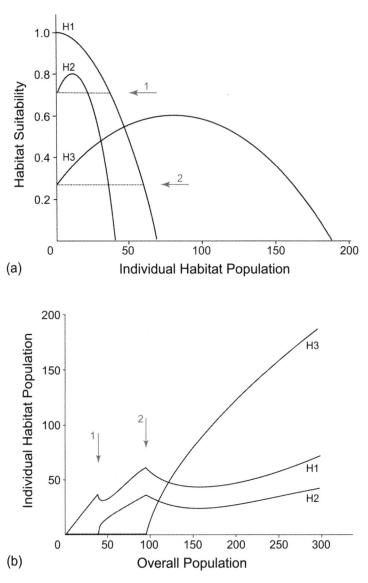

FIGURE 5.2. The ideal free distribution with Allee effects: (a) habitat suitability in three habitats as a function of habitat-specific density. H2 and H3 are characterized by Allee effects. (b) the overall population distribution as a function of total population size. We depict Allee effects causing the partial abandonment of high-suitability habitats; full abandonment is possible if the effects are sufficiently strong. Zero suitability is hypothetical. In practice, we expect in-fill to stop short of this point (after Winterhalder et al. 2010:473, Figure 3).

begins with an optimization premise: individuals elect to settle in the best available habitat; habitats differ in their basic suitability and their response to settlement and exploitation (Figure 5.2a). As population increases within a habitat, suitability decreases because of interference and exploitation competition, often in a nonlinear manner.

Once suitability of the best habitat has declined to the point that it is equal to the basic suitability of the next best habitat, newcomers will divide between them (Sutherland 1983:821, 1996:5). The system reaches equilibrium when no individual has further incentive to relocate.

The IFD is built around individual choice and

a simple optimization premise that integrates into its structure predictions about the relationships between environment, economy, and the population-level consequences of exploitation and competition. It is used by archaeologists to predict population distribution qualitatively (Kennett et al. 2006; Kennett et al. 2009) or quantitatively (Winterhalder et al. 2010). Habitat suitability generally will exhibit negative or declining density dependence; however, at low population density, the model can include Allee effects, or positive density dependence. Per capita opportunities for survival and reproduction may be enhanced as it becomes easier to find and defend food and mates. As such economies of scale are exhausted, suitability reaches a maximum and then decreases (Sutherland 1996:10–11; Greene and Stamps 2001).

Winterhalder et al. (2010:473) discuss in detail the primary predictions of the IFD model. Allee effects can produce a partial exodus or even complete abandonment of a high-ranked habitat (Winterhalder et al. 2010:473; Figure 5.2b). The form of the suitability curve for a given habitat is dictated by its response to human density increase and exploitation. Suitability in a habitat with many high-ranked food resources but only limited freshwater will decrease quickly with population density, as would a habitat containing only a few high-ranked resources of low yield. Conversely, suitability in habitats with abundant low-ranking but high-yield resources will decline only slowly. These habitats are less sensitive to density dependence. Allee effects also can vary. Low-density, ascending parts of the curve may be more or less steep, the peak representing a small or large increase over basic suitability. It may be placed at lower or higher human population densities.

Anthropogenic resource depression and habitat degradation from high population densities in island ecosystems is common (e.g., Hunt 2007; Hunt and Lipo 2009), the northern Channel Islands being an important example (Rick 2004, 2007; Kennett 2005; Braje 2007, 2010; Braje et al. 2007; Erlandson et al. 2008; Rick and Erlandson 2008; Erlandson and Rick 2010; Braje and Rick 2011). Empirical application of the IFD must, however, recognize that there may be lags in the linkage of human density and habitat suitability.

Especially depressed habitats may not recover immediately upon release from exploitation. By incorporating lag, the IFD can be adjusted to describe realistic habitat recovery and thus a mechanism for movement back into previously depleted habitats.

The typical IFD application (e.g., Winterhalder et al. 2010) invokes a density dependent situation. However, IFD predictions can be driven by changes of habitat suitability that are not population dependent. They may be environmental, technological, or sociocultural, and may affect all or only some habitats. Changes in sea surface temperature might affect the availability of food species in marine habitats (e.g., Arnold 1992a, 2001a; Arnold and Tissot 1993; Colten 2001; Kennett 2005; Kennett and Kennett 2000; Pletka 2001) but leave inland terrestrial resources relatively unchanged. The development of boat technology could have increased the suitability of coastal habitats with good launch and pull-out locations, but not those without them. Sociocultural change can alter the relative preference for some resources compared to others. Because these changes affect habitats independently of population, they are modeled as a displacement of the suitability curve or by a change in its shape (Figure 5.3).

In Figure 5.3, each graphic depicts suitability as a function of habitat-specific population density. For simplicity, we depict only negative density dependence—there are no Allee effects—and we have reduced the 46 watersheds of the northern Channel Islands to three hypothetical examples, habitats h_1 to h_3. Total population is a function of the number of individuals in all occupied habitats (Σp_n). Each of the four graphs represents a key stage in our hypothesized prehistory of Old Ranch Canyon: (a) as portrayed by Winterhalder et al. (2010), based solely on four habitat attributes of their analysis. ORC is highly ranked, but not so high that we predicted its early occupation at low cross-island population levels; (b) the prediction as it would be modified based on the recognition that the settlement sites rested in their early prehistory next to a rich estuary. We predict settlement much earlier, at higher suitabilities and at lower overall cross-island population levels; (c) ORC as characterized by the IFD after closure of the estuary. Although population

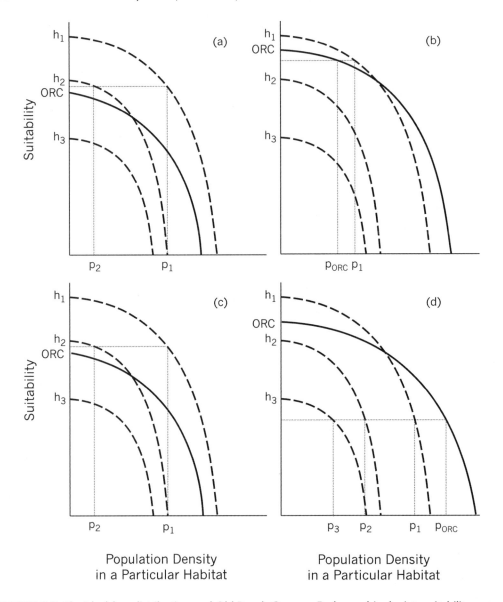

FIGURE 5.3. The ideal free distribution and Old Ranch Canyon. Each graphic depicts suitability as a function of habitat-specific population density: (a) ORC as portrayed by Winterhalder et al. (2010), based solely on the four habitat attributes of their analysis; (b) the ORC prediction as it would be modified based on the recognition that ORC rested in its early prehistory next to a rich estuary; (c) ORC as characterized by the IFD after closure of the estuary; (d) elevated suitability of ORC because of density-independent technical and socioeconomic developments.

has grown and the marginal suitability of occupied habitats has declined from that depicted in situation b, a strong density-independent decline in suitability associated with estuary closure has dropped ORC to just below a level at which the site would be occupied; (d) with further population growth, competition, and habitat exploitation, the marginal habitat suitability of occupied sites continues to decline, but density-independent technical and socioeconomic developments—the plank canoe, exploitation of the marine habitat around offshore kelp beds, and development of trade through *Olivella* bead production—significantly elevate and extend the suitability of ORC and assure its importance as a settlement up to the historic period.

Old Ranch Canyon

Old Ranch Canyon is on the eastern end of Santa Rosa Island (Figure 5.1). We assess whether or not IFD predictions are consistent with the available archaeological data from the mouth of this drainage as a means of evaluating their potential for broader applicability (see Winterhalder 2002).

Previous work established that ORC is a high-ranked drainage, sixth in rank using an intuitive environmental weighting (Kennett et al. 2009: 306, Table 20.1) and seventh based on a more statistical assessment (Winterhalder et al. 2010:483, Figure 9). The associated drainage is 18.59 km² in size, the second largest of the 46 drainages analyzed (range 1.28 to 34.35 km²). The canyon has 1.46 km of rocky intertidal shoreline adjacent to its mouth (ranked twenty-sixth; range 0 to 4.30 km) and 2.98 km of sandy beach (ranked sixth; range 0 to 3.74 km). Finally, there is 0.12 km² of offshore kelp forest (ranked twenty-sixth; range 0 to 1.86 km²). There is evidence for permanent village settlement at the mouth of Old Ranch Canyon during the middle Holocene and throughout the late Holocene and into the historic period (SRI-77, -81, -84, -85, -187, -191, -192 -666, -667; see Rick, Kennett, and Erlandson 2005), at which time it can be identified as the named village Qshiwqshiw (Johnson 1999).

Estuaries are rare on the northern Channel Islands, and the presence or absence of these resource-rich habitats was not a component of earlier IFD analyses (Kennett et al. 2009; Winterhalder et al. 2010). ORC and the adjacent Old Ranch House Canyon are unique in that they were situated next to a substantial estuary during the early and middle Holocene (Cole and Liu 1994; Rick, Kennett, and Erlandson 2005; Rick et al. 2006; Wolff et al. 2007; Rick 2009). Estuaries are often extremely productive (Bickel 1978:8), and the early presence of the Abalone Rocks estuary at the mouth of Old Ranch Canyon would have enhanced its suitability for permanent settlement. Barber (1979) has argued that the lower reaches of estuaries near their marine confluence are the most productive environments on earth, supporting a rich assemblage of fish, shellfish, and waterfowl.

Although rocky intertidal shellfish species dominate the ORC assemblages, Rick, Kennett, and Erlandson (2005) have also observed evidence for the early consumption of estuarine shellfish species, namely Venus clams (*Chione* sp.), Washington clams (*Saxidomas nuttalli*), and California oysters (*Ostrea lurida*), between ~8000 and 5900 cal BP. Although estuaries were not common on the northern Channel Islands, there were many settlements on the margins of estuaries on the adjacent mainland during the early and middle Holocene (Bickel 1978; Inman 1983; Erlandson 1994). The early and extensive use of these rich habitats, when present, is one indication of their resource value.

The life cycle of the Abalone Rocks estuary followed a pattern similar to that of mainland estuaries. Estuary formation requires a freshwater input from land and an open connection to the ocean (Bickel 1978:8), a configuration more common during periods of rapid sea level rise (Inman 1983:18–20; Erlandson 1994:34). Often, embayments form in coastal canyons that were cut deeply during periods of low glacial sea level (Bickel 1978:8; Erlandson 1994:34). On the Channel Islands, sea level rise began to slow around 6,000 years ago (Inman 1983; Rick, Kennett, and Erlandson 2005). This then allowed for the formation of sand bars, which eventually close the mouth of the estuary, causing it to stagnate, fill in, and lose productivity. Estuary extinction is particularly prominent in areas where freshwater input is limited, as is the case on Santa Rosa Island (Erlandson 1994). The current Abalone Rocks Marsh is located near the mouth of the relict estuary.

By contrast, on the adjacent California mainland, estuaries persist in areas of shallower topography where the convergence of flow from multiple sources forms larger sloughs and prevents estuary senescence (Jon Erlandson, personal communication, 2011). Estuary closure and static sea level are conducive to the formation of low-productivity marshes (Bickel 1978:11).

Because estuarine shellfish are present in the Old Ranch Canyon archaeological record from the earliest known occupation (Rick, Kennett, and Erlandson 2005; Rick 2009), they cannot be used to determine when the estuary formed. However, its projected closure corresponds to a decline in estuarine shellfish use between 6,000 and 5,000 years ago at multiple sites (SRI-77, -81, -84, -191, -192 -666, -667) (Rick, Kennett, and Erlandson 2005; Rick et al. 2006; Wolff et al. 2007; Rick 2009). This timing is coincident with the closure of estuaries throughout California.

Ideal Free Distribution Predictions

(a) In their discussion, Winterhalder et al. (2010) note that incorporating site-specific conditions affecting suitability as well as previously neglected environmental history in their model should improve the fit of IFD predictions to archaeological settlement data. Because of the unique and attractive resources provided by the Abalone Rocks estuary to early inhabitants of the Islands, their predicted settlement date for this location (3428–3068 cal BP; Winterhalder et al. 2010:476, Table 1) should significantly underestimate actual settlement. (b) The eventual loss of these resources associated with the closure of the estuary should have decreased ORC's settlement suitability, leading to partial or full abandonment as populations relocated to adjacent settlements with higher relative suitability. (c) Subsequently, as human population density throughout the northern Channel Islands continues to increase and the suitability of other locations declines, ORC should, after a hiatus, again become attractive to significant settlement. (d) The development of plank canoes (Arnold 1995, 2001a; Gamble 2002; Fagan 2004) and an increased emphasis on shell bead manufacture and trade (King 1990; Arnold and Munns 1994; Arnold and Graesch 2001; Munns and Arnold 2002) are resource-enhancing activities favored by the ORC environment with its long sandy beaches and access to prime *Olivella* habitat. Based on this, the IFD model predicts progressively intensified occupation from the Middle period through the MLT and Late period (starting after ~1500 cal BP). We note that these hypotheses reflect the combined effect of shifting density-dependent and density-independent sources of adaptive pressure on settlement.

Methods

Shifts in the relative habitat suitability of ORC have been observed using midden materials excavated by Doug Kennett and Don Morris from three well-dated sites near the mouth of the drain-

age: SRI-85 and the site complex including SRI-84 and -187 (henceforth, SRI-187). We include in this analysis data from two column samples (25 × 25 cm) excavated at SRI-85 and -187 from existing natural exposures in arbitrary 10 cm levels, from the surface to the base of the deposit. Exceptions to this protocol occurred in the lowest levels (below 50 cm) of Unit 2 of SRI-85 and Unit 1 of SRI-187, which followed natural strata. All excavated materials were water screened, dried, and then size sorted (½", ¼", and ⅛" mesh) and identified at California State University, Long Beach. Material from each successive screen size was sorted separately. More detailed sorting and checking was later conducted at the University of Oregon.

The data include chronological and dietary information. We submitted eight marine or estuarine shell samples for radiocarbon dating: one *Haliotis cracherodii* and one *Mytilus californianus* to Beta Analytic Inc. for standard radiometric dating, and one *Saxidomus nuttalli*, two *Olivella biplicata*, one *Mytilus californianus*, one *Septifer bifurcatus*, and one unidentified marine shell to the National Ocean Sciences Accelerator Mass Spectrometry Facility at the Woods Hole Oceanographic Institution for atomic mass spectrometry (AMS) dating. These were tested in 1999–2000 (Kennett 2005). Finally, we submitted three *Mytilus californianus* samples for AMS dating to the Keck Carbon Cycle AMS facility at the University of California, Irvine, in 2011 and 2012. We calibrated all dates in OxCal 4.1 (Bronk Ramsey 2009) using the most recent marine calibration curve, Marine09 (Reimer et al. 2009) and an updated ΔR value for the Santa Barbara Channel region (261 ± 21; B. Culleton, personal communication, 2012). The revised ΔR estimate incorporates five new AMS ^{14}C dates on pre-bomb (AD 1925) *Olivella* shells collected near Santa Barbara, California, with three existing dates on *Mytilus* reported by Ingram and Southon (1996; see also Kennett et al. 1997; Culleton et al. 2006), using the Marine09 calibration curve. We used a Bayesian statistical model in OxCal to further constrain error ranges on dates based on the relative stratigraphic position of the radiocarbon samples (see below).

Shellfish, other faunal constituents, and cultural materials were separated and quantified by trained undergraduate and graduate students.

For each level, all midden material collected in the ½" mesh was sorted in its entirety, as were a 100 g subsample of ¼" material and a 15 g subsample of ⅛" material. We also sorted the residual bulk material for artifacts, *Olivella biplicata* shells, and *Mytilus californianus* hinge fragments, as well as all bone, asphaltum, charcoal, and small gastropods. All other material was bagged separately. We sorted and weighed shells from ½", ¼", and ⅛" mesh separately, but added weights for each species together by level for analysis. Meat weights were calculated for the most important dietary constituents using the multipliers compiled and summarized by Rick (2004:79). Because *Olivella biplicata* was important for bead making rather than as a dietary component (e.g., Bennyhoff and Hughes 1987; King 1990; Arnold and Munns 1994), we analyzed this species by shell weight rather than meat weight.

In order to compare all data, including those levels that differed from the 10 cm arbitrary depth, we normalized shell and meat weight data to a volume of 1 m³. To assess long-term trends, we combined data into five time periods, the Early period prior to estuarine closure (before 5000 cal BP), the Early period after the estuary closed (5000–2550 cal BP), the Middle period (2550–800 cal BP), the Middle to Late period transition (MLT; 800–650 cal BP), and the Late period (650–168 cal BP) (King 1990; Arnold 1992a:66; Rick, Kennett, and Erlandson 2005).

Because of the long time span represented in Unit 2 of SRI-187, we dated all five levels of this unit. Two of the radiocarbon samples were from each of the other units. To obtain dates for each level, we calculated the weighted mean of the 2σ range for each available radiocarbon date and interpolated dates for the levels between them, assuming constant deposition rates (Braje et al. 2007). While this procedure is based on the tenuous assumption of constant deposition, we used it to assign ages to deposits that span a relatively short period of time (< 200 years).

Results
Chronology

Eleven radiocarbon dates from SRI-85 and -187 provide evidence that the mouth of Old Ranch Canyon was occupied from as early as 8,000 years ago through the middle and late Holocene (Table 5.1), consistent with previous observations by Rick (2009). The age of deposits in Unit 1 of SRI-85 are estimated to be between 440 and 590 cal BP (Late period). Deposits in Unit 2 of SRI-85 date to the Late period (0–10 cm, 600 cal BP; 10–20 cm, 630 cal BP) and the MLT (20–30 cm, 660 cal BP to 50–72 cm, 770 cal BP). Deposits in Unit 1 of SRI-187 date to the Middle period (1830 to 1880 cal BP) and predate the development of the *tomol*.

Unit 2 of SRI-187 spans a much longer time period, even though its deposits extended only 50 cm below the surface. The deepest deposits (40–50 cm) date to 8049–7835 cal BP (all radiocarbon dates are presented as 2σ cal BP), and the upper deposits (0–10 cm) date to 3305–3095 cal BP. In this case, we submitted samples from three intermediate levels to better determine when the Abalone Rocks estuary closed. The 20–30 cm (6472–6313 cal BP) and 30–40 cm (6517–6351 cal BP) levels predate closure of the estuary; the 10–20 cm (3325–3147 cal BP) level postdates it. This suggests an approximately 3,000 year gap in occupation at SRI-187.

Rick (2009) reports occupation dates for the eastern part of Santa Rosa Island for three sites that fit into this time period. SRI-191 and -192 also have a gap in occupation, however, with estuarine shell in earlier strata but not in later strata. SRI-191 has a gap between 6050–5730 and 4470–4150 cal BP, and SRI-192 has a gap between 5930–5690 and 2610–2280 cal BP. The only Old Ranch Canyon site that falls within this chronological gap is SRI-690, a shell midden that is deeply buried beneath culturally sterile sediments (~2.5 m below the surface) and has been dated to 4800–4520 cal BP. The buried midden deposit is ~50 cm thick and exposed for ~20 m in the creek bank (Rick 2009; unpublished site record). However, this site is closer to Southeast Anchorage and approximately 3 km from the mouth of Old Ranch Canyon. Therefore, these data are still consistent with the hypothesis that populations were reduced at the mouth of the canyon at this time.

Dietary Trends

Several estuarine shellfish species, including Venus clams (*Chione* sp.), Pacific littleneck clams (*Protothaca staminea*), Washington clams (*Saxidomas nuttalli*), and California oyster (*Ostrea lurida*) are present in the basal deposits of SRI-187.

TABLE 5.1. Chronology for CA-SRI-84/187 and CA-SRI-85

Site	Unit	Level	Sample	Uncalibrated Date	Uncalibrated Error	Calibrated Range (2σ)	Modeled Range (2σ)	Estimated Date (BP)	Cultural Period
SRI-85	1	0–10 cm	Beta-96870	1060	60	521–299	538–310	442	Late period
		10–20 cm						461	Late period
		20–30 cm						480	Late period
		30–40 cm						499	Late period
		40–50 cm						518	Late period
		50–60 cm						537	Late period
		60–70 cm						557	Late period
		70–80 cm	Beta-107044	1270	60	680–496	669–488	576	Late period
		80–84 cm						589	Late period
SRI-85	2	0–10 cm	OS-34576	1260	70	690–480	718–491	600	Late period
		10–20 cm						631	Late period
		20–30 cm						661	MLT
		30–40 cm						692	MLT
		40–50 cm						722	MLT
		50–72 cm	OS-34574	1500	30	885–694	875–680	771	MLT
SRI-187	1	0–10 cm						1831	Middle period
		10–20 cm	OS-32368	2500	30	1941–1730	1926–1737	1837	Middle period
		30–40 cm						1849	Middle period
		40–50 cm						1855	Middle period
		50–62 cm						1862	Middle period
		62–70 cm						1868	Middle period
		70–84 cm						1875	Middle period
		84–92 cm	OS-34474	2530	30	1983–1778	1976–1798	1881	Middle period
SRI-187	2	0–10 cm	OS-34475	3670	40	3392–3156	3305–3095	3204	Early period (no estuary)
		10–20 cm	UCIAMS-102545	3595	15	3305–3095	3325–3147	3238	Early period (no estuary)
		20–30 cm	UCIAMS-105613	6275	20	6518–6331	6472–6313	6399	Early period (estuary)
		30–40 cm	UCIAMS-105614	6260	20	6490–6313	6517–6351	6435	Early period (estuary)
		40–50 cm	OS-34564	7750	40	8054–7838	8049–7835	7945	Early period (estuary)

Notes: Radiocarbon dates are calibrated and stratigraphically modeled using OxCal 4.1.3 (Bronk Ramsey 2009) and the Marine09 calibration curve (Reimer et al. 2009).
Dates for undated levels are estimated by interpolating or extrapolating from weighted mean dates of dated levels.

Shellfish Meat Weight

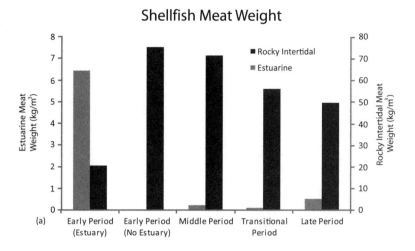

(a)

Fish, Sea Mammal, and Olivella

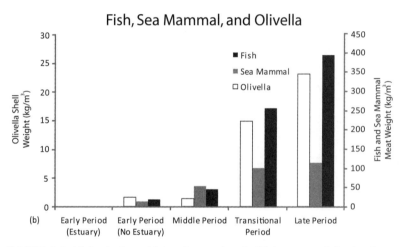

(b)

FIGURE 5.4. (a) Rocky intertidal and estuarine shellfish meat weight density, presented by cultural period. Note the different axes for the two shellfish types. (b) Fish and sea mammal meat weight density, and *Olivella* shell weight density, presented by cultural period. Again, note the two different axes.

Estuarine shellfish species are relatively unique for sites of any age on the northern Channel Islands (Rick, Kennett, and Erlandson 2005). To explore habitat changes through time, we divided shellfish into the most prevalent rocky intertidal (*Mytilus californianus*, *Haliotis rufescens*, and *Haliotis cracherodii*) and estuarine (*Protothaca staminea*, *Saxidomas nuttalli*, and *Ostrea lurida*) species (Tables 5.2 and 5.3). We do not believe that changes in abundance of different shellfish species reflect differential preservation; the estuarine shells, which were only in the basal levels of SRI-187, where they would have had more time to decompose, are more fragile than rocky in-

tertidal species. Grouped together by habitat, rocky intertidal species dominate the ORC sequence throughout, but this is less pronounced during the earliest part of the Early period (Figure 5.4a; Table 5.4). Rocky intertidal meat weight is approximately 270 percent higher after people reoccupy the site in the later part of the Early period (an increase from 20,461 g/m^3 to 75,616 g/m^3). In the absence of estuarine resources after the closure of Abalone Rocks estuary, later occupants apparently focused more heavily on rocky intertidal resources. This was followed by a decrease in rocky intertidal shellfish meat weight during the Middle period (71,739 g/m^3),

TABLE 5.2. Summary table of SRI-84/187 and SRI-85 midden constituents by shell/bone weight normalized to 1 m³

Site	Unit	Level	California Mussel wt (g/m³)	Black Abalone wt (g/m³)	Red Abalone wt (g/m³)	Abalone Total wt (g/m³)	California Oyster wt (g/m³)	Washington Clam wt (g/m³)	Pacific Littleneck Clam wt (g/m³)	Fish Bone wt (g/m³)	Sea Mammal Bone wt (g/m³)	Olivella biplicata wt (g/m³)
SRI-85	1	0–10 cm	55,630	1,361	1,496	4,352	0	0	160	6,606	2,446	31,646
		10–20 cm	167,518	0	0	506	0	0	3,242	6,699	5,075	56,843
		20–30 cm	133,149	1,778	859	4,052	0	0	2,856	27,389	11,606	23,806
		30–40 cm	150,724	1,973	1,486	3,459	0	0	1,225	11,968	6,875	43,755
		40–50 cm	385,323	272	256	528	0	0	0	14,667	16,666	31,870
		50–60 cm	284,872	795	1,182	2,330	0	0	0	35,979	6,514	21,816
		60–70 cm	102,793	0	0	432	0	0	224	16,331	2,006	14,344
		70–80 cm	189,320	0	1,128	1,128	0	0	269	20,944	1,363	6,955
		80–84 cm	8,653	0	4,760	4,760	0	0	0	2,032	716	624
	2	0–10 cm	106,465	0	191	191	0	0	0	7,520	587	2,406
		10–20 cm	78,506	0	0	948	0	0	756	3,360	3,205	3,715
		20–30 cm	139,295	0	1,827	1,915	0	0	128	2,565	3,149	6,968
		30–40 cm	252,633	0	3,120	3,546	0	0	438	11,451	11,832	30,877
		40–50 cm	215,405	970	9,912	14,407	0	0	0	15,805	1,179	15,435
		50–72 cm	46,935	0	3,214	6,376	0	0	0	7,079	581	6,500
SRI-187	1	0–10 cm	282,870	0	0	0	0	0	0	1,832	5,722	6,714
		10–20 cm	364,777	1,424	2,544	3,968	0	0	2,402	4,778	10,242	1,562
		30–40 cm	268,495	0	0	0	0	0	0	1,534	862	242
		40–50 cm	237,276	0	257	419	0	0	0	1,230	0	1,526
		50–62 cm	221,516	295	0	295	0	0	0	432	185	576
		62–70 cm	153,291	0	0	0	0	0	0	1,368	576	1,432
		70–84 cm	75,026	0	0	0	0	0	0	625	0	266
		84–92 cm	304,522	0	0	0	0	0	0	1,546	0	208
	2	0–10 cm	212,243	952	74	1,026	0	0	0	1,142	422	2,870
		10–20 cm	281,192	112	2,498	2,610	0	0	0	230	667	667
		20–30 cm	60,913	0	0	1,390	102	1,967	0	40	307	114
		30–40 cm	105,935	110	0	256	6,425	680	491	157	0	221
		40–50 cm	32,777	0	0	0	4,043	12,211	680	5	0	0

TABLE 5.3. Summary table of SRI-84/187 and SRI-85 midden constituents by raw shell/bone weight

Site	Unit	Level	California Mussel wt (g)	Black Abalone wt (g)	Red Abalone wt (g)	Abalone Total wt (g)	California Oyster wt (g)	Washington Clam wt (g)	Pacific Littleneck Clam wt (g)	Fish Bone wt (g)	Sea Mammal Bone wt (g)	Olivella biplicata wt (g)
SRI-85	1	0–10 cm	347.7	8.5	9.4	27.2	0.0	0.0	1.0	41.3	15.3	197.8
		10–20 cm	1,047.0	0.0	0.0	3.2	0.0	0.0	20.3	41.9	31.7	355.3
		20–30 cm	832.2	11.1	5.4	25.3	0.0	0.0	17.9	171.2	72.5	400.0
		30–40 cm	942.0	12.3	9.3	21.6	0.0	0.0	7.7	74.8	43.0	273.5
		40–50 cm	2,408.3	1.7	1.6	3.3	0.0	0.0	0.0	91.7	104.2	199.2
		50–60 cm	1,780.4	5.0	7.4	14.6	0.0	0.0	0.0	224.9	40.7	136.4
		60–70 cm	642.5	0.0	0.0	2.7	0.0	0.0	1.4	102.1	12.5	89.7
		70–80 cm	1,183.2	0.0	7.1	7.1	0.0	0.0	1.7	130.9	8.5	43.5
		80–84 cm	21.6	0.0	11.9	11.9	0.0	0.0	0.0	5.1	1.8	1.6
	2	0–10 cm	665.4	0.0	1.2	1.2	0.0	0.0	0.0	47.0	3.7	15.0
		10–20 cm	490.7	0.0	0.0	5.9	0.0	0.0	4.7	21.0	20.0	23.2
		20–30 cm	870.6	0.0	11.4	12.0	0.0	0.0	0.8	16.0	19.7	43.6
		30–40 cm	1,579.0	0.0	19.5	22.2	0.0	0.0	2.7	71.6	74.0	193.0
		40–50 cm	1,346.3	6.1	61.9	90.0	0.0	0.0	0.0	98.8	7.4	96.5
		50–72 cm	645.4	0.0	20.1	39.9	0.0	0.0	0.0	97.3	8.0	89.4
SRI-187	1	0–10 cm	1,767.9	0.0	0.0	0.0	0.0	0.0	0.0	11.5	35.8	42.0
		10–20 cm	2,279.9	8.9	15.9	24.8	0.0	0.0	15.0	29.9	64.0	9.8
		30–40 cm	1,678.1	0.0	0.0	0.0	0.0	0.0	0.0	9.6	5.4	1.5
		40–50 cm	1,483.0	0.0	1.6	2.6	0.0	0.0	0.0	7.7	0.0	9.5
		50–62 cm	1,661.4	2.2	0.0	2.2	0.0	0.0	0.0	3.2	1.4	4.3
		62–70 cm	766.5	0.0	0.0	0.0	0.0	0.0	0.0	6.8	2.9	7.2
		70–84 cm	656.5	0.0	0.0	0.0	0.0	0.0	0.0	5.5	0.0	2.3
		84–92 cm	1,522.6	0.0	0.0	0.0	0.0	0.0	0.0	7.7	0.0	1.0
	2	0–10 cm	1,326.5	6.0	0.5	6.4	0.0	0.0	0.0	7.1	2.6	17.9
		10–20 cm	1,757.5	0.7	15.6	16.3	0.0	0.0	0.0	1.4	4.2	4.2
		20–30 cm	380.7	0.0	0.0	8.7	0.6	12.3	0.0	0.3	1.9	0.7
		30–40 cm	662.1	0.7	0.0	1.6	40.2	4.3	3.1	1.0	0.0	1.4
		40–50 cm	204.9	0.0	0.0	0.0	25.3	76.3	4.3	0.0	0.0	0.0

TABLE 5.4. Meat/shell weight of each subdivision of the faunal record by time period and normalized to 1 m³

Time Period	Rocky Intertidal Meat Weight (g/m³)	Estuarine Meat Weight (g/m³)	Fish Meat Weight (g/m³)	Sea Mammal Meat Weight (g/m³)	Olivella Shell Weight (g/m³)
Late period	47,427	575	386,531	125,532	21,617
Transitional period	56,301	103	255,528	101,284	14,945
Middle period	71,739	217	46,209	53,200	1,566
Early period (no estuary)	75,616	0	19,013	13,184	1,769
Early period (estuary)	20,461	6,419	1,861	2,478	111

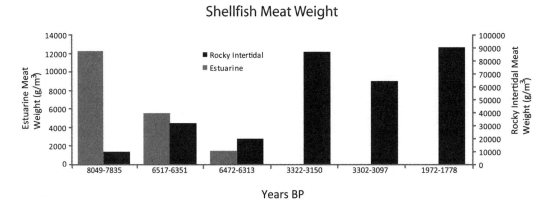

FIGURE 5.5. Shellfish meat weight density before and after the closure of Abalone Rocks Estuary.

the MLT (56,301 g/m³), and again during the Late period (47,427 g/m³), which may reflect greater focus on fish and sea mammals.

Estuarine species show a more pronounced pattern, dropping from 6,419 g/m³ in the earliest deposits to 0 g/m³ in the later part of the Early period. We suspect that small numbers of *P. staminea* later in time come from estuarine ponds at the mouth of Old Ranch Canyon or in adjacent pocket beaches that were targeted opportunistically. A stepwise decrease in estuarine meat weight is evident between 8049–7835 and 6472–6313 cal BP (Figure 5.5; Table 5.5). The abundance of rocky intertidal species does not show the reverse pattern, but fluctuates.

Variations in the meat weight of fish and sea mammal, and the shell weight of *Olivella biplicata* provide important information about environmental suitability and later occupation of ORC (Figure 5.4b; Table 5.4). All three show an increase through time. Fish meat weight increases from 1,861 g/m³ prior to closure of the es-

TABLE 5.5. Rocky intertidal and estuarine meat weight for each of the six oldest arbitrary excavation levels at SRI-187, normalized to 1 m³

Date (2σ cal BP)	Rocky Intertidal MW (g/m³)	Estuarine MW (g/m³)
1976–1798	90,748	0
3305–3095	64,431	0
3325–3147	86,802	0
6472–6313	19,754	1,498
6517–6351	31,863	5,499
8049–7835	9,767	12,260

tuary to 19,013 g/m³ after closure to 46,209 g/m³ during the Middle period. This was followed by a large jump during the MLT to 255,528 g/m³ and an additional increase during the Late period to 386,531 g/m³. *Olivella biplicata* shell weight follows a similar pattern. Like fish, *Olivella* jumps during the MLT to 14,945 g/m³ and then to 21,617 g/m³ during the Late period. Sea mammal meat weight increases more gradually, reaching 125,532 g/m³ during the Late period. These resource types generally became more prevalent over time as shellfish declined in importance.

Discussion

Midden data from SRI-85 and -187 have been correlated with environmental (estuary presence, then closure), technological (advent of *tomol*), and sociopolitical (*Olivella* shell bead) changes on the northern Channel Islands, all of which are density-independent factors. Such changes are consistent with IFD predictions, but require that we engage the model dynamically. The closing of the Abalone Rocks estuary can be represented, for instance, as a downward displacement of the suitability curve for this habitat location. Depending on the severity of the shift, this could have led to partial or full abandonment as people moved to other locations with relatively higher basic suitabilities. In fact, occupation of ORC appears to have decreased following the loss of the estuary, including the potential abandonment of SRI-187. The introduction of the *tomol* and the expansion of the shell bead industry should have raised density-dependent suitability because ORC offered enhanced access to marine resources and trade, and this also appears to be the case. Each of our four hypotheses appears to be supported by the available data from ORC.

Radiocarbon dates from SRI-85 and -187 suggest human occupation from the middle Holocene to the historic period, with a gap from approximately 6,300 to 3,300 years ago. This overall span is consistent with that suggested by Rick (2009), who estimated the occupational range of ORC and the surrounding area to between 8180 to 300 cal BP based on 51 radiocarbon dates from sites throughout the canyon. He and his collaborators (Rick 2009; Rick, Kennett, and Erlandson 2005; Rick et al. 2006; Wolff et al. 2007) have focused on seven sites from the Middle Holocene. SRI-191 and -192 have dates from before and after the closure of the estuary. Like SRI-187, these sites have estuarine shell in their earlier strata but not in their later strata. Both sites, however, have gaps in their radiocarbon records, although SRI-191 (between 6050–5730 and 4470–4150 cal BP) has a shorter one than SRI-187. The only published site potentially associated with ORC that falls within

the chronological gap for the canyon is SRI-690, which dates to 4800–4520 cal BP (Rick 2009) but is approximately 3 km from the mouth of the canyon and is relatively small. These dates support the hypothesis of either a short abandonment of ORC or at least an outmigration of a large part of the population as the estuary closed and became less productive.

Shellfish data from Unit 2 of SRI-187 also reflect estuarine closure. Like Rick, Kennett, and Erlandson (2005), we see clear evidence for estuarine shellfish in the midden assemblage prior to closure of the estuary (Inman 1983; Rick, Kennett, and Erlandson 2005) and for the subsequent shift away from the use of these estuarine species (Figure 5.4a). They are not found after the closure of the estuary, and, at the same time, there is a notable increase in the meat weight of rocky intertidal species. This is a significant shift but not a replacement because rocky intertidal species are always dominant in the shellfish assemblage. Even when the estuary was open, the total meat weight of estuarine shellfish species was only 31 percent of the total meat weight of rocky intertidal species.

The fact that estuarine species were consumed at all, given availability and abundance of rocky intertidal species, suggests that they were highly ranked. This is likely related to their abundance, meat yield, ease of collection, and possibly also to their resilience in the face of human predation (cf., Beaton 1991; Botkin 1980; Braje et al. 2007; Broughton 1997, 1999; Butler 2000; Cannon 2003; Hildebrandt and Jones 1992; Jones et al. 2008; Kelly 1995; Kennett 2005; Madsen 1993; Madsen and Schmitt 1998; Winterhalder 1986; Winterhalder and Smith 2000). Losing access to these species would have decreased the economic attractiveness of Old Ranch Canyon, represented by a downward shift in the suitability curve (Figure 5.3), leading to outmigration. When inhabitants again found it attractive to return to SRI-187 after a 3,000 year gap in occupation, they exploited rocky intertidal species more intensively than they did previously, with this increase more than making up for the loss of estuarine species in terms of meat weight.

The data from Unit 2 of SRI-187 show a significant decrease in estuarine shellfish dating from about 8000 to 6300 cal BP (Figure 5.5). This could be related to the stabilization of sea level and the associated closure of the estuary. There was another significant decrease in estuarine meat weight between the 30–40 cm and 20–30 cm levels of SRI-187, Unit 2, despite the fact that they are nearly contemporaneous, also suggesting that the estuary closure may have started by this time. In neither case, however, is there a clear obverse pattern in rocky intertidal meat weight that would suggest that it was exploited in higher quantities to make up for diminishing estuarine resources.

When people returned after the gap in the site's occupation, they did so to focus on rocky intertidal species. Similarly, fish and sea mammal started to become more prevalent (Figure 5.4b). The growing importance of these dietary components could have replaced meat consumption formerly satisfied by estuarine shellfish. Generally warm marine conditions and low marine productivity prevailed between 7500 to 3800 cal BP (Kennett et al. 2007), and the return to SRI-187 and an associated increase in rocky intertidal species near the end of this period may be related to an increase in marine productivity that ameliorated economic pressures on the site's inhabitants.

The development of the *tomol* after about 1500 BP would have also influenced the overall suitability of Old Ranch Canyon and other similar settlement locales. The appearance of this technology in the Santa Barbara Channel region is consistent with an increase in the consumption of fish at ORC. The quantity of fishbone for the MLT is more than 5.5 times what it was in the Middle period prior to the introduction of the *tomol*. The increase occurred largely because the *tomol* allowed more efficient exploitation of kelp forest fish species. Similarly, the meat weight of sea mammal nearly doubles from the Middle period to the MLT. These animals also were more easily hunted and transported to permanent settlements using *tomols*. Winterhalder et al. (2010:484) observe that sandy beach and kelp forests are more important predictors of settlement late in the precontact sequence, a result substantiated by our finding that fish were especially important during the MLT and Late period at ORC, along with a sandy beach to launch and land plank canoes, which could break apart on more rocky coastline.

Olivella biplicata also prefer sandy beach habitats. The increasing importance of bead manufacturing enhanced the suitability of areas like ORC with more extensive beach deposits. During the Late Middle, MLT, and Late periods there was a dramatic increase in *Olivella biplicata* shell bead production on the northern Channel Islands (Arnold 1987, 1990, 1992a, 1992b, 2001a; Arnold and Munns 1994; Munns and Arnold 2002:132–133; Kennett 2005; King 1990; Rick 2007). At ORC (SRI-85 and -187), *Olivella* bead manufacturing debris from the MLT is more than 9.5 times what it was during the preceding Middle period. Although not an important dietary species itself, *Olivella* was significant because of its use in trade that facilitated access to high-ranked resources from elsewhere. Beginning in the MLT, as many as 95-99 percent of the beads for the Santa Barbara Channel region were produced on the northern Channel Islands (Arnold 1987, 1992a:71, 2001a:18). This is consistent with the increasing importance of sandy beaches later in time.

The impact of the *tomol* and the expansion of the *Olivella* shell bead industry represent population-independent changes in the suitability of ORC. The relative suitability of areas with rich sandy beach habitat and offshore kelp forests increased with these technological and economic developments. Conversely, areas without these resources would have experienced a relative decline in suitability. These resources may also have been resilient to human exploitation, which would tend to broaden their IFD curve and sustainability at larger populations. The ORC faunal data show progressively larger amounts of fish, sea mammals, and *Olivella* from the Middle through the Late periods at the expense of rocky intertidal shellfish (Figure 5.4). Total marine meat weight increases through time, reflecting increasing human population.

Overall, the sequence of occupation at ORC was associated with at least three periods of change in population-independent suitability: the closure of the estuary (~5000–6000 cal BP), the significant reoccupation of the site with declining suitabilities elsewhere, the development of the plank canoe (~1500 cal BP), and the standardization and intensification of the *Olivella* shell bead industry (~1000 cal BP). The effects of these changes on suitability can be predicted qualitatively by changes in the IFD curves and, within the resolution of our faunal data, appear consistent with the settlement history of ORC.

Conclusion

Faunal data from Old Ranch Canyon provide an opportunity to apply the ideal free distribution model on a local scale and assess whether it facilitates a coherent explanation of the effects of environmental and cultural change on population and settlement. Radiocarbon dates from SRI-85, -187, and nearby sites (Rick 2009) indicate that the drainage was occupied from ~8,000 years ago until European contact, with at least one major gap in the record. This initial date is earlier than the prediction of the Winterhalder et al. (2010) model. This mismatch is consistent with IFD predictions, inasmuch as Winterhalder et al. (2010) purposely did not incorporate the unique and high-ranked estuarine resources of ORC into the original model.

Excavation data from SRI-85 and -187 provide evidence that major environmental, technological, and socioeconomic developments altered the conditions affecting the suitability of ORC and the settlement history, diet, and economy of its occupants. By and large, the resulting patterns are consistent with what we would predict using IFD reasoning. The rate of sea level rise slowed between 6000 and 5000 cal BP, causing closure of paleo-estuaries throughout Southern California. Abalone Rocks estuary in ORC was one of them. Prior to closure estuarine shellfish were a high-ranked resource that comprised a significant portion of the ORC diet. With estuary closure, these species were no longer available, causing a decrease in the suitability of the drainage. This decline apparently was large enough relative to the marginal suitabilities of other settlement locations on the northern Channel Islands to stimulate outmigration and perhaps site abandonment at SRI-187 and elsewhere in Old Ranch Canyon. This type of density-independent process is not visible in the regional IFD analysis of Winterhalder et al. (2010) but is fully accessible at the local level, where the specific environmental and socioeconomic changes affecting a particular site are identifiable.

During the time that ORC had a diminished population, surrounding settlement habitats presumably continued to experience population growth and gradual declines in suitability. These density-dependent declines in the suitability of alternative site locations made resettlement of SRI-187 attractive between about 3500 and 3000 cal BP. Subsequently, the development of the plank canoe enhanced cross-channel trade and increased the accessibility of kelp forest resources (fish and sea mammals), as well as the importance of sandy beaches for landing these watercraft. Island locations like ORC found their suitability enhanced independent of population as kelp forests, sea mammals, and trade became more accessible. This would be reflected in the IFD model by an upward shift in the suitability curves for locations with good canoe launch and pull-out areas. The standardization and intensification of the *Olivella* shell bead industry during the MLT augmented this effect. Consistent with these processes we find large increases in the relative quantity of faunal remains at ORC, reflecting an intensified economy and expanded population.

We believe the IFD to be an important analytical tool for understanding how human decisions, in a context of environmental and cultural change, influenced the character and pace of settlement on the northern Channel Islands. We expect the model to be similarly revealing elsewhere. We have highlighted features of its application not pursued in Winterhalder et al. (2010), especially the importance of density-independent factors in shaping IFD predictions. So far as we know, this is the first attempt to use site-specific archaeological data to assess IFD predictions. No less important, we hope to have aided understanding of human settlement on the California Channel Islands.

Acknowledgments

We would like to thank Jennifer Perry, Mark Raab, and an anonymous reviewer for comments on drafts of this chapter. Brendan Culleton provided important ideas about different approaches to the IFD model. We also appreciate the help of Don Morris during excavation.

Fieldwork for this project was supported by the National Science Foundation (SBR-9521974, Kennett) and a cooperative agreement with Channel Islands National Park (1443CA8120-96-003, Kennett).

References Cited

Allen, J., and J. F. O'Connell
2008 Getting from Sunda to Sahul. In *Islands of Inquiry: Colonisation, Seafaring and the Archaeology of Maritime Landscapes*, edited by G. A. Clark, F. Leach, and S. O'Connor, pp. 31–46. Australian National University, Canberra.

Arnold, J. E.
1987 *Craft Specialization in the Prehistoric Channel Islands, California*. University of California Press, Berkeley.
1990 Lithic Resource Control and Economic Change in the Santa Barbara Channel Region. *Journal of California and Great Basin Anthropology* 12(2):158–172.
1991 Transformation of a Regional Economy: Sociopolitical Evolution and the Production of Valuables in Southern California. *Antiquity* 65:953–962.
1992a Complex Hunter-Gatherer-Fishers of Prehistoric California: Chiefs, Specialists, and Maritime Adaptations. *American Antiquity* 57:60–84.
1992b Early-Stage Biface Production Industries in Coastal Southern California. In *Stone Tool Procurement, Production, and Distribution in California Prehistory*, edited by J. E. Arnold, pp. 67–130. *Perspectives in California Archaeology*, Vol. 2. Institute of Archaeology, University of California, Los Angeles.
1995 Transportation Innovation and Social Complexity among Maritime Hunter-Gatherer Societies. *American Anthropologist* 97(4): 733–747.
1997 Bigger Boats, Crowded Creekbanks: Environmental Stresses in Perspective. *American Antiquity* 62:337–339.
2001a The Chumash in World and Regional Perspectives. In *The Origins of a Pacific Coast Chiefdom: The Chumash of the Channel Islands*, edited by J. E. Arnold, pp. 1–20. University of Utah Press, Salt Lake City.
2001b Social Evolution and the Political Economy in the Northern Channel Islands. In *The Origins of a Pacific Coast Chiefdom: The Chumash of the Channel Islands*, edited by J. E. Arnold, pp. 287–296. University of Utah Press, Salt Lake City.

Arnold, J. E., R. H. Colten, and S. Pletka
1997 Contexts of Cultural Change in Insular California. *American Antiquity* 62(2):300–318.

Arnold, J. E., and A. P. Graesch
2001 The Evolution of Specialized Shellworking among the Island Chumash. In *The Origins of a Pacific Coast Chiefdom: The Chumash of the Channel Islands*, edited by J. E. Arnold, pp. 71–112. University of Utah Press, Salt Lake City.
2004 The Later Evolution of the Island Chumash. In *Foundations of Chumash Complexity*, edited by J. E. Arnold, pp. 1–16. Cotsen Institute of Archaeology, University of California, Los Angeles.

Arnold, J. E., and A. Munns
1994 Independent or Attached Specialization: The Organization of Shell Bead Production in California. *Journal of Field Archaeology* 21(4):473–489.

Arnold, J. E., and B. N. Tissot
1993 Measurement of Significant Paleotemperature Variation Using Black Abalone Shells from Prehistoric Middens. *Quaternary Research* 39:390–394.

Åström, M.
1994 Travel Cost and the Ideal Free Distribution. *Oikos* 69(3):516–519.

Barber, R. J.
1979 Human Ecology and the Estuarine Ecosystem: Prehistoric Exploitation in the Merrimack Valley. PhD dissertation. Harvard University, Cambridge, MA.

Beaton, J. M.
1991 Extensification and Intensification in Central California Prehistory. *Antiquity* 65(249):946–952.

Bennyhoff, J. A., and R. E. Hughes
1987 Shell Bead and Ornament Exchange Networks between California and the Western Great Basin. *Anthropological Papers of the American Museum of Natural History* 64(2): 79–175.

Bickel, P. M.
1978 Changing Sea Levels along the California Coast: Anthropological Implications. *The Journal of California Anthropology* 5:6–20.

Botkin, S.
1980 Effects of Human Exploitation on Shellfish Populations at Malibu Creek, California. In *Modeling Change in Prehistoric Subsistence Economics*, edited by T. Earle and A. Christenson, pp. 31–72. Academic Press, New York.

Braje, T. J.
2007 Archaeology, Human Impacts, and Historical Ecology on San Miguel Island, California. PhD dissertation. University of Oregon, Eugene.
2010 *Modern Oceans, Ancient Sites: Archaeology and Marine Conservation on San Miguel Island, California*. University of Utah Press, Salt Lake City.

Braje, T. J., D. J. Kennett, J. M. Erlandson, and B. J. Culleton
2007   Human Impacts on Nearshore Shellfish Taxa: A 7,000 Year Record from Santa Rosa Island, California. *American Antiquity* 72(4):735–756.

Braje, T. J., and T. C. Rick (editors)
2011   *Human Impacts on Seals, Sea Lions, and Sea Otters: Integrating Archaeology and Ecology in the Northeast Pacific.* University of California Press, Berkeley.

Bronk Ramsey, C.
2009   Bayesian Analysis of Radiocarbon Dates. *Radiocarbon* 51(1):337–360.

Broughton, J.
1997   Widening Diet Breadth, Declining Foraging Efficiency, and Prehistoric Harvest Pressure: Ichthyofaunal Evidence from the Emeryville Shellmound. *Antiquity* 71:845–862.
1999   *Resource Depression and Intensification during the Late Holocene, San Francisco Bay.* University of California Press, Berkeley.

Butler, V. L.
2000   Resource Depression on the Northwest Coast of North America. *Antiquity* 74:649–661.

Cannon, M. D.
2003   A Model of Central Place Forager Prey Choice and an Application to Faunal Remains from the Mimbres Valley, New Mexico. *Journal of Anthropological Archaeology* 22:1–25.

Cole, K. L., and G. Liu
1994   Holocene Paleoecology of an Estuary on Santa Rosa Island, California. *Quaternary Research* 41:326–335.

Colten, R. H.
2001   Ecological and Economic Analysis of Faunal Remains from Santa Cruz Island. In *The Origins of a Pacific Coast Chiefdom: The Chumash of the Channel Islands*, edited by J. E. Arnold, pp. 199–220. University of Utah Press, Salt Lake City.

Culleton, B. J.
2012   Human Ecology, Agricultural Intensification and Landscape Transformation at the Ancient Maya Polity of Uxbenká, Southern Belize. PhD dissertation. University of Oregon, Eugene.

Culleton, B. J., D. J. Kennett, B. L. Ingram, J. M. Erlandson, and J. R. Southon
2006   Intrashell Radiocarbon Variability in Marine Mollusks. *Radiocarbon* 48(3):387–400.

Erlandson, J. M.
1994   *Early Hunter-Gatherers of the California Coast.* Plenum, New York.

Erlandson, J. M., and T. L. Jones (editors)
2002   Catalysts to Complexity: Late Holocene Societies of the California Coast. Cotsen Institute of Archaeology, University of California, Los Angeles.

Erlandson, J. M., and T. C. Rick
2010   Archaeology Meets Marine Ecology: The Antiquity of Maritime Cultures and Human Impacts on Marine Fisheries and Ecosystems. *Annual Reviews of Marine Science* 2:165–185.

Erlandson, J. M., T. C. Rick, T. J. Braje, M. Casperson, B. Culleton, B. Fulfrost, T. Garcia, D. A. Guthrie, N. Jew, D. J. Kennett, M. L. Moss, L. Reeder, C. Skinner, J. Watts, and L. Willis
2011   Paleoindian Seafaring, Maritime Technologies, and Coastal Foraging on California's Channel Islands. *Science* 331:1181–1185.

Erlandson, J. M., T. C. Rick, T. J. Braje, A. Steinberg, and R. L. Vellanoweth
2008   Human Impacts on Ancient Shellfish: A 10,000 Year Record from San Miguel Island, California. *Journal of Archaeological Science* 35:2144–2152.

Erlandson, J. M., T. C. Rick, T. L. Jones, and J. F. Porcasi
2007   One If by Land, Two If by Sea: Who Were the First Californians? In *California Prehistory: Colonization, Culture and Complexity*, edited by T. L. Jones and K. A. Klar, pp. 53–62. Altamira, Landam, MD.

Fagan, B.
2004   The House on the Sea: An Essay on the Antiquity of Planked Canoes in Southern California. *American Antiquity* 69(1):7–16.

Fitzhugh, B., and T. L. Hunt
1997   Introduction: Islands as Laboratories: Archaeological Research in Comparative Perspective. *Human Ecology* 25(3):379–383.

Fitzhugh, B., and D. J. Kennett
2010   Seafaring Intensity and Island-Mainland Interaction along the Pacific Coast of North America. In *The Global Origins and Development of Seafaring*, edited by A. Anderson, J. Barrett, and K. Boyle, pp. 69–80. McDonald Institute for Archaeological Research, Cambridge, UK.

Fretwell, S. D.
1972   *Population in a Seasonal Environment.* Princeton University Press, Princeton, NJ.

Fretwell, S. D., and H. L. Lucas, Jr.
1969   On Territorial Behavior and Other Factors Influencing Habitat Distribution in Birds, Part 1: Theoretical Development. *Acta Biotheoretica* 19:16–36.

Gamble, L. H.
2002   Archaeological Evidence for the Origin of the

Plank Canoe in North America. *American Antiquity* 67(2):301–315.

Glassow, M. A.

1977   *An Archaeological Overview of the Northern Channel Islands, California, Including Santa Barbara Island.* National Park Service, Tucson.

1993   Changes in Subsistence on Marine Resources through 7,000 Years of Prehistory on Santa Cruz Island. In *Archaeology of the Northern Channel Islands of California: Studies of Subsistence, Economies, and Social Organization,* edited by M. A. Glassow, pp. 75–94. Archives of California Prehistory 34. Coyote Press, Salinas, CA.

Glassow, M. A., J. E. Perry, and P. F. Paige

2008   *The Punta Arena Site: Early and Middle Holocene Cultural Development on Santa Cruz Island.* Santa Barbara Museum of Natural History, Santa Barbara, CA.

Glassow, M. A., L. R. Wilcoxon, and J. Erlandson

1988   Cultural and Environmental Change During the Early Period of Santa Barbara Channel Prehistory. In *The Archaeology of Prehistoric Coastlines,* edited by G. Bailey and J. Parkington, pp. 64–77. Cambridge University Press, Cambridge.

Greene, C. M., and J. A. Stamps

2001   Habitat Selection at Low Population Densities. *Ecology* 82(8):2091–2100.

Hildebrandt, W. R., and T. L. Jones

1992   Evolution of Marine Mammal Hunting: A View from the California and Oregon Coasts. *Journal of Anthropological Archaeology* 11: 360–401.

Hunt, T. L.

2007   Rethinking Easter Island's Ecological Catastrophe. *Journal of Archaeological Science* 34:485–502.

Hunt, T. L., and C. P. Lipo

2009   Revisiting Rapa Nui (Easter Island) "Eocide." *Pacific Science* 63(4):601–616.

Ingram, B. L., and J. R. Southon

1996   Reservoir Ages in Eastern Pacific Coastal and Estuarine Waters. *Radiocarbon* 38(3):573–582.

Inman, D. L.

1983   Application of Coastal Dynamics to the Reconstruction of Paleocoastlines in the Vicinity of La Jolla, California. In *Quaternary Coastlines and Marine Archaeology: Towards the Prehistory of Land Bridges and Continental Shelves,* edited by P. M. Masters and N. C. Flemming, pp. 1–49, Academic Press, London.

Jazwa, C. S., D. J. Kennett, and D. Hanson

2012   Late Holocene Subsistence Change and Marine Productivity on Western Santa Rosa

Island, California. *California Archaeology* 4(1):69–97.

Jochim, M. A.

1976   *Hunter-Gatherer Subsistence and Settlement: A Predictive Model.* Academic Press, New York.

1981   *Strategies for Survival: Cultural Behavior in an Ecological Context.* Academic Press, New York.

Johnson, J. R.

1982   An Ethnographic Study of the Island Chumash. Master's thesis. Department of Anthropology, University of California, Santa Barbara.

1993   Cruzeño Chumash Social Geography. In *Archaeology on the Northern Channel Islands of California,* edited by M. A. Glassow, pp. 19–46. Coyote Press, Salinas, CA.

1999   The Chumash Social-Political Groups on the Channel Islands. In *Cultural Affiliation and Lineal Descent of Chumash Peoples in the Channel Islands and the Santa Monica Mountains,* Vol. 1, edited by S. McLendon and J. R. Johnson, pp. 51–66. Santa Barbara Museum of Natural History, Santa Barbara, CA.

Johnson, J. R., T. W. Stafford, Jr., H. O. Ajie, and D. P. Morris

2002   Arlington Springs Revisited. In *The Fifth California Islands Symposium,* edited by D. R. Brown, K. C. Mitchell, and H. W. Chaney pp. 541–545. Santa Barbara Museum of Natural History, Santa Barbara, CA.

Jones, T. L., J. F. Porcasi, J. W. Graeta, and B. F. Codding

2008   The Diablo Canyon Fauna: A Coarse-Grained Record of Trans-Holocene Foraging from the Central California Mainland Coast. *American Antiquity* 73(2):289–316.

Kelly, R. L.

1995   *The Foraging Spectrum: Diversity in Hunter-Gatherer Lifeways.* Smithsonian Institution Press, Washington, DC.

Kennett, D. J.

2005   *The Island Chumash: Behavioral Ecology of a Maritime Society.* University of California Press, Berkeley.

Kennett, D. J., A. J. Anderson, and B. Winterhalder

2006   The Ideal Free Distribution, Food Production, and the Colonization of Oceania. In *Human Behavioral Ecology and the Origins of Agriculture,* edited by D. J. Kennett and B. Winterhalder, pp. 265–288. University of California Press, Berkeley.

Kennett, D. J., and R. A. Clifford

2004   Flexible Strategies for Resource Defense on the Northern Channel Islands of California:

An Agent-Based Model. In *Voyages of Discovery: The Archaeology of Islands*, edited by S. M. Fitzpatrick, pp. 21–50. Praeger, Westport, CT.

Kennett, D. J., and C. A. Conlee
2002 Emergence of Late Holocene Sociopolitical Complexity on Santa Rosa and San Miguel Islands. In *Catalysts to Complexity: Late Holocene Societies of the California Coast*, edited by Jon M. Erlandson and Terry L. Jones, pp. 147–165. Cotsen Institute of Archaeology, University of California, Los Angeles.

Kennett, D. J., B. L. Ingram, and J. M. Erlandson
1997 Evidence for Temporal Fluctuations in Marine Radiocarbon Reservoir Ages in the Santa Barbara Channel, Southern California. *Journal of Archaeological Science* 24:1051–1059.

Kennett, D. J., and J. P. Kennett
2000 Competitive and Cooperative Responses to Climatic Instability in Coastal Southern California. *American Antiquity* 65(2):379–395.

Kennett, D. J., J. P. Kennett, J. M. Erlandson, and K. G. Cannariato
2007 Human Responses to Middle Holocene Climate Change on California's Channel Islands. *Quaternary Science Reviews* 26:351–367.

Kennett, D. J., J. P. Kennett, G. J West, J. M. Erlandson, J. R. Johnson, I. Hendy, A. West, B. J. Culleton, T. L. Jones, and T. W. Stafford, Jr.
2008 Wildfire and Abrupt Ecosystem Disruption on California's Northern Channel Islands at the Ållerød-Younger Dryas Boundary (13.0–12.9 ka). *Quaternary Science Reviews* 27: 2528–2543.

Kennett, D. J., B. Winterhalder, J. Bartruff, and J. M. Erlandson
2009 An Ecological Model for the Emergence of Institutionalized Social Hierarchies on California's Northern Channel Islands. In *Pattern and Process in Cultural Evolution*, edited by S. Shennan, pp. 297–314.

King, C. D.
1990 Evolution of Chumash Society: A Comparative Study of Artifacts Used in Social System Maintenance in the Santa Barbara Channel Region Before A.D. 1804. Garland, New York.

Madsen, D. B.
1993 Testing Diet Breadth Models: Examining Adaptive Change in the Late Prehistoric Great Basin. *Journal of Archaeological Science* 20:321–330.

Madsen, D. B., and D. N. Schmitt
1998 Mass Collecting and the Diet Breadth Model: A Great Basin Example. *Journal of Archaeological Science* 25:445–455.

Munns, A. M., and J. E. Arnold
2002 Late Holocene Santa Cruz Island: Patterns of Continuity and Change. In *Catalysts to Complexity: Late Holocene Societies of the California Coast*, edited by J. M. Erlandson and T. L. Jones, pp. 127–146. Cotsen Institute of Archaeology, University of California, Los Angeles.

Perry, J. E.
2003 Changes in Prehistoric Land and Resource Use among Complex Hunter-Gatherer-Fishers on Eastern Santa Cruz Island, California. PhD dissertation. Department of Anthropology, University of California, Santa Barbara.

Pletka, S.
2001 The Economics of Island Chumash Fishing Practices. In *The Origins of a Pacific Coast Chiefdom: The Chumash of the Channel Islands*, edited by J. E. Arnold, pp. 221–244. University of Utah Press, Salt Lake City.

Raab, L. M., J. Cassidy, A. Yatsko, and W. J. Howard
2009 *California Maritime Archaeology: A San Clemente Island Perspective*. Altamira, Lanham, MD.

Raab, L. M., and D. O. Larson
1997 Medieval Climatic Anomaly and Punctuated Cultural Evolution in Coastal Southern California. *American Antiquity* 62(2):319–336.

Raab, L. M., J. Porcasi, K. Bradford, and A. Yatsko
1995 Debating Cultural Evolution: Regional Implications of Fishing Intensification at Eel Point, San Clemente Island. *Pacific Coast Archaeological Society Quarterly* 31(3):3–27.

Reimer P. J., M. G. L. Baillie, E. Bard, A. Bayliss, J. W. Beck, P. G. Blackwell, C. Bronk Ramsey, C. E. Buck, G. S. Burr, R. L. Edwards, M. Friedrich, P. M. Grootes, T. P. Guilderson, I. Hajdas, T. J. Heaton, A. G. Hogg, K. A. Hughen, K. F. Kaiser, B. Kromer, F. G. McCormac, S. W. Manning, R. W. Reimer, D. A. Richards, J. R. Southon, S. Talamo, C. S. M. Turney, J. van der Plicht, and C. E. Weyhenmeyer
2009 IntCal09 and Marine09 Radiocarbon Age Calibration Curves, 0–50,000 years cal BP. *Radiocarbon* 51(4):1111–1150.

Rick, T. C.
2004 Daily Activities, Community Dynamics, and Historical Ecology on California's Northern Channel Islands. PhD dissertation. University of Oregon, Eugene.

2007 *The Archaeology and Historical Ecology of Late Holocene San Miguel Island, California*. Cotsen Institute of Archaeology, University of California, Los Angeles.

2009 8,000 Years of Human Settlement and Land

Use in Old Ranch Canyon, Santa Rosa Island, California. In *Proceedings of the Seventh California Islands Symposium*, edited by C. C. Damiani and D. K. Garcelon. Institute for Wildlife Studies, Arcata, CA.

Rick, T. C., and J. M. Erlandson

2008   Archaeology, Historical Ecology, and the Future of Ocean Ecosystems. In *Human Impacts on Ancient Marine Ecosystems: A Global Perspective*, edited by T. C. Rick and J. M. Erlandson, pp. 297–307. University of California Press, Berkeley.

Rick, T. C., J. M. Erlandson, T. J. Braje, J. A. Estes, M. H. Graham, and R. L. Vellanoweth

2008   Historical Ecology and Human Impacts on Coastal Ecosystems of the Santa Barbara Channel Region, California. In *Human Impacts on Ancient Marine Ecosystems: A Global Perspective*, edited by T. C. Rick and J. M. Erlandson, pp. 77–102. University of California Press, Berkeley.

Rick, T. C., J. M. Erlandson, R. L. Vellanoweth, and T. J. Braje

2005   From Pleistocene Mariners to Complex Hunter-Gatherers: The Archaeology of the California Channel Islands. *Journal of World Prehistory* 19:169–228.

Rick, T. C., D. J. Kennett, and J. M. Erlandson

2005   Preliminary Report on the Archaeology and Paleoecology of the Abalone Rocks estuary, Santa Rosa Island, California. In *Proceedings of the Sixth California Islands Symposium*, edited by D. Garcelon and C. Schwemm, pp. 55–63. National Park Service Technical Publication CHIS-05-01. Institute for Wildlife Studies, Arcata, CA.

Rick, T. C., J. A. Robbins, and K. M. Ferguson

2006   Stable Isotopes from Marine Shells, Ancient Human Subsistence, and Environmental Change on Middle Holocene Santa Rosa Island, California, USA. *Journal of Island and Coastal Archaeology* 1:233–254.

Sutherland, W. J.

1983   Aggregation and the "Ideal Free" Distribution. *Journal of Animal Ecology* 52(3):821–828.

1996   *From Individual Behaviour to Population Ecology*. Oxford University Press, Oxford.

Tregenza, T.

1995   Building on the Ideal Free Distribution. *Advances in Ecological Research* 26:253–307.

Wilcoxon, L. R.

1993   Subsistence and Site Structure: An Approach for Deriving Cultural Information from Coastal Shell Middens. In *Archaeology on the Northern Channel Islands of California*, pp. 137–150. Coyote Press, Salinas, CA.

Winterhalder, B.

1986   Diet Choice, Risk, and Food Sharing in a Stochastic Environment. *Journal of Anthropological Archaeology* 5(4):369–392.

2002   Models. In *Darwin and Archaeology: A Handbook of Key Concepts*, edited by J. P. Hart and J. E. Terrell, pp. 201–223. Bergin and Garvey, Westport, CT.

Winterhalder, B., D. J. Kennett, M. N. Grote, and J. Bartruff

2010   Ideal Free Settlement on California's Northern Channel Islands. *Journal of Anthropological Archaeology* 29:469–490.

Winterhalder, B., and E. A. Smith

2000   Analyzing Adaptive Strategies: Human Behavioral Ecology at Twenty-Five. *Evolutionary Anthropology* 9:51–72.

Wolff, C. B., T. C. Rick, and A. Aland

2007   Middle Holocene Subsistence and Land Use on Southeast Anchorage, Santa Rosa Island, California. *Journal of California and Great Basin Anthropology* 27:44–56.

6

Geographic Information Systems as a Tool for Analyzing Intrasite Spatial Variability on San Nicolas Island

Richard B. Guttenberg, René L. Vellanoweth, William E. Kendig, Rebekka G. Knierim, and Steven J. Schwartz

The use of geographic information systems (GIS) in archaeological research has greatly increased in recent years (Conolly and Lake 2006; Kvamme 1999; Lock and Stancic 1995; Wheatley and Gillings 2002). It is now widely used and has become an integral part of the archaeological tool kit (Katsianis et al. 2008; Knabb 2008; Lawson 2007; Lieff 2003; McCoy and Ladefoged 2009; Sharon et al. 2004); however, much of the archaeological use of GIS focuses on regional analysis of landscapes and settlement patterns (Afifi 2000; Kennett 2005; Kvamme 1999; 1995; McCoy and Ladefoged 2009; Pletka 2005; Teeter et al., Chapter 9). Less common is the application of GIS on an intrasite scale. In this chapter, we examine use of GIS as an effective tool to conduct an intrasite spatial analysis on San Nicolas Island.

In the following discussion we present preliminary results of a long-term research project that focuses on the spatial modeling of human activities that took place at the late Holocene village site of CA-SNI-25 on San Nicolas Island. We used GIS and cluster analysis to further examine the associations of artifacts, ecofacts, and features at the site. Using experimental and analytical methods, our results confirm the association of sandstone saws and circular shell fishhooks (Kendig et al. 2010). We also examined the pattern of distribution of red ochre within one locus of the site that shows evidence of ceremonial activity. Since ochre is often associated with ritualized behavior, we focused on its distribution around ceremonial features at CA-SNI-25. This approach has allowed us to shed light on the possible linkages of artifacts, as well as patterns of spatial and temporal variability in technology, subsistence, and behavior at the site.

Background

San Nicolas is the most remote of California's eight Channel Islands (Figure 6.1). It lies approximately 120 km (75 mi) southwest of Los Angeles and is approximately 98 km (60 mi) from the nearest point on the mainland (Martz 2008). Although it is one of the four southern Channel Islands, it is centrally located between the northern and southern island groups. San Nicolas is relatively small, measuring only 14.5 km long and 5 km wide, and has a maximum elevation of 277 m. The island is characterized by five topographic zones: the large, relatively flat central plateau; the northern, relatively steep southern cliffs; the northern and southern coastal terraces; and the dune fields of the west end (Martz 2002).

Geologically, the island is composed primarily of alternating beds of Eocene sandstones, siltstones, and interbedded marine sediments consisting of a conglomerate of metavolcanic and metasedimentary cobbles within a matrix of sandstone and mudstone (Vedder and Norris 1963:13).

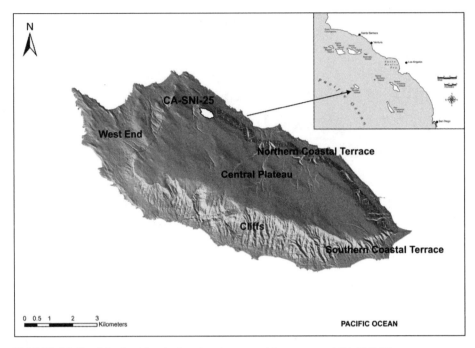

FIGURE 6.1. San Nicolas Island, showing topographic zones and CA-SNI-25.

Periodic exposures of these conglomerate beds and sandstone shingle beaches serve as primary sources of tool stone.

San Nicolas Island sandstone is often highly indurated, dense, and extremely hard (Thomas-Barnett 2004), making it useful as a raw material for both ground stone and expedient flake stone tools (Kendig et al. 2010). Constant cortical weathering of sandstone shingles within the island's surf zone produces an abundance of naturally polished sandstone cobbles thought to be used in the production of the sandstone saws discussed below (Kendig et al. 2010; Rogers 1930).

The island's size, isolation, lack of diverse habitats, and relatively arid landscape support a limited variety of flora, primarily coastal sage scrub, chaparral, and grasses, with few edible endemics (Junak 2008). Terrestrial native fauna are likewise limited to the island fox, deer mouse, island night lizard, land snails, and a variety of insects. None are particularly useful as sources of raw material or sustenance.

In contrast to its sparse terrestrial resources, San Nicolas is surrounded by highly productive and diverse marine habitats. The island's surroundings are home to the most extensive kelp forests per capita among the California Channel Islands and support a wide variety of shellfish,

fish, marine mammals, and seabirds (Mariani 2001; Pondella et al. 2005; Schoenherr et al. 1999: 345–346).

Culture History

Although the Channel Islands' oldest archaeological sites are believed to have been inundated by rising sea levels after the last glacial maximum (Inman 1983; Nardin et al. 1981; Curray 1965), 553 sites have been identified throughout the island (Martz 2002, 2005). A radiocarbon date (8400 cal BP) from a single *Mytilus* sp. shell from CA-SNI-339 represents the oldest known human habitation on San Nicolas Island. Other radiocarbon dates from sites representing villages, camps, seafood processing locations, and flake stone reduction areas indicate an increase in human habitation from the early to late Holocene (Martz 2005:65). At the time of contact, the Nicoleño spoke a language from the Takic family within the Uto-Aztecan linguistic group, associating them with Gabrielino (Tongva) groups on the southern islands (Munro 1999).

Tule Creek Village (CA-SNI-25)

The Tule Creek site (CA-SNI-25) is a large late Holocene village situated on the north end of the central plateau (Figure 6.1). The site over-

FIGURE 6.2. Open excavation of CA-SNI-25, showing East Locus hearths and pits.

looks Corral Harbor, a calm inlet that would have served as a favorable canoe launch (Bowers 1890: 57). The site is adjacent to Tule Creek and approximately 2 km southeast of Thousand Springs, both of which are excellent sources of freshwater. Malcolm Rogers (1930) conducted the earliest formal investigations of CA-SNI-25, characterizing it as a large village site with house pits, a communal structure, at least one cemetery, flaked stone tools, and a dense midden with numerous features that are well preserved (Rogers 1930). Because of these features, the Tule Creek site serves as an excellent example for exploring intrasite organization and use of space in both daily and ceremonial contexts.

More recent field investigations at CA-SNI-25 began in 2001 and were completed in 2009. Our fieldwork was focused primarily on two loci: East Locus and Mound B. We identified and tested several other loci and have incorporated these data into our analysis as well; however, we chose East Locus and Mound B because they were sampled using contiguous block excavations, which are conducive to identifying behavioral patterns (features) in the archaeological record.

We found numerous features at East Locus that are likely associated with ritualized behavior and ceremonial events. The space appeared to be organized and included several dog burials, multiple hearths, discrete pits, balancing stone caches, ochre, and other features and artifacts (Cannon 2006) (Figure 6.2). At Mound B, however, we encountered more domestic activities that were deposited during at least three major periods of habitation. We used more than 70 radiocarbon dates on well-preserved single pieces of shell, bone, and charcoal to establish a chronology for the site, suggesting it was inhabited between about 5000 cal BP and 500 cal BP. Although the site was occupied intermittently for about 5,000 years, the major village occupation occurred between about 800 and 500 cal BP (Kendig et. al 2010) (Table 6.1).

Spatial Studies and GIS in Archaeology

Over the last 50 years, archaeologists have incorporated different methods of spatial analysis into archaeological research designed to understand the distribution of sites, features, and artifacts (Hodder and Orton 1976; Dacey 1973; Bartlett 1974; Whallon 1973, 1974). Spatial statistics (e.g., nearest neighbor analyses) developed by researchers in other fields have been adopted and applied to a variety of archaeological settings

TABLE 6.1. Selected radiocarbon dates for features and loci at CA-SNI-25

Sample #	Unit and Context	Stratum/ Level	Depth (cm)	Material	Uncorrected ^{14}C Age (BP)	Calibrated Age Range (cal BP), 1 Sigma[a]	Calibrated Age Range (BP), 2 Sigma[a]
East Locus[b]							
OS-54411	Unit 8, Feature 6 (hearth)	IV/2	70	Charcoal	175 ± 30	220–170	225–73
OS-54562	Unit 7, Feature 9 (hearth)	V/1	60–70	Charcoal	395 ± 70	510–430	530–306
OS-54355	Unit 7H, fishing tackle kit feature	II/1	18	H. cracherodii	1090 ± 35	520–450	596–397
OS-54397	Unit 7L, Feature A (pit)	IIB/1	63	M. californianus	5700 ± 35	5910–4780	5966–5721
OS-55336	Unit 8E2, left-handed fishhook	II/4	—	Norrisia norrisi	1180 ± 35	512–598	637–486
OS-55465	Unit 8A, saddle bead	I/1	—	Olivella biplicata	1180 ± 35	512–598	637–486
OS-66789	Pit 7Q	II/8	125	H. cracherodii	900 ± 30	274–379	439–245
OS-66910	Dog burial	—	—	Canis familiaris	680 ± 25	570–670	677–563
Mound B[b]							
OS-54354	Unit 11, top of mound	II/3	46	H. cracherodii	880 ± 30	360–260	428–128
OS-54413	Unit 52, shell and lithic feature	I/3	63	H. cracherodii	225 ± 35	520–460	564–400
OS-54360	Unit 58, pit feature	IIB/1	93	H. cracherodii	4750 ± 35	4810–4670	4835–4569
OS-54358	Unit 57, hearth feature	I/3	94	H. cracherodii	4800 ± 30	4840–4770	4900–4623
OS-54357	Unit 55, pit feature	II/3–IIB/1	85	H. rufescens	4890 ± 35	4940–4830	5030–4796
Mound A[c]							
Beta-116352	Index unit	-	90–100	Charcoal	130 ± 40	147–62	152–54
Beta-116920	Index unit	-	20–30	Charcoal	550 ± 50	631–522	651–509
Beta-116351	Index unit	-	50–60	Charcoal	650 ± 90	672–553	733–513

[a] All dates were calibrated using Calib 6.02 (Reimer et al. 2009) and applying a ΔR of 225 ± 35 for all shell samples (see Kennett et al. 1997).

[b] Dates provided by Dr. René Vellanoweth, Department of Anthropology, California State University, Los Angeles.

[c] Dates provided by Dr. Patricia Martz, Department of Anthropology, California State University, Los Angeles.

(Clark and Evans 1954; Cox 1981; Getis 1964; Getis and Franklin 1987; Getis and Ord 1992; Hodder and Orton 1976; Ord 1975; Pinder et al. 1979). Researchers began using these methods to better interpret spatial patterning in the distribution of sites, features, and artifacts (Bartlett 1974; Dacey 1963, 1973; Hodder and Orton 1976; Whallon 1973, 1974).

It is important to note that we do not imply that the spatial statistics performed by GIS are a new development. In fact, the operations offered by GIS are well established and are not intended as a replacement for nonspatial statistics performed by other software programs (Sharon et al. 2004). Rather, we demonstrate that GIS can be used in tandem with nonspatial statistics and other forms of analysis as a method for testing and confirming hypotheses about relational and spatial associations. The intent of our research is to utilize GIS to enhance nonspatial statistical methods on data that are the subject of ongoing research at CA-SNI-25. We further contend that these methods may be effectively used in archaeological research throughout the Channel Islands and in other contexts where large, open-area excavations have yielded an abundance of data.

GIS in Archaeology on San Nicolas Island

Other studies using GIS and spatial analysis have been conducted on San Nicolas Island (Afifi 2000; Casaus 1998; Martz 2002; Merrill 2004). These studies focused on island-wide landscape analysis, comparing site and resource distributions. In the 1990s, Martz (2002) conducted the initial GIS work, which involved pedestrian surveys of the island and site mapping using a global positioning system (GPS). This work led to the creation of GIS data for the island's archaeological sites and features. Data from that initial survey was incorporated into our current research. Additional work used the compiled GIS data to describe settlement patterns on the island (Afifi 2000). More recent spatial studies have been conducted at CA-SNI-25 using mathematical models as well as statistical analysis (Merrill 2004; Cannon 2006).

Methods

For our work at CA-SNI-25, we constructed a map series of the site showing distributions and statistical clustering of excavated data using Arc-

GIS spatial autocorrelation and hot spot analysis (Getis and Ord 1992; Hodder and Orton 1976; Mitchell 2009). We first composed a base map using analog survey data collected in 2004 combined with GPS coordinates of datum points and unit locations recorded in the field in 2010. Locational data were collected using a Trimble GeoX with a Zephyr antenna, providing an accuracy of ±11 cm after differential correction. We tied in datum points from the 2004 survey (Merrill 2004) with additional coordinates of unit corners and feature locations to increase the accuracy of our field data.

We transposed the 2004 survey data by calculating the offset coordinates and combining them with recent georeferenced data, which converted our original analog data into a digital format. This process provided a base map showing the datum points and the outline of the unit grids in each locus (Figure 6.3). We then digitized unit grids using the Delta XY editing function and created individual polygons of exact size. The result was a direct representation of locus grids with accurate unit dimensions. These data were summarized and generalized to the unit grids of each respective locus. Data summarized into units (mostly 1 × 1 m) were treated in the same manner as population data in census tracts. Distance was measured from the unit centroid and must be analyzed in the context of scale, which in this case was on the locus level (Mitchell 2009).

With the locational data reconciled and fully digitized, we performed a data visualization analysis and conducted statistical operations using the ArcGIS 9.3 spatial statistics toolbox. Data visualization consisted of displaying the summarized data in distribution maps of features across each locus. Data were symbolized and displayed stratigraphically. Statistical operations included Moran's *I* spatial autocorrelation and Getis-Ord Gi* hot spot analysis (Getis and Ord 1992; Hodder and Orton 1976; Mitchell 2009).

Spatial autocorrelation is an operation that shows statistical clustering at defined distance intervals. Hodder and Orton (1976) discussed early applications of spatial autocorrelation and described the method in terms of scale and measure of distance between features (see also Whallon 1973, 1974). In ArcGIS, the Moran's *I* spatial autocorrelation tool is designed to run at different parameters to determine the distance interval

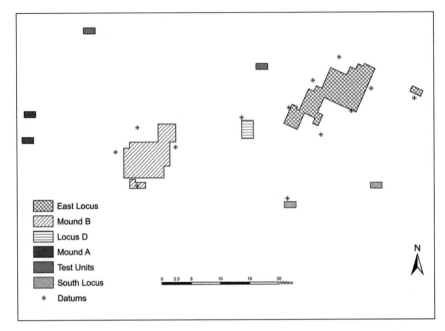

FIGURE 6.3. CA-SNI-25 site map.

(Mitchell 2009). Our replicative studies informally show debris fields from various tool manufacturing activities at approximately a 2 m radius (Kendig et al. 2010). Thus, we expected our distance interval to be around 2 m. The results from the spatial autocorrelation met our expectations, and our distance intervals were set between 2.5 and 3 m.

Hot spot analysis is based on the Getis-Ord-Gi* statistic (Getis and Ord 1992; Mitchell 2009). This method shows the patterns and locations of high and low values of statistical clustering based on the distance interval defined by the spatial autocorrelation tool. The values of clustering are actually z-scores produced as a result of the operation (Mitchell 2009). Statistically positive z-scores show visual clustering of features on the map, and small or negative z-scores show areas with little or no clustering (Figure 6.4).

Both statistical operations are based on Euclidean distance and nearest neighbor statistics that imply spatial context between features (Clark and Evans 1954; Dacey 1963, 1973; Getis 1964; Getis and Franklin 1987; Getis and Ord 1992; Mitchell 2009). Other authors have described the problems and limitations of nearest neighbor statistics in archaeological research (Merrill 2004; Merrill and Read 2010). We maintain, however, that these techniques are useful in archaeology,

especially when combined with other methods such as replicative experiments and nonspatial statistics that suggest relationships between variables.

Results

Our sample from CA-SNI-25 is ideal for intrasite GIS analysis. Large, open-area excavations allow for spatial dissection of the site across a temporal plane. Good preservation, excellent stratigraphic integrity, and numerous radiocarbon dates provide a solid foundation for spatial studies. By examining the distribution of artifacts as well as pigments, we highlight the utility of intrasite GIS as a tool to understand a variety of past cultural phenomena.

For instance, we examined the distribution of sandstone saws relative to shell fishhooks and hook making debris to confirm spatially what we derived experimentally about the use of sandstone saws as abraders for manufacturing shell fishhooks (Table 6.2) (Kendig et al. 2010). Documenting the spatial distribution of saws and hooks, and then analyzing their clustering across the site, allowed us to make inferences about the organization of shell fishhook production, one of the most important technological innovations of the late Holocene. To examine the role of pigments within a ceremonial context, we followed

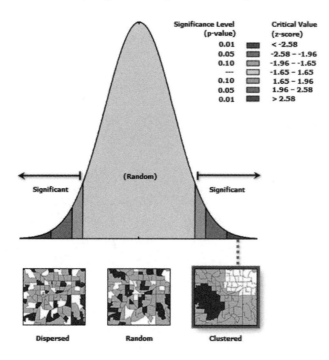

FIGURE 6.4. Example of output from spatial autocorrelation tool in ArcGIS showing areas of statistical significance.

TABLE 6.2. Stratigraphic distribution of fishhooks, ochre, and saws at East Locus

Stratum	Fishhooks (*n*)	Ochre Count	Weight (g)	Sandstone Saws (*n*)
Stratum I	190	129	169.43	25
Stratum II	56	814	510.47	47
Stratum III	0	0	0	0
Undifferentiated/Features	26	89	226.49	9
Totals	272	1,032	906.39	83

the distribution of red ochre (hematite) relative to ceremonial features such as pits, hearths, dog burials, and balancing stones. Understanding the distribution of ochre at East Locus has allowed us to address questions about how pigments were used in the past and how they were incorporated into ritualized activities, topics of global significance considering the great antiquity of pigment use by humans. In the discussion section we explore the application of these methods to data sets collected years ago and housed in museums, universities, and government agencies worldwide, but first we present the results of our study at CA-SNI-25.

Saws and Hooks

Once all spatial data were digitized and standardized, we performed a spatial autocorrelation and hot spot rendering of the distributions of sandstone saws and fishhooks across CA-SNI-25. In the stratigraphic visualization analysis of our data, we observed the greatest distribution of saws and hooks in Stratum II, which is consistent with the density of materials found throughout the site, particularly at East Locus (Table 6.2) (Cannon 2006). Saws were made of extremely hard sandstone cortical flakes with proximal edges thinned and straightened through the removal of striking platforms. Many of the saws were utilized

FIGURE 6.5. (a) Sandstone saw morphology and (b) fishhook production sequence.

on all margins and both faces, suggesting their use as cutting implements and abraders (Figure 6.5a). Red abalone (*Haliotis rufescens*) shell, once common in the deeper waters around San Nicolas, were the predominant material used for fishhook manufacture. Hooks were also crafted from black abalone (*Haliotis cracherodii*), mussel (*Mytilus californianus*), and Norris' top-shell (*Norrisia norrissi*) (Strudwick 1986) (Figure 6.5b).

The autocorrelation function indicated positive statistical clustering of both saws and hooks. The fishhooks showed clustering at a distance interval of 2.5 m, and the saws were clustered at 3.0 m. The distance intervals provided by the spatial autocorrelation were the parameters used to conduct the hot spot analysis. The hot spot map of saws shows clustering in roughly the same area of East Locus as the clustering of fishhook materials. The areas around the hearth and pit features show hot spots with positive z-scores greater than 2.0. Although both saws and hooks occur at Mound B and other loci, the pattern of distribution of these two artifact types is stronger at East Locus (Figure 6.6).

Ochre

Red ochre is found in the island's sedimentary deposits and occurs throughout the site, but for this study we focused on the distribution of ochre around areas at East Locus with evidence of ceremonial activity (Cannon 2006). The visual analysis of red ochre revealed that it occurs in

Stratum I at East Locus and Locus D, but the greatest distribution of ochre is clearly seen in Stratum II of East Locus (Figure 6.7). Here we see ochre distributed around the pit features at the north end of East Locus, as well as along the east side of the largest hearth.

We analyzed the occurrence of ochre at East Locus based on both the spatial distribution of the weight and number of individual pieces. The spatial autocorrelation operations performed for ochre suggested statistical clustering by count at a distance interval of 2.5 m, but its distribution by weight was randomly dispersed. The difference between clustering patterns by weight and total count are likely indicative of a problematic characteristic of the ochre sample. The numerous ochre fragments contribute to a greater distribution than the comparative measure of ochre by weight (Hodder and Orton 1976:41). The sample may either demonstrate a positively skewed pattern of clustering or be indicative of the widespread use of ochre across East Locus. The hot spots of red ochre at East Locus show clustering in areas around features believed to be associated with ceremonialism, such as the hearths, pits, and dog burials (Figure 6.7) (Bartelle et al. 2010; Cannon 2006; Vellanoweth et al. 2008).

Discussion

Our approach to using intrasite GIS provides a visual and interactive platform conducive to spatial studies in archaeology. By digitizing spatial

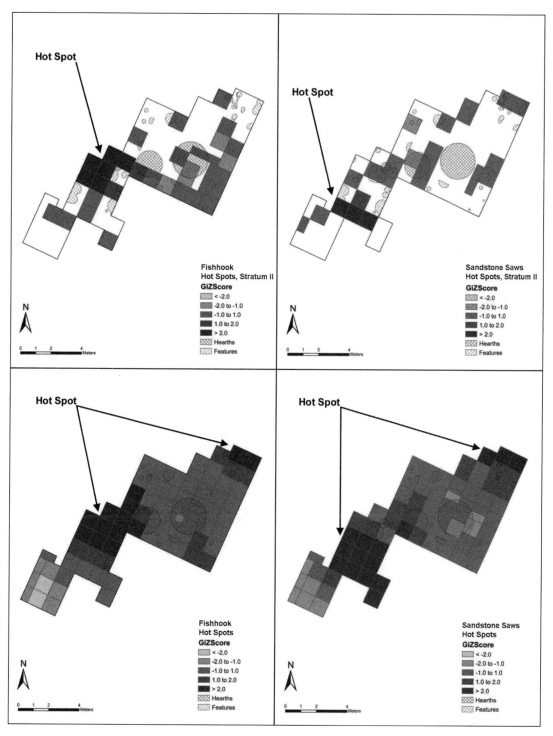

FIGURE 6.6. Hot spots of hooks and saws at East Locus in Stratum II (*top*). Hooks are clustered with a distance interval of 2.5 m, saws with a distance interval of 3 m; (*bottom*) hot spots of total distribution of hooks and saws at East Locus, all strata. Both hooks and saws are clustered at a distance interval of 2.5 m.

FIGURE 6.7. Distribution of ochre by weight (g) and total count at East Locus in Stratum II (*top*); hot spots of ochre by count in Stratum II at a distance interval of 2.5 m (*bottom*).

data from field notes and sketches, transit surveys and maps, and other analog forms, combining these with new georeferenced points, reconciling scales, and analyzing the distribution of archaeological finds, we created a powerful tool for examining the archaeological record. The correlations between saws and hooks, as well as ochre relative to ceremonial features, were made clear by GIS analysis. Although connecting spatially associated artifacts (saws/hooks) to functionality requires a variety of descriptive and analytical approaches, the results of our intrasite GIS analysis suggest that it is effective at finding and displaying in-ground relationships. Documenting and analyzing in situ spatial associations of objects and features form the basis for making behavioral inferences about how people organized and divided up their space to perform individual, social, and communal activities.

Our spatial analysis of CA-SNI-25 confirms previous studies on the association between saws and hooks, as well as assumptions about the role of ochre among Native Americans. Kendig et al. (2010), for example, suspected an association between saws and hooks based on field observations and literature searches, and then tested it with a series of replicative experiments, use-wear analyses, nonspatial statistics, and other analytical studies. The intrasite exploratory analysis described above strengthens the hypothesis that these two artifact types share not only a spatial association, but a functional one as well. Furthermore, the examination of red ochre across East Locus showed some interesting characteristics and raised questions about differences in the distribution of small fragments compared to weight. Our results suggest that although the use of ochre at East Locus was widespread, there was significant clustering of pigment in association with hearths and pit features.

Our focus on the potential use of sandstone saws in circular and J-shaped shell fishhook manufacture has additional implications for Channel Islands research. The introduction of the circular shell fishhook on San Nicolas and other Channel Islands was a significant factor in the rise of social and economic complexity observed in archaeological and ethnographic records (Arnold 2001; Kennett 2005; Strudwick 1986). The innovation

of the shell fishhook expanded the productivity of offshore fisheries used by Native Americans occupying the Channel Islands as well as the coastal mainland. The development of this technology was related to reliance on fishing as an effective subsistence strategy and contributed to other cultural developments observed in the archaeological record on San Nicolas and the other islands.

Evidence of pelagic fish remains and ceremonial feasting at CA-SNI-25 suggests an increased production from fishing harvests and a potential for food surplus (Bartelle et al. 2010). Martz (2005) argues that this development parallels a rise in population levels and densities on San Nicolas Island. Furthermore, this technology is believed to have set the stage for the development of craft specialization, the accumulation of personal wealth, and elite-based social stratification. These developments go hand in hand with the emergence of the plank canoe (*ti'at*) as a vehicle of food procurement, trade, and travel between the islands and the mainland, perhaps the most significant factors influencing the rise of social complexity documented throughout coastal and insular Southern California.

Inter-Island Implications

There are many implications for further research using GIS elsewhere on the Channel Islands. The application of GIS exploratory analysis allows for the visual display of spatial patterns that may not be immediately apparent in large data sets. Moreover, intrasite GIS provides a definitive direction for additional research on previously analyzed data. It may also prove useful to combine this type of intrasite approach with regional landscape analyses to examine source locations of materials and networks of trade and exchange. For instance, the spatial patterning of exotic trade materials (e.g., obsidian) on an intrasite scale may shed light on the nature and flow of trade goods between the islands and the mainland (Arnold 2001; Cannon 2006; Rick et al. 2001; Vellanoweth 2001).

Channel Islands sites excavated prior to the development of GIS could benefit from the application of the methods used in our study. If sites excavated many years ago have not been analyzed, or only partially analyzed, then intrasite

GIS can be used to predict and guide fruitful avenues of research. Sites such as Lemon Tank (CA-SCLI-1524) and Eel Point (CA-SCLI-43) on San Clemente Island and the El Montón site (CA-SCRI-333) on Santa Cruz Island are good candidates for intrasite spatial analysis using GIS and updated georeferenced data.

The Lemon Tank site, for example, has excellent potential for exploratory analysis in comparison to the Tule Creek site. Both sites have similar chronologies and have produced an abundance of data indicative of ceremonial activity. Hale (1995) has documented numerous features at the Lemon Tank site found within a ceremonial complex similar to those at East Locus, including dog burials, caches of ochre and seeds, artifacts made of exotic stone such as chert and steatite, hearths, and fishing kits (see Perry, Chapter 8). Many of these features exist within a ceremonial enclosure, which Hale has posited as being similar to those described in the *toloache* ceremony, or boy's puberty rite. Such ceremonial complexes are characteristic of Chingichngish, a religion practiced by Southern California peoples (see Boscana 1933; DuBois 1908; McCawley 1996; Raab et al. 2009). A similar sacred enclosure, or *yovaar*, is described at the Isthmus Cove site (CA-SCAI-39) on Santa Catalina Island in the ethnohistoric account of Sebastian Vizcaino's 1602 expedition (McCawley 1996). We have considered these possibilities as well at East Locus. The abundance of comparable features and artifacts at Lemon Tank and East Locus, coupled with a spatial analysis of both sites, would undoubtedly shed new light on possible religious ties between the island peoples, as well as connections with their mainland neighbors.

Perry (2007) described archaeological evidence of ritual activity on the northern Channel Islands from a landscape perspective. Sacred locales and shrines were viewed as part of a geographic and cultural landscape, ideal for using GIS at a regional scale. Perry (Chapter 8) also described intrasite ritual correlates on San Clemente Island similar to what we observed at CA-SNI-25. Our intrasite spatial analysis at CA-SNI-25 provided insight into archaeological signatures of ritual activity that can be applied elsewhere on both the northern and southern islands.

Teeter, Martinez, and Richardson (Chapter 9) have also applied GIS to indigenous trail systems across Santa Catalina Island. Using ethnographic data and a digital elevation model to produce a least-cost path, the authors suggested that trails functioned as more than just conduits of goods and information; trails also maintained social bonds, alliances, and geographic connections to sacred locales. This research on Catalina Island and Perry's work on Santa Cruz Island are both excellent examples of regional landscape approaches that can be used in tandem with our intrasite GIS work on San Nicolas Island. Understanding patterns of personal and social space on the Channel Islands requires both intrasite and landscape approaches, which are not mutually exclusive but complementary.

Conclusions

Perhaps one of the least understood aspects of the archaeology of the Channel Islands is the organization and use of space by native peoples in both domestic and ritualized contexts. The types of data necessary for such research demand large contiguous samples, excellent stratigraphic and chronological control, and the application of spatial analysis. It is also necessary to develop frames of reference (Binford 2001) for interpreting the spatial association of objects and features, and linking them to the dynamic behavioral and cultural processes that formed them (Binford 1980). Data sets derived from experimental, replicative/use-wear analyses, and ethnohistoric approaches, as well as computer modeling, provide excellent frames of reference and will prove useful in future studies on the Channel Islands. Despite the abundance of well-preserved sites on the Channel Islands, few have been excavated and analyzed using these approaches.

By combining the types of spatial analysis presented in this chapter with existing site-specific and regional data (see Perry 2007 and Chapter 8), it will be possible to model the use of space by native peoples through time on the Channel Islands. Perry's (2007 and Chapter 8) survey and synthesis of ceremonial sites on Santa Cruz Island provides an excellent backdrop against which site-specific spatial data can be compared. Modeling site-specific, island-wide, and regional data regarding the use of space for ceremonial and everyday purposes has the potential to illuminate differential land use patterns between the northern and southern Channel Islands.

We are hopeful that the new directions of intrasite spatial analysis will help to dispel some of the previous critiques of the use of GIS in archaeology. Often described as overgeneralizing and deterministic, GIS analysis has fallen under attack by critics implying that digital methods of analysis dehumanize human behavior (Conolly and Lake 2006; Kvamme 1999; Lock and Stancic 1995; McCoy and Ladefoged 2009; Wheatley 2004). Although these authors make some valid points, we argue that new technology is seeking to revive and enhance the spatial archaeology of the 1960s and 1970s (Holdaway and Wandsnider 2006; Jones and Munson 2005; McCoy and Ladefoged 2009; Wheatley and Gillings 2002:236). Our approach of integrating intrasite GIS with multiple methods of analysis retains the humanistic component of archaeological research necessary to properly interpret past human behavior (Challis and Howard 2006; Kvamme 2006; Kvamme et al. 2006; Rigaud and Simek 1991).

If shown to be successful, predictive models may be integrated into policies for managing cultural resources on the Channel Islands. This is particularly relevant to other sites on the islands where large, open-area excavations have yielded an abundance of data. At some point, we expect that georeferenced data will be generated for all Channel Island sites investigated in detail, allowing for intra-island and inter-island comparisons. Salient topics of interest—such as the development of innovative technologies, trade networks, craft specialization, the rise of social complexity, population demographics, and a host of other questions relevant to both the northern and southern islands, as well as to hunter-gatherer societies elsewhere in the world—can be integrated. By incorporating northern and southern island data sets, we can better understand the complexity and dynamics of the interactions that took place on the California Channel Islands.

Acknowledgments

We thank the U.S. Navy for its continued support for and access to the archaeological resources on San Nicolas Island. Excavation and lab work was funded by NAVAIR Weapons Division, Range Sustainability Office, Point Mugu, California, as well as Humboldt State University (HSU) and California State University, Los Angeles (CSULA). We thank Lisa Thomas-Barnett (NAVAIR) and Catherine Girod at the Naval Base of Ventura County for their assistance and logistical support. Special thanks to Dr. Patricia Martz for her many years of research on San Nicolas. Ray Corbett (Santa Barbara Museum of Natural History) and Jennie Allen (CSULA) assisted with editing early versions of this chapter. Kevin Smith (CSULA) offered insight and recommendations for our analysis, and William Hayden provided technical advice and support. We also thank Mark Raab and an anonymous reviewer for their comments. Finally, thanks to Chris Jazwa and Jennifer Perry for all of their hard work in assembling this volume.

References Cited

Afifi, A.
2000   Prehistoric Settlement Pattern on San Nicolas Island, California: A GIS Application. MA thesis. Department of Anthropology, California State University, Los Angeles.

Arnold, J. E. (editor)
2001   *The Origins of a Pacific Coast Chiefdom: The Chumash of the Channel Islands.* University of Utah Press, Salt Lake City.

Bartelle, B. G., R. L. Vellanoweth, E. S. Netherton, N. W. Poister, W. E. Kendig, A. F. Ainis, R. J. Glenn, J. V. Marty, L. Thomas-Barnett, and S. J. Schwartz
2010   Trauma and Pathology of an Articulated Dog from San Nicolas Island, California, U. S. A. *Journal of Archaeological Science* 37(12):2721–2734.

Bartlett, M. S.
1974   The Statistical Analysis of Spatial Pattern. *Advances in Applied Probability* 6(2):336–358.

Binford, L. R.
1980   Willow Smoke and Dogs' Tails: Hunter-Gatherer Settlement Systems and Archaeological Site Formation. *American Antiquity* 45(1):4–20.

2001   *Constructing Frames of Reference: An Analytical Method for Archaeological Theory Building Using Hunter-Gatherer Data Sets.* University of California Press, Berkeley.

Boscana, G.

1933   *Chinigchinich: A Revised and Annotated Version of Alfred Robinson's Translations of Father Gerónimo Boscana's Historical Account of the Belief of Usages, Customs and Extravagancies of this Mission of San Juan Capistrano Called the Acagchemem Tribe.* Fine Arts Press, Santa Ana, CA.

Bowers, S.

1890   San Nicolas Island. In *California State Mining Bureau Ninth Annual Report of the State Mineralogist for the Year Ending December 1, 1889.* Sacramento, CA.

Cannon, A. C.

2006   Giving Voice to Juana María's People: The Organization of Shell and Exotic Stone Artifact Production and Trade at a Late Holocene Village Site on San Nicolas Island, California. MA thesis. Department of Anthropology, Humboldt State University.

Casaus, K. R.

1998   Use of GIS for Natural and Cultural Resource Management: A Computerized Rule-Based Activity Planning System on San Nicolas Island, Point Mugu Naval Air Weapons Station. MA thesis. School of Renewable Natural Resources, University of Arizona, Tucson.

Challis, K., and A. J. Howard

2006   A Review of Trends Within Archaeological Remote Sensing in Alluvial Environments. *Archaeological Prospection* 13:231–240.

Clark, P. J., and F. C. Evans

1954   Distance to Nearest Neighbor as a Measure of Spatial Relationships in Populations. *Ecology* 35(4):445–453.

Conolly, J., and M. Lake

2006   *Geographical Information Systems in Archaeology.* Cambridge University Press, Cambridge.

Cox, T. F.

1981   Reflexive Nearest Neighbors. *Biometrics* 37(2):367–369.

Curray, J. R.

1965   Late Quaternary History: Continental Shelves of the United States. In *The Quaternary of the United States,* edited by H. E. Wright and D. G. Frey, pp. 723–735. Princeton University Press, Princeton, NJ.

Dacey, M. F.

1963   Order Neighbor Statistics for a Class of Random Patterns in Multidimensional Space. *Annals of the Association of American Geographers* 53(4):505–515.

1973   Statistical Tests of Spatial Association in the Locations of Tool Types. *American Antiquity* 38(3):320–328.

DuBois, C. G.

1908   The Religion of the Luiseño Indians of Southern California. *University of California Publications in American Archaeology and Ethnology* 8(3):69–186.

Getis, A.

1964   Temporal Land-Use Pattern Analysis with the Use of Nearest Neighbor and Quadrat Methods. *Annals of the Association of American Geographers* 54(3):391–399.

Getis, A., and J. Franklin

1987   Second-Order Neighborhood Analysis of Mapped Point Patterns. *Ecology* 68(3):473–477.

Getis, A., and J. K. Ord

1992   The Analysis of Spatial Association by Use of Distance Statistics. *Geographical Analysis* 24(3):189–206.

Hale, A.

1995   The World in a Basket: Late Period Gabrieliño Ceremonial Features from the Lemon Tank Site, San Clemente Island, CA. MA thesis. California State University, Northridge.

Hodder, I., and C. Orton

1976   *Spatial Analysis in Archaeology.* Cambridge University Press, Cambridge.

Holdaway, S. J., and L. Wandsnider

2006   Temporal Scales and Archaeological Landscapes from the Eastern Desert of Australia and Intermontane North Africa. In *Confronting Scale in Archaeology: Issues of Theory and Practice,* edited by G. Lock and B. Molyneaux, pp. 183–202. Springer, New York.

Inman, D. L.

1983   Application of Coastal Dynamics to the Reconstruction of Paleocoastlines in the Vicinity of La Jolla, California. In *Quaternary Coastlines and Marine Archaeology: Toward the Prehistory of Land Bridges and Continental Shelves,* edited by P. M. Masters and N. C. Flemming, pp. 1–49. Academic Press, London.

Jones, G., and G. Munson

2005   Geophysical Survey as an Approach to the Ephemeral Campsite Problem: Case Studies from the Northern Plains. *Plains Anthropologist* 50(193):31–43.

Junak, S.

2008   *A Flora of San Nicolas Island, California.* Santa Barbara Botanic Garden, Santa Barbara, CA.

Katsianis, M., S. Tsipidis, K. Kotsakis, and A. Kousou-
lakou
2008   A 3D Digital Workflow for Using Intra-Site
        Research in GIS. *Journal of Archaeological
        Science* 35:655–667.
Kendig, W. E., K. N. Smith, R. L. Vellanoweth,
J. A. Allen, C. M. Smith, and A. M. Points
2010   The Use of Replicative Studies to Understand
        the Function of Expedient Tools: The Sand-
        stone Saws of San Nicolas Island, California.
        *Journal of California and Great Basin Archae-
        ology* 30(2):193–210.
Kennett, D. J.
2005   *The Island Chumash: Behavioral Ecology of
        a Maritime Society.* University of California
        Press, Berkeley.
Knabb, K. A.
2008   Understanding the Role of Production
        and Craft Specialization in Ancient Socio-
        Economic Systems: Toward the Integration
        of Spatial Analysis, 3D Modeling and Virtual
        Reality in Archaeology. MA thesis. Depart-
        ment of Anthropology, University of Califor-
        nia, San Diego.
Kvamme, K. L.
1995   A View From Across the Water: The North
        American Experience in Archaeological GIS.
        In *Archaeology and Geographical Informa-
        tion Systems*, edited by Gary Lock and Zoran
        Stancic, pp. 1–14. Taylor and Francis, London.
1999   Recent Directions and Developments in
        Geographic Information Systems. *Journal of
        Archaeological Research* 7(2):153–201.
2006   There and Back Again: Revisiting Archaeo-
        logical Site Locational Modeling. In *GIS and
        Archaeological Site Location Modeling*, edited
        by Mark w. Meher and Konnie L. Wescott,
        pp. 3–38. Taylor and Francis, Boca Raton, FL.
Kvamme, K. L., J. K. Johnson, and B. S. Haley
2006   Multiple Methods Survey: Case Studies. In
        *Remote Sensing in Archaeology: An Explicitly
        North American Perspective*, edited by J. K.
        Johnson, pp. 251–267. University of Alabama
        Press, Tuscaloosa.
Lawson, K. S.
2007   Defining Activity Areas in the Early Neolithic
        Site at Foeni-Salas(Southwest Romania): A
        Spatial Analytic Approach with Geographi-
        cal Information Systems in Archaeology. MA
        thesis. Department of Anthropology, Univer-
        sity of Manitoba, Winnipeg, Canada.
Lieff, S.
2003   Applications of Geographic Information Sci-
        ence in the Archaeological Research of the

Fincastle Kill Site (DIOx 5) Alberta, Canada,
        and Tel Beth-Shemesh, Israel. MA thesis. De-
        partment of Geography, University of Leth-
        bridge, Alberta, Canada.
Lock, G., and Z. Stancic
1995   *Archaeology and Geographical Information
        Systems.* Taylor and Francis, London.
Mariani, R. R.
2001   Middle and Late Holocene Fishing Strategies
        on San Nicolas Island, California. MA thesis.
        Department of Anthropology, California
        State University, Los Angeles.
Martz, P. C.
2002   *San Nicolas Island Prehistoric Archaeological
        Sites Mapping and Recordation Project.* Pre-
        pared for Naval Air Weapons Station, China
        Lake, CA. On file, South Central Coastal Ar-
        chaeological Information Center, California
        State University, Fullerton.
2005   Prehistoric Context and Subsistence on San
        Nicolas Island. *Proceedings of the Sixth Cali-
        fornia Islands Symposium*, edited by D. K.
        Garcelon and C. A. Schwemm, pp. 65–82.
        Institute for Wildlife Studies, Arcata, CA.
2008   *4000 Years on Ghalas-At, Part One of the San
        Nicolas Island Index Unit Program.* Prepared
        for Naval Air Weapons Station, China Lake,
        CA. Through a Cooperative Agreement with
        California State University, Los Angeles,
        N68711-00-LT-0041.
McCawley, W.
1996   *The First Angelinos: The Gabrielino Indians
        of Los Angeles.* Malki Museum Press, Ban-
        ning, CA.
McCoy, M. D., and T. Ladefoged
2009   New Developments in the Use of Spatial
        Technology in Archaeology. *Journal of Ar-
        chaeological Research* 17:263–295.
Merrill, M. L.
2004   Intrasite Spatial Analysis and Interpretation
        of Mapped Surface Artifacts at CA-SNI-25,
        San Nicolas Island, California. MA thesis.
        Department of Anthropology, California
        State University Los Angeles.
Merrill, M. L., and D. Read
2010   A New Method Using Graph and Lattice
        Theory to Discover Spatially Cohesive Sets
        of Artifacts and Areas of Organized Activity
        in Archaeological Sites. *American Antiquity*
        75(3):419–451.
Mitchell, A.
2009   *The ESRI Guide to GIS Analysis*, Vol. 2: *Spa-
        tial Measurements and Statistics.* ESRI Press,
        Redlands, CA.

Munro, P.
1999   Takic Foundations of Nicoleño Vocabulary.
        In *Proceedings of the Fifth California Islands
        Symposium*. U.S. Minerals Management Ser-
        vice, Camarillo, CA. Published version of
        1994 manuscript.
Nardin, T. R., R. H. Osborne, D. J. Bottjer, and R. C.
Scheidermann
1981   Holocene Sea-Level Curves for Santa Mon-
        ica Shelf, California Continental Borderland.
        Science 213:331–333.
Ord, K.
1975   Estimation Methods for Models of Spatial
        Interaction. *Journal of the American Statisti-
        cal Association* 70(349):120–126.
Perry, J. E.
2007   Chumash Ritual and Sacred Geography on
        Santa Cruz Island, California. *Journal of Cal-
        ifornia and Great Basin Anthropology* 27(2):
        103–124.
Pinder, D., I. Shimada, and D. Gregory
1979   The Nearest-Neighbor Statistic: Archaeo-
        logical Application and New Developments.
        American Antiquity 44(3)430–445.
Pletka, N.
2005   Late Holocene Gabrielino Settlement Pat-
        terns in the Newport Coast Area of Cali-
        fornia: A Geographic Information Systems
        Based Approach. MA thesis. Department of
        Anthropology, California State University,
        Long Beach.
Pondella, D. J., B. E. Ginter, J. R. Cobb, and L. G. Allen
2005   Biogeography of the Nearshore Rocky-Reef
        Fishes at the Southern and Baja California
        Islands. *Journal of Biogeography* 32:187–201.
Raab, L. M., J. Cassidy, A. Yatsko, and W. J. Howard
2009   *California Maritime Archaeology: A San
        Clemente Island Perspective*. Altamira, Lan-
        ham, MD.
Rick, T. C., C. E. Skinner, J. M. Erlandson, and R. L.
Vellanoweth
2001   Obsidian Source Characterization and
        Human Exchange Systems on California's
        Channel Islands. *Pacific Coast Archaeological
        Society Quarterly* 37(3):27–44.
Rigaud, J., and J. F. Simek
1991   Interpreting Spatial Patterns at the Grotte
        XV: A Multiple Method Approach. In *The
        Interpretation of Archaeological Spatial Pat-
        terning*, edited by E. M. Kroll and T. D. Price,
        pp. 199–220. Plenum, New York.
Rogers, M. J.
1930   Field Notes: 1930 Expedition to San Nicolas

Island. Transcribed and edited by S. J.
Schwartz, 1994. On file, Naval Air Weapons
Station, Point Mugu, CA.
Schoenherr, A. A., C. R. Feldmeth, and M. J. Emerson
1999   *Natural History of the Islands of California*.
        University of California Press, Los Angeles.
Sharon, I., Y. Dagan, and G. Tzionit
2004   The [Awful?] Truth about GIS and Archae-
        ology. In *British School at Athens Studies*,
        Vol. 11: *Archaeological Field Survey in Cyprus:
        Past History, Future Potentials*, pp. 151–162.
        British School at Athens, Greece.
Strudwick, I. H.
1986   Temporal and Areal Considerations Re-
        garding the Prehistoric Circular Fishhook of
        Coastal California. MA thesis. Department
        of Anthropology, California State University,
        Long Beach.
Thomas-Barnett, L.
2004   A Sandstone Bowl Quarry Site on San Nico-
        las Island, California. MA thesis. Department
        of Anthropology, California State University,
        Los Angeles.
Vedder, J. G., and R. M. Norris
1963   *Geology of San Nicolas Island, California*.
        Professional Paper 369. U.S. Geological Sur-
        vey, Menlo Park, CA.
Vellanoweth, R. L.
2001   AMS Radiocarbon Dating and Shell Bead
        Chronologies: Middle Holocene Trade and
        Interaction in Western North America. *Jour-
        nal of Archaeological Science* 28:941–950.
Vellanoweth, R. L., B. G. Bartelle, A. F. Ainis, A. C.
Cannon, S. J. Schwartz
2008   A Double Dog Burial from San Nicolas Is-
        land, California, USA: Osteology, Context
        and Significance. *Journal of Archaeological
        Science* 35(12):3111–3123.
Whallon, R., Jr.
1973   Spatial Analysis of Occupation Floors, I: Ap-
        plication of Dimensional Analysis of Vari-
        ance. *American Antiquity* 38(3):266–278.
1974   Spatial Analysis of Occupation Floors, II:
        The Application of Nearest Neighbor
        Analysis. *American Antiquity* 39(1):16–34.
Wheatley, D.
2004   Making Space for an Archaeology of Place.
        Internet Archaeology 15. http://intarch. ac. uk
        /journal/issue15/wheatley_index. html.
Wheatley, D., and M. Gillings
2002   *Spatial Technology and Archaeology: The Ar-
        chaeological Applications of GIS*. Taylor and
        Francis, London.

7

Paleoethnobotanical Investigations on the Channel Islands

Current Directions and Theoretical Considerations

Kristina M. Gill

This chapter addresses subsistence and the relative importance of plants among the prehistoric maritime hunter-gatherer-fishers living on California's Channel Islands. While it is clear that island populations had a decidedly maritime focus, ethnographic and archaeological data indicate that plants were used in a variety of ways. Paleoethnobotanical research, in particular, has a crucial role to play in subsistence and settlement analysis, yet has not typically been given priority in Channel Islands research. The purpose of this chapter is to summarize the extant paleoethnobotanical research conducted on the islands and present some theoretical considerations for contextualizing the role of plants. Given the ethnographic and archaeological evidence, I argue that plants were of considerable importance in subsistence, trade, and ceremonial contexts and therefore should be given careful consideration in Channel Islands research.

Environmental Background

The terrestrial environments of each island vary considerably depending on topography, precipitation, and relative isolation (see Jazwa and Perry, Chapter 1). Generally, the northern islands receive significantly more rain than the southern islands, where more desertlike conditions exist, particularly on San Nicolas, the farthest from the mainland coast (Figure 7.1) (Moody 2000).

Although modern island vegetation communities are recovering, they have been severely affected by historic and modern ranching, overgrazing, and subsequent erosion, which limit our ability to accurately define the prehistoric distribution of vegetation communities (Junak et al. 1995). Also notable is the ethnohistorically documented landscape management by the Chumash through burning, which resulted in more productive resource patches and likely increased the extent of grasslands seen in modern times (Anderson 2005; Junak et al. 1995; Timbrook 1993, 2007; Timbrook et al. 1982). Despite the limitations of interpreting prehistoric vegetation communities based on modern observations, some general trends can be noted. Twelve plant community types described by Philbrick and Haller (1977) occur on the Channel Islands. The most dominant of these include southern coastal dune, coastal bluff, coastal sage scrub, island chaparral, valley/foothill grassland, southern coastal oak woodland, and island woodland. The extent to which each community is represented on the islands varies; the largest islands—Santa Cruz, Santa Rosa, and Santa Catalina—support most of the twelve communities, whereas the smallest islands, Anacapa and Santa Barbara, support only coastal communities (i.e., coastal dune, bluff, and sage scrub) and valley/foothill grasslands (Moody 2000; Philbrick and Haller 1977). While the diversity of plant resources available to prehistoric populations is directly correlated with the diversity of plant communities represented, a description of each plant community type is beyond the scope of this chapter. It is important to note, however, that the valley/foothill grassland community type occurs on all of the Channel Islands. Food plants available in this community

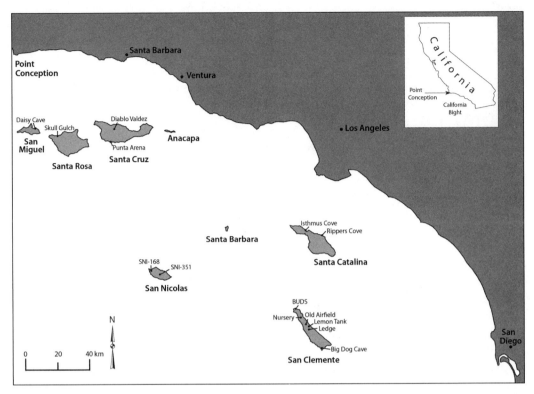

FIGURE 7.1. California's Channel Islands, with sites discussed in the text highlighted.

include a variety of small seeds, including grasses and red maids (*Calandrinia* sp.), and edible corms and bulbs, including blue dicks (*Dichelostemma* sp., on all eight islands) and mariposa lily (*Calochortus* sp., on the larger islands only) (Junak et al. 1995; Wallace 1985). As noted by previous researchers, the floral diversity of the eight Channel Islands is significantly lower than that of the mainland coast (Jazwa and Perry, Chapter 1; Rick et al. 2005).

Lower floral diversity aside, the extent to which plant resources were used on the islands in the past and how this changed through time has yet to be examined thoroughly. Ethnographic and archaeological evidence indicates that island populations used locally available plants for a variety of purposes, including basketry, roof thatching, woven mats, cordage, rope, nets, fishing line, storage containers, and skirts (Connolly et al. 1995; Cox 1989c; Erlandson et al. 1999; Martin and Popper 2001; Norris 1997; Orr 1968; Thomas 1995; Timbrook 1993, 2007; Raab et al. 2009; Rozaire 1978, 1989; Salls 1989a, 1989b). One of the most common plant materials used to make these

items is surf-grass (*Phyllospadix* sp.), a species commonly found along rocky shorelines in the intertidal and subtidal marine communities surrounding all of the Channel Islands (Junak et al. 1995). While surf-grass artifacts are commonly identified on the islands, they are virtually absent from the mainland. Timbrook (1993, 2007) suggests that island populations chose to substitute locally available plant materials (i.e., surf-grass) for materials that may have had more desirable properties but were either scarce or not available on the islands, such as Indian hemp (*Apocynum* sp.) and tule (*Scirpus* sp.).

In addition to the use of local, multipurpose plant materials, numerous ground stone artifacts typically associated with plant-processing activities (e.g., mortars, pestles, perforated stones) have been identified on all the Channel Islands (Conlee 2000; Cox 1989a, 1989b; Delaney-Rivera 2001; Erlandson et al. 1992; Fagan et al. 2006; Finnerty et al. 1981; Geiger 2000; Glassow et al. 2008; Meighan 2000; Orr 1968; Perry 2003; Rick 2007; Rick and Erlandson 2001; Rosenthal et al. 1988; Rozaire 1983; Thomas-Barnett 2004; Sutton 2010; Walker and Snethkamp 1984). Assumptions abound throughout California archaeology regarding (1) the reliance on particular plant resources (notably acorns and small seeds) and (2) the relationship between ground stone technology and the processing of acorns and seeds. These assumptions are largely based on Kroeber's observations; manos and metates have typically been associated with grinding small seeds, while acorn processing has been associated with mortars and pestles (Basgall 1987; Glassow et al. 1988; Glassow et al. 2007; Heizer 1974; Jones 1996; Kroeber 1925; Moratto 1984, 2002). Although ethnographic data from many areas of California indicate mortars and pestles were used for processing a variety of plants and animals, the assumption that the increased use of mortars and pestles directly indicates acorn intensification continues to be presented in the literature (Gamble and King 1997; Heizer 1974; Moratto 1984, 2002; but see Glassow 1996). Although increased use of mortars and pestles in the Channel region *may have been* associated with acorn intensification, especially on the mainland, caution should be employed when making such assumptions. Compared with the adjacent mainland, mano and metate technology is virtually absent from island assemblages; however, mortar and pestle technology appears on the islands around the same time it did on the mainland, around 6000 BP (Glassow et al. 2007). Interestingly, mortar and pestle technology has been identified on all of the Channel Islands, including Santa Barbara, the smallest and least terrestrially diverse (Erlandson et al. 1992; Geiger 2000; Glassow 1977). The appearance of this technology type on all the islands suggests that it was being used to process locally available resources; however, the extent to which plant versus animal resources, such as shellfish, were processed by mortar and pestle remains to be documented archaeologically. A second type of ground stone technology that appears to be strongly associated with the islands is the perforated stone. While variation among perforated stones does exist, suggesting they may have had a variety of uses, they are generally thought to be weights for digging sticks used to access bulbs and corms (Molitor 2000; Hollimon 1990; Sutton 2010).

The preponderance of ground stone technol-

ogy documented on the islands, combined with the diversity of artifacts made of locally available plant materials, suggests that local plant resources may have contributed to subsistence practices as well. If plant resources did compose a significant portion of resources targeted on the islands, seasonally or otherwise, decisions about settlement would likely have been tied to the location and seasonal availability of various plant resources. Thus, direct evidence for the use of plants on the Channel Islands is integral to understanding overall subsistence and settlement on the islands through time, which may have important implications for the development of sociopolitical complexity and the regional trade network seen in later time periods (Arnold 1987, 1992, 2001, 2010; King 1990).

Paleoethnobotanical Research

Paleoethnobotanical research on the Channel Islands began as early as the 1950s, and this field has become increasingly sophisticated since. Standardized methods for the recovery and presentation of paleoethnobotanical data have been refined substantially over the past few decades, including developments in sampling strategies, flotation methods, and quantitative analysis (Hastorf and Popper 1988; Pearsall 1989; VanDerwarker 2010a, 2010b). While these standardized methods have been employed in more recent paleoethnobotanical investigations on the Channel Islands, earlier researchers (e.g., Eisentraut 1990; Finnerty et al. 1981; McNulty 2000; Meighan 1954, 2000; Orr 1968; Young 2000; Wertman 1959; Williams 1992) often did not report data in a way useful for comparative analysis with more recent studies. In addition, several studies analyzed and reported data recovered from special-purpose features (i.e., hearths, storage pits) or ceremonial contexts only (Eisentraut 1990; Finnerty et al. 1981; Klug and Popper 1995; McNulty 2000; Meighan 1954, 2000; Orr 1968; Wertman 1959; Young 2000), rather than from general habitation debris (Klug and Popper 1993, 1997; Martin and Popper 1999, 2001; Popper 2003; Reddy and Erlandson 2012; Reddy 2000a, 2000b, 2003; Wohlgemuth 1997). While special-purpose features and ceremonial contexts are fascinating and clearly reflect important ideological and/or ritual patterns, we cannot make meaningful comparisons between feature, ceremonial, and midden contexts from different sites and time periods. As a result of the various contexts represented and differences in reporting standards, combined with the relatively small amount of paleoethnobotanical research conducted on the islands overall, a quantitative analysis comparing island assemblages is not possible at this time. Rather, the summary provided here illustrates the potential of paleoethnobotanical research in refining our understanding of subsistence and settlement among maritime hunter-gatherer-fishers in island contexts, and stresses the need for additional research to allow for future inter-island quantitative comparison (Tables 7.1 and 7.2).

Northern Islands

All rigorous paleoethnobotanical research on the northern Channel Islands is relatively recent, with data from eight sites on Santa Cruz Island, two on Santa Rosa Island, and one on San Miguel Island (Glassow et al. 2008; Gummerman 1992; Martin 2010; Martin and Popper 1999, 2001; Popper 2003; Reddy and Erlandson 2012). No data are currently available from Anacapa Island.

Of the eight sites on Santa Cruz Island for which paleoethnobotanical data are available, seven are located almost immediately adjacent to the coast (SCRI-191, -192, -240, -330, -474, -109, -427); one (SCRI-393) is located on a high ridge on the eastern end of the island. Most of these sites date to the late Holocene, from the Middle period (AD 700–1150) through the Historic period (AD 1769+), with the notable exception of the Punta Arena site (SCRI-109), which dates to the early and middle Holocene (7950–5250 cal BP) (Glassow et al. 2008). Santa Cruz Island samples analyzed for macrobotanical material were all column samples taken within midden deposits, combined with material recovered from the ⅛" mesh screens during excavation, where applicable. In addition, these samples were processed using flotation in order to aid in the recovery of macrobotanical remains (Gummerman 1992; Martin and Popper 1999, 2001; Popper 2003). Overall, good preservation of macrobotanical remains was reported for some sites (SCRI-191, -192, -240, -330, -474), but others had poor preservation (SCRI-109, -427, -393). Several factors affected preservation and recovery of

macrobotanical remains at these sites, including the age of the deposit, the depositional context, and possibly the flotation methods employed in the recovery of macrobotanical remains (e.g., varying mesh sizes, mechanical versus hand flotation techniques).

Nevertheless, the archaeobotanical remains recovered from Santa Cruz Island indicate that plants were used for a variety of purposes and were an important aspect of subsistence. A variety of small edible seeds have been identified at several sites, primarily those dating to later time periods (SCRI-191, -192, -240, -330, -474). Evidence of acorn use is also present, albeit in very low densities, in early, middle and late Holocene deposits at several sites (SCRI-191, -192, -330, and -109). Fragments of geophytes (i.e., corms and bulbs) have also been recovered in low densities from various contexts and time periods (SCRI-191, -192, -330, -474, and -109) (Glassow et al. 2008; Martin and Popper 1999, 2001).

Santa Rosa Island has limited paleoethnobotanical data from two sites. Orr (1968:200) reported a large amount (approximately 12 quarts) of red maids (*Calandrinia* sp.) seeds excavated from a burial context at Skull Gulch (SRI-2), although no additional paleoethnobotanical research has been conducted at this site. Erlandson et al. (1999:259) reported the recovery of a small amount of carbonized wood (.38 g) and two fragments of highly weathered and unidentifiable carbonized fruit seeds from screened (⅛") material at SRI-6, a 9,300–year-old site located at the mouth of Arlington Canyon, east of Skull Gulch. Flotation was not conducted at the time, but the recovery of carbonized material from an early Holocene site indicates a high potential for the recovery of macrobotanical remains on Santa Rosa Island.

Reddy and Erlandson (2012) recently reported the recovery of numerous corm fragments (totaling 3.71 g) from various strata spanning the early to late Holocene at Daisy Cave (SMI-261) on San Miguel Island. Small seeds, including bedstraw (*Galium* sp.) and chenopodium (*Chenopodium* sp.), were also recovered, although in very low densities. The nearly ubiquitous corm fragments recovered in cultural strata at Daisy Cave indicate its importance as a food source over a long period of time.

Southern Islands

Of the southern Channel Islands, most of the paleoethnobotanical research has been conducted on San Clemente Island, with data available from a total of 32 archaeological sites (Cummings 2000; Eisentraut 1990; Klug and Popper 1997; McNulty 2000; Meighan 2000; Reddy 2000a, 2000b, 2003; Young 2000; Wertman 1959; Wohlgemuth 1997). San Nicolas Island has paleoethnobotanical data available from two sites (SNI-168, -351) and a wood charcoal analysis from an additional site (SNI-56) (Klug and Popper 1993, 1995; Cummings 1993a, 1993b, 1993c; Williams 1992). Paleoethnobotanical data are minimal for Catalina Island, with only two studies suggesting the presence of macrobotanical remains (Finnerty et al. 1981; Meighan 1954). No data are currently available from Santa Barbara Island.

Thirty-two archaeological sites on San Clemente Island have been subject to archaeobotanical analysis, many of the samples coming from ceremonial feature contexts, which warrant some discussion. Seed caches have been found in apparent Late/Historic period ceremonial features at three sites located on the plateau of the island: the Ledge site (SCLI-126), the Old Airfield site (SCLI-1487), and the Lemon Tank site (SCLI-1524) (Figure 7.1). The contents of these features vary but commonly include abundant *Olivella* shell beads and whole abalone (*Haliotis* sp.) shells. Other items comprising feature contents in varying amounts include seeds, basketry, mortars, pestles, abalone shell bowls, perforated stones, steatite plaques and bowls, and tubular stone pipes (Madden 2000; Meighan 2000). In addition, dog, island fox, and raptor burials have been associated with several of these features (Salls and Hale 2000; Meighan 2000; Perry, Chapter 8). These unique features have been suggested as possible evidence for the ethnographically documented annual Mourning Ceremony (Meighan 2000), and raptor burials at Lemon Tank may be archaeological evidence for the *panes*, or bird ceremony (Salls and Hale 2000).

Undoubtedly, the unique context of these features limits comparative analysis with other feature types. Nevertheless, a brief description of archaeobotanical remains identified in these features is warranted, as they indicate the importance of plant resources not only for subsistence,

but for ceremonial purposes as well. Two of the features at the Ledge site contained seeds: Feature 1 contained a variety of plant remains, including acorn (*Quercus* sp.), cherry (*Prunus* sp.), and various small seeds, including domestic wheat (*Triticum* sp.) and red maids (*Calandrinia* sp.). Feature 5 is described as a small pit containing "thousands of seeds, only one species, *Calandrinia*" (McNulty 2000:64). The Old Airfield site also contained seeds in a feature context, consisting of cached morning glory (Convolvulaceae) seeds (Eisentraut 1990:106; McNulty 2000:63; Young 2000). Of particular interest are the seed caches at Lemon Tank, several of which were associated with animal burials. Six seed caches were identified during excavation, consisting exclusively of red maids (*Calandrinia* sp.) seeds contained in abalone (*Haliotis* sp.) shells. Curiously, several of these seed caches also contained human teeth (Eisentraut 1990). The number of red maids seeds varied between caches, ranging from 96 in Cache 6 to a staggering 273,240 in Cache 5 (Eisentraut 1990:100). Acorn (*Quercus* sp.) and cherry (*Prunus* sp.) were also noted during excavation but were not quantified or included in the final analysis (Eisentraut 1990).

Although not associated with the special feature contexts described above, macrobotanical remains from the Nursery site (SCLI-1215) were reported by Young (2000). It is unclear, however, whether the samples were taken from feature or midden contexts, and both carbonized and uncarbonized remains were included in the final analysis, making comparison with other data sets impossible. Interestingly, however, one manzanita berry pit (*Arctostaphylos* sp.), a resource that does not occur naturally on San Clemente Island, was identified in the analysis (Wallace 1985).

Macrobotanical analyses of samples from general midden contexts have been conducted at several sites on San Clemente Island, providing evidence for general subsistence practices: SCLI-1239, -1249, PL-100 (Reddy 2000a); LVTA-8, -9, LVTA/SE46 (Reddy 2000b); SCLI-1413, -1784, -1788, -1789, -1779 (Reddy 2002); LT-38, -43, -46, -60 (Reddy 2003); BUDS-4, -5, -8, -12, -13, -14, P5-7C, SCLI-1456, LT-22 (Klug and Popper 1997); SCLI-847 (Wohlgemuth 1997); and SCLI-1802, -1803 (Hildebrandt and Jones 1997). Many of these samples, with the exception of those

TABLE 7.1. Paleoethnobotanical remains recovered from Santa Catalina, San Nicolas, San Miguel, Santa Cruz, and Santa Rosa Islands

	Santa Catalina		San Nicolas		San Miguel
Site Number	SCAI-26	SCAI-39	SNI-168	SNI-351	SMI-261
Site Name	Ripper's Cove	Isthmus Cove			Daisy Cave
Context	Domestic	Burial	Domestic	Domestic	Domestic
Wood charcoal (g/liter)			9.06	0.175	5.5
Small seeds (n/liter)					
Atriplex spp. (Saltbush)					
Calandrinia spp. (Red maids)				0.149	
Chenopodium spp. (Goosefoot)					0.01
Galium spp. (Bedstraw)					0.02
Hemizonia spp. (Tarweed)					
Hordeum spp. (Wild barley)					
Malacothamnus spp. (Bushmallow)					
Opuntia spp. (Prickly pear)					
Phacelia spp. (Phacelia)					
Phalaris spp. (Maygrass)					
Plantago spp. (Plantain)					
Salvia spp. (Sage)					
Scirpus spp. (Tule)					
Sesuvium verrucosum (Sea purslane)					
Vaccinium spp. (Huckleberry)				0.153**	
Zea mays (Corn)		P			
Asteraceae (Sunflower family)					
Fabaceae (Legume family)				0.147	
Malvaceae (Mallow family)					
Poaceae (Grass family)					
Solanaceae (Nightshade family)					
Nuts and large seeds (g/liter)					
Juglans californica (Black walnut)					
Marah spp. (Wild cucumber)				0.843*	0.004
Prunus ilicifolia (Islay, Cherry)	P				
Quercus spp. (Acorn)	P				
Umbellularia californica (Bay laurel)					
Berry pits (n/liter)					
Arctostaphylos spp. (Manzanita)				0.077	
Geophytes (g/liter)					
Brodiaea-type corms (Blue dicks, Brodiaea)				0.42**	0.04

Notes: P = Present; *n/liter; **cf; ***1/8" screen.

Santa Cruz								Santa Rosa	
SCRI-191	SCRI-192	SCRI-240	SCRI-330	SCRI-109	SCRI-427	SCRI-393	SCRI-474	SRI-6	SRI-2
Christy	Morse Point	Prisoner's Harbor	Forney's Cove	Punta Arena			Posa Creek		Skull Gulch
Domestic	Domestic	Domestic	Domestic	Domestic	Domestic	Domestic	Domestic	Domestic	Burial
3.28	8.82	2.68	3.44	5.47	0.36	0.52	3.53	0.38***	
0.45	0.89	0.36	0.56				0.47		
18.82	6		3.42						1,000s
							1.48		
3.4			0.18						
			1						
	2.61		3.53				8.74		
0.5			0.24						
25.76	1		17.6				0.95		
1.25	0.5	0.36	3.5				0.53		
	0.18								
	7.22		0.33						
1.75	0.67		0.34						
21.08	0.6		6.6						
			2.5						
2.08**									
11.01	0.5								
9.68	17.2						2.37		
		0.36							
0.01									
13.25*	19.78*	0.36	7.34*	12.04*	0.05*		35.63*		
				0.07					
16.22	4.39		1.81				3.86		
0.11	0.8	0.01	0.11	0.454			0.09		

TABLE 7.2. Paleoethnobotanical remains recovered from San Clemente Island

Site Number	SCLI-126	SCLI-1487	SCLI-1524	SCLI-1215	
Site Name	Ledge	Old Airfield	Lemon Tank	Nursery	Big Dog Cave
Context	Ritual	Ritual	Ritual	Unknown	Domestic
Wood charcoal (g/liter)					
Small seeds (n/liter)					
Aclepias spp. (Milkweed)					
Atriplex spp. (Saltbush)					
Calandrinia spp. (Red maids)	1,000s		297,571*		
Chenopodium spp. (Goosefoot)					
Echinocactus spp. (Cactus)					
Eriogonum spp. (Buckwheat)					
Erodium spp. (Filaree)					
Galium spp. (Bedstraw)					
Hemizonia spp. (Tarweed)	P				P
Hordeum spp. (Wild barley)					P
Lavatera assurgentiflora (Island mallow)					
Lotus scoparius (Lotus/trefoil)	P				
Lupinus spp. (Lupine)					
Madia spp. (Tarweed)					
Opuntia spp. (Prickly pear)	P			P	P
Phacelia spp. (Phacelia)					
Phaseolus spp. (Domesticated bean)	P				
Plantago spp. (Plantain)					P
Rhus spp. (Lemonade berry)					
Stipa spp. (Needlegrass)	P				
Sueda spp. (Sea blight)	P**				
Triticum aestivum (Domestic wheat)	P				P
Vicia ludoviciana (Vetch)					
Aizoaceae (Fig-marigold family)					
Asteraceae (Sunflower family)	P				P
Boraginaceae (Borage family)					
Chenopodiaceae (Goosefoot family)					
Convolvulaceae (Morning glory family)		P			
Cyperaceae (Sedge family)					
Fabaceae (Legume family)					
Malvaceae (Mallow family)	P				
Poaceae (Grass family)					
Nuts and large seeds (g/liter)					
Quercus spp. (Acorn)					
Prunus ilicifolia (Islay, Cherry)	P				
Marah spp. (Wild cucumber)					
Umbellularia californica (Bay laurel)					
Berry pits (n/liter)					
Arctostaphylos spp. (Manzanita)				P	
Geophytes (g/liter)					
Brodiaea-type corms (Blue dicks, Brodiaea)					

Notes: P = present; *raw counts; **cf.

SCLI-1413	SCLI-1784	SCLI-1788	SCLI-1789	SCLI-1779	SCLI-1239	SCLI-1249	SCLI-1456	SCLI-847
Domestic	Domestic	Domestic	Domestic	Domestic	Domestic	Domestic	Domestic	Domestic
0.002	1.25	0.35	0.21	0.004	2.09	1.11		
					0.03	0.18		
					0.34	0.12		
	0.287	0.466	0.44	0.023	4.9			
					3.49	0.06		
	0.369	0.23	0.087					
		0.314	0.014					
0.035	0.419	0.138						
							1.923	
	0.085	0.035			3.46	0.36		
					0.03			
0.035	0.087	0.046					0.769	
						0.06		
			0.017					
1.31	1.47	1.22	0.93	0.023	6.48	0.67	0.385	8*
	0.022				1.21	0.06		1*
1.5	12.12	12.12	7.97	1.46	14.87	4.61	18.847	9*
							0.1	2*

TABLE 7.2. (cont'd.) Paleoethnobotanical remains recovered from San Clemente Island

Site Number	SCLI-1802	SCLI-1803	LVTA-8	LVTA-9	LVTA/SE46
Site Name					
Context	Domestic	Domestic	Domestic	Domestic	Domestic
Wood charcoal (g/liter)			5.42	0.01	0.415
Small seeds (n/liter)					
Aclepias spp. (Milkweed)					
Atriplex spp. (Saltbush)	0.38			0.47	
Calandrinia spp. (Red maids)					
Chenopodium spp. (Goosefoot)		0.13		0.53	3.42
Echinocactus spp. (Cactus)				0.94	1.82
Eriogonum spp. (Buckwheat)					
Erodium spp. (Filaree)					
Galium spp. (Bedstraw)					
Hemizonia spp. (Tarweed)		0.25			
Hordeum spp. (Wild barley)		0.38			
Lavatera assurgentiflora (Island mallow)					
Lotus scoparius (Lotus/trefoil)					
Lupinus spp. (Lupine)	1.13				
Madia spp. (Tarweed)					
Opuntia spp. (Prickly pear)					
Phacelia spp. (Phacelia)					
Phaseolus spp. (Domesticated bean)					
Plantago spp. (Plantain)					
Rhus spp. (Lemonade berry)					
Stipa spp. (Needlegrass)					
Sueda spp. (Sea blight)					
Triticum aestivum (Domestic wheat)					
Vicia ludoviciana (Vetch)	0.57		0.64		0.03
Aizoaceae (Fig-marigold family)					
Asteraceae (Sunflower family)				0.65	0.37
Boraginaceae (Borage family)					
Chenopodiaceae (Goosefoot family)			3.85		
Convolvulaceae (Morning glory family)					
Cyperaceae (Sedge family)					
Fabaceae (Legume family)	0.57				0.09
Malvaceae (Mallow family)		0.75			
Poaceae (Grass family)	15.3	0.88		0.18	0.03
Nuts and large seeds (g/liter)					
Quercus spp. (Acorn)					
Prunus ilicifolia (Islay, Cherry)					
Marah spp. (Wild cucumber)					
Umbellularia californica (Bay laurel)					
Berry pits (n/liter)					
Arctostaphylos spp. (Manzanita)					
Geophytes (g/liter)					
Brodiaea-type corms (Blue dicks, Brodiaea)					

Notes: P = present; *raw counts; **cf.

LT-22	LT-38	LT-43	LT-46	LT-60	BUDS-4	BUDS-5	BUDS-8	BUDS-12
Domestic	Domestic	Domestic	Domestic	Domestic	Domestic	Domestic	Domestic	Domestic
	0.008	0.11	0.007	0.012	0.31	0.315	0.018	3.15
		0.038						
								3
								1
			0.561	0.122				0.5**
						0.5**		
							0.588	
		0.019		0.046				
		0.667						
0.333								
		0.476	0.073	0.046				
0.667		1.257	0.879	1.239			0.294	
		0.001	0.001	0.000				
						0.01		

TABLE 7.2. (cont'd.) Paleoethnobotanical remains recovered from San Clemente Island

Site Number	BUDS-13	BUDS-14	P5-7C	PL-100
Site Name				
Context	Domestic	Domestic	Domestic	Domestic
Wood charcoal (g/liter)	0.01	5.347		1.06
Small seeds (n/liter)				
Aclepias spp. (Milkweed)				
Atriplex spp. (Saltbush)				
Calandrinia spp. (Red maids)		0.588		
Chenopodium spp. (Goosefoot)				0.16
Echinocactus spp. (Cactus)				
Eriogonum spp. (Buckwheat)				
Erodium spp. (Filaree)				
Galium spp. (Bedstraw)				
Hemizonia spp. (Tarweed)				
Hordeum spp. (Wild barley)			0.222	
Lavatera assurgentiflora (Island mallow)				
Lotus scoparius (Lotus/trefoil)				
Lupinus spp. (Lupine)				
Madia spp. (Tarweed)				
Opuntia spp. (Prickly pear)				
Phacelia spp. (Phacelia)				
Phaseolus spp. (Domesticated bean)				
Plantago spp. (Plantain)				
Rhus spp. (Lemonade berry)				
Stipa spp. (Needlegrass)				
Sueda spp. (Sea blight)				
Triticum aestivum (Domestic wheat)				
Vicia ludoviciana (Vetch)				
Aizoaceae (Fig-marigold family)				
Asteraceae (Sunflower family)				
Boraginaceae (Borage family)				
Chenopodiaceae (Goosefoot family)				
Convolvulaceae (Morning glory family)				
Cyperaceae (Sedge family)				
Fabaceae (Legume family)		0.588		0.11
Malvaceae (Mallow family)				0.03
Poaceae (Grass family)			3.778	0.24
Nuts and large seeds (g/liter)				
Quercus spp. (Acorn)				
Prunus ilicifolia (Islay, Cherry)				
Marah spp. (Wild cucumber)				
Umbellularia californica (Bay laurel)				
Berry pits (n/liter)				
Arctostaphylos spp. (Manzanita)				
Geophytes (g/liter)				
Brodiaea-type corms (Blue dicks, Brodiaea)				

Notes: P = present; *raw counts; **cf.

analyzed by Reddy, were small in volume, and only one sample per site was analyzed. Therefore, only general statements regarding patterns in the macrobotanical record can be made at this time. Overall, small seed densities are low at all sites, and acorn is present in low densities at LT-43, -46, and -60 (Reddy 2003). Corm fragments are also reported in low densities from three sites: BUDS-5, SCLI-1456, and -847 (Klug and Popper 1997; Wohlgemuth 1997).

Paleoethnobotanical studies on San Nicolas Island are relatively minimal and include data from only three sites. Williams (1992) conducted a wood charcoal analysis from a surface collection of 128 charcoal specimens from SNI-56. The majority (*n* = 114, or 89 percent) of specimens were identified as coyote brush (*Baccharis* sp.); just 3.9 percent (*n* = 5) were identified as pine (*Pinus* sp.), and 2.3 percent (*n* = 3) as manzanita (*Arctostaphylos* sp.) (Williams 1992:3). Coyote brush is common on San Nicolas Island; however, pine and manzanita do not occur there naturally (Wallace 1985; Williams 1992). One species of manzanita (*A. catalinae*) exists on Santa Catalina Island, whereas Santa Cruz and Santa Rosa Islands have several species. In addition, while these materials may have been obtained from the mainland, the geographically closest sources of pine include bishop pine (*P. muricata*) on Santa Cruz Island and the torrey pine (*P. torreyana*) on Santa Rosa Island. Alternatively, it is possible that these wood resources were obtained as driftwood. Two sites on San Nicolas have been subject to macrobotanical analysis: SNI-168 and -351. Four samples from a darkly stained basin-shaped feature at SNI-168 revealed only carbonized wood and bark remains, suggesting its use as a special-purpose feature (Klug and Popper 1995). Analysis of samples from both feature and midden contexts at SNI-351 indicated poor preservation at the site, with low densities of both wood charcoal and nonwood macrobotanical remains. Overall, small seeds were identified in low densities, and one geophyte was identified in a sample from the midden context at SNI-351 (Klug and Popper 1993).

Previous paleoethnobotanical research on Santa Catalina Island is nearly nonexistent, with only two somewhat vague references. McNulty (2000:62) describes a personal communication with Meighan (1954) indicating that he "recov-ered burned seeds in a fire hearth, including Catalina Cherry (*Prunus lyonii*) and charred acorns (*Quercus macdonaldii*) from the Empire Landing Site on Catalina Island." The Empire Landing site has been given several trinomial designations, including SCAI-31, -36, and -98, which were eventually combined as SCAI-26 and known locally as the Ripper's Cover site (Reinman and Eberhart 1980; South Central Coastal Information Center 2011). Unfortunately, additional information regarding archaeobotanical remains obtained from this site appears to be inaccessible at this time. The recovery of archaeobotanical remains at Isthmus Cove (SCAI-39) on Santa Catalina suggests that mainland plant foods were imported during the Mission period (Finnerty et al. 1981). According to Finnerty et al. (1981:14), "[c]arbonized seeds identified as corn by the UCLA Botany Department were found in association with the Burial 10 complex, and presumably came from the mainland mission farms." The archaeobotanical evidence identified at Isthmus Cove corroborates Jonathan Winship's 1807 observation that the native residents had "grain and vegetables" (Bancroft 1886, 19:84; Strudwick, Chapter 10).

Theoretical Considerations

Overall, previous paleoethnobotanical research on the Channel Islands has been intermittent at best. However, not only do available data indicate that archaeobotanical remains are present in island sites; they also have the potential to make a significant contribution in understanding overall subsistence practices, settlement decisions, and trade among these maritime hunter-gatherer-fishers. Models from optimal foraging theory, particularly diet breadth, have been applied extensively in hunter-gatherer subsistence studies, and the Channel Islands are no exception (Bettinger 2001; Bettinger et al. 1997; Bettinger and Baumhoff 1982; Broughton 1997; Erlandson 1991; Kennett 2005; Simms 1987; Yatsko 2000; Wohlgemuth 1996). However, despite ethnographic and archaeological data indicating the importance of plants in prehistoric diets for most areas of the world (Kelly 1995), prevailing subsistence research on the Channel Islands has tended to focus heavily on marine resources (e.g., Erlandson 1997; Glassow 2005; Glassow et al. 2008; Kennett 2005; Raab et al. 2002; Raab et al. 2009; Rick 2007; Sharp 2000; Yatsko 2000; Vellanoweth et al.

TABLE 7.3. Ranking of California plant resources

Rank	Resource Class	Example
1	Geophytes	Brodiaea (*Brodiaea* sp.), blue dicks (*Dichelostemma* sp.), Ithuriel's Spear (*Triteleia* sp.), mariposa lily (*Calochortus* sp.)
2	Nontoxic Nuts	Pine (*Pinus* sp.), bay (*Umbellularia californica*), hazel (*Corylus cornuta* var. *californica*), California walnut (*Juglans* sp.)
3	Toxic Nuts	Acorn (*Quercus* sp.; *Lithocarpus* sp.), buckeye (*Aesculus californica*), wild cherry (*Prunus ilicifolia*)
4	Small Seeds	Grasses (Poaceae), red maids (*Calandrinia* sp.), chia (*Salvia columbariae*), Farewell-to-Spring (*Clarkia* sp.), goosefoot (*Chenopodium* sp.), native barley (*Hordeum* sp.), tarweed (*Hemizonia* sp.; *Madia* sp.)
5	Aquatic Roots	Bulrush (*Scirpus* sp.), cattail (*Typha* sp.)

2002). While it is apparent that island populations had a decidedly maritime focus, examining the extent to which plant resources of different types were used must be contextualized within the framework of foraging theory.

Although resource ranking in terms of optimal foraging has been applied extensively in California archaeology to meat resources, plant resources have not been given the same consideration until recently. Wohlgemuth (2010) attempts to rank plant resources in California based on ethnographic and experimental caloric return rate data from the Great Basin and Columbia Plateau. While Wohlgemuth recognizes that the precise values of return rates may not translate directly for California resources, the general order of ranking should not change significantly. Simms (1987:38, 42) has conducted experiments suggesting that ranking in terms of morphological characteristics may be the most applicable cross-culturally. Ranking plant resources based strictly on caloric return rates is useful in that it provides a simple way to contextualize the potential importance of various plant resources in the Channel Region without bias of assumed importance through time based on the ethnographic record. It is important to note, however, that seasonality, storability, and nutritional content of plant resources are important attributes that are not included in this scheme and must be considered separately. The ranking of California plant resources in the simplest terms of return rates (kcal/hr) (following Wohlgemuth 2010:60–61) is presented in Table 7.3.

Although Wohlgemuth does not provide an indication of where the manzanita (*Archtostaphylos* sp.) berry pit might fit into this scheme, I suggest it be included with the nontoxic nuts as it requires little processing (dried and ground into a coarse meal) and is seasonally abundant. In addition, while aquatic roots are ranked lowest, ethnographic data do suggest that seasonally available pollen from aquatic plants such as cattail can be collected in large quantities, boiled, and made into gruel, resulting in very high return rates ranging from 2,700 to 9,400 kcal/hr (Mead 2003; Simms 1987:44; Timbrook 2007).

The seasonal availability, nutritional content, and storability of each plant food resource are important factors to take into consideration. Acorns, for example, have long been praised as an important food source throughout native California for their seasonal abundance, high caloric and protein content, and storability (Bean and Saubel 1972; Timbrook 2007). Intensive acorn use on the islands, however, has yet to be documented archaeologically, despite the role it has played in various arguments regarding regional exchange. It is possible, given the abundant marine resources available year-round, that acorns may not have been as important on the islands as they were elsewhere in prehistoric California. Other plant resources that require less processing time than acorns but contain higher carbohydrates, such as corms and bulbs, may have been more important to island populations who had access to abundant protein and fat from marine resources.

Stemming from optimal foraging theory, diet breadth models are useful in that they look at search costs versus pursuit and handling costs, where search costs are directly related to resource density and distribution, and pursuit and handling costs are dependent on resource type (Bettinger 2001; Kelly 1995; Winterhalder and Goland 1997). These expressions were developed primarily in terms of animal resources, where "search," "pursuit," and "handling" costs make sense for a hunter searching for, encountering, pursuing, and butchering game. Plant resources, however, must be considered in a slightly different light (O'Connell and Hawkes 1981; Simms 1987). First, search costs are determined by the amount of time it takes a forager to move from one patch of plant resources to another. Patches of plant resources are particularly predictable; they are stationary and usually only seasonally available. Unless a foraging group is new to an area, or environmental conditions change dramatically, it is reasonable to assume that the forager is familiar with the general locations of resource patches and their season of availability. Once a patch is encountered, pursuit (or gathering) of a particular resource begins and is dependent on the rate of procurement (Kelly 1995; Simms 1987). The rate of procurement, in turn, can be highly variable, depending on the individual gatherer, density within each patch, the level of difficulty involved with collecting specific resources, technology, and/or environmental conditions (Bettinger 2001; Bettinger and Baumhoff 1982; Simms 1987).

Handling time for plant resources is conceptually similar to that of animal resources: the amount of time needed to process the resource into an edible form, which is dependent on the particular resource (e.g., toxic nuts such as acorns have higher handling costs than edible corms such as blue dicks). Generally, foragers search for high-ranked resources first, and upon encountering a lower-ranked resource, they must decide to either pursue the encountered resource or continue searching. As high-ranked resources decline in abundance (for a number of possible reasons such as environmental change, overpredation, population growth, etc.), foraging efficiency for that particular resource declines, and the diet must expand to include lower-ranked resources (Bettinger 2001; Simms 1987).

Alternatively, if a change, such as a technological innovation, increases the efficiency of pursuit and handling of a previously unpursued resource, that resource may increase in rank sufficiently to be included in the diet (Bettinger 2001; Bettinger and Baumhoff 1982; Winterhalder and Goland 1997). Thus, changes in diet breadth can reflect changes in technology or cultural responses to external factors such as environmental stress. Overall, contextualizing California's plant resources in terms of foraging theory and diet breadth models is useful in developing and testing hypotheses and expectations for plant resource use, particularly in island contexts.

Geophytes: A High-Ranked Food Resource

Ethnographic data, while scant for the islands compared with that for the mainland, offer insight into the use of the highest-ranked plant resources on the islands: corms and bulbs. The Spanish term *cacomite* has been used to describe various plant species with edible bulbs/corms. Among Chumash informants, however, the term was most commonly applied to blue dicks (*Dichelostemma capitatum*), while other bulb/corm producing plants such as the mariposa lily (*Calochortus* sp.) were referred to as "another kind of *cacomite*" (Timbrook 2007:75). The Chumash name *shiqó'n* described the plant "as having blue flowers and a root like garlic" (Timbrook 2007: 75). Once the flowering stalks of the blue dicks died in early summer, the corms were harvested using a digging stick weighted with a perforated stone. They could then be eaten raw or, more commonly, taken back to the village or camp to be roasted in hot coals. On the islands in particular, several native families reportedly converged to harvest large quantities of *cacomites*, which were then communally roasted in a large roasting pit or oven, nearly 4 × 3 ft wide. A pit was excavated and a fire built inside; once the coals burned down, the corms were spread "out over the coals in a layer several inches thick" and then covered with more hot coals and ashes on top (Timbrook 2007:75). Dirt was then placed on top of the entire oven to keep air out. Once the corms were roasted, the oven was opened, and a designated person distributed the cooked corms to each of the families using an abalone scoop (Timbrook 2007).

While these ethnographic observations refer more specifically to the northern Channel Islands, a historic account pertaining to San Nicolas suggests the potential importance of corms on the southern islands as well. When George Nidever encountered the Lone Woman of San Nicolas Island in 1853, he wrote: "she took some roots of two different kinds, one called *corcomites* [*cacomite*] and the name of the other I do not know, and placed them in the fire which was burning within the inclosure [*sic*]. As soon as they were roasted she invited us to eat some" (Ellison 1937:83; Thomas 1995).

Although ethnographic data for the Chumash indicate the corms were dug in early summer, they potentially can be identified, dug up, and eaten at any time of the year, eliminating the need for long-term storage. The dried flowering stalks of the blue dicks typically remain upright throughout the year (except in areas subject to high winds) until new stalks emerge in spring. This attribute makes locating blue dicks corms very easy, the primary difference being the ease with which one can access the corm. Late summer and early fall can make for difficult digging depending on the location, as the ground is often dry and compact from little rainfall over the summer. Digging in other times of the year, in late fall through spring, may be easier because soil moisture content is higher. In addition, preliminary experimental data indicate that corms collected during different seasons may have different nutritional, textural, and/or taste qualities. For instance, corms dug in midsummer are often very starchy, whereas corms dug in mid-fall, when adventitious roots form to anchor the corm into the ground, often have a flavor that is sweeter and a texture that is less starchy (author's personal observation). In addition, experimental data on the sustainability of harvesting corms suggests that when the small cormlets are allowed to remain in the soil, approximately 50 percent of the corms can be harvested with no adverse effect on the overall population (Anderson and Rowney 1999). These experiments indicate that corms could be harvested in relatively large amounts with little or no impact on the plant population over time. In the context of ethnographic observations, theoretical considerations, and experimental data, corms and bulbs may indeed have made significant contributions not only to overall subsistence

and settlement on the islands, but to feasting events as well (Perry and Delaney-Rivera 2011). Furthermore, blue dicks are available, and in certain areas abundant, on *all* of the Channel Islands (Junak et al. 1995; Wallace 1985).

Discussion

Archaeologically, carbonized corm fragments have been identified from a wide range of time periods on nearly all of the larger islands, including San Miguel (Reddy and Erlandson 2012), Santa Cruz (Martin and Popper 1999, 2001), San Nicolas (Klug and Popper 1993), and San Clemente (Klug and Popper 1997; Wohlgemuth 1997). As part of my ongoing dissertation research, paleoethnobotanical analyses are fundamental to understanding settlement and subsistence patterns at a large, noncoastal site on the northern side of Santa Cruz Island. The Diablo Valdez Bedrock Mortar complex (SCRI-619/620) is a large residential site associated with bedrock outcrops that include a rockshelter for a portion of the site. It is located adjacent to a perennial stream, approximately 1 km northwest of Diablo Peak, the highest point of the Channel Islands at 750 m above mean sea level. The site consists of three loci with six bedrock mortars; a deep, dense shell midden extending to 214 cm below the surface (cmbs); five house depressions; and chipped stone debitage, projectile points, bowl mortar fragments, perforated stone fragments, and shell beads noted on the surface. Excavations during the summer of 2011 revealed numerous domestic features, including hearths, areas of burned earth, a large roasting pit, postholes, several possible living surfaces, and multiple pit features that appear to be hearth-clearing pits. Significantly, a large quantity of carbonized Brodiea-type corms, most likely blue dicks (*Dichelostemma* sp.), was recovered in the ⅛"-screened material and during careful hand excavation (Figure 7.2). These corms were identified as occurring in multiple strata, and they were found in particularly high density at Locus 2, within a small area of midden deposit at the 120–125 cmbs level, amounting to less than 1 liter of soil volume. While these corms were recovered within a general midden context rather than in a feature, the area within which they were recovered was discrete, representing a single

FIGURE 7.2. Blue dicks corms recovered from the Diablo Valdez site, Santa Cruz Island.

depositional event. The total weight of the corms from this context alone is 45.21 g. During ongoing laboratory analysis, we continue to recover additional whole and fragmented carbonized corms from nearly every stratum at both loci. Fragments of corms are fairly easy to identify as their internal structure is relatively uniform (Figure 7.3). These corms represent the most substantial recovery of carbonized corms yet reported for the islands or adjacent mainland.

Radiocarbon dates from the Diablo Valdez site indicate it was repeatedly occupied from circa 5700 cal BP through the Late period and after European contact. The deep, well-stratified deposits contain numerous domestic features, including a large roasting pit, living surfaces, and hearth clearing pits, suggesting occupation for relatively long durations, at least seasonally. The large quantity of carbonized corms recovered from nearly all strata, indicates that geophytes were an important food resource for island populations for at least 6,000 years. Early Holocene evidence of geophytes at Daisy Cave further point to the

importance of geophytes for island populations (Reddy and Erlandson 2012). In any case, the Diablo Valdez site appears to be a location that was occupied repeatedly over a long period of time, and one where blue dicks corms were used during various periods of habitation.

Conclusions

From a theoretical perspective, high-ranked plant resources should be expected to have supplemented the marine diet to balance protein from fish, shellfish, and sea mammals with carbohydrates (Kelly 1995). The ethnographic and archaeobotanical data presented here indicate that a variety of plant resources were used on the Channel Islands for food, as construction materials, and for ceremonial purposes. The ranking scheme presented here, using caloric return rate values, is intended as a heuristic device for reconsidering the potential importance of various plant resources on all of the islands within the framework of foraging theory. From this simplistic baseline, other factors affecting plant resource

FIGURE 7.3. Cross sections of three blue dicks corms recovered from the Diablo Valdez site, Santa Cruz Island.

subsistence and settlement decisions (i.e., season of availability, storability, and nutritional properties) must be considered independently. Accordingly, in order to effectively evaluate changes in overall subsistence, settlement, regional exchange, and sociopolitical complexity, paleoethnobotanical studies must be given a higher priority in research on the Channel Islands.

Acknowledgments

Thanks are due to many people, without whose assistance this chapter would not have been possible. First, thanks to the editors, Chris Jazwa and Jenn Perry, for pulling this all together. Funding for fieldwork was supported in part by the Peter F. Paige Memorial Fund through the Department of Anthropology at the University of California, Santa Barbara. To the folks who helped track down references and provided documents, often in the form of gray literature, I thank Jeanne Arnold, Lisa Barnett-Thomas, Jim Cassidy, Jon Erlandson, Tom Garlinghouse, Mike Glassow, Jenn Perry, Seetha Reddy, Ivan Strudwick, Wendy Teeter, Amber VanDerwarker, Julie Vanderweir, René Vellanoweth, Rob Wlodarski, Eric Wohlgemuth, Scott Wolf, and Andy Yatsko. I also thank Dana Bardolph, Mike Glassow, and Amber VanDerwarker for providing comments on earlier drafts, and Dana Bardolph and Greg Wilson for assistance with photographs and graphics. I also thank my amazing field crew, who schlepped hundreds of pounds of soil up and over a mountain, always in high spirits: Kelli Brasket, Henry Chodsky, Mike Glassow, Stephen Hennek, Chris Jazwa, Terry Joslin, Amber Marie Madrid, Dusty McKenzie, Sarah Mellinger, Jenn Perry, Tim Slowik, and Eric Wohlgemuth. I am particularly indebted to Eric Wohlgemuth, whose enthusiasm and willingness to rap anything plants is infectious.

References Cited

Anderson, M. K.
2005   *Tending the Wild: Native American Knowledge and Management of California's Natural Resources.* University of California Press, Berkeley.

Anderson, M. K., and D. L. Rowney
1999   The Edible Plant *Dichelostemma capitatum*: Its Vegetative Reproduction Response to Different Indigenous Harvesting Regimes in California. *Restoration Ecology* 7(3):231–240.

Arnold, J. E.
1987   *Craft Specialization in the Prehistoric Channel Islands, California.* University of California Press, Berkeley.
1992   Complex Hunter-Gatherer-Fishers of Prehistoric California: Chiefs, Specialists, and Maritime Adaptations of the Channel Islands. *American Antiquity* 57:60–84.
2001   Social Evolution and the Political Economy in the Northern Channel Islands. In

The Origins of a Pacific Coast Chiefdom: The Chumash of the Channel Islands, edited by J. E. Arnold, pp. 287–296. University of Utah Press, Salt Lake City.

2010 The Role of Politically Charged Property in the Appearance of Institutionalized Leadership: A View from the North American Pacific Coast. In *The Evolution of Leadership: Transitions in Decision Making from Small-Scale to Middle Range Societies*, edited by K. J. Vaughn, J. W. Eerkens, and J. Kantner, pp. 121–146. School for Advanced Research Press, Santa Fe, NM.

Bancroft, H. H.
1886 *The Works of Hubert Howe Bancroft*, Vol. 19: *History of California*, Vol. 2: 1801–1824. The History Company, San Francisco. Facsimile reprint, Wallace Hebberd, Santa Barbara, CA, 1966.

Basgall, M. E.
1987 Resource Intensification Among Hunter-Gatherers: Acorn Economies in Prehistoric California. *Research in Economic Anthropology* 9:21–52.

Bean, L. J., and K. S. Saubel
1972 *Temalpakh (From the Earth): Cahuilla Indian Knowledge and Usage of Plants*. Malki Museum Press, Banning, CA.

Bettinger, R. L.
2001 *Hunter-Gatherers: Archaeological and Evolutionary Theory*. Plenum, New York.

Bettinger R. L., and M. A. Baumhoff
1982 The Numic Spread: Great Basin Cultures in Competition. *American Antiquity* 47:485–503.

Bettinger, R. L, R. Malhi, and H. McCarthy
1997 Central Place Models of Acorn and Mussel Processing. *Journal of Archaeological Science* 24:887–899.

Broughton, J. M.
1997 Widening Diet Breadth, Declining Foraging Efficiency, and Prehistoric Harvest Pressure: Ichthyofaunal Evidence from the Emeryville Shellmound, California. *Antiquity* 71:845–862.

Conlee, C. A.
2000 Intensified Middle Period Ground Stone Production on San Miguel Island. *Journal of California and Great Basin Anthropology* 22(2):374–391.

Connolly, T. J., J. M. Erlandson, and S. E. Norris
1995 Early Holocene Basketry and Cordage from Daisy Cave, San Miguel Island, California. *American Antiquity* 60:309–318.

Cox, T.
1989a Food Procurement. In *A Step Into The Past:*

Island Dwellers of Southern California, curated by J. Smull and T. Cox, p. 17. Museum of Anthropology, California State University, Fullerton.

1989b Food Preparation. In *A Step Into The Past: Island Dwellers of Southern California*, curated by J. Smull and T. Cox, p. 19. Museum of Anthropology, California State University, Fullerton.

1989c Clothing and Decoration. In *A Step Into The Past: Island Dwellers of Southern California*, curated by J. Smull and T. Cox, p. 25. Museum of Anthropology, California State University, Fullerton.

Cummings, L. S.
1993a Exploratory Pollen and Phytolith Analysis at CA-SNI-351, a Shell Midden on San Nicholas Island, California. Manuscript on file, Department of Anthropology, California State University, Fullerton.

1993b Pollen Analysis of a Piece of Ground Stone from CA-SNI-351, San Nicolas Island, California. Manuscript on file, Department of Anthropology, California State University, Fullerton.

1993c Pollen Analysis of Tarring Pebbles and Beneath Shells in a Midden at CA-SNI-351, San Nicolas Island, California. Manuscript on file, Department of Anthropology, California State University, Fullerton.

2000 Phytolith Analysis. In *Archaeological Testing of Four Sites Near West Cove, Northern San Clemente Island, California*, edited by B. F. Byrd. Technical report on file, Natural Resource Office, Naval Region SW, Naval Air Station, North Island, San Diego.

Delany-Rivera, C.
2001 Ground Stone Tools as Indicators of Changing Subsistence and Exchange Patterns in the Coastal Chumash Region. In *Origins of a Pacific Coast Chiefdom: The Chumash of the Channel Islands*, edited by J. E. Arnold, pp. 71–112. University of Utah Press, Salt Lake City.

Eisentraut, P. J.
1990 Investigations of Prehistoric Seed Caches from Site CA-SCLI-1542, San Clemente Island. *Pacific Coast Archaeological Society Quarterly* 26(2–3):93–113.

Ellison, W. H. (editor)
1937 *The Life and Adventures of George Nidever [1802–1883]: The Life Story of a Remarkable California Pioneer Told in His Own Words, and None Wasted*. University of California Press, Berkeley.

Erlandson, J. M.

1991   Shellfish and Seeds as Optimal Resources:
        Early Holocene Subsistence on the Santa
        Barbara Coast. In *Hunter-Gatherers of Early
        Holocene Coastal California*, edited by J. M.
        Erlandson and R. H. Colten, pp. 89–101. Uni-
        versity of California, Los Angeles.

1997   The Middle Holocene on the Western Santa
        Barbara Coast. In *Archaeology of the Califor-
        nia Coast During the Middle Holocene*, edited
        by J. M. Erlandson and M. A. Glassow, pp. 91–
        109. Institute of Archaeology, University of
        California, Los Angeles.

Erlandson, J. M., M. A. Glassow, C. Rozaire, and
D. Morris

1992   4,000 Years of Human Occupation on Santa
        Barbara Island, California. *Journal of Cali-
        fornia and Great Basin Anthropology* 14(1):
        85–93.

Erlandson, J. M., T. C. Rick, R. L. Vellanoweth, and
D. J. Kennett

1999   Maritime Subsistence at a 9300 Year Old
        Shell Midden on Santa Rosa Island, Califor-
        nia. *Journal of Field Archaeology* 25:255–265.

Fagan, B., D. Grenda, D. Maxwell, A. H. Keller, and
R. Ciolek-Torello

2006   *Life on the Dunes: Fishing, Ritual and Daily
        Life at Two Late Period Sites on Vizcaino
        Point, Archaeological Testing at CA-SNI-39
        and CA-SNI-162, San Nicolas Island, Califor-
        nia*. Technical Series 88. Statistical Research
        Inc., Tucson, AZ.

Finnerty, W. P., D. A. Decker, N. N. Leonard III,
T. F. King, C. D. King, and L. B. King

1981   *Community Structure and Trade at Isthmus
        Cove: A Salvage Excavation on Catalina Is-
        land*. Pacific Coast Archaeological Society
        Occasional Paper No. 1. Originally pub-
        lished in 1970. Reprinted, Acoma Books,
        Ramona, CA.

Gamble, L. H., and C. King

1997   Middle Holocene Adaptations in the Santa
        Monica Mountains. In *Archaeology of the
        California Coast During the Middle Holocene*,
        edited by J. M. Erlandson and M. A. Glassow,
        pp. 61–72. Cotsen Institute of Archaeology,
        University of California, Los Angeles.

Geiger, D. C.

2000   Comparative Notes on San Clemente Ground
        Stone Artifacts. *Pacific Coast Archaeological
        Society Quarterly* 36(3):31–34.

Glassow, M. A.

1977   *An Archaeological Overview of the Northern
        Channel Islands, Including Santa Barbara Is-
        land*. Western Archaeological Center, Na-

tional Park Service, Tucson, AZ. Manuscript
on file, Central Coast Information Center,
University of California, Santa Barbara.

1996   The Significance to California Prehistory of
        the Earliest Mortars and Pestles. *Pacific Coast
        Archaeological Society* 32(4):14–26.

2005   Prehistoric Dolphin Hunting on Santa Cruz
        Island, California. In *The Exploitation and
        Cultural Importance of Sea Mammals*, edited
        by G. Monks, pp. 107–120. Oxbow Books,
        Oxford.

Glassow, M. A., L. H. Gamble, J. E. Perry, and G. S.
Russell

2007   Prehistory of the Northern California Bight
        and the Adjacent Transverse Ranges. In *Cal-
        ifornia Prehistory: Colonization, Culture, and
        Complexity*, edited by T. L. Jones and K. A.
        Klar, pp. 191–213. Altamira, Lanham, MD.

Glassow, M. A., J. E. Perry, and P. Paige

2008   *The Punta Arena Site: Early and Middle Ho-
        locene Development on Santa Cruz Island*.
        Contributions in Archaeology. Santa Bar-
        bara Museum of Natural History, Santa
        Barbara, CA.

Glassow, M. A., L. R. Wilcoxon, and J. M. Erlandson

1988   Cultural and Environmental Change During
        the Early Period of Santa Barbara Channel
        Prehistory. In *The Archaeology of Prehistoric
        Coastlines*, edited by G. Bailey and J. Parking-
        ton, pp. 64–77. Cambridge University Press,
        Cambridge.

Gummerman, G.

1992   *Paleoethnobotanical Analysis of Soil Samples
        from CA-SCRI-191, -192, -240, -330, -474,
        Santa Cruz Island*. Report prepared for Bob
        Peterson by Paleoethnobotany Laboratory,
        Cotsen Institute of Archaeology, University
        of California, Los Angeles.

Hale, A., and R. A. Salls

2000   The Canine Ceremony: Dog and Fox Burials
        of San Clemente Island. *Pacific Coast Archae-
        ological Society Quarterly* 36(4):80–94.

Hastorf, C. A., and V. S. Popper (editors)

1988   *Current Paleoethnobotany: Analytical
        Methods and Cultural Interpretations of Ar-
        chaeological Plant Remains*. University of
        Chicago Press, Chicago and London.

Heizer, R. F.

1974   Studying the Windmiller Culture. In *Ar-
        chaeological Researches in Retrospect*, edited
        by G. R. Wiley, pp. 179–204. Winthrop,
        Cambridge.

Hildebrandt, W. R., and D. A. Jones

1997   *Data Recovery Excavations at Two Prehis-
        toric Sites Associated with the JSOW Impact*

*Area, San Clemente Island, California: CA-SCLI-1802 and CA-SCLI-1803.*Technical report submitted to NAS North Island, San Diego, CA. Far Western Anthropological Research Group, Davis, CA.

Hollimon, S. E.

1990 Division of Labor and Gender Roles in Santa Barbara Channel Area Prehistory. PhD dissertation. Department of Anthropology, University of California, Santa Barbara.

Jones, T. L.

1996 Mortars, Pestles, and Division of Labor in Prehistoric California: A View from Big Sur. *American Antiquity* 6:243–264.

Junak, S., T. Ayers, R. Scott, D. Wilken, and D. Young

1995 *A Flora of Santa Cruz Island.* Santa Barbara Natural History Museum, Santa Barbara, CA.

Kelly, R. L.

1995 *The Foraging Spectrum: Diversity in Hunter-Gatherer Lifeways.* Smithsonian Institution Press, Washington, DC.

Kennett, D. J.

2005 *The Island Chumash: Behavioral Ecology of a Maritime Society.* University of California Press, Berkeley.

King, C.

1990 *Evolution of Chumash Society: A Comparative Study of Artifacts Used for Social System Maintenance in the Santa Barbara Channel Region Before A.D. 1804.* Garland, New York.

Klug, L., and V. Popper

1993 *Archaeobotanical Analysis of Soil Samples from CA-SNI-351, San Nicolas Island, California.* Manuscript on file, Paleoethnobotany Laboratory, University of California, Los Angeles.

1995 *Macrobotanical Analysis of Soil Samples from CA-SNI-168, San Nicolas Island, California.* Manuscript on file, Paleoethnobotany Laboratory, University of California, Los Angeles.

1997 Macrobotanical Analysis of Nine Soil Samples from San Clemente Island, California. In *Archaeological Site Significance Evaluation Report of Nine Sites on San Clemente Island, California,* edited by C. Doolittle, D. Grenda, and R. Ciolek-Torrello. Technical report submitted to Southwest Division Naval Facilities Engineering Command. Statistical Research Inc., Tucson, AZ.

Kroeber, A. L.

1925 *Handbook of the Indians of California.* Bureau of American Ethnology Bulletin 78. Washington, DC: Smithsonian Institution.

Madden, S. A.

2000 Analysis of Features at the Ledge Site. *Pacific Coast Archaeological Society Quarterly* 36(4): 8–13.

Martin, L.

2010 Reconstructing Paleoenvironmental Instability and Plant Resource Availability on Santa Cruz Island Using Macrobotanical Analysis. M.A. thesis. Department of Anthropology, University of California, Los Angeles.

Martin, S. L., and V. S. Popper

1999 *Macrobotanical Analysis of Flotation Light Fractions from CA-SCRI-109 and -427, Santa Cruz Island, Santa Barbara County, California.* Technical report submitted to Michael Glassow, Department of Anthropology, University of California, Santa Barbara.

2001 The Chumash in World and Regional Perspectives. In *The Origins of a Pacific Coast Chiefdom: The Chumash of the Channel Islands,* edited by J. E. Arnold, pp. 1–19. University of Utah Press, Salt Lake City.

McNulty, A.

2000 The Seed Caches at Ledge, San Clemente Island. *Pacific Coast Archaeological Society Quarterly* 36(4):59–65.

Mead, G. R.

2003 *The Ethnobotany of the California Indians.* E-Cat Worlds, Le Grande, OR.

Meighan, C.

1954 Personal communication with A. McNulty. In The Seed Caches at Ledge, San Clemente Island. *Pacific Coast Archaeological Society Quarterly* 36(4):59–65.

2000 The Old Air Field Site, San Clemente Island. *Pacific Coast Archaeological Society Quarterly* 36(4):69–79.

Molitor, M.

2000 Perforated Stones from the Ledge Site. *Pacific Coast Archaeological Society Quarterly* 36(2): 53–59.

Moody, A.

2000 Analysis of Plant Species Diversity with Respect to Island Characteristics on the Channel Islands, California. *Journal of Biogeography* 27(3):711–723.

Moratto, M.

1984 *California Archaeology.* Academic Press, New York.

2002 Culture History of the New Melones Reservoir Area, Calaveras and Tuolumne Counties, California. In *Essays in California Archaeology: A Memorial to Franklin Fenenga,* edited by W. J. Wallace and F. A. Riddell, pp. 25–54. Contributions of the University of California Archaeological Research Facility No. 60. Berkeley.

Norris, S. E.

1997 Early Holocene Cordage and Perishable Arti-facts from the Daisy Cave Site (CA-SMI-261), San Miguel Island, California. M.A. thesis. Department of Anthropology, University of Oregon, Eugene.

O'Connell, J. F., and K. Hawkes

1981 Alyawara Plant Use and Optimal Foraging Theory. In *Hunter-Gatherer Foraging Strat-egies*, edited by B. Winterhalder and E. A. Smith, pp. 99–125. University of Chicago Press, Chicago.

Orr, P.

1968 *Prehistory of Santa Rosa Island*. Santa Bar-bara Museum of Natural History, Santa Bar-bara, CA.

Pearsall, D. M.

1989 *Paleoethnobotany: A Handbook of Procedures.* Academic Press, San Diego.

Perry, J. E.

2003 Changes in Prehistoric Land and Resource Use Among Complex Hunter-Gatherer-Fishers on Eastern Santa Cruz Island. PhD dissertation. Department of Anthropology, University of California, Santa Barbara.

Perry, J. E., and C. Delaney-Rivera

2011 Interactions and Interiors of the Coastal Chumash: Perspectives from Santa Cruz Island and the Oxnard Plain. *California Ar-chaeology* 3(1):103–125.

Philbrick, R. N., and J. R. Haller

1977 The Southern California Islands. *Terrestrial Vegetation of California*, edited by M. G. Bar-bour and J. Major, pp. 893–906. Wiley, New York.

Popper, V. S.

2003 *Macrobotanical Analysis of Soil Samples and Charcoal from CA-SCRI-393, Santa Cruz Is-land, California.* Technical report submitted to Channel Islands National Park.

Raab, L. M., J. Cassidy, A. Yatsko, and W. Howard

2009 *California Maritime Archaeology: A San Clemente Island Perspective*. Altamira, Lan-ham, MD.

Raab, L. M., A. Yatsko, T. S. Garlinghouse, J. F. Porcasi, and K. Bradford

2002 Late Holocene San Clemente Island: Notes on Comparative Social Complexity in Coastal Southern California. In *Catalysts to Complex-ity: Late Holocene Archaeology of the Califor-nia Coast*, edited by J. M. Erlandson and T. L. Jones, pp. 13–26. Perspectives in California Archaeology. Cotsen Institute of Archaeol-ogy, University of California, Los Angeles.

Reddy, S.

2000a Paleoethnobotanical Study of Carbonized Plant Remains from SCLI-1239, SCLI-1249, and PL-100. *Archaeological Testing of Three Sites along the LVT Road, North-Central San Clemente Island, California*, edited by B. F. Byrd. Technical report on file, Natural Re-source Office, Naval Region SW, Naval Air Station, North Island, San Diego, CA.

2000b Paleoethnobotany on San Clemente Island: Plant Remains from SCLI-154, LVTA-9, and LVTA/SE46. *Archaeological Testing of Four Sites Near West Cove, Northern San Clemente Island, California*, edited by B. F. Byrd. Tech-nical report on file, Natural Resource Office, Naval Region SW, Naval Air Station, North Island, San Diego, CA.

2002 Prehistoric Usage and Natural Fires: Eluci-dating Plant Usage at Five Sites in the Old Airfield, San Clemente Island, California. In *Archaeological Testing of Five Sites in the Old Airfield Area, North-Central San Clemente Is-land, California*, edited by Brian F. Byrd and Sherri Andrews, pp. 133–150. Technical re-port on file, Natural Resource Office, Naval Region SW, Naval Air Station, North Island, San Diego, CA.

2003 Prehistoric Plant Usage at Four Highland Sites in the Vicinity of Lemon Tank on San Clemente Island, California. *Archaeological Testing of Four Sites in the Lemon Tank Area, Central San Clemente Island, California*, edited by B. F. Byrd and S. Andrews. Tech-nical report on file, Natural Resource Office, Naval Region SW, Naval Air Station, North Island, San Diego, CA.

Reddy, S., and J. M. Erlandson

2012 Macrobotanical Food Remains from a Trans-Holocene Sequence at Daisy Cave (CA-SMI-261), San Miguel Island, California. *Journal of Archaeological Science* 39(1):33–40.

Reinman, F., and H. Eberhart

1980 Test Excavations at the Ripper's Cove Site (SCAI-26). *Pacific Coast Archaeological Soci-ety Quarterly* 16(1):61–105.

Rick, T. C.

2007 *The Archaeology and Historical Ecology of Late Holocene San Miguel Island*. Perspectives in California Archaeology Vol. 8. Cotsen In-stitute of Archaeology, University of Califor-nia, Los Angeles.

Rick, T. C., and J. M. Erlandson

2001 Late Holocene Subsistence Strategies on the South Coast of Santa Barbara Island, California. *Journal of California and Great Basin Anthropology* 23(2):297–308.

Rick, T. C., J. M. Erlandson, R. L. Vellanoweth, and T. J. Braje
2005 From Pleistocene Mariners to Complex Hunter-Gatherers: The Archaeology of the California Channel Islands. *Journal of World Prehistory* 19:169–228.

Rosenthal, E. J., S. L. Williams, M. Roeder, W. Bonner, and I. Strudwick
1988 The Bulrush Canyon Project: Excavations at Bulrush Canyon Site (SCAI-137) and Camp Cactus Road Site, Santa Catalina Island. *Pacific Coast Archaeological Society Quarterly* 24(2–3):1–104.

Rozaire, C.
1978 *Archaeological Investigations on Santa Barbara Island, California*. Report on file, Central Coast Information Center, University of California, Santa Barbara.
1983 Mortar and Pestle Manufacturing on San Miguel Island, California. *The Masterkey* 57(4): 131–143.
1989 Woven Materials in the Murphy Collection. In *A Step Into The Past: Island Dwellers of Southern California*, curated by J. Smull and T. Cox, pp. 21–24. Museum of Anthropology, California State University, Fullerton.

Salls, R. A.
1989a Marine Adaptation of the California Islands as Viewed from a Prehistoric "Tackle Box." In *A Step Into The Past: Island Dwellers of Southern California*, curated by J. Smull and T. Cox, p. 16. Museum of Anthropology, California State University, Fullerton.
1989b To Catch a Fish: Some Limitations on Prehistoric Fishing in Southern California, with Special Reference to Native Plant Fiber Fishing Line. *Journal of Ethnobiology* 9(2):173–206.

Salls, R. A., and A. Hale
2000 Messenger to the Great Spirit: The *Panes* Ceremony on San Clemente Island. *Pacific Coast Archaeological Society Quarterly* 36(4): 95–101.

Sharp, J. T.
2000 *Shellfish Analysis from the Punta Arena Site, a Middle Holocene Red Abalone Midden on Santa Cruz Island, California*. MA thesis. Sonoma State University. Coyote Press, Salinas, CA.

Simms, S.
1987 *Behavioral Ecology and Hunter-Gatherer Foraging: An Example from the Great Basin*. BAR International Series 381. Oxford.

South Central Coastal Information Center
2011 Information Accessed on October 5, 2011. Department of Anthropology, California State University, Fullerton.

Sutton, E. A.
2010 An Analysis of Perforated Stones from the Santa Barbara Channel Region. Manuscript on file, Department of Anthropology, University of California, Santa Barbara.

Thomas, L. D.
1995 Archaeobotanical Research on San Nicolas Island: Current Directions. *Pacific Coast Archaeological Society Quarterly* 31(4):23–32.

Thomas-Barnett, L.
2004 A Sandstone Bowl Quarry Site on San Nicolas Island, California. MA thesis. Department of Anthropology, California State University, Los Angeles.

Timbrook, J.
1993 Island Chumash Ethnobotany. In *Archaeology on the Northern Channel Islands of California: Studies of Subsistence, Economics and Social Organization*, edited by M. A. Glassow, pp. 47–62. Archives of California Prehistory 34. Coyote Press, Salinas, CA.
2007 *Chumash Ethnobotany: Plant Knowledge Among the Chumash People of Southern California*. Santa Barbara Museum of Natural History Monographs No. 5, Publications in Anthropology No. 1. Heyday Books, Berkeley.

Timbrook, J., J. R. Johnson, and D. D. Earle
1982 Vegetation Burning by the Chumash. *Journal of California and Great Basin Anthropology* 4:163–186.

VanDerwarker, A. M.
2010a Simple Measures for Integrating Plant and Animal Remains. In *Integrating Zooarchaeology and Paleoethnobotany: A Consideration of Issues, Methods, and Cases*, edited by A. M. VanDerwarker and T. M. Peres, pp. 65–74. Springer Science and Business Media, New York.
2010b Correspondence Analysis and Principal Components Analysis as Methods for Integrating Archaeological Plant and Animal Remains. In *Integrating Zooarchaeology and Paleoethnobotany: A Consideration of Issues, Methods, and Cases*, edited by A. M. VanDerwarker and T. M. Peres, pp. 65–74. Springer Science and Business Media, New York.

Vellanoweth, R. L., P. Martz, and S. Schwartz
2002 The Late Holocene Archaeology of San Nicolas Island. In *Catalysts to Complexity: Late*

Holocene Archaeology of the California Coast, edited by J. M. Erlandson and T. L. Jones, pp. 82–100. Perspectives in California Archaeology. Cotsen Institute of Archaeology, University of California, Los Angeles.

Walker, P. L., and P. E. Snethkamp
1984   Archaeological Investigations on San Miguel Island, 1982, Vol. 1: Prehistoric Adaptations to the Marine Environment. Manuscript on file, Central Coast Information Center, University of California, Santa Barbara.

Wallace, G. D.
1985   *Vascular Plants of the Channel Islands of Southern California and Guadalupe Island, Baja California, Mexico*. Contributions in Science No. 365. Natural History Museum of Los Angeles County, Los Angeles.

Wertman, F. L.
1959   Identified Plant Seeds from Big Dog Cave, San Clemente Island. In *Introduction to San Clemente Island Archaeology*, by M. B. McKusick and C. B. Warren. *Annual Reports of the Archaeological Survey* 1:160–183. University of California, Los Angeles.

Williams, S. L.
1992   Reconstruction of Aboriginal Fuel Wood Collecting Strategies on San Nicolas Island. Paper presented at the Society for California Archaeology annual meeting, Pasadena.

Copy on file, Naval Air Weapons Station, Point Mugu, CA.

Winterhalder, B., and C. Goland
1997   An Evolutionary Ecology Perspective on Diet Choice, Risk, and Plant Domestication. In *People, Plants and Landscapes: Studies in Paleoethnobotany*, edited by K. J. Gremillion, pp. 123–160. University of Alabama Press, Tuscaloosa.

Wohlgemuth, E.
1996   Resource Intensification in Prehistoric Central California: Evidence from Archaeobotanical Data. *Journal of California and Great Basin Anthropology* 18:81–103.
1997   Results of Preliminary Scan of Two Flotation Samples from CA-SCLI-847. Technical report submitted to Tom Garlinghouse, University of California, Davis.
2010   Plant Resource Structure and the Prehistory of Plant Use in Central Alta California. *California Archaeology* 2(1):57–76.

Yatsko, A.
2000   Late Holocene Paleoclimatic Stress and Prehistoric Human Occupation on San Clemente Island. PhD dissertation. University of California, Los Angeles.

Young, J.
2000   Plant Seeds from the Nursery Site. *Pacific Coast Archaeological Society Quarterly* 36(3): 76–78.

8

The Archaeology of Ritual on the Channel Islands

Jennifer E. Perry

California's Channel Islands have yielded a rich body of archaeological data that are helping to answer questions about human colonization of the Americas, human-environment interactions, and the emergence of complex societies. Although archaeological evidence of ritual has also been documented on the islands for more than 100 years, ceremonial facets of island life have received comparatively less attention in the scholarly literature. Discussions have focused on unique sites, such as the Cave of the Whales on San Nicolas Island, and interesting features, such as animal burials, but there has yet to be a pan-island synthesis that incorporates different categories of evidence. In this chapter I discuss ethnographic, historic, and archaeological evidence relating to ritual throughout the Channel Islands. Archaeological correlates include portable items (such as shamanic regalia), shrines, rock art, animal effigies and burials, and ceremonial enclosures. In general, this evidence has been found on the larger islands where there were larger and more permanent habitations. There is no obvious evidence of ritual activity on Anacapa or Santa Barbara Islands, although that does not rule out the possibility that they were also important elements of the sacred landscapes and seascapes of the Channel Islands.

Ethnography of the Channel Islands

In historic times, the northern and southern islands were inhabited by the Chumash and Gabrielino (Tongva), respectively. The northern islands, from east to west, are Anacapa, Santa

Cruz, Santa Rosa, and San Miguel Islands; the southern islands include Santa Catalina, San Clemente, San Nicolas, and Santa Barbara Islands (Figure 8.1). The largest villages were on Santa Cruz, Santa Rosa, and Santa Catalina, the largest islands. Islanders began to relocate to missions on the mainland starting in late 1700s, with the last attempts at island life ending in the 1810s (Strudwick, Chapter 10). People from Santa Cruz Island went to Mission San Buenaventura and Mission Santa Barbara, whereas those from Catalina and San Clemente Islands went primarily to Mission San Gabriel (McLendon and Johnson 1999; Johnson and McLendon 2002). Spanish priests at these missions not only recorded the names of their island neophytes, but also their villages of birth and occupations (Johnson 2001). Mission records include descriptions of different social, economic, and ceremonial roles, such as shamans and dancers (Geiger and Meighan 1976). After mission secularization, Chumash and Tongva islanders returned to living in separate villages on the mainland and retained their distinct identities and practices through the late 1800s (Johnson and McLendon 2002:649).

Cosmologies, Symbols, and Rituals

A fundamental concept in native societies of California is that of power, which is manifested in a variety of objects, beings, and locations that may be accessed by individuals for purposes of both healing and harm (Bean 1976, 1992). Some places in the landscape have power because of their spatial proximity to supernatural realms. In

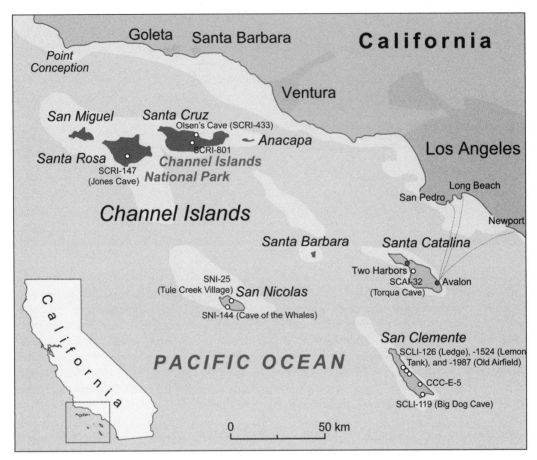

FIGURE 8.1. Channel Islands map showing major sites discussed in text (Lencer 2009, Creative Commons Attribution).

the three-tiered universe, native Californians occupy the middle realm, mountains are connected to the upper world, and both water and caves provide access to the lower world (Bean 1992; Hudson and Underhay 1978). Among the historic Chumash, the middle world was conceptualized as the 'antap plain of the mainland and all of the islands. West of the islands, beyond the horizon, is the Land of the Dead, where Chumash spirits were believed to reside (Hudson and Underhay 1978:40–41).

Evident in coastal societies throughout the Pacific Rim is an emphasis on the interface between land, sky, and sea. The sea and its inhabitants play important roles in Chumash and Tongva cosmologies; among the Chumash, the sea was a reality parallel to land, and every marine being had its terrestrial correlate (e.g., swordfish and humans)

(Blackburn 1975). Swordfish, dolphins, whales, and other sea creatures are recurring themes in mythologies and ceremonies (e.g., dances), as well as portable and permanent media (Blackburn 1975; Davenport et al. 1993; Hudson and Underhay 1978).

As Meighan (2000) emphasized, despite their differences in languages and origins, the Chumash and Tongva shared commonalities by virtue of occupying similar coastal environments in close proximity, and by their direct interactions. Specific to coastal groups is the emphasis placed on symbolism associated with the sea, including marine animals depicted in stories, rock art, and stone effigies. Also common to both societies, along with others in Southern California, was a ceremonial emphasis on birds, as is evident in the common use of regalia such as feathers, claws, and whistles made of bird bones (Corbett 2004). Consistent with other shamanistic societies, different animals such as birds were thought to be able to travel between different realms and therefore were used as messengers to the spirit world, which was the purpose of bird-killing ceremonies performed by the Tongva and other societies in Southern California (Boscana 1978).

Historically, Chumash and Tongva on the mainland and islands participated in two regional ritual organizations: the 'antap of the Chumash and the Chingichngish of the Tongva and other Takic-speaking neighbors (Kroeber 1976; McCawley 1996). Both societies were organized politically at the village level; aside from instances of intervillage alliances, these ritual organizations were the primary ways in which different villages were interconnected through ceremonial obligation (Blackburn 1974; Gamble 2008; Hudson and Underhay 1978). In villages located on the boundaries between Chumash and Tongva territories, it was common to participate in each other's ritual organizations and ceremonies (McCawley 1996).

'Antap

In historic times, there were members of the regional 'antap organization in each Chumash village (Bean and King 1974; Blackburn 1974; Hudson and Underhay 1978). "The Twenty" included "the Twelve," who were the major officials, and the *shan* (the other eight), who played lesser roles as assistants. 'Antap members, some of whom were shamans, were responsible for healing, rain making, predicting the future, making astronomical observances, and organizing feasts and ceremonies, such as those related to winter solstice ceremonies (Bean and King 1974; Hudson et al. 1977:50–63; Hudson and Underhay 1978:62). As in other societies, the Chumash regard the winter solstice as a critical time when the Sun, the giver of life and death, is farthest south. Different ceremonies to ensure the Sun's return, and thereby restore cosmic balance, were conducted in ceremonial enclosures (*siliyik*) in villages as well as at mountain shrines (Blackburn 1974:104; Hudson and Blackburn 1986:56–60, 84–90; Hudson et al. 1977). Central to these shrines is the construction, use, and destruction of feathered poles that represented the *axis mundalis*, the

connection between Earth and Sky, and associated offerings of seeds and beads (see summary in Perry 2007). Evidence of winter solstice ceremonies conducted on the northern Channel Islands includes references to 'antap members residing in the "Island Province," which included all of the northern Channel Islands (Hudson et al. 1977:17–18; Hudson and Underhay 1978:31; Johnson 2001).

Based on mission records from San Buenaventura and Santa Barbara, Johnson (2001) was able to identify particular social, economic, and ceremonial roles among villagers on Santa Cruz Island who later became incorporated into the mission system. He mentions the following ritual roles specifically: dancers, singers, those who "made offerings to the sea," those who had sweat lodges, those who administered *toloache* (*Datura wrightii*), one of "the Twenty," and shamans (Johnson 2001:61–62, Table 3.4). References to participants in the winter solstice and Xutash ceremonies, and 'antap members, illustrate the rich and complex ceremonial life that existed on the islands in historic times and earlier, for which there are specific archaeological correlates. Such ritual practices may have been continued on Santa Cruz Island until 1824, the time of the Chumash revolt, when people returned to the island temporarily (Hudson 1976); these ceremonies were continued on the mainland by descendants of the Island Chumash into the 1870s (Hudson and Underhay 1978:69).

Chingichngish

At the time of European contact, the Chingichngish ritual organization was spreading throughout Southern California among Takic speakers, including the Gabrielino (Tongva), Juaneño (Acagchemem), and Luiseño (Payomkowishum) (Boscana 1978; Moriarty 1969). Important similarities exist in Chingichngish practices cross-culturally and through time, as is evident in descriptions written by Spanish explorers and priests, including Vizcaino in 1602, Boscana in the early 1800s, and Harrington in the early 1900s (McCawley 1996:168). *Chingichngish* refers to the belief in a supreme deity who established rules of conduct and passed judgment on humans by helping the good and punishing evil doers. The deity retained animal spies and avengers, and possessed the ability to inflict harm ranging from minor injury to death (Harrington 1933; McCawley 1996:146).

According to different accounts, Chingichngish ceremonies were held annually around the time of winter solstice (Kroeber 1971; McCawley 1996). They included inducement of altered states of consciousness through singing, whistle or flute playing, dancing, sleep deprivation, and/or the ingestion of datura. The ceremony involved a series of mourning rituals that traditionally required property destruction, bird killing, and offerings. Some of these activities were conducted inside the *yovaar*, an unroofed sacred enclosure that was constructed from brush within Tongva villages (Bean and Smith 1978:542). Chingichngish is attributed with teaching the Tongva how to construct and use the *yovaar* (Boscana 1978). Based on the instructions from Chingichngish, the *yovaar* was restricted to the elites and/or ritual specialists, known as the Toovat, who had access to greater supernatural knowledge (McCawley 1996:28, 104, and 173). Those who did not have access were referred to as the Saorem, meaning "persons who do not know how to dance." The earliest written description of the *yovaar* was in 1602 at the large village at Isthmus Cove on Catalina Island by Father Antonio de la Ascensión, who was a member of the Vizcaino expedition (McCawley 1996:85).

One of the ceremonies conducted inside the *yovaar* was the annual eagle killing, or Panes, ceremony, which Father Boscana described in great detail, having served at Mission San Juan Capistrano from 1814 to 1826 and at Mission San Gabriel from 1826 until 1831 (Hanna 1933; McCawley 1996:7; Moriarty 1969). According to mission baptismal records, most of the Tongva from Catalina and San Clemente Islands went to Mission San Gabriel. Therefore, the ceremonies that Boscana described may have included mainland and island participants.

According to Boscana (1978), the eagle killing ceremony was performed inside the *yovaar*, and any kind of raptor, including red-tailed hawks, falcons, and ravens, could be used (Hale 1995). A bird was captured, ceremonial activities were performed, and then the participants "killed the bird without losing a single particle of blood" (Hanna 1933:37). During the rite, the birds were danced

with, talked to, and given messages to send to the dead. The bird was then killed by the participants applying pressure to its lungs. The skin was removed, the feathers were kept, and then the remains were placed in a prepared hole within the "temple." Boscana's description of the temple correlates with the *yovaar* as described by Kroeber (1971). It is traditionally believed that this mourning ritual was first conducted after the death of the deity Wiyot (also spelled "Wewyoot") (Bean and Smith 1978:544; Boscana 1978; McCawley 1996:93; Strong 1929:309). Among the Luiseño, it served as an annual memorial for chiefs (Kroeber 1976).

Datura and the Toloache

One of the shared characteristics of the 'antap and Chingichngish is the *toloache* ritual (Kroeber 1976). Datura was used in ceremonial contexts throughout Southern California, including for puberty rites and shamanic flight (McCawley 1996; Geiger and Meighan 1976:89), and it is one of the few plants to be thought of as a female supernatural being (Timbrook 2007). In particular, McCawley (1996:146) mentions a possible association between Maniishar, one of the lesser Chingichngish deities, and the psychoactive plant known as datura or jimsonweed. Ethnographic evidence suggests that the *toloache* ceremony originated on one of the southern Channel Islands, was dispersed to coastal mainland groups, and then spread into the interior of Southern California along networks between Takic-speaking groups. As Kroeber (1976:621–622) noted, "all southern accounts mention Santa Catalina and San Clemente Islands as the seat of the source of the cult."

Although evidence of ritual activities, such as burials, extends deep into prehistory, the majority of island research has focused on sites with Late and historic period components. Some of these sites have mission-related artifacts that may have been obtained directly or from family members from the very same missions at which Father Boscana and others were making their observations (see story recounted in Hudson 1979). Given these relationships, and those exemplified by informants such as Fernando Librado Kitsepawit, it is possible to make connections between written accounts and the archaeological

FIGURE 8.2. Steatite sucking tube in archaeological collections at the Fowler Museum, Los Angeles.

record on the Channel Islands. In fact, the very same individuals and/or their relatives could have been involved in some of the rituals described on the mainland and those evidenced materially on the islands.

Archaeological Correlates

Archaeological correlates of ritual have tended to be organized in terms of different categories of sites, features, and artifacts. On the Channel Islands, such categories include human burials and cemeteries, animal burials, and rock art. It is important to recognize, however, that some of these categories tend to overlap (see Ehringer 2003), such as animal burials associated with humans, and with other site functions, such as rock art in habitation sites. It is also important to note that ritual activities may necessarily occur off-site within less humanized spaces of a community's territory, such as mountaintop shrines. In addition, they may be conducted in the context of either permanent or temporary structures, such as ceremonial enclosures that were rebuilt, and it may involve the intentional destruction of material items, such as solstice poles and mourning caches. Archaeological evidence of ritual includes shamanic regalia, shrines and offerings, rock art, and animal burials. For brevity's sake, human internment is not discussed as its own category, but as a context for these other categories of ritual evidence.

Portable Items: The Shaman's Tool Kit

Among the Tongva, "island shamans were held in special awe" (McCawley 1996:95) for their supernatural strength. Archaeological evidence of their presence on the Channel Islands includes artifacts found in habitations, burials, and isolated contexts. Throughout native California, it was believed that power could be manifested in a wide variety of objects and could be used by a wide variety of people. Shamans and other ritual specialists, such as those conducting winter solstice ceremonies, had great abilities to harness this power by employing specific regalia. The shaman's tool kit includes bone whistles, quartz crystals (the Sun lived in a quartz crystal house, according to the Chumash), raptor claws, charm stones, stone pipes, and sucking tubes (Figure 8.2). Shamans and medicine men possessed different combinations of regalia that they used as personal amulets or talismans (Bean 1992; Hudson and Underhay 1978; Hudson and Blackburn 1986; McCawley 1996; Walker and Hudson 1993).

Shamanic regalia among the Chumash and Tongva included items used for purposes of healing, controlling the weather, ensuring safe travel, and predicting the future (Hudson and Underhay 1978; Hudson and Blackburn 1986; McCawley 1996; Walker and Hudson 1993). Charm stones, quartz crystals, and animal effigies are all referred to as having been used to induce rain (Hudson and Underhay 1978:34; Hudson and Blackburn 1986:154–158; Johnson 2000:306; Lee 1981, 1997; McCawley 1996:97). Chumash and Tongva informants also discussed how these items were worn as protective amulets when engaging in warfare, travel, or other dangerous activities (Hudson and Blackburn 1986:159). Charm stones were also used in healing and *toloache* ceremonies (Grant 1993:64; Hudson and Blackburn 1986:160; Walker and Hudson 1993). Portable ritual items such as these, as well as stone pipes, are described in detail in a thematic issue on the "Archaeology of San Clemente Island" in the *Pacific Coast Society Quarterly* (Cameron 2000; Meighan 2000; Wood 2000).

Regalia associated with shamans—including charm stones, plummet stones, and sucking tubes—have been found in habitation and burial contexts on the northern Channel Islands (see Figure 8.1; Olson 1930; Hollimon 1990; Hoover 1971; Orr 1968; Rogers 1929). In 1927–1928, Olson (1930) excavated two cemeteries at Smugglers' Cove on Santa Cruz Island associated with residential bases (SCRI-504 and SCRI-506) that are regarded as the historical village of Nanawani (Johnson 1988, 1993). Associated with the 69 burials were ritual items that included stone pipes, bone whistles, quartz crystals, an eagle claw, and red ochre (Hollimon 1990:145; Hoover 1971:199). Archaeological examples of bone whistles are made of deer and bird tibia (Corbett 2004) and are not unique to the northern islands. They have also been found in habitation and burial contexts on the southern islands in association with other shamanic regalia, such as at Big Dog Cave on San Clemente Island (Ehringer 2003:21) and on Catalina Island (Wendy Teeter, personal communication, 2011). Among the Tongva, it was believed that Chingichngish gave shamans the ability to influence nature through the power of song, which could be accomplished through the use of a whistle or flute (McCawley 1996:179–180).

Similarly, unmodified pebbles with iron concretions from the islands were regarded as magical stones. There has been some confusion about their particular origins, whether San Nicolas or Santa Barbara Island, although Timbrook (2002) has made a convincing case for San Nicolas Island. Regardless, their supernatural significance was widespread among the Tongva and Chumash, and known to mission priests. Referred to as *toshaawt* or *tosaut*, they were used for healing, rain making, and puberty rites (Hudson and Blackburn 1986:166–170; McCawley 1996:98; Merriam 1955:86; Timbrook 2002). Among coastal villages, they were connected directly to the creation of the world. Father Boscana documented the story of the deity Nocuma, who made the world by securing it with a *toshaawt* stone that was brought to him by a large fish or whale (Boscana 1978; Conti et al. 2002; Harrington 1978: 145–146; Timbrook 2002). These stones have been found at ceremonial sites on San Nicolas, such as Tule Creek Village (SNI-25), in association with animal burials, quartz crystals, and ochre (Vellanoweth et al. 2008:3113; see Guttenberg et al., Chapter 6, for a discussion of SNI-25).

Another category of portable items is the in-cised stone, discussed in detail by Lee (1997). As defined by Lee (1997:59), these stones are "made of mudstone, siltstone, or diatomaceous earth, they made be flat or rounded, and are further embellished with incising." Incised stones do not correlate with any particular time period and occur in a variety of contexts, including habitations, ceremonial complexes, and cemeteries (Hale 1995; Lee 1997). Incised stones and charm stones have also been found as isolates on the ground surface near the prominent Montañon Ridge on Santa Cruz Island (Perry 2003:267–269). Whereas most incised stones have geometric designs, those of the southern islands also include possible animal motifs (Lee 1981:40–45; McCawley 1996:99). Regardless, despite their prevalence and general association with shamanism, their specific functions continue to be unclear; however, Lee (1997:59) suggests that their intentional destruction may have been part of mourning ceremonies.

On the opposite end of the representational spectrum are animal effigies made of stone, primarily locally occurring steatite. On the southern islands, bird and whale effigies were carved out of steatite from Catalina Island and circulated to San Clemente and San Nicolas Islands. The most common effigies are birds, specifically pelicans (Figure 8.3), and killer whales. In Lee's (1981) study of steatite effigies from Southern California, there was a relatively equal distribution of birds and whales at 110 and 102, respectively ($n = 212$). On San Clemente Island, they are dispersed throughout the landscape and have been found on the surfaces of sites with deflated middens and few other artifacts. In particular, pelicans and cormorants were regarded as "crewmen" for boat captains, providing supernatural support for safe travel (Blackburn 1975:175; Lee 1997:27), which may shed insight into their prevalence on remote islands such as San Clemente.

Shrines

In addition to ritual portable items, certain places held spiritual significance, including those related to cardinal directions, mountains, and freshwater sources (Bean 1976; Hudson and Underhay 1978). For example, the highest point on Santa Cruz Island is today referred to as Mount Diablo, or Devil's Peak, and is regarded as the origin of

FIGURE 8.3. Steatite pelican effigy in archaeological collections at the Fowler Museum, Los Angeles.

the Rainbow Bridge that allowed people to travel to the mainland in mythical times. Some sacred locales were marked with the construction and use of shrines. The characteristics and functions of shrines are described in detail in the historical and ethnographic literature (Hudson et al. 1977; Hudson and Blackburn 1986; Hudson and Underhay 1978; Perry 2007). Specifically, descriptions exist of shrines on the mainland that were constructed and used by important individuals who had relocated from Santa Cruz Island, including members of the 'antap (Hudson et al. 1977; Hudson and Blackburn 1986; McLendon and Johnson 1999:144).

The landscape of Santa Cruz Island, the largest and most topographically varied of the Channel Islands, is defined by rugged ridgelines that bound a central valley. The highest peak on the Channel Islands is Mount Diablo at 750 m in elevation on the North Ridge. The eastern end of the island is defined by the Montañon Ridge, which tops out at 550 m in elevation. I have proposed elsewhere that rock features intentionally constructed along these prominent ridgelines

are remnants of shrines (Figure 8.4; Perry 2003, 2007). Twenty rock features of similar sizes and in similar locales have been found on both ridges, and these could have been used to anchor the feathered wooden poles (Perry 2007:104). On El Montañon, associated evidence includes the presence of dark carbonaceous soil and large chunks of charcoal. Given the absence of fish and shellfish fragments, it is possible that the dark soil includes remnant of plants that served as offerings. Furthermore, burnt wood is one of the expected archaeological correlates of winter solstice shrines, given the intentional construction and destruction of the wooden poles each year (Hudson et al. 1977; Hudson and Underhay 1978: 67–69; Hudson and Blackburn 1986:84–90, 93–98; Perry 2007:107). Another reference to a possible shrine on Santa Cruz Island is a cluster of glass trade beads found on Mount Pleasant, another prominent point on the landscape (Glassow 2010:6.43–6.44). Taken together, these lines of evidence indicate how ritual activities may have been embedded within the supernatural properties of the local environment, and how these

FIGURE 8.4. Rock feature on Santa Cruz Island interpreted as a possible shrine (Feature F at CA-SCRI-406) (photograph courtesy of Sam Spaulding).

traditions were subsequently continued on the mainland by people who retained distinct island identities.

Rock Art

Other sacred places on island landscapes were marked with rock art. Limited rock art research has been conducted on the Channel Islands since the early 1900s, in part because little evidence has been found since then. Reasons for this include the lack of suitable geologic material, erosion that has occurred since historic times, limited survey in island interiors (Perry 2007), and the impact of military operations that restrict access (Andy Yatsko, personal communication, 2011). Rock art has been found on all of the larger islands, but none of the smaller islands (i.e., San Miguel, Anacapa, and Santa Barbara Islands; see Lee and Clewlow 1979). The most common symbols depicted in petroglyph and pictograph form include geometric designs, cupules or pitted grooves, and the widely distributed "aquatic motif" in the form of fish and sea mammals (Hudson and Conti 1981; Knight 2001; Meighan 2000).

The best examples of petroglyphs are etched into sandstone on Santa Rosa and San Nicolas Islands, whereas the best examples of red ochre pictographs are on Catalina and San Clemente Islands (Andrews 2009; Conti et al. 2002; Jones 1956; Knight 2001; Quist 1978). In contrast, there is only one recorded site on Santa Cruz Island with definitive rock art, Olsen's Cave (SCRI-433) on the northern shore (Glassow 2010:6.24–6.26; Knight 2001; Steward 1929). Olsen described the presence of pictographs of red ochre as including smears, crosses, and rakes, which are similar to the shapes depicted in petroglyphs at Jones' Cave on Santa Rosa Island. John Johnson (personal communication, 2012) has noted that the weathered pictographs at Olsen's Cave are not as elaborate as those on the mainland. Both rock art sites are associated with dense shell middens indicative of long-term habitation.

On Santa Rosa Island, the only documented example of rock art is located in Jolla Vieja Canyon, in the island's interior. First documented by Jones (1956) in 1901, the trans-Holocene site of SRI-147, or Jones' Cave, is a large, multicomponent site situated near reliable freshwater. It consists of five rockshelters, dense shell middens

FIGURE 8.5. Cave of the Whales (CA-SNI-144) on San Nicolas Island (photograph courtesy of Lisa Thomas).

exposed in the stream terrace, one bedrock mortar, and petroglyphs (Braje et al. 2007; Kennett 2005). In the sandstone alcoves above the thick layers of human occupation is limited evidence of rock art consisting of grooved cupules, lines, and rakes (Jones 1956). The only other known example of rock art on Santa Rosa Island is a cluster of undocumented geometric motifs, including zigzag lines, inscribed in eroding sandstone along the beach (Sam Spaulding, personal communication, 2008).

The most famous example of island rock art is the Cave of the Whales (SNI-144) (Figure 8.5), which is the only known rock art site on San Nicolas Island despite intensive survey (Conti et al. 2002; Meighan 2000). Rozaire and Kritzman (1960) provided the most thorough description of the petroglyphs prior to their erosion. The most noticeable motifs are fish cut or grooved into the sandstone, which are thought to be killer whales, dolphins, or porpoises (Meighan 2000:21). In total, there are 32 aquatic or fish motifs, 3 double zigzags, and 7 lines (Conti et al. 2002:669). In addition, there is an iron concretion, or *toshaawt*, embedded below one of the rock art panels, which further supports interpretations of the cave being a sacred place (Conti et al. 2002:674).

Fish or aquatic motifs are also portrayed in rock art on San Clemente Island. Pictographs of red ochre have been found at the south end of the island but cannot be evaluated further because of military operations (Conti et al. 2002; Andy Yatsko, personal communication, 2011). Most recently, Andrews (2009) recorded a rockshelter, site CCC-E-5, in which three fish elements were painted in red ochre. Similar elements were found at SCLI-1724 (McCarthy 1980), but some researchers have disputed their authenticity (Meighan 2000:26). Regardless, these are comparable to the elements depicted at Cave of the Whales and, despite the difference in medium, suggest artistic similarities throughout the southern islands.

On Catalina Island, Torqua Cave (SCAI-32), or "Holder's Cove," also contains elaborate rock art with at least 25 red ochre pictographs, including anthropomorphs and a sun symbol (Knight 2001; Meighan 2000). Similar to Jones' Cave on Santa Rosa Island, Torqua Cave is situated in the island's interior and is associated with thick shell midden deposits (Wendy Teeter, personal communication, 2011). Other rock art on Catalina includes unrecorded pictographs as well as cupules at several locales (SCAI-92, SCAI-94,

SCAI-104, SCAI-120, and SCAI-127), and these are also found on the other islands. As discussed in Meighan (2000:17), "it is reasonably well documented that cupule rocks are places of supplication for some desired event, the pits being made an accompaniment to individual prayers."

Places such as Cave of the Whales and Torqua Cave stand out among the rock art on the Channel Islands because of the quantity, diversity, and symbolic nature of their images; however, when combined with other lines of evidence, other sites appear to be equally significant based on the duration of occupation, artifact diversity, and other features, such as at Jones' Cave (SRI-147) on Santa Rosa Island. Furthermore, other sites have no rock art but substantial evidence of other ritual activities. They arguably played important, yet different, roles in the ceremonialism and sacred geography of the islanders.

Animal Burials

Animal burials have been found on the Channel Islands and adjacent mainland within the traditional territories of the Chumash, Tongva, Luiseño, and Kumeyaay (Collins 1991; Hale 1995; Hale and Salls 2000). Animal motifs, however—in rock art, animal effigies, and animal burials—appear to be more common on the southern islands (Cameron 2000; Meighan 2000; Vellanoweth et al. 2008). Dogs, foxes, and birds are the most common animals depicted, and they tend to co-occur in different combinations. Three types of animal burials are encountered: (1) animal burials resulting from economic activities, (2) animal skeletons associated with human burials, and (3) animal remains associated with other ceremonial activities. On the mainland, one of the largest collections of animal burials was found during the excavation of the Encino Village site (LAN-43) in Los Angeles County (Langenwalter 1986). Eighteen animal skeletons were recovered, including a red-tailed hawk, a fox cremation in an abalone shell, and 11 dog burials in association with human remains.

Dog burials are present on six of the eight Channel Islands, although they are seemingly more common on the southern islands. A total of 95 dogs have been recovered from 41 archaeological sites: 40 from the northern islands and 55 from the southern islands, of which 29 are from San Nicolas Island (Vellanoweth et al. 2008:3119). The concentration of dog burials on San Nicolas Island may indicate that dogs served a variety of roles. It appears that while some of these dogs were put to work and may have served largely economic functions, others were treated with ritual significance. In particular, Vellanoweth et al. (2008) discuss the excavation of a double dog burial at Tule Creek Village (SNI-25), a site that was occupied for about 4,000 years and used intensively during the Late period. The dogs are carefully oriented near "prepared ochre; morning glory and wild cucumber (*Marah macrocarpus*) seeds; iron concentrations known as *toshaawt* stones; calcite crystals; and other reliquary" (Vellanoweth et al. 2008:3113).

Dogs, foxes, and other material elements of these rituals were imported from other places, requiring interactions with other communities. Interestingly, foxes originated on the northern islands and were subsequently transported to the southern islands around 5,000 years ago, although the reasons for doing so are unclear. Tentative evidence of the economic importance of foxes comes from San Nicolas Island. Twenty partial and complete fox skeletons were recovered from SNI-7 in close proximity to one another. Butcher marks on some of the skeletons possibly indicate that the foxes were skinned for pelts (Collins 1991). At least three complete fox skeletons were identified at Eel Point (SCLI-43) and one at the Nursery site (SCLI-1215) on San Clemente Island. On the northern islands, fox remains, including single or multiple crania, are associated with human burials at several sites (i.e., SRI-1, SRI-2A, SRI-41, and SRI-131) on Santa Cruz and Santa Rosa Islands.

Animal burials within a ritual context have also been found at Big Dog Cave (SCLI-119), Lemon Tank (SCLI-1524), and Ledge (SCLI-126) on San Clemente Island. In 1939, excavations at Big Dog Cave yielded ceremonial bundles, canoe planks, mission cloth, and animal interments (Hale and Salls 2000; Salls 1990). One bundle consisted of a Spanish chicken and another contained a "big dog" wrapped in a sea otter robe, sea grass, and mission cloth. In total, five humans, two birds, and one dog were interred (Ehringer 2003:16). As described in Raab et al. (2009:209), "the burial of mission-era cloth, the wooden canoe effigy, wheat seeds, and other objects at Big Dog Cave (Coleman and Wise 1994) also has parallels in the features at Lemon Tank in the form of basketry, cordage, steatite (soapstone effigies), fishhooks, and a seed cache containing the deciduous teeth of children" (Eisentraut 1990). As suggested by Ehringer (2003:17), another similarity relates to the bird burials; it is possible that chickens at Big Dog Cave and Ledge were substitutes for raptors, given that they were wrapped in mission cloth in association with seeds and abalone shells.

In 1988 and 1989, 136 pit features were identified during the excavation of the Lemon Tank site located on the high plateau of San Clemente Island facing Catalina Island (Raab et al. 2009:204). Ritual elements include a smashed turtle rattle, one stone pipe, seed caches, and 19 animal burials, most of them located within or near an area identified as a ceremonial structure. Based on the configuration of 25 excavated postholes, it appears that the structure was repeatedly constructed within a specific location and remained relatively consistent in size, about 4 m long and 3 m wide. Hale (1995) describes how this correlates to the *yovaar* enclosure described by Kroeber (1976) as being used for mourning rituals. A total of six foxes, eight raptors, and five dogs were ceremonially interred at the Lemon Tank site. Most of the raptors were buried inside the enclosure, whereas most of the foxes were buried outside.

Of the two dogs found outside, one was buried in quarters with a chalcedony knife blade fragment located next to cut marks on the sacrum (Hale 1995). An adult dog within the structure was also buried in quarters. The dog was decapitated, the ribs were ochre-stained, and the femur shafts were absent. Associated artifacts included shell beads, abalone shells, and a seed cache. One of the central features within the structure was another adult dog burial that was capped with a rock on which there were beads, basket trays, an asphaltum-covered water bottle, and at least two seed caches. Within the burial were a chert biface in the abdominal cavity, a white quartz crystal, basketry, lithics, and a seed cache. Next to the dog's hind paws was a bird. Given the spatial association with what are interpreted as offerings, shamanic regalia, and a ceremonial enclosure, it seems reasonable to interpret these particu-

lar dogs as having had ritual significance in life or death, unlike some of the dogs on San Nicolas Island.

Collectively, Big Dog Cave (SCLI-119), Lemon Tank (SCLI-1524), Ledge (SCLI-126), and Old Airfield (SCLI-1987) were all occupied into historic times based on the presence of mission artifacts and corroborating radiocarbon dates (Ehringer 2003; Raab et al. 2009), and they share the same kinds of material culture associated with Tongva ceremonies. At the Ledge site, 1 km south of Lemon Tank, 40 pit features have yielded more than 1,000 steatite plaques and a Catholic medal. About 1 km north of Lemon Tank is the Old Airfield site, with 22 pit features containing artifact offerings that were ritually burned or broken (Eisentraut 1990). All four sites have evidence of the ceremonial destruction of property, small offerings including seed caches, and human burials, and three have animal burials (Ehringer 2003:27).

Based on ethnographic and archaeological evidence, it has been posited that these sites represent aspects of the Chingichngish religion, specifically mourning ceremonies (Hale 1995; Raab et al. 2009). The birds at Lemon Tank were redtail hawks, peregrine falcons, and a raven, which strongly correlate with descriptions of bird interment during the Panes and Chingichngish ceremonies (Boscana 1978; Hale 1995). It is also possible that the fox burials were ritual sacrifices associated with property or image-burning rites. Destroying images and items of the deceased was an important element of the Chingichngish ceremony. Given the similarities in their ceremonial structures, artifacts, and chronologies, as well as their geographic proximity, Lemon Tank, Ledge, and Old Airfield may have been part of the same ceremonial complex, one that may have been interconnected with people and Chingichngish practices on other islands.

Ceremonial Complexes and Feasting

Sites such as those on San Clemente Island are one example of what may be interpreted as a ceremonial complex that incorporated different aspects of the physical environment. Important facets of the public ceremonies were feasting events held for large groups of people. Interestingly, some of these site complexes have been found in island interiors, despite the strong coastal orientation of historic villages. For example, in the Central Valley of Santa Cruz Island is an interior shell midden (SCRI-801) with a possible feasting feature (Perry and Delaney-Rivera 2011) that may be associated with other midden components and structures in the vicinity (SCRI-324 and SCRI-384) (Sutton 2009). The remains of animals of great social and supernatural importance to the Chumash were present in the ashy lens excavated at SCRI-801, including dolphin bones and fragments of a swordfish bill, along with shell beads (Perry and Delaney-Rivera 2011:119).

What sites such as SCRI-801 and Lemon Tank have in common is being situated in flat and open environments where larger groups of people could assemble to dance, feast, and perform other rituals. Distinctions were made between sacred and secular, such as inside and outside ceremonial enclosures, as well as what was situated "off-site," or in the spaces between and beyond habitation. Not all ceremonies took place within the confines of the village; rather, sacred places were present inside and outside of the sphere of daily activities and could be constructed or natural (see Bradley 2000). These places were embedded within the broader landscapes and seascapes of the Channel Islands that informed the identities and relationships of island residents.

Sacred Landscapes and Seascapes

Meighan (2000) proposed that the islanders, both Chumash and Tongva, had more in common with one another than with their mainland relatives by virtue of the inhabited environment and their lived experiences. Such similarities are evident in the oceanic details of their cosmologies and the emphasis on "portable rock art," among other characteristics (Lee 1981, 1997; Perry 2007). In fact, distinct island identities were perpetuated on the mainland as evidenced by the establishment of communities of islanders after mission secularization and the perpetuation of island subsistence and ritual practices (McLendon and Johnson 1999; Johnson and McLendon 2002). Despite geographic displacement and missionization, island ancestry informed patterns of residence well into the 1800s and continues to influence identity today.

Island Commonalities

Although the archaeology of ritual may be interpreted through a variety of theoretical lenses, these linkages to place may be approached through landscape archaeology (see Perry and Delaney-Rivera 2011; Robinson et al. 2011). Relevant concepts include "seascapes" (Cooney 2003; McNiven 2003), "taskscapes" (Ingold 1993); "places" and "routes" (Tilley 1994, 2008); and "landscapes of movement" (Snead et al. 2009). In McNiven's (2003:332) discussion of seascapes, he emphasizes that they "are defined by cosmologies that frame and constrain perception, engagement and use of seas. Seascapes are animated spiritscapes." Among the "tasks" conducted by islanders were ceremonial ones associated with the supernatural power of particular places, such as mourning rituals in the Tongva *yovaar* and Chumash winter solstice ceremonies at shrines. Such activities required the movement of individuals between places using different modes of transportation and routes that crossed different landscapes and seascapes.

Ritual activities referenced sacred points on the islands and mainland, including boundaries between and portals to different realms. Rockshelters such as Jones' Cave on Santa Rosa, Cave of the Whales on San Nicolas, Big Dog Cave on San Clemente, and Torqua Cave on Catalina Island were significant sacred places because of their unique properties as caves, which are regarded as portals to the supernatural realm among indigenous societies throughout the world. Conti et al. (2002:673) discuss this in the context of the rock art at the Cave of the Whales: "the visual effect of marine mammals 'swimming' on the rock surface may be another indication of crossing the boundary between water and land." Movement was manifested in the form of spirit helpers who travel between realms, such as dolphins and killer whales between sea and sky, dogs and foxes that can dig and burrow into the ground, and birds that interact with land, sky, and sea. Significantly, the depictions of fish or whales above the *toshaawt* stone at the Cave of the Whales on the San Nicolas Island suggest a direct connection to Nocuma's creation of the world (Conti et al. 2002). Ceremonies were also associated with physical movement, ranging from dances to processions outside of the *yovaar* and *siliyik* (Blackburn 1974; McCawley 1996) to those between shrines positioned along ridgelines (Hudson and Underhay 1978; Perry 2007).

In addition, public ceremonies, such as the mourning rites of Chingichngish, required the invitation and assembly of larger groups of people, some of whom traveled from other islands and the mainland. One example of this is a letter written in 1805 regarding Chumash feasts on Santa Cruz Island that involved an estimated 1,800 people, which exceeds population estimates for the island. Some of these feasts may have taken place in the interior of the island based on archaeological evidence at SCRI-324, SCRI-384, and SCRI-801 (Johnson 1982:61-62; Perry and Delaney-Rivera 2011:119; Sutton 2009). Minimally, this would have involved walking, and for some people, it entailed making boat trips that presented tangible risks and symbolic transitions between land and sea.

Some of the "portable rock art" found on the Channel Islands, such as animal effigies, were talismans that protected shamans against the dangers of travel, whether in the realms of supernatural or ordinary reality. They facilitated movement, and to obtain them required traveling along pathways through seascapes and "landscapes of transportation" (Snead et al. 2009:3). The shaman's tool kit (e.g., whistles, magical stones, quartz crystals, stone pipes, and animal effigies) necessitated access to different local and imported resources. Several of these items were made of stone and therefore were obtained from particular geologic contexts. Boat trips to places such as San Nicolas Island to obtain magical stones could have been conceptualized as journeys with supernatural significance, and/or the stones themselves could be markers of successful trips. As Conti et al. (2002:672) discussed with respect to traveling to San Nicolas Island, "To the extent that a successful trip represented a victory over the threat of death, items returned from the island were also likely to be imbued with power. For the canoeist, one could travel no further towards the horizon and survive to return to the mainland."

Furthermore, intervisibility between different features of landscapes and seascapes would have been important for navigation within the ordinary and supernatural realms (see Phillips 2003). Along the main boat route from the mainland to Santa Cruz Island (Hudson et al. 1978), Anacapa Island is one example of this, as suggested by its Chumash names (Applegate 1975). The original Chumash word for Anacapa (Anyapakh) has been translated as "mirage or illusion," which refers to its ever-changing appearance that informs boaters of weather conditions (Perry and Delaney-Rivera 2011:111). However, islanders also referred to it as "big, high like a peak." That it may have been regarded as a sacred mountain is suggested by the possible presence of a shrine at San Pedro Point, the easternmost point of Santa Cruz Island, which was referred to as "it points toward the big, high peak" of Anacapa Island (Perry and Delaney-Rivera 2011:120). Another example is found on San Clemente Island. Most of the possible Chingichngish sites are situated in proximity to one another on the island's high plateau overlooking the steep slopes and narrow beaches below. Comparatively speaking, this area does not provide the most convenient access to the coast or other subsistence resources. However, the viewshed of Catalina Island, 52 km to the northeast, is significant, and would have afforded a visual link between people who were interrelated through marriage and interconnected through ritual and trade. Furthermore, except for San Miguel Island, all of the Channel Islands are visible from Santa Barbara Island, including San Nicolas Island at the western edge of the 'antap plain.

Island Differences and Cultural Change

It would be misleading to emphasize pan-island similarities at the exclusion of discussing contrasts in the evidence of ritual on the northern and southern islands. Such differences may relate to differences in Chumash and Tongva belief systems, as well as the unique physical characteristics of each Channel Island. When considering all of the archaeological evidence together, several important differences stand out. The first relates to animal burials; although animal burials occur on the northern islands, it appears to have been a more common practice within Tongva territory on the southern islands and adjacent mainland.

The second relates to the motifs depicted in rock art, which may be an artifact of the limited evidence and its limited study. Animal symbolism, specifically aquatic motifs, is found throughout Tongva and Chumash territory in the form of rock art and effigies; however, animals and anthropomorphs are seemingly absent from the rock art of the northern islands, which consists primarily of geometric or abstract elements. This pattern holds regardless of whether they are pictographs or petroglyphs, which requires thinking about the idea that the specific medium may not have been as important as the locational context (e.g., rockshelter) and the symbolism being depicted.

Another locus of difference relates to responses to climatic events such as drought and cultural ones such as European contact. Droughts are a recurring phenomenon in Southern California and are of as much concern today as they were in the past. One of the major functions of shamanic regalia was to induce rain (Hudson and Blackburn 1986; Hudson and Underhay 1978), and one of the purposes of Chumash winter solstice ceremonies was to predict drought based on the supernatural actions of the Sun (Johnson 2000). The effects of drought on human populations varied between and within island landscapes, as indicated by the bioarchaeological evidence (e.g., Walker 1996). Whereas smaller or more remote islands such as San Clemente may have been abandoned episodically (Yatsko 2000), the communities of other islands, such as Catalina, may have served as refuges for their displaced relatives. Larger islands such as Santa Cruz, with evidence of permanent habitation, may have continued to serve as important places for conducting activities such as winter solstice ceremonies.

Island communities experienced, interpreted, and responded in different ways to drought and other crises, including European contact. As emphasized in Raab et al. (2009:197–198), the Channel Islands were the first place in Alta California to be visited by Spanish explorers and one of the earliest points of contact in North America. More than 200 years before the first mission was established in this region, islanders and their mainland relatives were responding to the effects of European-introduced disease, population shifts, and significant cultural change. Several scholars have argued that Chingichngish and 'antap were revitalization movements, or crisis cults, that arose in response to these changing circumstances (Bean and Vane 1978; Hudson and Underhay 1978:72; Kroeber 1976). Chingichngish ceremonies may have been conducted on San Clemente Island during mission times because, as Raab et al. (2009:210) suggest, they would be away from the control of Spanish authorities.

From this perspective, the geographic positioning of the Channel Islands not only facilitated the entry of the Spanish into Alta California (Strudwick, Chapter 10), but also provided the literal and metaphorical ground for cultural transformation and survival. As mountains in the sea at the edge of the middle realm, the islands, their shamans, and their material resources (e.g., steatite sucking tubes and animal effigies) were sources of power (Teeter, Martinez, and Richardson, Chapter 9; Strudwick, Chapter 10). Although the particular expressions varied, these are significant ways in which social and supernatural relationships of native California were mapped onto the landscapes and seascapes of the Channel Islands. The worlds of islanders extended far beyond their particular islands of residence, the surface of the sea, and the middle realm (see McNiven 2003:330–331), permeating the consciousness of people living in Southern California, past and present.

Conclusion

In this survey of the evidence of ritual on the Channel Islands, it is evident that the particular properties of the islands and their surrounding seascapes had profound influences on the cosmologies and identities of the Chumash and Tongva (Gabrielino), regardless of their respective origins and affiliations. This is comparable to other coastal societies, such as those of Polynesia, Scandinavia, and the Pacific Northwest, whose landscapes and seascapes were integral to their cosmologies, ceremonies, and identities. In the edited volume by Fitzhugh and Habu (2002), Ames (2002) placed emphasis on the unique characteristics of maritime societies (i.e., boat transportation) with respect to the forager-collector continuum. In the thematic issue on "Seascapes" in *World Archaeology*, Cooney (2003) expanded on discussions of coastal subsistence and settlement to incorporate the supernatural properties of the sea. The archaeological and ethnographic records of places such as the Channel Islands allow us to explore these different layers of island living, subsistence and supernatural alike, to garner insights into the complex and dynamic relationships that have existed between coastal environments and human societies through time.

Acknowledgments

I thank Mike Glassow, John Johnson, Mark Raab, Sam Spaulding, Wendy Teeter, and Andy Yatsko for their assistance in finding relevant historical and archaeological information, as well as their insights into interpreting the evidence of ritual on the Channel Islands. I am also grateful to Dan Reeves for reading a previous version of this chapter. The photographs in Figures 8.2 and 8.3 are of artifacts housed in the collections at the Fowler Museum in Los Angeles and are included here with the assistance of Wendy Teeter. Figure 8.4 was taken and provided by Sam Spaulding and Figure 8.5 by Lisa Thomas. I thank all of them for generously allowing me to use these images. I am also grateful to Ann Huston, Lyndal Laughrin, Kelly Minas, the University of California Natural Reserve System, and Channel Islands National Park for their ongoing support of archaeological research on the Channel Islands.

References

Ames, K. M.

2002 Going by Boat: The Forager-Collector Continuum at Sea. In *Beyond Foraging and Collecting: Evolutionary Change in Hunter-Gatherer Settlement Systems*, edited by B. Fitzhugh and J. Habu, pp. 19–52. Kluwer Academic/Plenum, New York.

Andrews, S.

2009 Unpublished site record for CCC-E-5.

Applegate, R.

1975 An Index of Chumash Placenames. In *Papers on the Chumash*, pp. 19–46. Occasional Papers No. 9. San Luis Obispo County Archaeological Society, San Luis Obispo.

Bean, L. J.

1976 Power and Its Application in Native California. In *Native Californians: A Theoretical Perspective*, edited by L. J. Bean and T. C. Blackburn, pp. 407–420. Ballena, Ramona, CA.

1992 *California Indian Shamanism*. Ballena, Menlo Park, CA.

Bean, L. J., and T. F. King (editors)

1974 *'Antap: California Indian Political and Economic Organization*. Ballena, Ramona, CA.

Bean, L. J., and C. R. Smith

1978 Gabrielino. In *Handbook of North American Indians*, Vol. 8: *California*, edited by R. F.

Heizer and W. C. Sturtevant, pp. 538–549. Smithsonian Institution, Washington, DC.

Bean, L. J., and S. B. Vane

1978 Cults and Their Transformations. In *Handbook of North American Indians*, Vol. 8: *California*, edited by R. F. Heizer and W. C. Sturtevant, pp. 538–549. Smithsonian Institution, Washington, DC.

Blackburn, T. C.

1974 Ceremonial Integration and Social Interaction in Aboriginal California. In *'Antap: California Indian Political and Economic Organization*, edited by L. J. Bean and T. F. King, pp. 93–110. Ballena, Ramona, CA.

1975 *December's Child: A Book of Chumash Oral Narratives, Collected by J. P. Harrington*. University of California Press, Berkeley.

Boscana, G.

1978 *Chinigchinich*. Malki Museum Press, Banning, CA.

Bradley, R.

2000 *The Archaeology of Natural Places*. Routledge, London and New York.

Braje, T. J. , D. J. Kennett, J. M. Erlandson, and B. J. Culleton

2007 Human Impacts on Nearshore Shellfish Taxa: A 7000 Year Record from Santa Rosa Island, California. *American Antiquity* 72(4): 735–756.

Cameron, C.

2000 Animal Effigies from Coastal Southern California. *Pacific Coast Archaeological Society Quarterly* 36(2):30–52.

Coleman, C. D., and K. Wise

1994 Archaeological Field Research by Los Angeles Museum-Channel Islands Biological Survey 1939–1941. In *The Fourth California Islands Symposium: Update on the State of Resources*, edited by W. L. Halvorson and G. J. Maender, pp. 183–192. Santa Barbara Museum of Natural History, Santa Barbara, CA.

Collins, P. W.

1991 Interaction Between Island Foxes (*Urocyon littoralis*) and Indians on Islands off the Coast of Southern California: I. Morphologic and

Archaeological Evidence of Human Assisted Dispersal. *Journal of Ethnobiology* 11(1):51–81.

Conti, K. , W. D. Hyder, and A. Padgett
2002   Cave of the Whales: Rock Art on San Nicolas Island. In *Proceedings of the Fifth California Islands Symposium*, edited by D. Brown, K. Mitchell, and H. Chaney, pp. 669–676. Santa Barbara Museum of Natural History, Santa Barbara.

Cooney, G.
2003   Introduction: Seeing Land from the Sea. *World Archaeology* 35(3):323–328.

Corbett, R.
2004   Chumash Bone Whistles: The Development of Ceremonial Integration in Chumash Society. In *Foundations of Chumash Complexity*, edited by J. E. Arnold, pp. 65–74. Perspectives in California Archaeology Vol. 7. Cotsen Institute of Archaeology, University of California, Los Angeles.

Davenport, D. , J. R. Johnson, and J. Timbrook
1993   The Chumash and the Swordfish. *Antiquity* 67(255):257–272.

Ehringer, C. R.
2003   Roosters and Raptors: Cultural Continuity and Change at Big Dog Cave, San Clemente Island, California. Master's thesis. Department of Anthropology, California State University, Northridge.

Eisentraut, P. J.
1990   Investigations of Prehistoric Seed Caches from Site CA-SCLI-1524, San Clemente Island. *Pacific Coast Archaeological Society Quarterly* 26(2–3):93–111.

Fitzhugh, B., and J. Habu
2002   *Beyond Foraging and Collecting: Evolutionary Change in Hunter-Gatherer Settlement Systems*. Kluwer Academic/Plenum, New York.

Gamble, L. H.
2008   *The Chumash World at European Contact: Power, Trade, and Feasting among Complex Hunter Gatherers*. University of California Press, Berkeley.

Geiger, M., and C. Meighan
1976   *As the Padres Saw Them: California Indian Life and Customs as Reported by the Franciscan Missionaries, 1813–1815*. Santa Barbara Mission Archive Library, Santa Barbara, CA.

Glassow, Michael A. (editor)
2010   *Channel Islands National Park Archaeological Overview and Assessment*. Prepared for and on file at the Cultural Resources Division, Channel Islands National Park, Ventura, CA.

Grant, C.
1993   *The Rock Paintings of the Chumash: A Study of a California Indian Culture*. University of California Press, Berkeley.

Hale, A.
1995   *The World in a Basket: Late Period Gabrielino Ceremonial Features from the Lemon Tank Site, San Clemente Island, California*. Master's thesis. California State University, Northridge.

Hale, A., and R. A. Salls
2000   The Canine Ceremony: Dog and Fox Burials on San Clemente Island. *Pacific Coast Archaeological Society Quarterly* 36(4):80–94.

Hanna, P. T.
1933   *Chinigchinich: A Revised and Annotated Version of Alfred Robinson's Translation of Father Geronimo Boscana's Historical Account of the Beliefs, Usages, Customs and Extravagancies of the Indians of This Mission of San Juan Capistrano Called the Acagchemem Tribe*. Fine Arts Press, Santa Ana, CA.

Harrington, J. P.
1933   Annotations of Alfred Robinson's Chinigchinich. In *Chinigchinich: A Revised and Annotated Version of Alfred Robinson's Translation of Father Geronimo Boscana's Historical Account of Belief, Usages, Customs and Extravagances of the Indians of This Mission of San Juan Capistrano Called the Acagchemem Tribe*, edited by P. T. Hanna, pp. 91–228. Fine Arts Press, Santa Ana, CA.
1978   Annotations. In *Chinigchinich*, edited by G. Boscana. Malki Museum Press, Banning, CA.

Hollimon, S. E.
1990   Division of Labor and Gender Roles in Santa Barbara Channel Area Prehistory. PhD dissertation. University of California, Santa Barbara.

Hoover, R. L.
1971   Some Aspects of Santa Barbara Channel Prehistory. PhD dissertation. University of California, Berkeley.

Hudson, D. T.
1976   Chumash Canoes of Mission Santa Barbara: The Revolt of 1824. *Journal of California Anthropology* 2(1):5–14.
1979   A Rare Account of Gabrielino Shamanism from the Notes of John P. Harrington. *Journal of California and Great Basin Anthropology* 1(2):356–362.

Hudson, D. T., and T. C. Blackburn
1986   *The Material Culture of the Chumash Inter-*

action Sphere, Vol. 4: *Ceremonial Paraphernalia, Games, and Amusements*. Ballena and Santa Barbara Museum of Natural History, Santa Barbara, CA.

Hudson, D. T. , T. Blackburn, R. Curletti, and J. Timbrook
1977 *The Eye of the Flute: Chumash Traditional History and Ritual as Told by Fernando Librado Kitsepawit to John P. Harrington*. Malki Museum Press, Banning, CA.

Hudson, D. T., and K. Conti
1981 The "Aquatic Motif" in Chumash Rock Art. *Journal of California and Great Basin Anthropology* 3(2):224–231.

Hudson, D. T., J. Timbrook, and M. Rempe (editors)
1978 *Tomol: Chumash Watercraft as Described in the Ethnographic Notes of John P. Harrington*. Ballena Press Anthropological Papers No. 10. Ballena Press and Santa Barbara Museum of Natural History, Santa Barbara.

Hudson, D. T., and E. Underhay
1978 *Crystals in the Sky: An Intellectual Odyssey Involving Chumash Astronomy, Cosmology, and Rock Art*. Ballena Press Anthropological Papers No. 10, edited by L. J. Bean and T. C. Blackburn. Ballena Press, Socorro, NM.

Ingold, T.
1993 The Temporality of the Landscape. *World Archaeology* 25(2):152–174.

Johnson, J. R.
1982 An Ethnohistoric Study of the Island Chumash. Master's thesis. University of California, Santa Barbara.
1988 Chumash Social Organization: An Ethnohistoric Perspective. PhD dissertation. Department of Anthropology, University of California, Santa Barbara.
1993 Cruzeño Chumash Social Geography. In *Archaeology on the Northern Channel Islands*, edited by M. A. Glassow, pp. 19–46. Archives of California Prehistory 34. Coyote Press, Salinas, CA.
2000 Social Responses to Climate Change among the Chumash Indians of South-Central California. In *The Way the Wind Blows: Climate, History, and Human Action*, edited by R. J. McIntosh, J. A. Tainter, and S. K. McIntosh, pp. 301–327. Columbia University Press, New York.
2001 Ethnohistoric Reflections on Cruzeño Chumash Society. In *The Origins of a Pacific Coast Chiefdom: The Chumash of the Channel Islands*, edited by J. E. Arnold, pp. 53–70. University of Utah Press, Salt Lake City.

Johnson, J. R., and S. McLendon
2002 Social History of Native Islanders After Missionization. In *Proceedings of the Fifth California Islands Symposium*, Ventura, CA, edited by D. Brown, K. Mitchell, and H. Chaney, pp. 646–653. Santa Barbara Museum of Natural History, Santa Barbara, CA.

Jones, P. M.
1956 *Archaeological Investigations on Santa Rosa Island in 1901*. Anthropological Records 17(2), edited by R. F. Heizer and A. B. Elsasser. University of California Press, Berkeley and Los Angeles.

Kennett, D. J.
2005 *The Island Chumash: Behavioral Ecology of a Maritime Society*. University of California Press, Berkeley.

Knight, A.
2001 Notes on the Rock Art of the California Channel Islands. Unpublished manuscript accessed online at http://www. californiaprehistory. com/reports01/rep0022. html.

Kroeber, A. L.
1971 Elements of Culture in Native California. In *The California Indians: A Source Book*, edited by R. F. Heizer and M. A. Whipple, pp. 3–65. University of California Press, Berkeley.
1976 *Handbook of the Indians of California*. Dover, New York.

Langenwalter, P. E., II
1986 Ritual Animal Burials from the Encino Village Site. *Pacific Coast Archaeological Society Quarterly* 22(3):63–97.

Lee, G.
1981 *The Portable Cosmos: Effigies, Ornaments, and Incised Stones from the Chumash Area*. Ballena, Socorro, NM.
1997 *The Chumash Cosmos: Effigies, Ornaments, Incised Stones, and Rock Paintings of the Chumash Indians*. Bear Flag Books, Arroyo Grande, CA.

Lee, G., and C. W. Clewlow, Jr.
1979 *Rock Art of the Chumash Area: An Annotated Bibliography*. Institute of Archaeology Occasional Paper No. 3. University of California, Los Angeles.

McCarthy, D.
1980 Unpublished site record for CA-SCLI-1724.

McCawley, W.
1996 *The First Angelinos: The Gabrielino Indians of Los Angeles*. Malki Museum Press, Banning, CA.

McLendon, S., and J. R. Johnson
1999 *Cultural Affiliation and Lineal Descent of*

Chumash Peoples in the Channel Islands and the Santa Monica Mountains. Report prepared for the Archeology and Ethnography Program, National Park Service, Washington, DC. Santa Barbara Museum of Natural History, Santa Barbara, and Hunter College, City University of New York, New York.

McNiven, I. J.
2003   Saltwater People: Spiritscapes, Maritime Rituals and the Archaeology of Australian Indigenous Seascapes. *World Archaeology* 35(3):329–349.

Meighan, C.
2000   Rock Art on the Channel Islands of California. *Pacific Coast Archaeological Society Quarterly* 36(2):15–29.

Meriam, C. H.
1955   *Studies of California Indians*. University of California Press, Berkeley.

Moriarty, J. R., III
1969   *Chinigchinix: An Indigenous California Religion*. Southwest Museum, Los Angeles.

Olson, R. L.
1930   Chumash Prehistory. *University of California Publications in American Archaeology and Ethnology* 28(1):1–21.

Orr, P. C.
1968   *Prehistory of Santa Rosa Island, Santa Barbara, California*. Santa Barbara Museum of Natural History, Santa Barbara, CA.

Perry, J. E.
2003   Prehistoric Land and Resource Use among Complex Hunter-Gatherer-Fishers on Eastern Santa Cruz Island. PhD dissertation. University of California, Santa Barbara.
2007   Chumash Ritual and Sacred Geography on Santa Cruz Island, California. *Journal of California and Great Basin Anthropology* 27(2):103–124.

Perry, J. E., and C. Delaney-Rivera
2011   Interactions and Interiors of the Coastal Chumash: Perspectives from Santa Cruz Island and the Oxnard Plain. *California Archaeology* 3:103–126.

Phillips, T.
2003   Seascapes and Landscapes in Orkney and Northern Scotland. *World Archaeology* 35(3):371–384.

Quist, R.
1978   Channel Island Pictographs. *Journal of New World Archaeology* 2(4):40–45.

Raab, L. M., J. Cassidy, A. Yatsko, and W. J. Howard
2009   *California Maritime Archaeology: A San Clemente Island Perspective*. Altamira, Lanham, MD.

Rogers, D. B.
1929   *Prehistoric Man of the Santa Barbara Coast*. Santa Barbara Museum of Natural History, Santa Barbara, CA.

Rozaire, C. E., and G. Kritzman
1960   A Petroglyph Cave on San Nicolas Island. *Masterkey* 34(4):147–151.

Salls, R. A.
1990   Return to Big Dog Cave: The Last Evidence of a Prehistoric Fishery on the Southern California Bight. *Pacific Coast Archaeological Society Quarterly* 26(2–3):38–60.

Snead, J. E., C. L. Erickson, and J. A. Darling
2009   Making Human Space: Archaeology of Travel, Path, and Road. In *Landscapes of Movement: Trails, Paths, and Roads in Anthropological Perspective*, edited by J. E. Snead, C. L. Erickson, and J. A. Darling, pp. 1–19. University of Pennsylvania Museum of Archaeology and Archaeology, Philadelphia.

Steward, J. H.
1929   *Petroglyphs of California and Adjoining States*. Publications in American Archaeology and Ethnology 24(2). University of California, Berkeley.

Strong, W. D.
1929   *Aboriginal Society of Southern California*. University of California Publications in American Archaeology and Ethnology 26(1):1–358. Malki Museum Press, Banning, CA.

Sutton, E. A.
2009   *Update on the Status of Research at Nimatlala, a Historic Period Chumash Village on Santa Cruz Island*. Paper presented at the 43rd annual meeting of the Society for California Archaeology, Modesto, CA.

Tilley, C.
1994   *A Phenomenology of Landscape: Places, Paths, and Monuments*. Berg, Oxford.
2008   Phenomenological Approaches to Landscape Archaeology. In *Handbook of Landscape Archaeology*, edited by B. David and J. Thomas, pp. 271–276. Left Coast Press, Walnut Creek, CA.

Timbrook, J.
2002   Search for the Source of the Sorcerer's Stones. In *Proceedings of the Fifth California Islands Symposium*, edited by D. Brown, K. Mitchell, and H. Chaney, pp. 633–640. Santa Barbara Museum of Natural History, Santa Barbara, CA.
2007   *Chumash Ethnobotany: Plant Knowledge*

among the Chumash People of Southern California. Santa Barbara Museum of Natural History, Santa Barbara, CA.

Vellanoweth, R. L., B. G. Bartelle, A. F. Ainis, A. C. Cannon, and S. J. Schwartz
2008   A Double Dog Burial from San Nicolas Island, California, USA: Osteology, Context, and Significance. *Journal of Archaeological Science* 35:3111–3123.

Walker, P. L.
1996   Integrative Approaches to the Study of Ancient Health: An Example from the Santa Barbara Channel Area of Southern California. In *Notes on Populational Significance of Paleopathological Conditions: Health, Illness, and Death in the Past*, edited by A. Pérez-

Pérez, pp. 97–105. Fundación Uriach, Barcelona.

Walker, P. L., and T. Hudson
1993   *Chumash Healing: Changing Health and Medical Practices in an American Indian Society.* Malki Museum Press, Banning, CA.

Wood, F. W.
2000   Stone Pipes and Cloud Blowers from San Clemente Island. *Pacific Coast Archaeological Society Quarterly* 36(2):76–78.

Yatsko, A.
2000   *Late Holocene Paleoclimatic Stress and Prehistoric Human Occupation on San Clemente Island.* PhD dissertation. Department of Anthropology, University of California, Los Angeles.

9

Cultural Landscapes
of Santa Catalina Island

Wendy G. Teeter, Desireé Reneé Martinez,
and Karimah O. Kennedy Richardson

California's southern Channel Islands, and in particular Santa Catalina Island, located just 32 km off the coast of Los Angeles from the Palos Verde Peninsula, provide a microcosm in which to investigate how prehistoric people utilized and managed essential resources within a well-defined area (see Jazwa and Perry, Chapter 1, Figure 1.1). Professional and vocational archaeological investigations have occurred since the 1890s, resulting in the identification of more than 1,500 individual cultural sites on the island (Figure 9.1). Much of the published research on Catalina has revolved around describing life in a particular village or documenting Catalina's connections to the mainland via a large interregional trade network (e.g., Bennyhoff et al. 1987; Jackson and Ericson 1994; Meighan 1959; Raab et al. 1995). However, in order to understand the complex and unique contributions of Catalina Island and its inhabitants, one must delve further into the archaeological record and further synthesize the extant research.

Since 2007, the Pimu Catalina Island Archaeology Project (PCIAP) has been expanding the knowledge of inter- and intravillage relationships and cultural life of the Catalina Island Gabrielino (Tongva) by compiling and reanalyzing previous research; accurately remapping, reassessing, and redocumenting previously recorded sites using GPS and GIS technology; and identifying and documenting new sites while working with members of the Gabrielino (Tongva) community to complete these tasks. Previous interpretations of Catalina's archaeological record do not adequately explain the distribution, quantity, or variety of cultural phenomena identified across the island. Prior investigations invoked models of cultural ecology to explain how the island environment influenced human behavior. It is equally important, however, to recognize how human behavior has shaped the island environment. Acknowledging these dynamic interactions, PCIAP has incorporated landscape theory into its research design in order to evaluate "the dynamic, interdependent relationships that" Catalina islanders have "maintain[ed] with the physical, social, and cultural dimensions of their environments across space and over time" (Anschuetz et al. 2001). By examining trails and pathways, the very landscape alterations that link people and resources, PCIAP hopes to better understand how these connections, both physical and social, were constructed and maintained.

Accordingly, our research is influenced by different theoretical and methodological approaches to documenting and interpreting trails, pathways, and movement within cultural landscapes. In particular, this chapter describes our application of landscapes of movement, a dimension of landscape theory, and GIS techniques such as least cost path (LCP) models on Catalina (Snead et al. 2009; Melmed and Apple 2009). In addition, we discuss how ethnographic and ethnohistoric information gathered from Southern California tribes provides insights into trail use and connections to the island landscape that are not visible otherwise. By applying a landscape approach, PCIAP intends to expand on previous in-

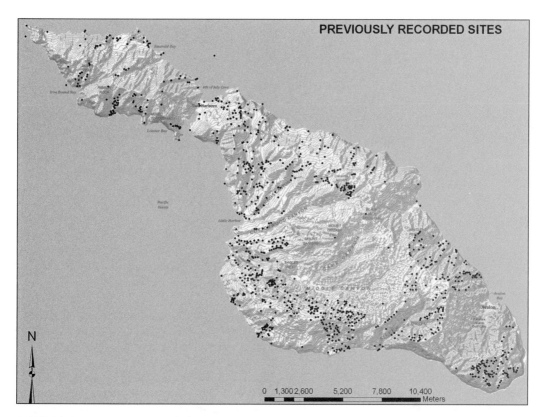

FIGURE 9.1.PREVIOUSLY recorded sites on Santa Catalina Island (current through 2011).

terpretations of Catalina's archaeological record to include other social and ritual dimensions of island living.

Cultural and Landscape Setting

Santa Catalina Island, also known as Pimu or Pimungna, is one of three southern Channel Islands—along with Kiinkepar (San Clemente) and Xaraashnga (San Nicolas)—that were determined to be inhabited by the Gabrielino (Tongva) prior to European contact based on linguistic, ethnographic, and archaeological cultural affiliation (McCawley 1996).

The closest of the southern Channel Islands to the mainland, Catalina measures 34 km (21 mi) long and 12 km (8 mi) wide from Long Point to China Point. At the narrowest point, the island measures 0.8 km (0.5 mi) across the isthmus. A high central ridge runs almost the length of the island from northwest to southeast, with most drainages perpendicular to it. Few areas are level, and several peaks rise more than 600 m (2,000 ft) above mean sea level (amsl), the highest being

Mount Orizaba at 670 m (2,097 ft). Avalon Bay, Catalina/Isthmus Bays, and Little Harbor are natural bays big enough to accommodate large ships, with smaller landings spread along both sides of the island (Strudwick, Chapter 10). The leeward side, however, facing northeast, provides the best anchorages. Compared to the northern Channel Islands, the climate is mild and dry, with an average temperature of 70°F in the daytime and an annual average of 12 inches of rain.

Despite its rugged terrain and arid environment, Catalina Island has been attractive to human inhabitants for thousands of years because of freshwater available from the hundreds of year-round springs, plentiful marine resources, and lithic resources such as soapstone, among other features (Schoenherr et al. 1999). At the time of European contact by Juan Cabrillo in 1542, the Tongva were using a wooden plank canoe called a *ti'at* to travel to and from the southern Channel Islands, allowing for intra-island and island–mainland trade, exchange, and communication. Island items such as soapstone artifacts, dried fish, and marine mammal pelts and meat were traded for mainland resources, including furs, skins, grass seeds, worked deer bone, chert, and obsidian (Bean and Vane 1978; Meighan 1959; Schumacher 1879). The distribution of these items was accomplished not just by boat, but also through the construction, maintenance, and use of footpaths on the island and the mainland.

Tongva villages were composed of extended families and clans that came together for harvests, trade, ceremonies, and other cooperative activities. Major village sites on Catalina Island have been identified at Two Harbors (Nájquqar) (SCAI-39), Avalon (SCAI-29), Toyon (SCAI-564), White's Landing (SCAI-34), Ripper's Cove (SCAI-26), Johnson's Landing (SCAI-24), Starlight Beach (SCAI-106), Little Harbor (SCAI-17), and Big Springs (SCAI-50). Meighan and Johnson (1957:24) estimated that the total number of Tongva on Catalina Island at the time of European contact to be around 2,000 to 3,000 individuals; however, without more research and radiocarbon dating, the island's population size through time cannot be evaluated further (McCawley 2002).

The lack of dated sites on Catalina has limited the ability to temporally associate and compare its archaeological record to that of the other Channel Islands and the mainland. Only three sites on Catalina (SCAI-17, -26, -137) have associated radiocarbon dates (Cottrell et al. 1980; Raab et al. 1994:246, 1995). The earliest radiocarbon date, from 7529 to 7892 years cal BP (calibrated 1σ range), comes from SCAI-17, a large habitation on Little Harbor Mesa on the windward side of the island, which has a view of San Nicolas and Santa Barbara Islands (Raab el al. 1994:246). Four other sites (SCAI-39, -45, -118, and the Cottonwood Creek site) have been assigned relative dates based on temporally diagnostic shell beads (Rosen 1980; Bickford and Martz 1980; Finnerty et al. 1970; Strudwick, Chapter 10).

Tongva society and culture were severely affected by the colonization of their territory by the Spanish, the establishment of San Gabriel Mission in 1771, the founding of Pueblo de Los Angeles, and the distribution of numerous Spanish/Mexican land grants encompassing Tongva villages and the islands (McCawley 2002). Places such as Two Harbors were often visited and re-corded by European explorers as Catalina Harbor is the only all-weather port between San Diego and San Francisco. It is believed that the last Tongva had left Pimu by the early 1830s (Meighan and Johnson 1957; Howard 2002; Strudwick, Chapter 10).

Previous Archaeological Investigations

There were many early nineteenth- and twentieth-century archaeological explorations of Catalina Island (see Wlodarski 1982 for a complete list). One of the first researchers on Catalina was naturalist William Dall. As part of the United States Coast Survey, Dall collected natural resource samples from along the Pacific Coast. He is best known for his time in Alaska and his notes on Native Alaskan life (Smithsonian 2011). During his time on Catalina Island, from 1873 to 1874, he collected various examples of the natural environment and archaeological artifacts that he sent to the United States National Museum, now called the Smithsonian (U.S. Congress 1877:533). Paul Schumacher was another significant early collector. From 1875 to 1879, under contract with the United States National Museum and the Harvard Peabody Museum, Schumacher joined the Expedition for Explorations West of the One Hundredth Meridian to collect artifacts from California's Channel Islands and from sites on the southern California mainland. Schumacher's explorations on Catalina focused on soapstone quarries (Schumacher 1877, 1878, 1879; Wheeler et al. 1879), native plants, and examples of mainland basketry (e.g., Peabody Museum No. 78-40-10/14757-59). Other collectors followed, with most being categorized as "pot hunters." Ralph Glidden was the most prolific member of this group.

A modern scientific approach to Catalina archaeology did not occur until the UCLA Archaeological Survey began conducting research projects from the late 1950s through 1970s (e.g., Meighan 1959; Finnerty et al. 1970). Other, more compliance-driven archaeological work has been completed from the 1970s to the present (e.g., Wlodarski 1982; Strudwick et al. 2007). Also conducted during this time were smaller research and field school projects run through the University of California, Riverside (Leonard 1976); California State University, Los Angeles (Reinman and Eberhart 1980); and California State University, Long Beach (Rosenthal et al. 1988). Additionally, Nelson Leonard (1976) led a major cultural resources survey project as part of a recreational easement and comprehensive management study for Los Angeles County under the Center for Natural Areas to prepare for the transfer of land from the Santa Catalina Island Company to the Catalina Island Conservancy. While many sites were recorded as a result of these projects, the haste with which this was done often meant that little detailed information was recorded, resulting in inaccurate locational data and incomplete site characterizations.

The major research questions of these projects were centered on trade and the procurement of marine resources on the Channel Islands through the lens of cultural ecology (e.g., Meighan 1959; Porcasi 1998, 2000; Raab et al. 1995; Reddy 2006). Only a few researchers have attempted to interpret the archaeological data of Catalina at the regional level. Decker (1969) synthesized early burial excavations by Ralph Glidden and tried to understand socioeconomic patterns between village sites, while Wlodarski (1982) compiled all references and data from previous archaeological investigations on Catalina in order to encourage new research. PCIAP is currently attempting to bring both professional and amateur excavations into one large research project using multiple methodologies and interdisciplinary collaborations.

Landscape Theory

Although a landscape approach to archaeological sites can be traced to the 1920s (Stoddard and Zubrow 1999), its application began in earnest in the mid-1970s in Britain as a way to meld field archaeology with landscape history (Fleming 2006:267; Aston and Rowley 1974:11). Since that time, scholars have taken landscape archaeology in a variety of directions. Early archaeological studies viewed the landscape solely as the backdrop onto which material cultural was placed. It was seen as a factor that influenced how past peoples arranged themselves, whether by the landscape's available resources and/or its physical characteristics (e.g., settlement patterns) (Ashmore and Knapp 1999:1; Wandsnider 1992).

Recent landscape archaeology studies have recognized that the landscape is more than just a synonym for the natural environment. Instead, landscapes represent "a way in which... people have signified themselves and their world through their... relationship with nature, and through which they have underlined and communicated their own social role and that of others with respect to external nature" (Cosgrove 1985: 55). Also important is the recognition that the so-called "empty" spaces, areas lacking sites or clusters of material remains, may be just as significant as those with tangible cultural phenomena (Wobst 2005; Anschuetz et al 2001:161). Thus, consideration of the entire landscape surrounding an archaeological site, including its physical and metaphysical properties, must be included in order to gain more-nuanced understandings of the past.

Using a landscape archaeology approach to studying and documenting trails, Snead et al. (2009) describe the theory of landscapes of movement, which refers to understanding the environmental context of a trail or pathway in addition to its function. A trail cannot be understood as an isolated feature because it is connected to the landscape that surrounds it. Applying the landscapes of movement approach broadens our view by recontextualizing trails with cultural knowledge systems, cosmology, normative behaviors, historical memory, and surrounding aesthetics.

Snead et al. (2009) also describe a number of theoretical approaches applicable to trails. Through the lens of political economy, the movement of people and goods along a trail or pathway reflects not only the socioeconomic connections of villages but also their sociopolitical ones. Direct ties via a trail can indicate the social control of one group of people by another, while the lack of a connecting trail can indicate a group's political independence or social isolation.

A phenomenological view considers the experience of the person taking the trail (Snead et al. 2009; Tilley 1997). "This visual or imaginable scape may include stars and alignments, fauna and flora, geomorphology, and landscapes, colors, sounds and smells" (Wobst 2005). The trail's sole purpose may be to guide the user to certain experiences or feelings, leading them to reconnect with cultural memories; to reenact oral traditions; or to travel through time, real or imaginative, to reach a sacred space, idea, or being (Snead et al. 2009). "We will have to allow for the 'natural' (that is 'non-artefactual') and 'cultural' (that is, 'artefactual') variables to be enculturated, to be significant to human action, and to articulate, like artifacts, with social life" (Wobst 2005).

Practice theory and structuration are used to explain the relationship between human agency and the structure of trails. Pathways are created by human use and are the result of the physical alteration of the landscape. Once established, the paths become a cultural norm through continued use, thus shaping subsequent human behavior (Snead et al. 2009).

Finally, an ethnogeographical approach uses ethnography to understand the cultural significance and perception of landscape and movement from an emic perspective. By working with Native American communities, researchers can incorporate their understanding of space and place, and how they situate themselves in relation to their trails or pathways (Snead et al. 2009; McCarthy 1986; Rivers and Jones 1993). An example of an ethnographical approach is Ian McNiven's (2003) work with Aboriginal Australians. He describes how Aboriginal Australians see the ocean as more than just a means to provide subsistence, but as a seascape imbued with spiritual properties. The sea directs how they view themselves and their interactions with it (McNiven 2003:330).

There are several hurdles to applying these approaches on Catalina Island, especially the ethnogeographical approach. Although there is a lack of Tongva ethnography on trails, a landscape of movement perspective can still be applied by using trail ethnographies from neighboring communities that inhabit similar biogeographic territories. Additionally, PCIAP has compiled information regarding members of neighboring communities who traveled to Catalina for a variety of reasons, and therefore their ethnographies are integral to understanding trail use on the island.

Furthermore, it is important to recognize that trails and pathways extend beyond the island landscape; they continue into and across the ocean via boats. Thus, acknowledging and integrating seascapes into research about trails becomes imperative to understanding inter- and intra-island relationships (Cooney 2003; Perry, Chapter 8).

California Landscape Studies

Landscape theory has been applied in a number of regional and temporal contexts in California (e.g., Fleming 1997; Kryder-Reid 2007; Eerkens et. al. 2007; Robinson et al. 2011; Whatford 1994; Perry and Delaney-Rivera 2011; Allen 2011; Robinson 2011; Laylander and Schaefer 2010). A subsection of these studies includes understanding how people and places are connected via trails and pathways, on land and sea. For example, Perry and Delaney-Rivera (2011) utilized taskscapes, places, routes, and viewsheds to understand "how travel routes and the distribution of resources, of both land and sea, were facilitated and/or controlled through site placement, intermarriage, and ceremonial integration of Santa Cruz Island and the Oxnard plain on the mainland."

On the mainland, the Bureau of Land Management and the California Energy Commission have incorporated a landscape approach into studies of prehistoric trails in northern Riverside County. The Chuckwalla Valley Prehistoric Trails Network Cultural Landscape study was generated in response to the destruction of archaeological sites by recent massive renewable energy development in the California desert. The study aims to understand how "sites that may lack individual distinction" may have "greater significance and research value when contributing to a larger data base" (Laylander and Schaefer 2010). Documenting these types of connections allows us to transcend traditional interpretations of site type, placement, and significance, and to align more squarely with Native American understandings of how "everything is connected" within cultural landscapes.

Trails Research in California

Santa Catalina Island has been, and continues to be, an important hub for the intermingling of people and the exchange of ideas and objects. Research on trails within the ancestral Tongva territory has included their participation in an extensive trade network that covered the western United States. Emphasis has been placed on the origin and destination of traded cultural materials (e.g., Bennyhoff et al. 1987; Jackson and Ericson 1994; Davis 1961). Previous research has documented that the prehistoric and historic residents of Catalina traded lithic resources (e.g., soapstone) for grooved axes (Heizer 1946), textiles (Hulbert 1902), and pottery (Ruby and Blackburn 1964) from the northern Channel Islands, central California, and the American Southwest.

Southern California and southwestern trails research has also focused on identifying and documenting trails used by European pioneers, traders, and missionaries during the historic period. For example, over the past 20 years, many researchers have uncovered segments and branches of the Old Spanish Trail, designated as the fifteenth national trail by Congress in 2002 (Old Spanish Trail Association 2011). The Old Spanish Trail was used to bring woolen goods and other items from Santa Fe, New Mexico, to Los Angeles, and to return with mules and horses to be traded all the way to Missouri. Researchers have pointed out that portions of the Old Spanish Trail are overlaid on other historic and prehistoric trails (Warren 2004). Therefore, the survival and economic growth of non–Native American communities were based on Native American knowledge of the local landscape and its resources, thus shaping how subsequent people, including Europeans, interacted with the environment.

In recent years, researchers have collected oral histories from Native American community members and gathered information about trails in order to relocate, document, and understand their use by Native American peoples. In their article "Archaeological Trails and Ethnographic Trails: Can They Meet?" Musser-Lopez and Miller (2010) worked with the Nuwuvi (Southern Paiute) people and other researchers to show that the "Salt Song Trail" was not only a cultural idea expressed in ritual song cycles but also had an actual physical imprint. The Salt Song Trail includes associated shrines and networked pathways within a sacred landscape. This route existed not only in dreams and the spirit world, but also in the physical world.

Trails, therefore, do more than just connect people to goods for economic reasons (Benny-hoff et al. 1987; Jackson and Ericson 1994; Davis 1961). Trails, pathways, and roads move people to people, new ideas to people, stories to hearts, and sacredness to those seeking it. From an emic perspective, an item carried along a trail to a village may not signify trade but something totally different, such as spiritual or social obligations, or some combination thereof. For example, Willie Pink, a Luiseño/Cupeño, has been exploring many of the extant trails within the Luiseño territory and contemplating their use. He posits that each trail extended from the main road required social obligations at the ending destination. At each intersection, travelers chose to visit and assume those obligations or continue on down the road (William Pink, personal communication, 2010).

Other ethnohistoric and ethnographic information connects trails to cultural and religious activities. In the seminal study *Power and Persistence*, Bean and Vane (1978) collected ethnographic information from several Native American communities located between the Coachella Valley and the Colorado River. The study discussed the Pacific Ocean–Great Plains trade system and demonstrated that the Tongva, Cahuilla, Panya (Halchidoma), and Northern Pima were trade partners historically and prehistorically. The Tongva were the western anchor of the trade route (Bean and Vane 1978:5–3; Dobyns 1984). Additionally, Daniel McCarthy (1982) has spent his career documenting trails within the California deserts, including the Mojave, and has connected them to the rock art sites that dot the landscape.

These studies are applicable to trails within Tongva territory because other Native American communities, such as the Cahuilla, used the trails not only for direct access to raw materials but also for religious purposes. Francisco Patencio, a Cahuilla *net* for Agua Caliente, stated that the trails were everywhere and "led from the land of one tribe to another. The trails were sacred to Indians" (Patencio 1943:70). In Patencio's medicine bundle was a string of shell beads that he said were given to the Cahuilla *kauisik* clan by the Native Americans of San Fernando, who in turn received them from the people on Catalina. Thus, a Cahuilla perspective of trails is relevant to understanding the pathways that connected them to the Tongva, and the Tongva to each other, including on the southern islands.

Connections to Catalina Island

Previous researchers have also documented the connections of Catalina's people to other Native American communities on the mainland. In 1926, Helen H. Roberts collected songs from Celestino Awai'u, a Luiseño from Pechanga, which describe how the *sen'yam* came from Catalina Island to what is now called Carlsbad, approximately 55 km north of present-day San Diego. The *sen'yam* attempted to displace the community living there, the *palem'yum* (Helen H. Roberts American Indian and Pacific Island Recordings Collection, AFS 751-754, American Folklife Center; Strudwick, Chapter 10). Furthermore, a Luiseño informant told DuBois (1908) that the Chingichngish religion came from the north, then to Catalina and San Clemente Islands, to San Juan Capistrano, to San Luis Rey, and finally to the San Diego Kumeyaay/Diegueño territory.

Tribal oral histories also provide interesting descriptions of non-Tongva journeys to Catalina for different purposes. The late Jane Penn, a Cahuilla *wanikik* clan elder, recounted that her father told her that the *wanikik* would travel down to the Pala reservation for sea fishing and then make raft boats to sail to Catalina Island to collect flat serrated shells (Johnson and Johnson 1967). Other Native American community members have described oral histories that speak of spiritually powerful people meeting on Catalina Island once a year and speaking in a language that only those at the meeting could understand (anonymous, personal communication, 2011).

Pink (personal communication, 2010) has found references to Catalina in his study of oral histories, including that the Cahuilla and Luiseño visited Catalina in seven-years cycles to directly obtain soapstone. This particular oral tradition is intriguing and ties to John Eddy's work (2009) on determining soapstone sources using their unique signatures through laser ablation inductively coupled plasma time of flight mass-spectrometer (LA-ICP-TOFMS). Eddy's research has identified several soapstone sources to the north and south of the Los Angeles Basin. These areas are physically closer and easier to get to

than Catalina, and yet the artifacts that he tested indicated a Catalina origin. What was so special about Catalina soapstone and, by extension, the objects made from it that the Cahuilla and Luiseño would go to great distances and expense to obtain it?

Modeling Least Cost Paths

While the ethnographic record can be used to understand the location and use of trails, Melmed and Apple (2009) have acknowledged that the reverse can also be true. Identifying potential trails using GIS can assist ethnographic work by showing connections between locations used for ritual, habitation, or other activities. Melmed and Apple (2009) describe how to evaluate the geographical features of possible travel corridors to hypothesize where prehistoric trails may be located using the LCP digital elevation model (DEM). By combining intensive field surveys and GIS analysis in Imperial County, their model identified potential pathways from previously recorded trail segments to sites. This methodology requires the use of slope and elevation to estimate potential routes for the extension of known trail segments. The LCP model identifies potential paths that would require the least amount of energy exertion as compared to other paths. Melmed and Apple (2009) field-tested the predictions by looking for cultural materials along the possible trail extensions. Since large invasive mammals such as bison, goats, pigs, deer, and tourists have obscured or destroyed the locations of prehistoric trails, this model can be beneficially applied to Catalina to reconstruct possible routes.

Apple (2005) showed in her study of the Colorado River culture area that cultural features are often directly associated with the trails. She noted that the type of sites in association with the pathways, such as quartz scatters, rock art, and rock alignments, were correlated with more spiritual or non-utilitarian uses of trails. This methodology is being used on Catalina, and several potential pathways have been identified.

Apple (2005) also investigated potential behavioral uses associated with the trails. Based on the type of sites found along a trail, the trail was characterized as either utilitarian or non-utilitarian. Using similar criteria on Catalina, potential trails have both ceremonial (e.g., locations with petro-

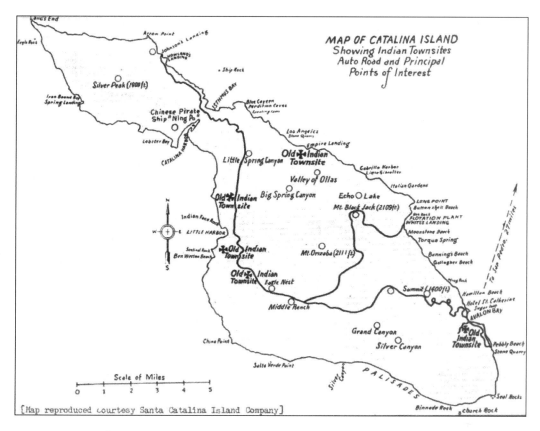

FIGURE 9.2. Map from ca. 1917–1938 of Catalina Island showing Native American villages and stage-coach trails (courtesy of Santa Catalina Island Company).

glyphs or pictographs) and utilitarian sites (e.g., midden sites and lithic reduction locations) along their routes. It may be too simple to expect a single type of behavioral use for each pathway and that the activity being performed is what designates the pathway as ceremonial or utilitarian at any specific time. Examples of temporal changes in trail significance are found in village processions for saints and festivals throughout the world (e.g., Goldfrank 1923; Mines 2002).

Victoria Kline (2009) also applied the LCP model to study trails and evaluate the landscape in Southern California. Kline (2009) postulated that many of the current highways were built on top of early trails, and she set out to demonstrate that the primary commonality between these early footpaths and modern highways is topography. Kline (2009) used LCP to show that topography influences distance and direction, which in turn influences routes of contact and trade. Specifically, she focused on the possible travel routes

through the San Luis Rey Watershed using the Lost Valley as a central location. Kline created GIS layers and DEMs to hypothesize where prehistoric trails may have existed. She determined that Lost Valley had more than one LCP, which ultimately connected it to other trail networks. She also identified connections between the LCPs and previously documented sites. This methodology is being incorporated into current Catalina research by using old maps to identify stagecoach roads and horse trails that may overlay prehistoric trails (Figure 9.2).

PCIAP Application of Landscape Models

By incorporating different models of landscape and movement, PCIAP is attempting to redefine sites more meaningfully to understand the long history of Pimu and its intra-island, inter-island, and island–mainland relationships. Documenting geomorphological changes in Catalina's

topography, synthesizing and incorporating previous research, conducting extensive island survey, and identifying Catalina's specific lithic
signatures are necessary components for understanding the origin and nature of Catalina's cultural resources.

In the context of the PCIAP, we are working
to locate and map previously recorded and new
sites, as well as noting the presence of important
natural resources. Previous research has often focused on the large Catalina coastal villages and
their relationship to the other coastal villages,
other islands, and the mainland through canoe
travel; however, many resources, such as freshwater, soapstone, and better protection from
the weather, are found in the island's interior. As
a result, PCIAP is looking at the most practical
way of moving around the island on foot, which
is along the sloping ridgelines or just above seasonal drainages that contain springs and where
there are fairly flat contours. Within ArcGIS,
the LCP approach was applied to mapped sites
to see whether their locations implied possible
trails or pathways that connected them to other
sites, natural resources, and/or ceremonial spaces
(e.g., Robinson's [2010] approach for understanding pictograph sites on the Hulkuhku Chumash
landscape). The project selected various intuitive starting and ending points (such as protected
bays, large springs, and soapstone quarries) to review with the DEMs and identify the LCPs to get
from one place to another.

Little Harbor, Airport Quarries,
Little Gibraltar

The Little Harbor Mesa site is one of the most
well known sites on Catalina because of its antiquity (more than 7,000 years) and the extensive research that has taken place there (Meighan 1959;
Raab et al. 1995). The antiquity and extent of occupation may relate to the rich marine resources
of Little Harbor, including its protected embay-
ment, larger gastropods (such as red abalone),
and dolphins that were attracted by a nearby submarine canyon (Raab et al. 1995; Porcasi 2000;
Porcasi and Fujita 2000). Furthermore, it would
have been one of the most viable landing areas for
those traveling between Catalina and San Clemente Islands.

PCIAP has investigated possible trails within
the Little Harbor area, including the Little Harbor site (SCAI-17), located on an adjacent mesa,
and sites positioned closer to shore (SCAI-18, -15,
-20, -21, and -128). This area forms a large village
complex surrounded by a ring of shell midden
that extends from the beach to the plateaus high
above (Meighan 1959; Raab et al. 1995). Also near
the beach are two known areas of red ochre pictographs that require further documentation.

Figure 9.3 displays a possible trail between
Little Harbor Mesa (SCAI-17) and the interior of
the island heading east along a ridge. As PCIAP
completed pedestrian surveys in the area, a pattern of concentrated cultural remains emerged,
with sites spaced no more than 500 m apart.
While the ridgeline has not been completely
documented, there are previously recorded sites
along the projected path, which continues toward a soapstone quarry district below the modern Catalina Island Airport. Soapstone artifacts
have been recovered from the Little Harbor site
(Meighan 1959:388). Therefore, it seems plausible that those living at Little Harbor were connected to interior resources and other people via
pathways such as the one projected to follow this
ridgeline.

The Airport Quarry area is one of the dens-
est soapstone concentrations on the island, with
more than 30 quarry sites and a large central habitation area (SCAI-61, -87, 91, 131) (Figure 9.3).
The number of quarries in this area was larger
in the past because many were destroyed by the
construction of the Catalina Island Airport. One
boulder was described as having more than 80
bowl scars (Meighan and Johnson 1957:25). A
second pathway, indicated by the string of previously documented archaeological sites along the
ridge, leads towards Little Gibraltar, which is another possible boat landing location. To confirm
this possible path, PCIAP will use DEMs to determine if this is an LCP, followed by continued
survey to identify and characterize unrecorded
cultural remains.

The site density of the quarry area raises the
question of whether or not this district was a
communal soapstone tool production area possibly used by non-Pimu people. This is a tantalizing
prospect given the Luiseño and Cahuilla ethno-

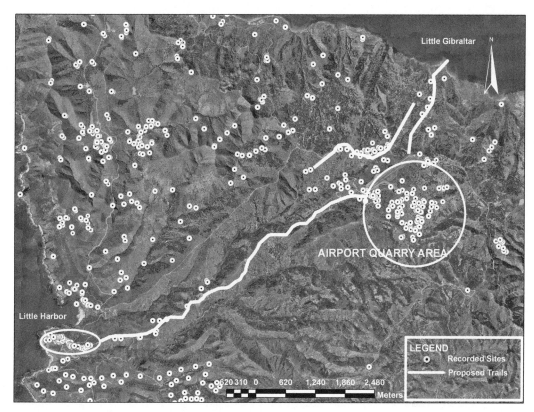

FIGURE 9.3. Map showing potential pathways from Little Harbor to a soapstone quarry district near the airport. Another potential pathway leads from Little Gibraltar to the quarry district.

historic stories of traveling to Catalina, as retold by Pink (personal communication, 2010). It is one that could be corroborated if specific kinds of nonlocal material culture are found there in the future.

PCIAP has also documented that most of the larger Pimu villages are located near soapstone quarries, and thus villagers would not have needed to travel far to find material for household use. The distribution of Catalina soapstone may help to show where trails likely existed on the island and who was using them. Catalina soapstone has been documented on the other southern islands, in Tongva villages on the Palos Verdes Peninsula, and in the Chumash area, including on the northern Channel Islands (Howard 2002; Perry 2003). In particular, soapstone artifacts are common on San Clemente Island, and places such as Little Harbor and Little Gibraltar could have served as important interfaces with respect to inter-island conveyance. These re-

lationships with other communities in Southern California are further supported based on mission marriage records that intimately connect the island and mainland Tongva with the Chumash, Tataviam, Luiseño, and Serrano (Perry, Chapter 8; King 2003: Figure 12).

KBRT Road, Salta Verde, and Toyon

Another area that PCIAP has surveyed is along the western ridge of Coffee Pot Canyon (Figure 9.4). As shown in Figure 9.4, a string of previously identified but undocumented cultural sites line the ridgetop along what is currently referred to as the KBRT Station Road. This proposed pathway heads towards Thunder Beach, east of Salta Verde Point. Although Thunder Beach is not ideal for *ti'at* landing due to the roughness of the waves crashing on the rocky shore, the trail may lead to the Salta Verde rock art site (Pimu 2009.1). Identified by PCIAP in 2009, the site is located in a densely vegetated drainage. The face of this 2.5 m

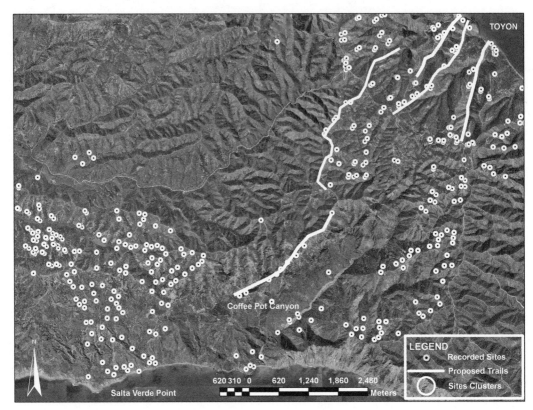

FIGURE 9.4. Map showing potential pathways along ridges in the Salta Verde, KRBT Road, and Toyon areas.

tall metavolcanic boulder is etched with zigzag lines and cross-hatching typical of the Southwest Coast petroglyph style. The top of the boulder has what looks like a snake pecked into the rock. Although not painted, this "snake" element, as well as the other shallow "cupules," may be associated with the girl's puberty ceremony that has been documented in other Southern California tribal areas, specifically that of the Luiseño (McCawley 1996).

Another line of sites extends along a ridge that ends at the large coastal village complex of Toyon (including SCAI-562, -563, and -564). Along the ridgeline between these sites there is evidence of clusters of shallow midden deposits and lithic scatters that may represent subsistence activities associated with larger coastal village sites; however, radiocarbon dating is required to further evaluate these potential relationships. Several other connecting lines in Figure 9.4 also show possible trails. In addition to ridgelines, there are other wide canyon drainages with reliable fresh-

water sources that supported communities in Middle Canyon, Cottonwood Canyon, and Bullrush Canyon.

Issues in Identifying Cultural Sites

It is important to note that PCIAP survey methods include investigating the sides of potential ridgeline pathways, something previous researchers have not done consistently. The slopes of ridgelines are often dismissed as possible areas for cultural material because of their steepness. With some areas having almost an 80-degree drop, PCIAP has found that site deflation has caused cultural materials to erode down from the tops of the ridges. As a result, a site might not have been previously identified since its remnants now only exist downslope. Furthermore, it has become evident that these steep ridgelines often lead to small plateaus and other flat areas that have evidence of cultural activities that are not easily identified from above.

FIGURE 9.5. Photograph of Eagle's Nest Hunting Lodge and Middle Canyon River after the flood of 1995 (courtesy of *Catalina Islander*).

Finally, understanding Catalina's geomorphology is a necessary component in trying to identify cultural sites on the landscape. As an example, in Middle Canyon during the late 1800s, the Banning brothers built Eagle's Nest, which included a lodge, a barn, horse stables, several outbuildings, and chicken and goat pens. Used subsequently as a tourist destination, much of the land on which it was located has been washed away by periodic and intense Middle River floods. The last major flood occurred there in 1995, causing the Thompson Reservoir to overflow and the Middle Canyon Road to collapse in several spots (Muir 1995). At least 10 m of land has been lost there in less than a hundred years (Figure 9.5). These historic floods are reminders that many prehistoric trails and sites will never be identified because they are beneath several meters of fluvial deposits.

Conclusions

The PCIAP has been expanding the knowledge of inter- and intravillage relationships and cultural life of the Catalina Island Tongva. To better understand these relationships, PCIAP is applying landscape theory, through the use of trails and pathways, to investigate social connections of and resource acquisition from various areas throughout the island and to/from the mainland.

The examples that we have presented offer several potential pathways that will be used in future LCP digital elevation modeling. PCIAP will continue to identify new sites and cultural features, redefine previously recorded sites, date cultural components, and evaluate patterns across the landscape. Once LCPs are compiled for areas such as from Little Harbor to Little Gibraltar, and from Toyon to Salta Verde, survey and site documentation will be conducted to evaluate the validity of these hypotheses.

In addition, ethnographic and ethnohistoric information from other Southern California tribes regarding their use and connection to the other Channels Islands may also offer potential explanations of the data results. Different scales and modes of movement across landscapes and, in this case, seascapes must always be acknowledged when doing comparative studies, but the data enrichment more than makes the endeavor worthwhile. PCIAP will continue to refine and assess the archaeological record of Catalina Island through a landscape approach to better understand the relationships not only between the landscape, resources, and residents of Pimu, but also their connections to and influences on people throughout Southern California.

Acknowledgments

The authors wish to thank their families and the Tongva people who support our project, especially Cindi Alvitre and Craig Torres, who have provided endless guidance and assistance. The Pimu Catalina Island Archaeology Project could not exist without the Catalina Island Conservancy, including Ann Muscat, Carlos de la Rosa, Frank Starkey, Lenny Altherr, Chuck Wright, and Frank Hein, to name only a few of the many people who provide intellectual and logistical support whenever asked. We would also like to thank the Nakwatsvewat Institute, the Catalina Island Museum, and Ran Boytner for all their support. The residents of Catalina Island, especially Tom Cushing, and the Lopez, Saldana, Stein-Brannock, and Warner families, have been important contributors to our understanding of Catalina sites. The Cotsen Institute of Archaeology at UCLA Director's Council deserves special thanks, especially Charles Steinmetz, Patti and Roger Civalleri, Lisa and Leroy Watson, and of course Charles Stanish (the director himself). Field seasons from 2007 to 2011 provided the information, and we humbly thank all the students and assistants involved, notably David Jacobsen, Lylliam Posadas, Elizabeth Connelly, Ivan Strudwick, Claudia Nocke, Lucius Martin, and Andrew Perdue, who come whenever duty calls. We appreciate all the suggestions and edits provided for this chapter by Christopher Jazwa and Jennifer Perry. Any errors or omissions are entirely our own.

References Cited

Allen, M. W.
2011   Of Earth and Stone: Landscape Archaeology in the Mojave Desert. *California Archaeology* 3(1):11–30.

Anschuetz, K. F., R. H. Wilshusen, and C. L. Scheick
2001   An Archaeology of Landscapes: Perspectives and Directions. *Journal of Archaeological Research* 9(2):157–211.

Apple, R. M.
2005   Pathways to the Past. *Proceedings of the Society for California Archaeology* 18:106–112.

Ashmore, W., and A. B. Knapp
1999   Archaeological Landscapes: Constructed, Conceptualized and Ideational. In *Archaeologies of Landscape: Contemporary Perspectives*, edited by W. Ashmore and A. B. Knapp, pp. 1–32. Blackwell, Malden, MA.

Aston, M., and T. Rowley
1974   Landscape Archaeology: An Introduction to Fieldwork Techniques on Post-Roman Landscapes. David and Charles, Newton Abbot.

Bean, L. J., and S. Brakke Vane (editors)
1978   *Persistence and Power: A Study of Native American Peoples in the Sonoran Desert and the Devers-Palo Verde High Voltage Transmission Line*. Report submitted to Southern California Edison by Cultural Systems Research, Menlo Park, CA.

Bennyhoff, J. A., R. E. Hughs, and D. Hurst-Thomas
1987   Shell Bead and Ornament Exchange Network between California and the Western Great Basin. *Anthropological Papers of the American Museum of Natural History* 64(2): 83–175

Bickford, V., and P. Martz
1980   Test Excavations at Cottonwood Creek, Catalina Island, California. *Pacific Coast Archaeological Society Quarterly* 16 (1–2):106–124.

Cooney, G.
2003   Introduction: Seeing Land from the Sea. *World Archaeology* 35(3):323–328.

Cosgrove, D. E.
1985   Prospect, Perspective and the Evolution of the Landscape Idea. *Transactions of the Institute of British Geographers* 10:45–62.

Cottrell, M. G., J. M. Clevenger, and T. G. Cooley
1980   Investigation of CA-SCaI-137, Bulrush Canyon, Catalina, California. *Pacific Coast Archaeological Society Quarterly* 16(1–2):5–25.

Davis, J. T.
1961   *Trade Routes and Economic Exchange among the Indians of California*. Archaeological Survey Reports No. 54. University of California, Berkeley.

Decker, D. A.
1969   *Early Archaeology on Catalina Island: Potential and Problems*. Archaeological Survey Annual Report Vol. 11. University of California, Los Angeles.

Dobyns, H. F.
1984   Trade Centers: The Concept and a Rancherian Culture Area Example. *American Indian Culture and Research Journal* 8(1): 23–35.

DuBois, C. G.
1908   The Religion of the Luiseño Indians of Southern California. *University of California Publications in American Archaeology and Ethnology* 8:69–166.

Eddy, J. J.
2009   Source Characterization of Santa Cruz Island Chlorite Schist and Its Role in Stone Bead and Ornament Exchange Networks. In *Proceedings of the Seventh California Islands Symposium*, edited by T. J. Coonan and M. J. Potter, pp. 67–79. Institute for Wildlife Studies, Arcata, CA.

Eerkens, J. W., J. S. Rosenthal, D. C. Young, and J. King
2007   Early Holocene Landscape Archaeology in

the Coso Basin, Northwestern Mojave Desert, California. *North American Archaeologist* 28(2):87–112

Finnerty, W. P., D. A. Decker, N. N. Leonard III, T. F. King, C. D. King, and L. B. King
1970   *Community Structure and Trade at Isthmus Cove: A Salvage Excavation on Catalina Island.* Pacific Coast Archaeological Society Occasional Papers No. 1.

Fleming, A.
2006   Post-Processual Landscape Archaeology: A Critique. *Cambridge Archaeological Journal* 16(3):267–280.

Fleming, K.
1997   Cultural Landscape Study of Lost Valley, San Diego County, California. *Proceedings of the Society for California Archaeology* 10: 29–35, edited by J. Reed, G. Greenway, and K. McCormick.

Goldfrank, E. S.
1923   Notes on Two Pueblo Feasts. *American Anthropologist* n.s. 25(2):188–196.

Heizer, R. F.
1946   The Occurrence and Significance of Southwestern Grooved Axes in California. *American Antiquity* 11(3):187–193.

Howard, V.
2002   Santa Catalina's Soapstone Vessels: Production Dynamics. In *Proceedings of the Fifth California Islands Symposium*, edited by D. R. Browne, Mitchell, K. L., and Chaney, H. W., pp. 598–606. U. S. Department of the Interior, Washington, DC.

Hulbert, A.
1902   *Indian Thoroughfares: His Historic Highways of America.* Vol. 2. A. H. Clark, Cleveland.

Jackson, T., and J. Ericson
1994   Prehistoric Exchange Systems in California. In *Prehistoric Exchange Systems in North America*, edited by T. Baugh and J. Ericson, pp. 385–411. Plenum, New York.

Johnson, F., and P. Johnson
1967   Letter to Jay Ruby. March 7. In possession of the authors.

King, C.
2003   Japchibit Ethnohistory. Prepared for the U.S. Department of Agriculture, Southern California Province, Angeles National Forest, Arcadia. Prepared by Topanga Anthropological Consultants, Topanga, CA.

Kline, V. L.
2009   Regional Network Analysis Situating Lost Valley in the Inter-Site Landscape. Master's thesis. Anthropology Department, San Diego State University.

Kryder-Reid, E.
2007   Sites of Power and Power of Sight. In *Sites Unseen: Landscape and Vision*, edited by D. Harris and D. Fairchild Ruggles, pp. 181–212. University of Pittsburgh Press, Pittsburgh.

Laylander, D., and J. Schaefer
2010   Draft Chuckwalla Valley Prehistoric Trails Network Cultural Landscape: Historic Context, Research Questions, and Resource Evaluation Criteria. California Energy Commission, Sacramento.

Leonard, N. N., III
1976   *Archaeological Element for the Conservation and Recreation Plan for Santa Catalina Island, Phase I: The Data Base.* Submitted to the Center of Natural Areas. Copies available at the California South Central Coastal Information Center, Fullerton.

McCarthy, D. F.
1982   The Coco-Maricopa Trail Network. Appendix C of *Cultural Resource Inventory and National Register Assessment of the Southern California Edison Palo Verde to Devers Transmission Line Corridor (California Portion)*, edited by R. L. Carrico, D. K. Quillen, and D. R. Gallegos. Submitted to Southern California Edison. WESTEC Services, San Diego.

McCarthy, H. D.
1986   Salt Pomo: An Ethnogeography. *Journal of California and Great Basin Anthropology* 8(1): 24–36.

McCawley, W.
1996   *The First Angelinos: The Gabrielino Indians of Los Angeles.* Malki Museum Press, Banning, CA.
2002   A Tale of Two Cultures: The Chumash and the Gabrielino. In *Islanders and Mainlanders*, edited by J. Altschul and D. Grenda, pp. 41–65. SRI Press, Tucson.

McNiven, I.
2003   Saltwater People: Spiritscapes, Maritime Rituals and the Archaeology of Australian Indigenous Seascapes. *World Archaeology* 35(3):329–349.

Meighan, C. W.
1959   The Little Harbor Site, Catalina Island: An Example of Ecological Interpretations in Archaeology. *American Antiquity* 24(4):383–405.

Meighan, C. W., and K. L. Johnson
1957   Isle of Mines. *Pacific Discovery* 10(1):24–29.

Melmed, A., and R. Apple
2009   Trails through the Landscape of the Colorado Desert. *Proceedings of the Society for California Archaeology* 21:226–230.

Mines, D. P.
2002   Hindu Nationalism, Untouchable Reform, and the Ritual Production of a South Indian Village. *American Ethnologist* 29:58–85.

Muir, F.
1995   Catalina Takes a Beating: Islanders Worry About Tourism, Isolation as Storms' Toll Rises. *Los Angeles Times*, January 21.

Musser-Lopez, R. A., and S. Miller
2010   Archaeological Trails and Ethnographic Trails: Can They Meet? *Proceedings of the Society for California Archaeology* 24:1–24.

Old Spanish Trail Association
2011   Trail Notes. http://www. oldspanishtrail.org /learn/trail_notes. php. Accessed October 2, 2012.

Patencio, F.
1943   *Stories and Legends of the Palm Springs Indians*. Reprinted, Palm Springs Desert Museum, Palm Springs, CA, 1969.

Perry, J. E.
2003   Prehistoric Land and Resource Use among Complex Hunter-Gatherer-Fishers on Eastern Santa Cruz Island. PhD dissertation. University of California, Santa Barbara.

Perry, J. E., and C. Delaney-Rivera
2011   Interactions and Interiors of the Coastal Chumash: Perspectives from Santa Cruz Island and the Oxnard Plain. *California Archaeology* 3:103–126.

Porcasi, J. F.
1998   Middle Holocene Ceramic Technology on the Southern California Coast: New Evidence from Little Harbor, Santa Catalina Island. *Journal of California and Great Basin Anthropology* 10(2):270–284.
2000   Updating Prehistoric Maritime Subsistence at Little Harbor, Santa Catalina Island, California. In *Proceedings, Fifth California Islands Symposium*, edited by D. R. Browne, K. L. Mitchell, and H. W. Chaney, pp. 580–589. U.S. Department of the Interior, Minerals Management Service, Washington, DC.

Porcasi, Judith F., and Harumi Fujita
2000   The Dolphin Hunters: A Specialized Prehistoric Maritime Adaptation in the Southern California Channel Islands and Baja California. *American Antiquity* 65(3):543–566.

Raab, M. L., K. Bradford, J. F. Porcasi, and W. J. Howard
1995   Return to Little Harbor, Santa Catalina Island, California: A Critique of the Marine Paleotemperature Model. *American Antiquity* 60(2):287–308.

Raab, M. L., K. Bradford, and A. Yatsko
1994   Advances in Southern Channel Islands Ar-

chaeology: 1983 to 1993. *Journal of California and Great Basin Anthropology* 16(2):243–270.

Reddy, S.
2006   *Archaeological Survey of Ben Weston Beach Access Road, Santa Catalina Island, California*. Report submitted to the Catalina Island Conservancy. Copy available at the South Central Coastal Information Center, Fullerton. Statistical Research Inc., Tucson, AZ.

Reinman, F., and H. Eberhart
1980   Test Excavations at the Ripper's Cove Site, SCAI-26. *Pacific Coast Archaeological Society Quarterly* 16(1–2):61–105.

Rivers, B., and T. L. Jones
1993   Walking Along Deer Trails: A Contribution to Salinan Ethnogeography Based on the Field Notes of John Peabody Harrington. *Journal of California and Great Basin Anthropology* 15(2):146–175.

Robinson, D. W.
2010   Land Use, Land Ideology: An Integrated Geographic Information Systems Analysis of Rock Art Within South-Central California. *American Antiquity* 75(4):792–818.
2011   Placing Ideology: Rock Art Landscapes of Inland and Interior South-Central California. *California Archaeology* 3(1):31–52.

Robinson, D. W., J. E. Perry, and G. Grasse-Sprague
2011   Landscape Archaeology in Southern and South-Central California. *California Archaeology* 3(1):5–10.

Rosen, M. D.
1980   Archaeological Investigations at Two Prehistoric Santa Catalina Sites: Rosski (SCaI-45) and Miner's Camp (SCaI-118). *Pacific Coast Archaeological Society Quarterly* 16(1–2):26–60.

Rosenthal, E. J., S. L. Williams, M. Roeder, W. Bonner, and I. Strudwick
1988   The Bulrush Canyon Project: Excavations at Bulrush Canyon Site (ScaI-137) and Camp Cactus Road Site, Santa Catalina Island. *Pacific Coast Archaeological Society Quarterly* 24(2–3):1–104.

Ruby, J., and T. Blackburn
1964   Occurrence of Southwestern Pottery in Los Angeles, County, California. *American Antiquity* 30(2):209–210.

Schoenherr, A. A., C. R. Feldmeth, and M. J. Emerson
1999   *Natural History of the Islands of California*. University of California Press, Berkeley.

Schumacher, P.
1877   Method and Manufacture of Several Articles by the Former Inhabitants of Southern California. *Peabody Museum Eleventh Annual Report* 7:258–268.

1878   Ancient Olla Manufactory of Santa Catalina Island, California. *American Naturalist* 12(9): 629.

1879   The Method and Manufacture of Soapstone Pots. In *Report Upon United States Geographical Surveys West of the One Hundredth Meridian: Archaeology*, pp. 117–121. Government Printing Office, Washington, DC.

Smithsonian Museum

2011   Smithsonian Scrapbook: Letters, Diaries and Photographs from the Smithsonian Archives. http://siarchives. si. edu/history/exhibits/doc uments/dall. htm. Accessed October 5, 2011.

Snead, J. E., C. L. Erickson, and J. A. Darling

2009   Making Human Space: The Archaeology of Trains, Paths, and Roads. In *Landscapes of Movement: Trails, Paths, and Roads in Anthropological Perspective*, edited by J. Snead, C. Erickson, and J. A. Darling, pp. 1–19. University of Pennsylvania Museum of Archaeology and Anthropology, Philadelphia.

Stoddard, S., and Zubrow, E.

1999   Changing Places. *Antiquity* 73:686–688.

Strudwick, I. H., R. McLean, J. Michalsky, B. Smith, and J. E. Baumann

2007   A Glimpse of the Past on Pimu: Cultural Resource Survey, Santa Catalina Island, Los Angeles County, California. report submitted to Southern California Edison. Copy available at the South Central Coastal Information Center, Fullerton. LSA Associates, Irvine, CA.

Tilley, C.

1997   *A Phenomenology of Landscape: Places, Paths and Monuments*. Bloomsbury Academic, New York.

U.S. Congress. House.

1877   Appendices of the Report of the Chief of Engineers. In *Report of the Secretary of War*, Vol. 2, Part 3, Index to the Executive Documents of the House of Representatives of the United States for the Second Session of the Forty-Fourth Congress, 1876–1877. Government Printing Office, Washington, DC.

Wandsnider, L.

1992   Archaeological Landscape Studies. *In Space, Time and Archaeological Landscapes*, edited by J. Rossignol and L. Wandersnider, pp. 285–292. Plenum, New York.

Warren, E.

2004   The Old Spanish National Historic Trail. In *Pathways Across America*. Partnership for the National Trail System, Madison, WI.

Whatford, J. C.

1994   Patterns on the Land: Landscape Archaeology at Annadel State Park. *Proceedings of the Society for California Archaeology* 7:159–164.

Wheeler, G. M., A. A. Humphreys, and H. G. Wright

1879   *Report Upon United States Geographical Surveys West of the One Hundredth Meridian: Archaeology*. Government Printing Office, Washington, DC.

Wlodarski, R.

1982   *A Bibliography of Catalina Island Investigations and Excavations (1850–1950)*. Occasional Paper 9. Institute of Archaeology, University of California, Los Angeles.

Wobst, M.

2005   Artifacts as Social Interference: The Politics of Spatial Scale. In *Confronting Scale in Archaeology: Issues of Theory and Practice*, edited by G. Lock and B. L. Molyneaux, pp. 55–66. Springer, New York.

10

The Native Depopulation
of Santa Catalina Island

Ivan H. Strudwick

Over 7,000 years of native occupation of Santa Catalina Island culminated in a prehistoric population that likely exceeded 500 individuals. Within 50 years after the 1769 European occupation of the adjacent coastal mainland, Catalina's native population was gone. When did the last native Catalina islanders leave their island home, what caused their decline, and is it possible to identify where they relocated?

The rescue of the last native inhabitant of San Nicolas Island is legendary and is known to have occurred in the summer of 1853, when, after living a solitary island life for 18 years, the "Lone Woman" was rescued and taken to live with Mr. and Mrs. George Nidever in Santa Barbara, where she died after just seven weeks (Ellison 1937:89). Had it not been for that sensational story, the earlier 1835 relocation of the last 17–18 of her tribal relatives from San Nicolas Island to San Pedro and then on to Los Angeles and Mission San Gabriel might not have been documented (Ellison 1937:37; Heizer and Elsasser 1961:12; McCawley 1996:67). Lacking a romantic tale of solitary life from Catalina Island, the truth concerning the last native Catalina islanders may be doomed to eternal obscurity. In an effort to follow the faded trail of the final decline and ultimate fate of the native Catalina Island population, this chapter examines four basic lines of evidence: (1) ethnohistoric and historic accounts; (2) recorded island and mainland village names; (3) mission and church baptismal and marriage records, and (4) native songs.

Information presented here has been referenced from many sources. The earliest descrip-tions of California come from journals of exploration kept in the sixteenth through eighteenth centuries. The early nineteenth century brought additional firsthand accounts, including some of the first based on American exploration, but by then native cultures had changed from their pre-contact conditions. One of the first identifiable results of the introduction of European culture to coastal California was a substantial reduction in the native population.

Three principal authors are referenced: Williamson (1904); Johnson (1988), who has compiled data from mission and church records; and McCawley (1996), whose seminal work on the Gabrielino contains information on all four of the above-listed research areas. The basis for this chapter had its inception in Strudwick et al. (2007), originally prepared for a Southern California Edison (SCE) power pole project on Catalina. What this chapter offers is a consolidated review of native Santa Catalina Island depopulation and subsequent relocation in relation to patterns from other California Channel Islands.

Gabrielino Territory

Although the geographical and cultural relationships of California's eight Channel Islands are presented elsewhere in this volume (e.g., Jazwa and Perry, Chapter 1), some basic information is worth repeating here. Of the four southern Channel Islands, Santa Catalina is the largest (76 mi²/ 122 km²) and nearest to the mainland (20 mi/ 32 km south of the Palos Verdes Peninsula) (Schoenherr et al. 1999:147) (Figures 10.1 and 10.2). While the Chumash occupied the north-

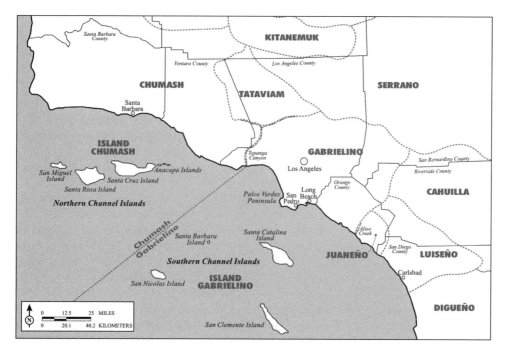

FIGURE 10.1. Map of Southern California showing the Channel Islands and native cultural areas.

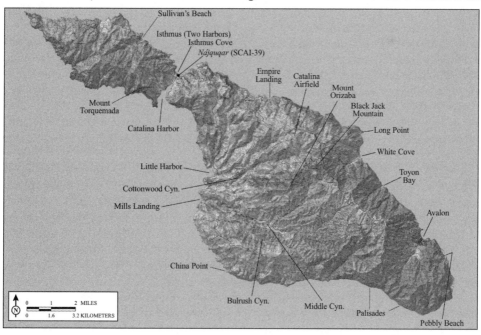

FIGURE 10.2. Map of Santa Catalina Island showing major geographical features.

ern Channel Islands and adjacent Santa Barbara mainland, the southern Channel Islands were occupied by the "Gabrielino," a name first used about 1852 (William McCawley, personal communication, 2012; see Reid 1968:98). A third native group discussed here, the Luiseño, were named after Mission San Luis Rey and occupied the coastal area near Carlsbad in what is now northern San Diego County.

The Gabrielino, Chumash, and Luiseño spoke mutually unintelligible languages. Gabrielino territory centered in what is now Los Angeles

TABLE 10.1. Historic accounts of Santa Catalina Island's native population

Date	Discoverer	Account	Reference
1542	Juan Rodriguez Cabrillo	A "great number"	Wagner 1941:46
1602	Sebastián Vizcaíno	More than 450 "Indians"	Bolton 1908:84 Wagner 1929:401
1769	Fr. Juan Vizcaíno	Unidentified number of "Indians"	Vizcaíno 1959:17
1805	Cpt. William Shaler	"about 150 men, women, and children"	Shaler 1935:47
1807	Cpt. Jonathan Winship	40 or 50 native residents	Bancroft 1886, 19:84

and Orange Counties and included the watersheds of the Los Angeles, San Gabriel, and Santa Ana Rivers, spanning the coast from Aliso Creek north to a point between Topanga and Malibu Creeks (Kroeber 1925:620–621; Bean and Smith 1978:538; McCawley 1996:3, 2002:41; Schwartz 2003:1–2). The "Island Gabrielino" were permanent residents of Catalina, San Clemente, and San Nicolas Islands, but the small size and limited resources of Santa Barbara Island made permanent occupation there unfeasible (McCawley 2002:44).

In order to classify native habitation of the Channel Islands, McCawley (2002:42–44) grouped the islands into three categories: primary, secondary, and peripheral. Primary islands contain large landmasses, stable supplies of freshwater, and several terrestrial habitats. Secondary islands are smaller, have less reliable freshwater supplies, and fewer biotic habitats. Peripheral islands are small islands unable to support permanent settlement. Two northern Channel Islands, Santa Cruz and Santa Rosa, are primary islands. Santa Catalina is the only primary southern Channel Island.

Depopulation and Relocation: Lines of Evidence
Ethnohistoric and Historic Accounts

On October 7, 1542, Juan Rodriguez Cabrillo first observed Catalina and San Clemente Islands, naming them "San Salvador" and "La Victoria," after his ships. Landing on San Salvador (Catalina), Cabrillo is thought to have anchored at Avalon, where "a great number of Indians" made signs for the Spaniards to come ashore (Wagner 1941:46, Johnson 1988:2; McCawley 1996:77) (Table 10.1).

Beginning in 1565, voyages from Mexico to the Philippines and back were made by what became known as "Manila galleons," merchant transport ships returning with profits from trade with Manila in the Philippines (Cowan 1988:7). Westerly trade winds in higher latitudes took these ships eastward across the Pacific to the Mendocino area, where they turned south, traveling rapidly down the California coast, usually without landing until they reached their destination, Acapulco. Records from at least three of these voyages—the first in 1565, the second in 1595, and a third in 1598—are thought to describe Catalina (Wagner 1929; Johnson 1988:2–3), although native populations are not mentioned.

The best known of these three Manila galleon voyages was that of Cermeño aboard the *San Agustin* in 1595. After having lost his ship in the San Francisco Bay area, Cermeño and his crew took their launch and traveled south. On December 16, 1595, they stopped at what is believed to be Catalina Island (Wagner 1929:162; Johnson 1988:3).

In 1598, the galleon *San Pedro* is thought to have sunk off Catalina (Wlodarski et al. 1984:61; Johnson 1988:3), although this has recently been disputed (Johnson 2010:42). The ship sank on the Pacific side of the island near the isthmus, the survivors spending several months on Catalina before being rescued by a ship sent from Mexico. In 1601 and 1603, the Spanish sent salvage expeditions to recover material from the wreck, reportedly relying on native Catalina islanders as divers (Wlodarski et al. 1984:61; Johnson 1988:3).

In 1602–1603, Sebastián Vizcaíno sailed along California surveying the coast for safe harbor should future landings be necessary. On November 24, 1602, the eve of the feast day of Saint Catherine, Vizcaíno landed at what is thought to have been Avalon, where mass was given with more than 150 native men and women present (Bolton

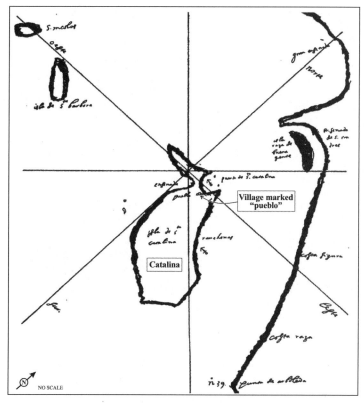

FIGURE 10.3. Father Antonia de la Ascensión's 1602 map of Catalina Island showing the village of Nájquqar (SCAI-39) (marked "pueblo") (from Wagner 1929:235).

1908:84; Wagner 1929:401; McCawley 1996:77). Two days later, the party visited the isthmus, where they observed a "pueblo and more than 300 Indians, men, women and children" (Bolton 1908:85) (Table 10.1).

On the 1602 Vizcaíno expedition, Father Antonio de la Ascensión drew a map of Catalina that clearly identifies the pueblo at the isthmus (Wagner 1929:234–235; McCawley 2002:42–43; Figure 10.3). The village of Nájquqar (SCAI-39) is located at Isthmus Cove in Two Harbors (McCawley 1996:78–79; Figure 10.4). This village is one of the principal prehistoric villages on Catalina and may also have been the center for steatite trade. Ascensión's map identifies *rancherías* (native settlements) along the eastern shore where an anchor marks the location of safe anchorage. There are many safe anchorages along Catalina's eastern shore, beginning in the south with Avalon Bay and continuing northward to Toyon Bay and White Cove. That Ascensión specifically identi-

fied the pueblo at Isthmus Cove while only generally identifying other settlements along the eastern shore as *rancherías* suggests that he perceived the village at Isthmus Cove to be the island's principal one.

Catalina was visited again in 1769 by the *San Antonio*, a provision supply ship for the Portolá expedition, on which Captain Juan Pérez and Father Juan Vizcaíno were traveling to San Diego Harbor to meet with the overland portion of the expedition coming from mainland Mexico (Avina 1932:5). Led by Captain Gaspar de Portolá, the 1769–1770 expedition was the first European land expedition through California. Before reaching San Diego, one of the supply ships, the *San Antonio*, landed on Catalina Island, where Vizcaíno described a level area, most likely the isthmus, "where there are Indians" (Vizcaíno 1959:17; McCawley 1996:77) (see Table 10.1). Here, Vizcaíno made many observations about Catalina's native material culture.

FIGURE 10.4. View of Isthmus Cove looking southeast at the location of the village of Nájquqar (SCAI-39) on the bluff to the left of the pier.

On March 14, 1805, Captain William Shaler in the *Lelia Byrd* visited Catalina Island to locate a harbor to repair his ship after collecting sea otter skins that he intended to sell in Canton, China. Returning to Catalina on May 1, Shaler careened his ship at what has been described as Avalon (Gudde 1998:21), but was actually the isthmus (see Shaler 1935:70), which he named Port Roussillon (Shaler 1935:47). Staying six weeks for repairs, Shaler described "Indian inhabitants of this island, to the amount of about 150 men, women, and children" (Shaler 1935:47) (see Table 10.1). It was on this same voyage in early 1803 that second-in-command, supercargo Richard J. Cleveland, reported 11 naked Indians living in a cave on the south side of San Clemente Island. Cleveland believed these individuals to be the sole inhabitants of that island (Bancroft 1886, 19:11; see also Johnson 1988:5).

In February of 1807, Captain Jonathan Winship in the *O'Cain* visited Catalina Island with native Kodiak sea otter hunters. According to Bancroft (1886, 19:84), Winship found 40 or 50 native residents on Catalina with grain and vegetables to sell (see also Williamson 1904:20; Johnson 1988:5; McCawley 1996:79). The is the last substantiated date documenting natives on Catalina Island.

Erroneous Accounts

The misinterpretation of native California Channel Island names has led to incorrect conclusions concerning Santa Catalina Island natives. The native Gabrielino name for Santa Catalina Island, Pimu, has been confused in the literature with the native Chumash name for Santa Cruz Island, Limu (Johnson 1988:6; 2010:40). Because of this, some descriptions of Channel Island villages and events have been incorrectly assigned to Catalina. In one example, Williamson (1904:19) states that in 1804, California Mission president Estevan Tapis "did favor the founding of a mission on the isle [of Catalina] which he calls 'Limu,'" where there was an abundance of timber, water, and soil, and where there were 10 *rancherías*, the three largest of which, Cajatsa, Ashuael, and Liam, contained 124, 145, and 122 adults, respectively. Williamson (1904:19–20) states that in 1806, Tapis reported that measles had killed more than 200 natives on "Catalina" and Santa Rosa Islands, and that founding a mission on Catalina was doubtful due to the lack of freshwater and suitable land. In both instances, Tapis was describing Santa Cruz Island, not Catalina.

In a second example, Bancroft (1886, 19:578–579) states that in 1822 there were still some pagans on Santa Catalina Island and that the padres

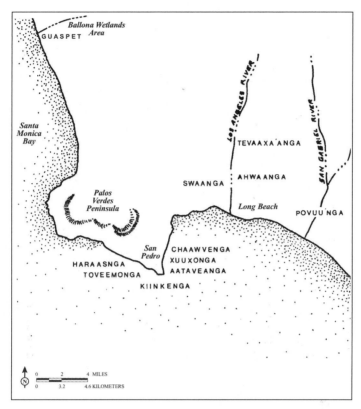

FIGURE 10.5. Map of the Palos Verdes Peninsula area showing native villages (after McCawley 1996:56, map.)

thought the island should be settled with the remaining original inhabitants. However, this is attributable to Bancroft confusing the Chumash name for Santa Cruz Island, Limu, with Pimu.

Recorded Island and Mainland Village Names

Knowing the name and location of native villages can provide a clearer understanding of cultural relationships and population movements. The Gabrielino called Santa Catalina Island Pimu, Pipimar, or Pemuu'nga, and the islanders referred to themselves as Pepimaros or Peppi'maris (Kroeber 1925:621, 634; Johnston 1962:113; Bean and Smith 1978:540; McCawley 1996:10). The word *Pipimar* may have been a general term meaning "island Indian" (Harrington 1933; Johnson 1988: 9). San Clemente was called Kinki or Kinkipar (also spelled Quinqui and Guinguina) (Kroeber 1925:621; Heizer 1968:106; Johnson 1988:8; McCawley 1996:10). Suffixes attached to the *Pimu* root, such as *-nga* and *-na* (as in Pimunga and Pimuna), refer to the location itself. Suffixes such

as *-vit*, *-bit* or *-pat* (as in Pimubit) designate an individual from the location of the root word (Johnson 1988:9; McCawley 1996:10). The Chumash name for Catalina Island was Juyà, and for San Clemente Island, Kinkin (Johnson 1988:8, 18).

The Gabrielino names for San Clemente and San Nicolas Islands, Kiinkenga and Haraasnga, appear in San Gabriel Mission baptismal registries from the late 1700s and early 1800s (Johnson 1988). This suggests that those baptized may have been living on the mainland coast near the mission.

McCawley (1996) presents information from J. P. Harrington's informant José Zalvidea in order to map specific village locations (Figure 10.5). Zalvidea described the village of Kínkina (Kiinkenga) as having been located on the Palos Verdes Peninsula (McCawley 1996:18). Johnston (1962:89, 112) places the village of Kinki near San Pedro. Heizer (1968:107) believes that the mainland village of Kinki may have been named by a group of resettled San Clemente islanders.

Notably, Zalvidea reported that Gabrielino were still living at Kiinkenga in the early 1900s (McCawley 1996:206).

There is some confusion concerning the location of some native villages. In 1852, Hugo Reid (1968:8) listed Harasg-na without a location, although Zalvidea placed it in San Pedro near Kiinkenga (Johnston 1962:112; McCawley 1996:67). As Kimkiharasa was the Luiseño name for San Clemente Island (Johnston 1962:112), a similar name, Xarasngna, could have been the Gabrielino name for San Clemente Island.

The similarity between the names Harasg-na and Xarasngna with Kiinkenga (Kínkina/Kinki) and Kimkiharasa has also led to some confusion. Ghalas-at is the Chumash name for San Nicolas Island, and Kroeber (1925:635; see also Johnston 1962:113) states that the Chumash pronunciation of Haraasnga is "Ghalas-at." For many years the village of Guaspet (also known as Guasna, Guaschna, Guaaschna, and others) was thought to be a variation of Ghalas-at and thus a reference to San Nicolas Island. Recently, the location of Guaspet has been identified as lying within the Ballona Wetlands of west Los Angeles (McCawley 1996:61–63; King and Johnson 1999; Stoll et al. 2009; Douglass and Hackel 2011). Knowing the location of Guaspet is important since there are more Mission San Gabriel–recorded baptisms from Guaspet than almost any other native village (Stoll et al. 2009), and nearly half of recorded Island Gabrielino marriages occur with individuals from Guaspet (discussed in the following section on marriage).

Researchers believe that some villages on the Palos Verdes Peninsula were settled by relocated Gabrielino islanders (Heizer 1968:107; McCawley 1996:66, 203). Although some Island Gabrielino may have relocated to the nearby Ballona Wetlands village of Guaspet, the site was occupied prehistorically (see Stoll et al. 2009; Douglass and Hackel 2011) and was not created by historic-era native relocation. In the case of the San Nicolas islanders (Nicoleño), "It may be that groups of Island Gabrielino relocated to the mainland and founded the community of Haraasnga, bestowing upon it the name of their traditional home" (McCawley 1996:67). Similarly, Chumash villages on Santa Cruz Island are known to have relocated to the nearby mainland (McLendon and Johnson 1999; Johnson 2001:59). Although informants

identified mainland villages with native names for San Clemente Island (Kinki) and San Nicolas Island (Haraasnga), no mainland village named for Catalina Island is known.

Mission and Church Baptismal and Marriage Records

In order to identify patterns of social relations between Gabrielino islanders, John Johnson (1988: 8–24) reviewed existing marriage and baptismal records from Missions San Fernando and San Gabriel, and from the Plaza Church of Los Angeles (Table 10.2). From 1804 to 1826, 18 marriages are recorded with at least one Island Gabrielino partner, one-third of them in 1805 (Johnson 1988:17). Nine of these marriages occurred in the first three years, 1804–1806. This suggests that the principal initial movement of Island Gabrielino to the mainland began in 1804.

Fourteen of the 18 marriages include native Catalina islanders, although only one marriage (in 1811) was between two Catalina islanders. Island Gabrielino were exogamous, marrying those from other islands far more often than someone from their own island. One of the 18 marriages is notable: in 1805, Pio Chapray (Saplay), a chief of Humaliu (Malibu, the southernmost coastal Chumash village), married Pia Siliyenahuan from Humaliu (Johnson 1988:18). Saplay was originally from Juyà (Catalina). Baptismal registries also identify two other Catalina Island chiefs: the first, Juyibam, was listed as the father of a Pimubit child baptized at Mission San Gabriel in 1820; the second, Cano of Pimunga, was baptized at Mission San Fernando in 1825 (Johnson 1988:20). Johnson (1988:20) found that Ramona Huitchi, the mother of the Pimubit child (son of Juyibam), was baptized at Plaza Church in 1830. The entry identified Ramona as coming from Quinqui (San Clemente Island), suggesting to Johnson (1988:20) the likelihood "that a chief from Pimunga had taken a San Clemente Island wife."

From 1789 to 1836, 93 adult Gabrielino islanders were baptized at the two missions and at the Plaza Church of Los Angeles (Johnson 1988:21–24) (Figure 10.6). Of this number, nearly half ($n = 43$, 46.2 percent) of the baptisms were of individuals from Catalina Island, and the majority of these ($n = 27$, 63 percent) were baptized at Mission San Gabriel. An initial group of 13 bap-

TABLE 10.2. Island Gabrielino (Tongva) marriages in mission registries

Date	No. of Marriages	(Catalina) Pimu	(S. Clemen.) Quinqui	(Island) "Island"	(Ballona) Guaspet
		Number of Individuals			
1804	2	3	0	0	0
1805	6	4	3	0	4
1806	1	0	0	1	1
1811	1	2	0	0	0
1813	2	2	0	0	2
1819	1	1	0	0	1
1822	1	1	1	0	0
1823	2	2	2	0	0
1825	1	1	1	0	0
1826	1	0	2	0	0

Note: Data adapted from Johnson 1988:17, Table 1.

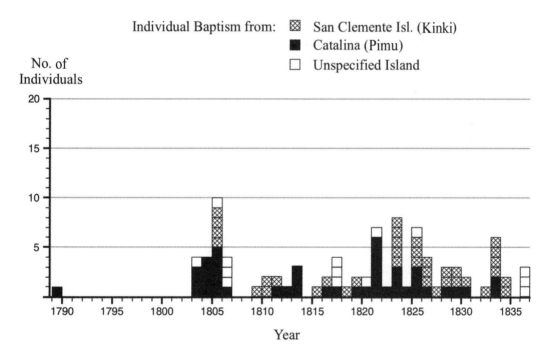

FIGURE 10.6. Adult Island Gabrielino (Tongva) baptized at Missions San Fernando and San Gabriel and at the Plaza Church of Los Angeles between 1789 and 1836 (after Johnson 1988:23, Figure 2).

tisms occurred in 1803–1806, not unexpectedly mirroring the initial group of Island Gabrielino marriages in 1804–1806. However, most adult Island Gabrielino, including those from Catalina, were not baptized until Plaza Church was established in the 1820s (Johnson 1988:21). Many adult islanders were never baptized, and many others were baptized on their deathbeds as a final rite. Nonetheless, recorded baptisms indicate that an initial wave of Island Gabrielino migrated to the mainland beginning in 1803.

Johnson (1988) identified 69 children baptized to unbaptized parents from 1789–1836. He believes that Island Gabrielino adults avoided baptism at the missions to avoid having to leave their new mainland villages. "The establishment of Plaza Church at Los Angeles in 1826 allowed the islanders of the Indian community to remain in homes near the pueblo without having to join the mission work forces" (Johnson 1988:21, 24).

It has been argued that baptismal records may not accurately date the migration of Island Gabrielino from the islands to the mainland (Johnson 1988:20). The attempt to avoid joining the mission workforce may explain why there was an initial 1803–1806 increase in Island Gabrielino baptisms, followed by a hiatus of baptisms until 1809, and then only a minimal number of baptisms until the late 1810s and 1820s. The islanders who moved to the mainland in 1803–1806 may not have considered the implications of baptism as carefully as those who were baptized later. This is a much different scenario than what occurred with the Island Chumash, who mass-migrated to adjacent mainland missions during the late 1810s; 42 percent of all recorded Island Chumash baptisms occurred from 1816 to 1820 (Johnson 1988:13, 20). Despite arguments for the postponement of Island Gabrielino baptisms, the initial group of Catalina islander baptisms began in 1803.

Native Songs

Because few survive, native songs are a limited data source for patterns of native Catalina islander migration. Nonetheless, song was integral to Gabrielino ritual and was a crucial element in recording and commemorating historical events. Gabrielino songs were inherited along family lines and often preserved genealogical and territorial information. Individuals and lineages owned songs that could not be sung by others without permission (McCawley 1996:179; see Teeter, Martinez, and Richardson, Chapter 9, regarding the significance of song among native Californians).

Kroeber (1925:622) states that the Luiseño and Diegueño (a San Diego area native group; see Figure 10.1) sang nearly all of their ceremonial songs in the Gabrielino language, not even understanding the words. Johnston (1962:97) states that native Luiseño men had a great respect for the men of Catalina, attributing to them extreme longevity and strength. Songs sung by a Santa Catalina Island clan that had recently migrated to the mainland were said by the Luiseño to empower this clan. Johnston (1962:97) states that Helen H. Roberts obtained this information from an informant, although the informant's name was not identified.

McCawley (1996:179) references Roberts (1933) for two Gabrielino songs about Catalina lineages. One song commemorates the migration of a Catalina lineage to the mainland at Carlsbad near San Luis Rey (see McCawley 1996:202), describing the conflict that arose between the Catalina lineage and a previously settled group (Teeter, Martinez, and Richardson, Chapter 9). A second song describes how the Catalina lineage settled into their new home and began raising crops. These songs indicate that Island Gabrielino migrated to settle in Luiseño territory, although exactly when and where is unknown.

Although Kroeber (1925:622) states that the Franciscans brought the San Clemente Island Indians to Mission San Luis Rey, others suggest that there is no connection between the Island Gabrielino and Mission San Luis Rey or San Juan Capistrano (Merriam 1968:122–148, cited in Johnson 1988:8). Aside from Kroeber's statement, these songs are the only evidence that any Island Gabrielino group relocated to Luiseño territory.

Causes of Native Depopulation of Santa Catalina Island

Native depopulation of the Channel Islands began with exposure to European culture that disrupted native culture and social relationships through: (1) changes in population dynamics, (2) disease, and (3) violence.

Changes in Population Dynamics

Unprecedented village movement due to European pressure may have decreased food gathering abilities, stressing the native social fabric and impeding population growth. Depopulation was inexorably set in motion by the introduction of European culture, which disrupted native cultural continuity and social relationships in at least the three ways listed above. Decreasing native populations made trade between the Catalina islanders and mainland groups more difficult. Steatite (soapstone or talc-schist) originating on Catalina was used prehistorically for items such as pendants, effigies, and cooking pots (Schumacher 1878:629; Meighan and Rootenberg 1957; Meighan 1959:391–394; Williams and Rosenthal 1993). These and other items from the island, such as otter pelts (Rosen 1980:27) and jicamas (small edible roots; Wagner 1929:236), were traded to natives on the mainland (refer to McGuire 1883:589). In 1602, Father Ascensión (McGuire 1883:589) observed that "They [the native Catalina islanders] live by buying, selling and bartering." As native populations on the adjacent mainland declined, the demand for trade items decreased. This created a situation where there was less incentive to inhabit distant islands such as Catalina. As shown on the northern Channel Islands, the native Chumash village of Lu'upsh at China Harbor on Santa Cruz Island, apparently situated for lithic procurement purposes, was abandoned as island-mainland trade relations changed during the historic era (Arnold 2001).

Disease

A measles epidemic in about 1806 killed nearly 200 natives on Santa Cruz and Santa Rosa Islands (Williamson 1904:19). Cholera, rabies, and smallpox are all reported in mission death records from San Luis Obispo south to San Juan Capistrano (Douglass and Stanton 2010). Similar epidemics occurred repeatedly throughout California (Castillo 1978:102; King 1978:65), and although spared from much of the initial wrath of disease due to their distant, somewhat inaccessible locale, the native Catalina population could not have been immune. Based on observations from the 1803–1805 portion of his circum-Pacific voyage in the *Lelia Byrd*, Captain Shaler (1935:58) described the natives of Lower California as "almost universally infected with the venereal disease, and numbers perish daily, in the most deplorable manner.... Upper California is still populous... [but] the same disorder rages there with the same violence."

Violence

Beginning in 1803, Aleut sea otter hunters brought to California are known to have killed native San Nicolas islanders and may have factored into the native depopulation of Santa Catalina and other California Channel Islands. In 1852, Reid (1968:100–101) stated that the Northwest Coast Indians had once killed great numbers of those on the islands. Alfred Robinson (1846) suggested that the onslaught by Alaskan natives who had been brought to hunt sea otter induced both northern and southern California Channel Islanders to seek refuge and protection among mainland missions (see also Williamson 1904:20–21). McCawley (1996:66) suggests that these attacks may have caused Island Gabrielino to relocate to the Palos Verdes Peninsula on the mainland, where they established villages such as Kiinkenga and Haraasnga.

In 1803, Joseph O'Cain sailed the ship *O'Cain* from Boston to the Aleutian Island of Kodiak in Alaska. O'Cain worked out an agreement with Alexander Baranov, chief manager of the Russian American Company, whereby Baranov supplied 40 Aleut hunters to hunt sea otter along the California coast. O'Cain supplied the transport in his ship, and any sea otter furs obtained were to be sold in Canton, China (Batman 1985:137–144). The year 1803 marks the first recorded instance of the use of native Alaskans (Northwest Coast Indians) to hunt sea otter in California.

Bringing 20 of their own skin boats, known as *bidarkas*, as well as spears and darts of bone and ivory, the Aleuts accompanied the *O'Cain* southward. As did the *Lelia Byrd*, the *O'Cain* carried several cannons, a supply of guns, and ammunition. In June of 1804, the *O'Cain* returned to Kodiak Island with 1,800 sea otter furs after having traveled as far south as Baja California (Batman 1985:142–143). Within a short time other American ships voyaged to California to hunt sea otter, many with armed Aleut hunters. This eventually resulted in situations where relatively peaceful California Channel Islanders were killed by native Alaskans (Kroeber 1925:634; Heizer and Elsasser 1961; McCawley 1996:203).

As reported by Heizer and Elsasser (1961:3), it was in 1811 that Kodiak (Aleut) Indians temporarily left on San Nicolas Island by an American captain killed nearly all of the Nicoleño. However, recent research (Morris et al. in press) documents that the massacre of an unknown number of Nicoleño by native Alaskan sea otter hunters from the Russian American Company ship *Il'mena* (formerly the *Lydia*) actually occurred in 1814. Though not specifically mentioned in the literature, native Catalina islanders must have experienced similar depredations from Alaskan sea otter hunters. Lacking guns, the islanders would have had little or no defense against such attacks.

George Nidever, the captain who in 1853 rescued the Lone Woman of San Nicolas Island, describes being attacked by "N.W. Indians" on January 1, 1836, while hunting sea otter on the northeastern side of Santa Rosa Island (Ellison 1937:40–44). Nidever states that he and several colleagues were attacked by Northwest Coast Indians in 13 canoes, each containing at least two and sometimes a third Indian. Although the Northwest Coast Indians used buckshot to hunt otter, they attacked Nidever using English muskets loaded with lead ball that carried over a mile, past some of Nidever's men who had escaped to an inland location (Ellison 1937:42). Nidever and his men eventually shot and killed three of the marauding Aleut and wounded another five or six, stating that this dealt a severe blow to them as for several years they had been terrorizing the coast, running hunters off the islands and stealing supplies and furs. Nidever (Ellison 1937:44) explains:

> They usually come in brigs or large vessels being almost invariably owned or fitted out by Americans or English and manned and officered by men of the same nationalities, the [NW Coast] Indians being employed to hunt. Landing occasionally on the Islands, they attacked the almost defenseless natives, killing many of them....

It is not known if the Island Chumash experienced similar attacks or if such attacks hastened native depopulation of the northern Channel Islands. Other than the attacks on the natives from San Nicolas Island, there is no record of any native Island Gabrielino or Island Chumash group being attacked by Aleut sea otter hunters.

The Final Exodus of Native Catalina Islanders

The sum total of known recorded native sightings on Santa Catalina Island is five (Table 10.1). From these recorded sightings, the native Santa Catalina Island population appears to have decreased significantly from 1602, when there were probably at least 450 islanders, to 1805, when there were

an estimated 150. In 1807, just two years later, only 40–50 native Catalina islanders remained. Corresponding with the final documented instances of native Catalina population decline, mainland mission registries record the initial surge of Catalina islander baptisms in 1803–1806. This is the same period as the first mission-recorded Island Gabrielino marriages, in 1804–1806, and immediately follows the first use of Alaskan sea otter hunters in California, which began in 1803. Based on Nidever's 1836 account (Ellison 1937:40–44), Robinson (1846) and Reid (1968 [1852]:100–101)) were correct in claiming that Northwest Coast sea otter hunters slaughtered Channel Islanders. The result was that beginning in 1803, a noticeable number of Island Gabrielino began immigrating to the mainland.

The final exodus of native Catalina islanders to the adjacent mainland occurred soon after 1807, most likely sometime between 1810 and 1818. McCawley (1996:202) states that the island was largely abandoned by 1818, although the last inhabitant was not removed until 1832 (Meighan and Johnson 1957:24). Forcible removal of native Catalina islanders from 1789 to 1818 is mentioned (Rosen 1980:54), but specifics are lacking. If the Catalina natives were forcibly removed, ostensibly by the missionaries, then the padres would have brought the natives to the mission for baptism. The few recorded baptisms during this period do not reflect forced removal, and supporting documentation is currently unknown.

There are other reasons to question the veracity of forcible removal of the last Catalina natives. McCawley (1996:202) reports that J. P. Harrington informant Sétimo López described Maria and José Chári, siblings from Catalina, as living in "Calabazas" (Calabasas, 15 mi west-northwest of Los Angeles). Around 1916, Harrington stated that "the last Indian woman, named Maria...died at Las Calabazas 10 or 15 years ago" (McCawley 1996:202). Sétimo's half-brother, Martin Violin, had a father named Nicanor Guandía, who, according to Sétimo, was the one who removed the islanders in a canoe (McCawley 1996:202). Unfortunately, neither the date when Nicanor Guandía is said to have removed the Catalina natives by canoe nor a description of whether force was used during their removal is provided. Did some natives inhabit Catalina until 1832, as reported by Meighan and Johnson (1957:24)? Logical conjecture suggests removal by canoe with relatives was probably a matter of personal choice. Based on the date of Harrington's interview, Maria Chári died about 1901–1906. Had Maria lived into her 90s, it is possible that she could have lived on Catalina as a child in the 1810s. However, insufficient information was recorded by Harrington to accurately estimate when these activities occurred.

Had natives inhabited Catalina as late as 1832, the historical political climate of California makes it unlikely that their removal was forcible, as the missions were in the process of secularization, and little effort would likely have been made by missionaries to increase their number of converts. More likely, the documented threat from Aleut sea otter hunters exerted more influence on whether or not native islanders chose to remain on Catalina. Beginning in 1803, native Catalina islanders would have been exposed to the Aleut, who were known to attack unprovoked (Ellison 1937:40–44). As described, in 1811 native San Nicolas Islanders were slaughtered by Aleut hunters (Heizer and Elsasser 1961:3). Living under such a threat would have provided strong motivation for the natives to leave Catalina, rendering forcible removal unnecessary.

On Catalina, items of European origin have been found on native habitation sites (Holder 1901; Meighan and Johnson 1957; Finnerty et al. 1970; Wlodarski et al. 1984). This material includes glass trade beads, cloth, and metal objects. Holder (1901:15) describes his observations at the Isthmus Cove site of Nájquqar (SCAI-39), the same site visited in 1805 by William Shaler, captain of the *Lelia Byrd* (Shaler 1935:47):

> One of the largest prehistoric settlements was at the isthmus….As near as I could judge, the graves of the lowest strata here long antedate the Cabrillo discovery, as in them I found nothing but native beads made from shell and bone, while from upper layers of graves I took mortars and pestles, beads of glass of Venetian pattern, bell-clappers, old knife-blades, bits of copper wire, an iron ax-head and mattock, which the Indians had doubtless received from the Spaniards in exchange for native products. All these had been buried with the dead, the

iron implements being carefully wrapped with cloth, which had rusted away, leaving merely the impression. (Holder 1901:15)

The presence of European trade goods at archaeological sites on Catalina may eventually show that Catalina natives inhabited the island well into the 1800s. Since precise dates on historic material from archaeological sites on Catalina do not exist, it is not known exactly when natives ceased occupying those sites with European items. Some sites on San Clemente Island (Rechtman 1985; Raab and Yatsko 1990:16; Raab et al. 2009; Perry, Chapter 8), as well as several mainland coastal Chumash sites (Gamble 2008: 202–211), have also been found with European material, but rarely can the material be dated more accurately than to within a decade or two. Some of the metal items from Chumash sites, such as knives, appear to have been made of hoop iron or other scrap metal (Gamble 2008:210).

In 1969, Nájquqar (SCAI-39) was excavated by the UCLA Archaeological Survey and described as a distribution center for island-mainland trade (Finnerty et al. 1970:22). During the extensive excavation at what remained of the site following more than a century of looting and previous "archaeological" exploration, burials were found with glass trade beads and carbonized corn reported to have come from mainland mission farms (Finnerty et al. 1970:15, 17). This appears to validate Jonathan Winship's 1807 description of the Catalina natives, who he said had "grain and vegetables" (Bancroft 1886, 19:84). One adult male burial from SCAI-39 was described as having "two probable bullet holes in his skull" (Finnerty et al. 1970:21). A steatite pipe, an abalone shell, and glass beads were associated with this burial. Quantities of glass trade beads and shell disk beads with small perforations from SCAI-39 reportedly date from 1771/1785 to "around 1820" (Finnerty et al. 1970:15), indicating that the site was occupied for some time after 1771/1785. The absence of metal implements from the 1969 excavation of SCAI-39 (Finnerty et al. 1970) is likely the result of the items having rusted away, as described by Holder (1901:15) in the previous quote.

Wlodarski et al. (1984:60) conducted a replicative study of the use of metal for soapstone quarrying and found that metal tools appear to have been used during the later sequence at the Jane Russell Quarry (SCAI-72). Other than Meighan and Johnson (1957:27), who report iron axe heads near some steatite quarries, no metal artifacts have been recovered in direct association with steatite quarries (Wlodarski et al. 1984:51). Glass trade beads from a steatite quarry known as Miner's Camp (SCAI-118), below Catalina Airfield, are thought to date to circa 1800 (Rosen 1980:54–55), providing evidence that natives continued to inhabit Catalina and quarry steatite on the island after the arrival of Europeans (Teeter, Martinez, and Richardson, Chapter 9).

European goods were given and traded directly to the islanders in 1542 by the Cabrillo expedition, in 1602 by the Vizcaíno expedition, and also in 1769 by those aboard the *San Antonio*, supply ship for the Portolá expedition. Material from the 1598 wreck of the *San Pedro*, a Manila galleon that sank near the isthmus (Wlodarski et al. 1984:61), could have been obtained directly by native islanders both by diving and beachcombing. European trade goods could also have been obtained by the islanders prior to 1800 through barter with mainland natives who were observed to have such items just prior to the land portion of the 1769–1770 Portolá expedition (Vizcaíno 1959 [1769]:25). Thus, native Catalina islanders had items of European manufacture beginning in 1542.

None of the above examples of historic items from Catalina provides a precise post-1807 date. Inasmuch as no other post-1807 historic data or references to native Catalina islanders exist, identifying the year of the final native departure from Catalina is conjecture. Although it is possible that a few natives continued inhabiting Catalina after 1810, the inherent social aspects of native life would have been absent. In other words, a small number of natives surviving on Catalina after about 1810 would have lived in virtual confinement, without the advantages of trade and communication with those on the mainland, and possibly in fear of attack from Aleut sea otter hunters. For these reasons, it is unlikely that the natives would have continued inhabiting Catalina for any length of time following a reduction in their population below 20–30 individuals, which is here estimated to have occurred about 1810.

Although currently undocumented, it is likely that the last native inhabitants departed Catalina during the 1810s. A later date, although possible, will require documentation.

Historic Accounts: Subsequent Relocation of Native Catalina Islanders

From their mainland villages, the relocated Catalina islanders dispersed into the surrounding populace. Although some appear to have initially relocated to the Carlsbad area in Luiseño territory, most islanders stayed in the Gabrielino area. They moved into or near the pueblo of Los Angeles, near Mission San Gabriel, and to a lesser extent to the Mission San Fernando area. The majority of Catalina islander baptisms occurred at Mission San Gabriel. Native chiefs from Catalina are known from records at Missions San Gabriel (Juyibam in 1820) and San Fernando (Cano in 1825). In 1805, one Catalina chief, Saplay, became a chief of Humaliu (Malibu). Also, two songs recorded in the Luiseño area by a Gabrielino group document the migration of a Catalina Island clan to somewhere in the Carlsbad area near Mission San Luis Rey.

1830–1853

An 1830 census identifies some Indians from the islands inhabiting the pueblo of Los Angeles (Johnson 1988:24). In 1835, when the final 17–18 Nicoleño (with the exception of "the Lone Woman") relocated from San Nicolas Island, they were taken to San Pedro and then to Los Angeles and Mission San Gabriel (Ellison 1937:37; see also Heizer and Elsasser 1961:12; McCawley 1996:67). This may have been to join an existing mainland village community of San Nicolas islanders already living in the San Pedro area. The village named Haraasnga or Ghalas-at (also called Guasna, Guaschna, and Guaaschna) appears to fit this description.

In 1845, a group of four households of islanders known as the "village of the Pipimares" existed near another Indian *ranchería* on the outskirts of Los Angeles. The Pipimares may have included some Catalina islanders. They, along with those in the nearby, larger Indian village, were moved away from Los Angeles by an order from the Los Angeles City Council, ostensibly due to management and health issues (Robinson 1952; Johnson 1988:24). It is not known what became of the four islander households.

Kroeber (1925:634) states that in 1853, when the last native survivor was rescued from San Nicolas Island and brought to Santa Barbara, native "Pepimaros" (islanders) were sent for from Los Angeles in an attempt to communicate with her. This suggests that islanders were still known in the Los Angeles area as late as 1853, when the Lone Woman was rescued, although no one was ever found who could speak her language. It is possible that just eight years after the four Island Gabrielino households comprising the "village of the Pipimares" were forcibly moved away from the outskirts of Los Angeles, that they were living in obscurity and could not be found, or that the households consisted of Island Gabrielino other than San Nicolas islanders. Perhaps it was not common knowledge that the San Nicolas islander village of Haraasnga existed on the Palos Verdes Peninsula. According to Harrington, a locale on the Palos Verdes Peninsula known as "Fisherman's Camp" was occupied by Indians into the 1890s (McCawley 1996:206). Assuming that the village contained some individuals who spoke Nicoleño, perhaps none of those journeyed to Santa Barbara to see the Lone Woman, who died just seven weeks after being rescued (Ellison 1937:89).

Cano of Pimunga and José Zalvidea

In 1852, Reid (1968:27) wrote:

> ...one of the Chief's from Santa Catharine; who was ordered by the priest to San Gabriel, and there baptized. He had *three* wives, the *first* of which was allowed him, and the others discarded. The Priest joined him in the holy bonds of matrimony according to the form of the Catholic Church, which to him appeared highly ridiculous. He is still alive and now resides at San Fernando; his name, as known at present, is *Canoa*, or *Canoe*; he is still a Captain and accounted a great wizard.

The fact that a tribal chief from Catalina Island lived in San Fernando in 1852 suggests that other Catalina islanders may have resided nearby. Canoa, or Cano, was related to José Zalvidea's father. Zalvidea said (ca. 1914–1917) that Josefa,

Cano's daughter and thus also Zalvidea's relative, lived in Colton (McCawley 1996:18).

José Zalvidea was a Gabrielino informant to Kroeber, Gifford, Merriam, and Harrington (Johnson 1988:26; McCawley 1996:17). Zalvidea was Harrington's informant from 1914 to 1917 and claimed to have known Hugo Reid (McCawley 1996:18), who died December 12, 1852. Zalvidea did not speak Gabrielino, but spoke Serrano and some Cahuilla (McCawley 1996:17–18). He was raised in the San Gabriel Valley and later lived in Highland and on the nearby San Manuel Indian Reservation in San Bernardino County. Zalvidea had a son who lived on the Morongo Reservation in the Cabezon–Palm Springs area (Johnson 1988:27). He also had siblings who lived in Oklahoma and San Gabriel (McCawley 1996:18). While McCawley states that Zalvidea claimed his father was born and raised on Santa Catalina Island, Johnson (1988:27) reports that Zalvidea said it was his grandfather, 'ukimovit, who may have been from San Clemente Island. Further confusing Zalvidea's patrilineage is the name of Zalvidea's relative: "San Gabriel and Plaza Church registers record several children born to an islander from Quinquina named Aquimobit, which is how 'ukimovit may well have been written by a Spanish speaker" (Johnson 1988:27). This suggests Zalvidea's grandfather may have originally come from San Clemente Island, and it is entirely possible that his grandfather may have subsequently lived on Santa Catalina Island. However, if Zalvidea was younger than about 70 in 1920, meaning that he was born about 1850, it is unlikely that his father was born and raised on Catalina. If, as he claimed, Zalvidea knew Hugo Reid, who died in 1852, Zalvidea would have been born prior to the mid-1840s. Nevertheless, if either Zalvidea's father or grandfather was truly a native Catalina islander, Catalina islanders relocated to San Gabriel, and from there their descendants moved to such places as Colton, Highland, the Cabezon-Palm Springs area, and as far away as the state of Oklahoma.

1890–Early 1900s

Harrington stated that a site on the Palos Verdes Peninsula known as Fisherman's Camp was occupied by Indians into the 1890s (McCawley 1996:

206). Harrington informant José Zalvidea also stated that in the early 1900s Gabrielino were still living at Kiinkenga, the village named after San Clemente Island (McCawley 1996:206). Fisherman's Camp may have been Kiinkenga, although this is conjecture.

Maria and José Chári

As stated previously, in about 1916 Harrington mentioned that "the last [native Catalina] Indian woman, named Maria...died at Las Calabazas 10 or 15 years ago" (McCawley 1996:202). Harrington's informant, Sétimo López, stated that Maria and José Chári were brother and sister from Catalina who lived together at "Calabazas."

Post-2000 Research

Using mitochondrial DNA, Johnson and Lorenz (2006:44, 58) identified a direct matrilineal link from modern populations to an individual from San Clemente Island. This is the same matriline to which Harrington's consultant Felicitas Montaño belongs.

Recently, Sétimo López (aka Sétimo Moraga) was identified as Cano's son (Johnson 2006:29). Baptized as "Fernando" at Mission San Fernando on October 15, 1855, Sétimo's local descendants confirmed that his full name, as written on his grave stone, was Fernando Sétimo Moraga. Although nearly two centuries have elapsed since the last native Catalina islanders left their island home, the examples above show that it is possible

to follow their now faded trail into the twentieth and twenty-first centuries.

Conclusion

It is always sad when a group of people must leave their home for the unknown promise of a new life elsewhere. Perhaps they leave for the purpose of bettering their lot, or perhaps, as may have happened to the native islanders of Catalina, they leave for their own safety. It was a scene undoubtedly repeated innumerable times throughout history the world over. Violence was just one of three factors thought to have contributed to the native depopulation of Santa Catalina Island and probably other southern and northern Channel Islands. Combined with disease and changes in population dynamics resulting from population reduction, the downward spiral of the native Catalina population eventually led to the exodus of natives from the island, most likely sometime between 1810 and 1818. Historical documentation shows that the majority of native Catalina islanders stayed within Gabrielino territory, moving to the Pueblo of Los Angeles and the Mission San Gabriel area, with somewhat fewer moving to the Mission San Fernando area. Some are thought to have relocated to Carlsbad near Mission San Luis Rey, in Luiseño territory. From these locations, the last native Catalina islanders mixed into the surrounding populace, some of their descendants staying in the Southern California area and some, like other intrepid humans, moving to distant lands.

Acknowledgments

A long-time interest in the history of events on Catalina was rekindled by an island power pole survey recently completed by LSA Associates for SCE, in which SCE archaeologist Adam Sriro figured largely. At LSA, archaeologist Rod McLean was instrumental in managing and conducting fieldwork and research for that project, and later provided encouragement with his knack for straightforward thought. LSA principals Frank Haselton, Deborah McLean, and Steve Conkling provided company resources; key among them was allowing graphic artist Gary Dow to produce report figures. Professor Wendy Teeter at UCLA and Harvard doctoral candidate Desireé Martinez provided the opportunity to lecture at the annual Pimu–Catalina Island field school and then an invitation to join the sympo-

sium for which this chapter was written. Discussions with William McCawley led to his expert review, and he is also thanked for his map of Gabrielino villages near the Palos Verdes Peninsula (Figure 10.5). Dr. John Johnson provided thoughtful discussion, review, several key references, data for Table 10.2, and permission for use of Figure 10.6. Steven Schwartz and John Douglass also provided references, as did Pacific Coast Archaeological Society president Scott Findlay and board member Bob Brace. SCE archaeologist Natasha Tabares reviewed an early draft of this chapter. Symposium co-chairs and volume editors Christopher Jazwa and Jennifer Perry provided many helpful comments. My wife, Diane Valko Strudwick, as always, provided expert editorial review, advice, and helpful insight. To those listed, as well as to anyone I may have unintentionally omitted, I offer my most sincere and grateful appreciation.

References Cited

Arnold, J. E.
2001   The Chumash in World and Regional Perspectives. In *The Origins of a Pacific Coast Chiefdom: The Chumash of the Channel Islands*, edited by J. E. Arnold, pp. 1–19. University of Utah Press, Salt Lake City.

Avina, R. H.
1932   Spanish and Mexican Land Grants in California. MA thesis. Department of History, University of California, Berkeley.

Bancroft, H. H.
1886   *The Works of Hubert Howe Bancroft*, Vol. 19: *History of California*, Vol. 2, *1801–1824*. The History Company, San Francisco. Facsimile reprint, Wallace Hebberd, Santa Barbara, 1966.

Batman, R.
1985   *The Outer Coast*. Harcourt, Brace, Jovanovich, San Diego.

Bean, L. J., and C. R. Smith
1978   Gabrielino. In *Handbook of North American Indians*, Vol. 8: *California*, edited by R. Heizer, pp. 538–549. W. C. Sturtevant, general editor. Smithsonian Institution, Washington, DC.

Bolton, H. E.
1908   *Spanish Exploration in the Southwest, 1542–1706*. Charles Scribner's Sons, New York. (Reprinted, Barnes and Noble, New York, 1952.)

Castillo, E. D.
1978   The Impact of Euro-American Exploration and Settlement. In *Handbook of North American Indians*, Vol. 8: *California*, edited by R. Heizer, pp. 99–127. W. C. Sturtevant, general editor. Smithsonian Institution, Washington, DC.

Cowan, R. G.
1988   Preface to California's Land Grants. In *California Ranchos: Patented Private Land Grants Listed by County*, by Burgess McK. Shumway, pp. 7–9. Stokvis Studies in Historical Chronology and Thought No. 11. Borgo Press, San Bernardino, and Sidewinder Press, Glendale, CA.

Douglass, J. G., and S. W. Hackel
2011   The Ethnohistory and Archaeology of the Gabrielino/Tongva During the Mission Period: A Perspective from the Ballona Lagoon Area, West Los Angeles. Paper presented at the annual meeting of the American Society of Ethnohistory, Pasadena, CA.

Douglass, J. G., and P. B. Stanton
2010   *Living During a Difficult Time: A Comparison of Ethnohistoric, Bioarchaeological, and Archaeological Data During the Mission Period, Southern California*. Proceedings of the Society for California Archaeology 24. Riverside.

Ellison, W. H. (editor)
1937   *The Life and Adventures of George Nidever (1802–1883)*. University of California Press, Berkeley.

Finnerty, W. P., D. A. Decker, N. N. Leonard III, T. F. King, C. D. King, and L. B. King
1970   *Community Structure and Trade at Isthmus Cove: A Salvage Excavation on Catalina Island*. Occasional Paper No. 1. Pacific Coast Archaeological Society, Costa Mesa, CA.

Gamble, L. H.
2008   *The Chumash World at European Contact: Power, Trade, and Feasting among Complex Hunter-Gatherers*. University of California Press, Berkeley and Los Angeles.

Gudde, E. G.
1998   *California Place Names: The Origin and Etymology of Current Geographical Names*. 4th ed. Revised and enlarged by William Bright. University of California Press, Berkeley and Los Angeles.

Harrington, J. P.
1933   Annotations of Alfred Robinson's Chinigchinich. In *Chinigchinich: A Revised and Annotated Version of Alfred Robinson's Translation of Father Geronimo Boscana's Historical Account of Belief, Usages, Customs and Extravagances of the Indians of This Mission of San Juan Capistrano Called the Acagchemem Tribe*, edited by P. T. Hanna, pp. 91–228. Fine Arts Press, Santa Ana, CA.

Heizer, R. F.
1968   Introduction and Notes. In *The Indians of Los Angeles County: Hugo Reid's Letters of 1852*, edited and annotated by R. Heizer. Southwest Museum Papers No. 21. Southwest Museum, Highland Park, CA.

Heizer, R. F., and A. B. Elsasser (editors)
1961   *Original Accounts of the Lone Woman of San Nicolas Island*. University of California Archaeological Survey Reports No. 55.

Holder, C. F.
1901   *An Isle of Summer: Santa Catalina Island*. R. Y. McBride, Los Angeles.

Johnson, J. R.
1988   The People of *Quinquina*: San Clemente Island's Original Inhabitants as Described in

Ethnohistoric Documents. Anthropology Department, Santa Barbara Museum of Natural History. Manuscript on file at the Natural Resources Office, Naval Air Station, North Island, San Diego.

2001 Ethnohistoric Reflections of Cruzeño Chumash Society. In *The Origins of a Pacific Coast Chiefdom: The Chumash of the Channel Islands*, edited by J. E. Arnold, pp. 53–70. University of Utah Press, Salt Lake City.

2006 *Ethnohistoric Overview for the Santa Susana Pass State Historic Park Cultural Resources Inventory Project*. Ethnographic Study Services No. A05E0023. On file, Southern Service Center, California Department of Parks and Recreation.

2010 The Earliest European Contacts with the Chumash Islanders. In *Pacific Seafarers and Maritime Cultures*, pp. 38–45. Maritime Museum of San Diego.

Johnson, J. R., and J. G. Lorenz

2006 Genetics, Linguistics, and Prehistoric Migrations: An Analysis of California Indian Mitochondrial DNA Lineages. *Journal of California and Great Basin Anthropology* 26(1):33–64.

Johnston, B. E.

1962 *California's Gabrielino Indians*. Frederick Webb Hodge Anniversary Fund Publication Vol. 8. Southwest Museum, Los Angeles.

King, C.

1978 Protohistoric and Historic Archeology. In *Handbook of North American Indians*, Vol. 8: *California*, edited by R. Heizer, pp. 58–68. W. C. Sturtevant, general editor. Smithsonian Institution, Washington, DC.

King, C., and J. R. Johnson

1999 The Chumash Political Groups in the Santa Monica Mountains. In *Cultural Affiliation and Lineal Descent of the Chumash Peoples in the Channel Islands and Santa Monica Mountains*, edited by S. McLendon and J. Johnson, pp. 67–92. Santa Barbara Museum of Natural History, Santa Barbara, CA.

Kroeber, A. L.

1925 *Handbook of the Indians of California*. Bulletin 78. Bureau of American Ethnology, Smithsonian Institution, Washington, DC.

McCawley, W.

1996 *The First Angelinos: The Gabrielino Indians of Los Angeles*. Malki Museum Press, Banning, CA, and Ballena Press, Novato, CA.

2002 A Tale of Two Cultures: The Chumash and the Gabrielino. In *Islanders and Mainlanders*,

edited by J. Altschul and D. Grenda, pp. 45–65. SRI Press, Tucson.

McGuire, J. D.

1883 Aboriginal Quarries: Soapstone Bowls and the Tools Used in Their Manufacture. *American Naturalist* 17(6):587–595.

McLendon, S., and J. R. Johnson

1999 Cultural Affiliation and Lineal Descent of Chumash Peoples in the Channel Islands and the Santa Monica Mountains. Report on file at the Santa Barbara Museum of Natural History, Santa Barbara, CA.

Meighan, C. W.

1959 The Little Harbor Site, Catalina Island, California: An Example of Ecological Interpretation in Archaeology. *American Antiquity* 24(4):383–405.

Meighan, C. W., and K. L. Johnson

1957 Isle of Mines: Catalina's Ancient Indian Quarries. *Pacific Discovery* 10(1):24–29.

Meighan, C. W., and S. Rootenberg

1957 A Prehistoric Miner's Camp on Catalina Island. *Masterkey* 31(6):176–184.

Merriam, C. H.

1968 *Village Names in Twelve California Mission Records*. Archaeological Survey Report No. 74. University of California.

Morris, S. L., G. J. Farris, S. J. Schwartz, I. V. L. Wender, and B. Dralyuk

In press Murder, Massacre, and Mayhem on the California Coast, 1814–1815: Newly Translated Russian American Company Documents Reveal Concern over Violent Clashes. *Journal of California and Great Basin Anthropology*. Spring 2014.

Raab, L. M., J. Cassidy, A. Yatsko, and W. J. Howard

2009 *California Maritime Archaeology: A San Clemente Island Perspective*. Altamira, Lanham, MD.

Raab, L. M., and A. Yatsko

1990 Prehistoric Human Ecology of *Quinquina*: A Research Design for Archaeological Studies on San Clemente Island, Southern California. *Pacific Coast Archaeological Society Quarterly* 26(2–3):10–37.

Rechtman, R. B.

1985 The Historic Period Occupation at the Aboriginal Site of Ledge, San Clemente Island: An Analysis of Historic Artifacts. MA thesis. Department of Anthropology, University of California, Los Angeles.

Reid, H.

1968 *The Indians of Los Angeles County: Hugo Reid's Letters of 1852*. Edited and annotated by

R. Heizer. Southwest Museum Papers No. 21. Southwest Museum, Highland Park, CA.

Roberts, H. H.

1933   *Form in Primitive Music: An Analytical and Comparative Study of the Melodic Form of Some Ancient Southern California Indian Songs.* W. W. Norton, New York.

Robinson, A.

1846   *Life in California during a Residence of Several Years in That Territory.* Wiley and Putnam, New York.

Robinson, W. W.

1952   *The Indians of Los Angeles: Story of the Liquidation of a People.* Glen Dawson, Los Angeles.

Rosen, M. D.

1980   Archaeological Investigations at Two Prehistoric Santa Catalina Island Sites: Rosski (SCaI-45) and Miner's Camp (SCaI-118). *Pacific Coast Archaeological Society Quarterly* 16(1–2):27–60.

Schoenherr, A. A., C. R. Feldmeth, and M. J. Emerson

1999   *Natural History of the Islands of California.* University of California Press, Berkeley and Los Angeles.

Schumacher, P.

1878   Ancient Olla Manufactory on Santa Catalina Island, California. *American Naturalist* 12(9):629.

Schwartz, S. J.

2003   Some Observations on the Material Culture of the Nicoleño. Paper presented at the Sixth California Islands Symposium. Ventura, CA.

Shaler, W.

1935   *Journal of a Voyage between China and the North Western Coast of America, Made in 1804 by William Shaler.* Saunders Studio Press, Claremont, CA.

Stoll, A. Q., J. G. Douglass, and R. Ciolek-Torrello

2009   *Searching for Guaspet: A Mission Period*

Rancheria in West Los Angeles. Proceedings of the Society for California Archaeology 22.

Strudwick, I. H., R. McLean, J. Michalsky, B. Smith, and J. E. Baumann

2007   A Glimpse of the Past on *Pimu*: Cultural Resource Survey of Selected Areas on Santa Catalina Island, Los Angeles County, California. LSA Associates. Report on file at the South Central Coastal Archaeological Information Center, University of California, Fullerton.

Vizcaíno, J.

1959   *The Sea Diary of Fr. Juan Vizcaíno to Alta California, 1769.* Translated by Arthur Woodward. Early California Travel Series 49. Glen Dawson, Los Angeles.

Wagner, H. R.

1929   *Spanish Voyages to the Northwest Coast of America in the Sixteenth Century.* California Historical Society Special Publications 4.

1941   *Juan Rodriguez Cabrillo: Discoverer of the Coast of California.* California Historical Society, San Francisco.

Williams, S. L., and E. J. Rosenthal

1993   Soapstone Craft Specialization at the Upper Buffalo Springs Site Quarry, Santa Catalina Island. *Pacific Coast Archaeological Society Quarterly* 29(3):22–50.

Williamson, M. B.

1904   History of Santa Catalina Island. *Annual Publication of the Historical Society of Southern California and of the Pioneers of Los Angeles County 1903* 1(6):14–31.

Wlodarski, R. J., J. F. Romani, G. R. Romani, and D. A. Larson

1984   Preliminary Evidence of Metal Tool Use in Soapstone Quarry-Mining, Catalina Island: Jane Russell Quarry. *Pacific Coast Archaeological Society Quarterly* 20(3):35–66.

11

Island Perspectives

Michael Jochim

This collection of current research on the Channel Islands reflects many of the recent trends and enduring issues of hunter-gatherer archaeology. These include such topics as research approaches, demography, settlement organization, interaction, and ritual. It also presents an opportunity to reflect upon the state of research on the islands and the broader context of investigations into these topics. This chapter will discuss some of the topics presented in this volume as well as suggest ways to place the islands in wider theoretical and regional arenas.

Research Approaches

There are many different field methods used in the study of prehistoric hunter-gatherers, two of which — regional survey and site sampling — have formed the predominant recent approaches used on the Channel Islands, supplementing earlier extensive excavations. These techniques — exemplified in this volume by the work of Braje, Erlandson, and Rick (Chapter 2) in discovering terminal Pleistocene sites, by Gusick's study (Chapter 3) of early Holocene sites on Santa Cruz Island, and by Perry's work (Chapter 8) on probable ceremonial ridgetop sites — have produced significant new knowledge about different aspects of the islands' prehistory. Such approaches also form the basis for most of the other chapters in the volume, providing a necessary baseline for the examination of settlement history, changes in subsistence and settlement organization, and the creation and use of paths.

Another common archaeological field approach, broad area excavations, has been rela-tively scarce in recent research, with some no-table exceptions, including the work at Eel Point on San Clemente Island (Raab et al. 1994; Raab et al. 2009) and the excavation of Tule Creek Village on San Nicolas Island (see Guttenberg et al., Chapter 6). It is difficult to believe that column samples can adequately capture spatial variation and artifact proportional representation in sites. Broad excavations are absolutely necessary for pursuing many questions of archaeological relevance, including the reliability of existing column samples for characterizing site contents and functions, spatial variation and patterning of activities within sites, and variations among households and their implications for social relations and cultural change. Given the long scholarly interest in the development of social complexity on the Channel Islands, variation among households is one of the key arenas in which this will be evident, and this requires larger exposures, particularly in sites with house depressions. The work by Guttenberg et al. (Chapter 6) in this volume analyzing the intrasite spatial distribution of different artifact classes was only possible in a site like Tule Creek Village with substantial excavated exposures. In this regard, I am echoing Glasgow's call (Chapter 4) for larger samples from sites whenever possible (given regulatory restrictions) as an important direction for future island research.

Although plant resources are known to have been important ethnohistorically, especially on the mainland, their role in prehistoric subsistence has been difficult to determine. Consequently, it is exciting to see the increased attention that such resources receive here, as exemplified by

Gill's contribution to this volume (Chapter 7). Research on the islands has frequently invoked marine resources and their fluctuations related to environmental changes as important factors in explaining cultural developments. Without denying the maritime emphasis of island subsistence economies, it is clear from ethnohistoric accounts (and now, increasingly, from archaeological studies) that plants were important components of many aspects of life, including subsistence, manufacturing, curing, clothing, and ritual. Understanding the role of plants in these arenas may have implications for patterns of labor organization, settlement, and exchange; however, the significance of plant foods in these settings has yet to be determined, surely varied through time, and may be highly relevant to processes of culture change. With Timbrook's (2007) extensive compendium and discussion of historic plant use among the Chumash, archaeologists are uniquely equipped to investigate the various roles of plants as well as their implications for other aspects of life. Of course, this requires considerable effort in collection, flotation, and analysis, now added to the already arduous work required for careful faunal analysis of midden deposits.

The scale at which research questions are posed is another, quite different aspect of research approaches, and this is an area in which greater dialogue among scholars should be encouraged. Work in this volume does, indeed, reflect research at different scales, from the single site (Guttenberg et al., Chapter 6) to groups of sites (Glassow, Chapter 4; Gusick, Chapter 3; and Jazwa, Kennett, and Winterhalder, Chapter 5) to islands (Strudwick, Chapter 10; and Teeter, Martinez, and Richardson, Chapter 9), to multiple islands (Gill, Chapter 7; Braje, Erlandson, and Rick, Chapter 2; and Perry, Chapter 8). Yet the framing and organization of research could provide rich results if more explicitly developed and tested at different spatial scales. For example, Meighan's (2000) characterization of island culture as distinct in some ways from that of the mainland (cited by Perry, Chapter 8) deserves further research. In what ways are the islands—all of the islands—different, and how is this reflected in their history of cultural development and change? At another level, Perry cites cultural and ritual distinctions between the northern and southern

groups of islands. This would appear to represent an ideal context in which to investigate the roles of cultural background and ecology in shaping cultural development. Distinguishing between large and small islands is another way of viewing groups of islands, in this case reflecting ecological differences that seem to have had a major impact on settlement history. Hypotheses should be developed and tested by research designed with this specific ecological contrast as guidance. Similarly, individual islands could form the basic unit of comparison, with each uniquely characterized by such attributes as size, shoreline characteristics and marine productivity, available freshwater and plant species, raw materials, proximity to other islands and the mainland, and even characteristics of adjacent mainland societies. Hypotheses could then be devised about their patterns of settlement and development.

Demography

Colonization, settlement shifts, and depopulation are interrelated issues dealing with the occupation of the landscape and are the focus of innovative studies in this collection. To expand upon the work by Braje, Erlandson, and Rick (Chapter 2) documenting surprisingly abundant evidence of pioneering settlement of the islands, one might consider that if the kelp "highway" and, ultimately, the Channel Islands exerted a "pull" on human colonization, we should also continue to expand investigations (and scale) to examine conditions in Asian source areas in terms of maritime technology and possible "push" factors to encourage population movements. Because the very early sites on the northern islands containing stemmed points and crescents date largely to the period before and during the breakup of Santarosae, it would be interesting to determine their distribution relative to that island's configuration, and whether the varying density of these sites among the modern islands informs us about initial settlement choices and site functions in this pioneering phase. Would the ideal free distribution predict these patterns of distribution? Jazwa, Kennett, and Winterhalder (Chapter 5) utilize the IFD in an ingenious manner to examine the sequence of occupation of different locations on Santa Rosa Island; this approach might also usefully be applied to the sequence of settlement of different islands. Moreover, theories of migration derived from geography often include proximity to initial settlements as an important determinant of patterns of population expansion and might be considered in relation to the patterns predicted by the IFD. It also might be the case that as settlements shifted because of sea level rise, they were somewhat tethered by the location of earlier (ancestral?) sites. In this case, history as well as proximity to other contemporary sites could have played a role in characterizing settlement locations. As suggested by Teeter, Martinez, and Richardson's research on Santa Catalina Island (Chapter 9), proximity to trails is another locational characteristic deserving attention in models of settlement. Building upon the work by Strudwick (Chapter 10), a different use of the IFD might be to examine the history of native depopulation of all of the islands, in light of how the various islands rank in attractiveness to Westerners and their subsequent use of each island.

Settlement Organization

A focus on site function and seasonality has played a large role in island research and is exemplified here by the chapters by Glassow, Gusick, and, to some extent, Gill. Such studies are at the core of investigations into past adaptations and use of the landscape, but as pointed out by Glassow, they face serious problems. The similarity in contents among Gusick's early Holocene sites indeed suggest a common functional role for all and present a different picture from the later sites discussed by Glassow, which display much more intersite variability. As he discusses, however, interpretations of this variability must deal with considerable ambiguity. The search for specific functional signatures of different site types may be frustrated by a variety of plausible interpretations. It also should be considered whether attempts to place sites into specific functional categories (and then to aggregate them into proposed settlement systems) ignore much hunter-gatherer literature that documents different functional or seasonal uses of the same locations, or whether this approach at least has varying utility across time periods with differing socioeconomic organizations. Much depends upon the strength of correlation between a site's locational characteristics (especially locally available resources) and the site's activities and ultimate role

in a settlement system. The Diablo Valdez site on Santa Cruz Island, discussed by Gill, may be a site with a high correlation.

Tying together several issues already discussed is the problem of assigning weight to the role of different factors— plants, marine resources, view, proximity to trails— in developing models of settlement. Optimal foraging models underlie several studies in this volume, but such models have difficulty incorporating both animal and plant foods, much less the spatial implications for settlement when viewsheds or other less comparable factors are also deemed relevant. I have previously suggested that we need multiple foraging models, at least two ("male" activities and "female" activities; perhaps "children," "elderly," etc.), to accurately characterize hunter-gatherer patterns of labor division, primarily because different goals apparently guide different foraging activities (Jochim 1988). In a sense, this simply pushes the problem of incorporating various factors to a new level; how does one reconcile the two (or more) models in terms of their implications for the optimal location of settlements? The magnitude of this problem depends on the distribution of different categories of resources and their spatial congruence at different times of the year. Questions specific to the islands must be asked, such as, "Does the collection and processing of blue dicks interfere with other subsistence tasks that might be optimal at the same time but in a different place?" If so, then the settlement choices must find a compromise between the attractions exerted by different locations. Several such compromises might be possible. The problem still remains, however, of determining the importance of blue dicks relative to other resources available at the same time.

Interaction

Much research has been done investigating patterns of interaction between islanders and mainland populations, citing ethnohistoric evidence for exchange and participation in ceremonies. A number of the contributors to this volume, however, suggest that interactions among the islanders themselves were significant as well. A greater focus on these might help counteract what I see as a "mainland-centric" perspective on island culture and reveal important aspects of island life. Trade was certainly one aspect of this interisland interaction. In this volume, Teeter, Martinez, and Richardson (Chapter 9) cite the exchange of steatite items from Catalina to the northern islands, and Perry (Chapter 8) mentions specifically the exchange of steatite effigies from Catalina to San Clemente and San Nicolas. Stone bowls were also traded from San Miguel to other islands, and other items most likely were exchanged as well. Ceremonial participation was another form of inter-island interaction. Perry cites the attendance of mourning rites of Chingichngish on the southern islands by groups from neighboring islands, including some from the northern islands. She also suggests that the placement of a shrine on Santa Cruz and of Chingichngish sites on San Clemente are in part related to views of neighboring islands (Anacapa and Catalina) with ritual significance. Even in the subsistence realm, Glassow (Chapter 4) suggests the remote possibility that the foraging radius of groups on the west end of Santa Cruz included the east end of Santa Rosa. Additional study and sourcing of materials may enlarge the archaeological picture of such interaction and help determine how much of island-to-island interactions were mediated through the mainland.

Ritual

Only briefly discussed in this collection, and devilishly hard to determine prehistorically, the relationship between economic and sacred landscapes is a topic of growing interest in the discipline. For prehistoric hunter-gatherers in particular, the sacred landscape is elusive. Nevertheless, we know from ethnographic and ethnohistoric accounts, as well as recent land claim disputes, that such landscapes exist and are critical to understanding patterns of land use. Given

the rich ethnohistoric literature of the region, the Channel Islands may offer great potential for research in this area, as well as guidance for future archaeological research. Perry (Chapter 8) has surveyed much of the existing ethnohistoric and archaeological evidence for ritual life on the islands, convincingly demonstrating the important role this played, with implications for settlement location and landscape use, population travel and aggregation, and extraction, working, and exchange of raw materials. A holistic approach to island lifeways must include attention to this domain, and archaeologists must be ingenious in its investigation. The research discussed by Teeter, Martinez, and Richardson on Santa Catalina (Chapter 9) is one example, using least-cost pathways developed in a GIS framework to examine potential routes of movement, in part related to aspects of a sacred landscape.

Conclusions

The chapters presented in this volume bode well for the future of Channel Islands archaeology. New data and innovative approaches place this research in the mainstream and, in some ways, at the forefront of archaeological research into hunter-gatherers. The islands represent a unique laboratory for investigation, combining recognizable boundaries with excellent conditions of preservation and a valuable cadre of ethnohistoric information. The contributors to this volume have taken advantage of these conditions to good effect, and have laid the groundwork for future research that should be even more significant, including research that has implications for topics as broad as the peopling of the Americas, the organization of maritime adaptations, and the development of social complexity.

References

Jochim, M.
1988   Optimal Foraging and the Division of Labor. *American Anthropologist* 90:130–36.
Meighan, C.
2000   Rock Art on the Channel Islands of California. *Pacific Coast Archaeological Society Quarterly* 36(2):15–29.
Raab, L., M. K. Bradford, and A. Yatsko
1994   Advances in Southern Channel Islands Archaeology: 1983–1993. *Journal of California and Great Basin Anthropology* 16:243–270.

Raab, L. M., J. Cassidy, A. Yatsko, and W. J. Howard
2009   *California Maritime Archaeology: A San Clemente Island Perspective.* Altamira, Lanham, MD.
Timbrook, J.
2007   *Chumash Ethnobotany.* Santa Barbara Museum of Natural History Monograph No. 5. Heydey Books, Berkeley, CA.

Contributors

Todd J. Braje
San Diego State University
Department of Anthropology

Jon M. Erlandson
University of Oregon
Museum of Natural and Cultural History

Kristina M. Gill
Department of Anthropology
University of California, Santa Barbara

Michael A. Glassow
Department of Anthropology
University of California, Santa Barbara

Amy E. Gusick
Department of Anthropology
University of California, Santa Barbara

Richard B. Guttenberg
California State University, Los Angeles

Christopher S. Jazwa
Department of Anthropology
Pennsylvania State University

Michael Jochim
Department of Anthropology
University of California, Santa Barbara

William E. Kendig
California State University, Los Angeles

Douglas J. Kennett
Department of Anthropology
Pennsylvania State University

Rebekka G. Knierim
California State University, Los Angeles

Desireé Reneé Martinez
Department of Anthropology
Harvard University

Jennifer E. Perry
Department of Anthropology
California State University, Channel Islands

Karimah O. Kennedy Richardson
Southwest Museum of the American Indian
Autry National Center of the American West,
Los Angeles

Torben C. Rick
National Museum of Natural History
Smithsonian Institution, Department of
Anthropology, Program in Human Ecology and
Archaeobiology

Steven J. Schwartz
NAVAIR
Range Sustainability Office, San Nicholas
Island, CA

Ivan H. Strudwick
LSA Associates, Inc., Irvine, CA

Wendy G. Teeter
Fowler Museum
University of California, Los Angeles

René L. Vellanoweth
California State University, Los Angeles

Bruce Winterhalder
Department of Anthropology and Graduate
Group in Ecology
University of California, Davis

Index

Numbers in *italics* refer to figures.